HOUSING ALLOWANCES IN COMPARATIVE PERSPECTIVE

Edited by Peter A. Kemp

First published in Great Britain in 2007 by

The Policy Press
University of Bristol
Fourth Floor
Beacon House
Queen's Road
Bristol BS8 1QU
UK

Tel +44 (0)117 331 4054
Fax +44 (0)117 331 4093
e-mail tpp-info@bristol.ac.uk
www.policypress.org.uk

British Library Cataloguing in Publication Data
A catalogue record for this book is available from the British Library.

Library of Congress Cataloging-in-Publication Data
A catalog record for this book has been requested.

ISBN 978 1 86134 754 5 hardcover

Cover design by Qube Design Associates, Bristol
Front cover: photograph supplied by kind permission of Hugo Martínez Téllez
Printed and bound in Great Britain by MPG Books, Bodmin

Contents

List of tables and figures

Tables

Figures

—

Acknowledgements

I would like to thank the contributors for giving up their time to write their chapters for this book and for doing so with such good humour. It goes without saying that without their involvement this book would not have been possible. Thanks are also due to an anonymous reader for very helpful comments on both the book proposal and the completed manuscript. I am grateful to Professor Joanne Neale (Oxford Brookes University) for comments on Chapter Twelve; to Steve Wilcox (University of York) for providing Table 6.8 in my chapter on Great Britain; and to Mike Gautrey, editor of the *International Social Security Review*, for allowing me to draw on an article of mine published in that journal. I would also like to thank Lisa Southwood for helping to prepare the typescript for publication. Finally, I am grateful to Emily Watt and Philip de Bary at The Policy Press for their patience and support in the preparation of this volume.

Peter A. Kemp
University of Oxford

Notes on contributors

Per Åhrén is a senior adviser at the Norwegian State Housing Bank, Oslo, Norway. He received his PhD from the Stockholm School of Economics. His most recently published work includes 'The duration of housing allowance claims and labour market disincentives: The Norwegian case' (2005) *European Journal of Housing Policy*, vol 5, no 2, pp 131–46, and 'Housing allowances in the Nordic countries', in M Lujanen (ed) (2004) *Housing and housing policy in the Nordic countries*, Copenhagen: Nordic Council of Ministers.

Marja Elsinga works as a senior researcher at the OTB Research Institute for Housing, Urban and Mobility Studies, Delft University of Technology, the Netherlands. She is leader of the research programme 'Housing Systems' and specialises in housing policy, risks of homeownership and developments in social housing.

Dr Kath Hulse is Director of the Swinburne-Monash Research Centre of the Australian Housing and Urban Research Institute, and Programme Leader for Cities and Housing at the Institute for Social Research, Swinburne University of Technology, Melbourne, Australia.

Peter A. Kemp is the Barnett Professor of Social Policy at the University of Oxford, England. He previously held professorial posts at the universities of York and Glasgow. He has been researching housing allowances since 1983 and has published extensively on the topic. He has also undertaken research on privately rented housing, homelessness, the management of social housing and housing history; recent work also includes research on social security. His numerous books and monographs include *Housing and social policy* (Macmillan, 1990), *A comparative study of housing allowances* (The Stationery Office, 1997) and *Private renting in transition* (Chartered Institute of Housing, 2004).

Stefan Kofner has lectured on housing policy and housing finance at Zittau University in Saxony, Germany, since 1997. His publications include two textbooks and a column for a housing journal. He is also a board member of a municipal housing organisation.

Martin Lux is Head of the Socio-economics of Housing Research Team at the Institute of Sociology, Academy of Science of the Czech Republic, Prague. His field of specialisation is housing and social policy, social housing, housing subsidies and simulation modelling. He is a member of the Housing Economics Working Group of the European Network for Housing Research, the Advisory Board of the *European Journal of Housing Policy*, the Association for the Development of the Property Market in the Czech Republic, and the Board for Popularisation of Science of the Academy of Sciences of the Czech Republic. In 2004 he was awarded the Austrian Erhard Busek Prize and in 2006 the Prize of the Czech Academy of Sciences for outstanding scientific work. He is co-author of two studies for the United Nations Economic Commission for Europe (UN/ECE), and author of comparative housing studies, books and articles.

Sandra J. Newman is Professor of Policy Studies at Johns Hopkins University, Chair of the Graduate Programme in Public Policy and Director of the Hopkins Institute for Policy Studies, Johns Hopkins University, US. She holds joint appointments with the departments of Sociology and Health Policy and Management. Her interdisciplinary research focuses on the effects of housing and neighbourhoods on children and families, and on the dynamics of neighbourhood change. She is author or co-author of numerous journal articles, monographs and books, including *Low-end rental housing: The forgotten story in Baltimore's housing boom* (2005), *The home front: Implications of welfare reform for housing policy* (1999), and *Beyond bricks and mortar* (1992). She is on the editorial board of the *Journal of Policy Analysis and Management* and *Housing Studies* and an associate editor of *Housing Policy Debate*.

Hugo Priemus was educated as an architect and an economist. From 1977 to 2003 he was Professor of Housing at Delft University of Technology, the Netherlands. Since 2003 he has been Professor of System Innovation and Spatial Development and Dean at the Faculty of Technology, Policy and Management, Delft University of Technology. He is the author of numerous books and other publications, including *Housing allowances in the Netherlands: Product of a conservative or progressive ideology?* (Delft University Press, 1984).

Madhu Satsangi is a senior lecturer in the Department of Applied Social Science, University of Stirling, Scotland. In addition to research on housing subsidies, his recent work has been on the social relations of rental housing supply, with a particular focus on rural areas. His most recent publications are '"The best laid plans?" An assessment of housing association provision in Scotland' (in *Policy & Politics*, 2006) and 'Land tenure change and rural housing in Scotland' (in *Scottish Geographical Journal*, 2007).

Marion Steele is Emeritus Associate Professor, Department of Economics, University of Guelph and resident Research Fellow, Centre for Urban and Community Studies, University of Toronto, Canada. Among her work on housing allowances is a monograph for the Ontario Economic Council and a comparison with US Section 8, published in *Urban Studies*. Her other research investigates renter residential mobility, the effects of homeownership on household characteristics, house prices, and tax aspects of housing. Her most recent article,

'The Canadian home buyers' plan: tax benefit, tax expenditure and policy assessment', was published in *The Canadian Tax Journal*, 2007.

Petr Sunega is a member of the Socio-economics of Housing Research Team at the Institute of Sociology, Academy of Science of the Czech Republic, Prague. His field of specialisation is housing allowances in comparative perspective, housing economics and simulation modelling. He participates in most of the research projects undertaken by the Socio-economics of Housing Research Team.

David C. Thorns is Director of the Social Science Research Centre and Professor of Sociology at the University of Canterbury, New Zealand. He has over 30 years' experience as an urban researcher working in the fields of housing, social policy, social inequality, tourism, research methodology and the implications of globalisation. He is a board member of the Centre for Housing Research Aotearoa/New Zealand.

ONE

Housing allowances in context

Peter A. Kemp

Introduction

Most of the advanced welfare states are committed to ensuring that housing is affordable to ordinary citizens. Shelter is not only a necessity, but for most households it is also the largest single item in their budget. For low-income households in particular, the ratio of housing expenditure to income can be high. In fact, most of the advanced welfare states provide, in one form or another, assistance with housing expenditure. Although the aims and instruments employed vary from one country to another, a common concern is to ensure that ordinary people can afford to occupy decent housing at a price within their means.[1]

The policy instruments that governments employ to ensure this basic goal vary between countries and over time (Doling, 1997). Governments can seek to provide assistance on the supply side, that is, to builders, landlords and financiers. Typically, supply-side assistance is geared towards lowering the price or rent that households have to pay for their housing. This may be achieved through the provision of direct subsidies to builders or landlords, such as low interest loans or capital grants, which are often referred to as 'bricks-and-mortar' subsidies (Oxley, 1987). It may also be achieved by indirect subsidies such as tax relief to private landlords. Whether by these direct or indirect means, supply-side subsidies to providers make it possible for them to charge less than the market price or the economic cost of the dwelling. It may also take the form of price regulation, such as rent controls, that limit the amount that landlords or other suppliers of accommodation may charge to consumers (Robinson, 1979).

Governments may also provide assistance to the demand side, that is, directly to the consumers (home buyers and renters), thereby helping to ensure that they can afford to pay the price or rent charged for their dwelling. Demand-side assistance can take a number of forms, including both direct subsidies such as low interest loans for home buyers, and indirect assistance such as mortgage interest tax relief. However, perhaps the most common form of demand-side assistance is housing allowances. These are income-related subsidies tied to housing that are paid to consumers (or directly to landlords on their behalf).[2]

Although such schemes are commonly called housing allowances (for example in Finland), they are also known as Housing Benefit (Britain), Rent Assistance (Australia), Shelter Allowance (Canada), Accommodation Supplement (New Zealand) and housing vouchers (the US). Some liberal welfare regimes – including

Australia, Canada, Ireland and New Zealand – provide subsidised housing with rents that are related to the income of the tenant. Similarly, in Britain in the 1930s some local authorities charged income-related rents – which were referred to as 'differential rent schemes' – on their council housing (Malpass, 1990). Income-related rents can be regarded as an implicit housing allowance (Kemp, 1997).

In some countries, income-related assistance with housing expenditure is also provided within social assistance schemes (see Eardley et al, 1996). The way in which social assistance provides such help can, however, have implications for housing allowance caseloads and costs. Three basic approaches appear to be used towards housing expenditure – rent or mortgage payments – in social assistance schemes (Kemp, 1997). First, in some countries, social assistance benefit rates are implicitly meant to be sufficient to allow recipients to afford at least part of their housing expenditure out of their benefit payments. Where this is the case, recipients with high housing expenditures are usually expected to apply for help from the housing allowance scheme. Examples of countries taking this approach include Australia, New Zealand and the Netherlands. Second, in other countries, social assistance benefit payments are enhanced to take into account recipients' full housing expenditure (usually subject to a ceiling). Canada, Germany and Sweden employ this approach, as does Great Britain in relation to homeowners. Third, in other countries, social assistance is not intended to meet housing expenditure and recipients are expected to rely on a separate housing allowance scheme. Perhaps the only country that takes this approach to the treatment of housing expenditure in social assistance is Great Britain (see Chapter Six).

Shifting assistance

Although the details vary from one country to another, most of the advanced welfare states first intervened on the supply rather than the demand side to tackle their housing problems. During the First World War, many countries involved in the hostilities introduced rent controls in the privately rented housing market. Housing subsidies also began to be introduced at around this time and, until the 1960s, they tended mainly to take the form of 'bricks-and-mortar' subsidies, often provided to non-profit landlords such as housing associations or local authorities. Such intervention was often the result of pressure 'from below' and tended to come from organised labour and the better-paid working class rather than the poorest tenants (Merrett, 1979; Harloe, 1985, 1995; Ball et al, 1988). This is important because what they demanded was not the introduction of housing allowances, but rent controls and subsidised, social rented housing. Housing allowances would have benefited the poorest tenants rather than the labour aristocracy and moderate-income groups that tended to benefit from social housing.

One driver of the pressure for building new social housing was the absolute housing shortages that developed during and after both the First and Second World Wars. Producer subsidies seemed to be a more effective instrument than housing allowances for tackling those shortages (Howenstine, 1986). It is also important to remember that social protection was not well developed in most countries before the Second World War. In so far as social protection existed, it tended to focus on basic pensions schemes and poor relief. In that context, the introduction of housing allowances on a wide scale would have been more or less unthinkable in many countries.

In recent decades, income-related housing allowance schemes have become a central feature of many advanced welfare states. In particular, governments have sought to shift assistance with housing costs from the supply side to the demand side. Many nations have reduced or eliminated bricks-and-mortar subsidies, which enable social housing landlords to charge below market rents. Instead, they have placed more emphasis on income-related housing allowance schemes and market or near-market rents (Oxley, 1987; Kemp, 1990). Income-related housing allowances have been used by governments as a way of cushioning (to some extent) the poorest households from the effects of reductions in bricks-and-mortar subsidies and the shift towards market rents (Harloe, 1985; Howenstine, 1986).

This shift from bricks-and-mortar subsidies to personal support through income-related housing allowance schemes reflects changing attitudes among governments in the advanced welfare states about how best to provide assistance with housing costs. A number of factors have been at work. To some extent the trend towards increasing reliance on income-related housing allowances instead of bricks-and-mortar subsidies mirrors a view that the problem to be tackled is increasingly an *income* rather than a *housing* one (Kemp, 1990). This change reflects the end to absolute housing shortages and the fact that housing standards have improved very considerably since the Second World War. Meanwhile, affordability has become a more important policy concern in recent decades (Grigsby and Bourassa, 2004). It follows that the more appropriate policy response is to give households an income supplement – which may or may not be tied to their housing expenditure – rather than to provide them with a low rent dwelling.

The shift towards housing allowance schemes also reflects a belief that assistance with housing expenditure can be better targeted if directed only to those households that 'really need' help. This of course mirrors the wider debate about universal versus selective approaches to welfare provision (Titmus, 1968; Deacon and Bradshaw, 1983). Because housing allowance schemes are means tested, the amount of assistance provided is more or less finely tuned to the financial circumstances of the recipients. In contrast, bricks-and-mortar subsidies are criticised for being 'indiscriminate'; helping all households living in subsidised housing irrespective of their need for financial help.[3] A related argument is that housing allowances are a more cost-effective way to enable low-income households to afford decent housing than providing help in the form of bricks-and-mortar subsidies to builders or landlords.

In addition, governments have placed increasing emphasis on market and quasi-market housing and less on public sector provision. In this respect, income-related housing allowances are a policy instrument that helps to make market- or near-market-based housing feasible for lower-income households (Ball et al, 1988).

Thus, income-related housing allowances can help to 'recommodify' housing provision (see Doling, 1999). A related factor is that housing allowances are perceived by neo-liberal and conservative governments as giving low-income households greater consumer choice than social rented housing (Mayo and Barnbrock, 1985). The emphasis on consumer choice reflects the renewed romance with markets and disenchantment with public provision – not just in housing, but in the welfare state more generally – that have influenced governments in the advanced economies to a greater or lesser degree since the mid-1970s (Piven, 1986). As well as offering more consumer choice, housing allowances are often seen as being a much less paternalistic way to help people than providing them with social housing.

Explanations of the growing importance of housing allowances have generally focused on changes in housing policy (eg Ball et al, 1988). Yet while *policy* changes have been very important, the growing importance of income-related housing allowance schemes also reflects rising 'needs'. The drivers here are common to those facing social security benefits in the modern era. These rising needs reflect socio-economic and demographic trends that have occurred over recent decades. These include the growth in unemployment from the 1970s, which led to an increase in the number of households needing help with their rent or mortgage payments. The associated rise in long-term unemployment meant that some claimants had exhausted their entitlement to social insurance and had to rely on less generous social assistance safety-net benefits, which again increased the demands on housing allowance schemes. The increase in part-time jobs and the growth of more precarious forms of employment since the 1970s have also helped to increase the demand for housing allowances from people on the margins of the labour market. In addition, the growing numbers of economically inactive people of working age – including lone-parent households, early retirees and people receiving long-term sickness and disability benefits – has also helped to increase housing allowance costs and caseloads. Finally, population ageing has resulted in an increasing number of people above official retirement age, including many low-income pensioners, who are entitled to housing allowances.

Despite the trend towards greater reliance on housing allowances, some countries do not have a national housing allowance scheme. These include Austria, Belgium (Winters, 2005), Canada (Steele, 1984, 1998) and Switzerland. In addition, the so-called 'rudimentary welfare states' (Leibfried, 1993) of southern Europe (Greece, Portugal, Spain and Italy) do not have national housing allowance schemes (Kemp, 1990). So far as the latter are concerned, the lack of a national housing allowance scheme is perhaps not surprising. In the first place, these countries have less well-developed systems of social protection more generally (Eardley et al, 1996). They rely more heavily on family support networks, which in effect provide alternatives to state social protection. Moreover, relatively high proportions of young adults in these countries live in their parental home until their 30s. Finally, these countries have very high levels of owner occupation and a substantial tradition of self-build housing. Arguably, these factors help to reduce the need for financial assistance from housing allowances.

Since the early 1990s, housing allowance schemes have been introduced into many of the transition economies of eastern and central Europe. Thus the Czech Republic, Hungary, Poland, Russia, Slovakia, Slovenia and the Ukraine (Struyk et al, 1997; Lux, 2003; Lykova et al, 2004; Hegedus and Teller, 2005) all introduced housing allowances in one form or another. Although the details vary from one country to another, such schemes have helped to make it possible to increase rents as part of the process of privatisation and restitution of formerly state-owned rental housing in the transition to a market economy. Hegedus and Teller argue that the introduction of housing allowances in central and eastern Europe was essentially "a response to the affordability hardships caused by the transition and had nothing to do with the trends in developed countries" (2005, p 203). The allowances are often of relatively marginal significance and confined to the very poorest households (Lux, 2003).

The role of housing allowances

Income-related housing allowances can have housing policy or social security objectives. In practice, however, schemes invariably have both functions, though one or the other is usually dominant (Kemp, 1997). From a *housing policy* perspective, the purpose of housing allowances is to allow low-income households to afford 'adequate' housing, that is, accommodation that meets minimum standards in terms of its condition and its size relative to household needs. Put differently, the role of housing allowances is to enable recipients to raise their level of housing consumption above that which they would otherwise be able to afford (but not to so high a level that they can be regarded as 'over-consuming' accommodation).[4] That is one reason why some housing allowance schemes have, or had in the past, a requirement that households must live in accommodation that meets a minimum standard. Less emphasis seems to be placed on minimum standards within housing allowance schemes these days, perhaps because the quality of housing has improved considerably since the Second World War.

From a *social security* perspective, the role of housing allowances is not to enable low-income households to move to better-quality or larger accommodation, but rather to enable them to reduce the share of their income devoted to housing expenditure. In other words, the purpose of housing allowances, when looked at from a social security perspective, is to enable recipients to reduce their rent-to-income ratio to an 'affordable' level. By spending less of their income on housing, they can devote more of it to non-housing items in their budget. With the improvement in housing conditions in many countries in recent decades, the emphasis within housing allowance schemes has shifted more towards the income support or affordability role (Grigsby and Bourassa, 2004).

Thus housing allowances are a hybrid policy instrument. The money that is given to recipients can be spent on housing (thereby enabling them, for example, to move to better-quality dwellings) or it can be used to reduce their rent-to-income ratio and consequently be spent on other budgetary items. These two roles – housing consumption and housing affordability – are not necessarily compatible and can generate conflicting objectives between different government departments. For example, the ministry responsible for housing may be more likely to view housing allowances as a housing policy instrument, whereas the social security ministry may be more interested in the affordability role. This kind of policy conflict was apparent in Great Britain during the 1980s and early 1990s, when the Department of Social Security made cuts in housing benefit entitlement that threatened to undermine the Department of the Environment's policies of rent deregulation in the privately rented sector (Kemp, 1994).

Designing housing allowances

In general, income-related housing allowances are relatively complicated policy instruments, though the extent to which this is the case varies from one scheme to another. A major reason for this complexity is that the amount of help that such schemes provide is usually based on the individual circumstances of the recipients. That complexity may make housing allowances appear to be highly technical, or even rather boring, policy instruments. However, it is important to remember that governments that decide to introduce or reform housing allowance schemes have to make a number of important decisions about their design. Those decisions are not merely technical matters, but may crucially affect who is eligible to apply for housing allowances, how much money they are entitled to, and on what terms or conditions they may receive it.

Entitlement to income-related housing allowance schemes is generally calculated according to formulae or tables that take into account three main variables: financial resources, household size or composition ('needs'), and eligible housing expenditure. The *resources* that are taken into account are income and, usually but not always, assets such as savings. Income may be calculated either before or after income tax and social security contributions have been deducted. Housing allowance entitlement may be assessed on current income or income in a previous tax year. Entitlement may also vary by *household* size or type. In some countries, eligible *housing expenditure* may be confined to rent payments, while in others homeownership costs may be eligible as well. Australia, Britain and the Netherlands fall into the former category, while Germany, New Zealand and Sweden fall into the latter category. Eligible rent may be defined to include the cost of fuel and other services or may exclude them. Eligible homeownership costs may be confined to mortgage interest payments or may include capital repayments and other costs such as insurance and maintenance (Doling, 1997).

The three core variables – resources, household size or type, and housing expenditure – are combined into a formula to calculate entitlement levels. Most housing allowance formulae are variants of the so-called 'housing gap' approach (Howenstine, 1986). In such schemes, housing allowance entitlement is defined as a percentage of the difference – the gap – between recipients' eligible housing expenditure and a minimum contribution (or 'entry threshold' as it is referred to in New Zealand).Very often, the minimum contribution is a function of income. In housing gap schemes, the general formula can be represented as follows:

$$HA = a(H - bY)$$

where

HA is housing allowance entitlement
a is a fraction that is usually less than 1.0
H is eligible housing expenditure
b is the household contribution rate
Y is assessed income

Expressed in words, this formula means that housing allowance entitlement is equal to a percentage of the difference between housing expenditure and a set percentage of income. The proportion of the difference a covered by the allowance varies between schemes, but is usually less than 100%. Even within schemes, it can vary according to client group or level of income. Likewise, the household contribution rate b varies from one country to another. In some countries, the contribution rate varies within schemes depending, for example, on client group, income or rent level. In the Netherlands and Sweden the minimum contribution is expressed as a monetary amount rather than a percentage of income (though this sum may itself have been originally calculated in percentage terms, as in Germany).

There are several rationales for the presence of the minimum contribution rates or 'entry thresholds' in housing allowance schemes (Kemp, 1997). The most common reason is almost tautological in that it is felt that households should make a contribution from their own pockets to their housing expenditure. The entry threshold also formally identifies which households are entitled to receive help. Because households only become entitled to assistance if their housing expenditure is in excess of the minimum contribution, it permits allowances to be targeted on households who have higher housing outgoings. In other words, households whose housing expenditure is below the entry threshold are not, by definition, 'in need' and therefore do not require financial assistance. A further important reason for the minimum contribution built into housing allowance scheme design relates to concern about moral hazard, an issue that is discussed in the next section.

The precise way in which the housing allowance scheme variables are combined into a formula varies from one country to another.Very often these formulae are based on rough and ready assumptions rather than on detailed analysis of their impact on, or their consequences for, particular types of recipient.Variations in the details of housing allowance design are not merely technical matters, however, of interest only to the officials responsible for administering the scheme. Differences in the way that the three core variables are combined into a formula can make a significant difference to the amount of financial assistance that particular types of household receive. Hence the design details can have important distributional implications. Schemes may favour or disadvantage particular sizes or types of household or give relatively more or less help to people with high as opposed to low rents, and so on.

The distributional – and, hence, political – implications of housing allowance formulae often become apparent when major adjustments are made or proposed. Unless accompanied by an expanded budget, such changes invariably create groups of 'winners' and 'losers' (Kemp, 2000a). Equally, however, the complexity of income-related housing allowances can make it easier than might otherwise be the case for governments to cut back entitlement levels. This can be achieved, for example, by changing some of the more obscure rules or the parts of the scheme with incomprehensible names such as 'tapers' or 'non-dependent deductions' (to use two British examples). In other words, scheme complexity facilitates the process referred to by Pierson (1994) as 'retrenchment by stealth'.

Moral hazard: housing and labour market disincentives

Most income-related housing allowance schemes use *actual* rather than *notional* housing expenditure to calculate entitlement. They are *ex post* rather than *ex ante* schemes (see Gibb, 1995). This is because rents and mortgage payments vary widely and take up a large share of household expenditure. Beveridge (1942) referred to this as 'the problem of rent'. This is also an important reason for the need for such schemes in the first place. However, the fact that income-related housing allowance schemes usually take into account claimants' actual housing expenditure has important moral hazard implications. In a social security context, 'moral hazard' refers to the possibility that claimants may manipulate the system by changing their behaviour in ways that increase their benefit entitlement (Barr, 1999).

While all means-tested social security benefits are subject to moral hazard to some degree, housing allowance schemes based on actual rather than notional housing costs are particularly prone to this problem. This is because claimants living in private rental accommodation are able to exercise a degree of choice over which house or flat they occupy; and hence they have some say over the rent they pay. This choice may be very limited but it nonetheless does exist in most cases (Kemp, 2000b). Faced with a number of possibilities, private tenants may opt to live in more or in less expensive accommodation. Some claimants might try to negotiate with the landlord over the rent level when taking up a tenancy, but others might not do so. In general, the amount of housing allowance received increases as the rent increases. Hence, these marginal housing decisions can influence the amount of housing allowance paid and, therefore, the cost of the scheme. For this reason, housing allowances invariably employ a range of methods to prevent recipients from 'over-consuming' housing.

The minimum contribution incorporated into housing gap schemes, previously discussed, is intended among other things to give recipients an incentive to 'shop around' for accommodation or to minimise the risk of collusion between the landlord and tenant in setting the rent. If housing allowances covered all of the rent for the poorest recipients, they would have little financial incentive to economise on their housing expenditure. They might agree to pay a higher rent for their accommodation than it is really worth in the marketplace, or they might move upmarket to unreasonably expensive, or unnecessarily large, accommodation. The latter has been referred to as 'upmarketing' (Hills, 1991). Minimum contributions ensure that some proportion of the marginal cost of recipients' housing decisions is paid for out of their own pocket.

The question of moral hazard raises another crucial question for the design of any housing allowance scheme and that is whether (and, if so, how) to define a maximum amount of housing expenditure that is eligible to be taken into account when calculating benefit entitlement. The rationale behind such limits is generally to prevent recipients from living in unduly expensive accommodation and to help restrain the cost of housing allowance schemes. The household contribution rate discussed above is partly intended to inhibit 'over-consumption' of housing. In general, three further strategies tend to be employed by governments to prevent such 'over-consumption' resulting from the provision of housing allowances:

- housing expenditure ceilings;
- housing allowance maxima; and
- administrative rules.

First, the housing allowance schemes in most countries have rent ceilings, which may vary by household size or area. In some cases, such as the Netherlands, people living in accommodation that has a rent above the ceiling are disqualified from receiving an allowance. More commonly, however, the excess rent above the ceiling is ignored, as in Germany and Great Britain. Second, several countries place limits on the amount of housing allowance that may be awarded to recipients. For example, the New Zealand Accommodation Supplement scheme incorporates caps of this sort, which vary between different parts of the country. Third, the British Housing Benefit scheme has a number of administrative rules that aim to reduce the possibility of benefit being paid on unreasonably high rents or unreasonably large accommodation (Kemp, 2000b).

As well as seeking to prevent over-consumption, housing expenditure ceilings may be used to limit the possibility that housing allowances may be capitalised into higher rents (or house prices) within housing markets that are not subject to rent controls. This possibility exists because housing allowances increase the effective demand for accommodation, which in turn may allow landlords to charge higher rents than would otherwise be possible. Hence, if rents rise, housing allowances, in effect, may be 'captured' by landlords rather than by the claimants who formally receive them (technically, this distinction is known as the *effective* versus the *formal incidence* of a benefit or tax).

Whether or not housing allowances do result in higher rents in the private market depends upon a complex array of factors and is likely to vary depending upon the characteristics of individual housing markets. There is a relatively small body of research evidence about the market impacts of housing allowances, most of which has been conducted in the US. In particular, a 10-year social research experiment in the US found that housing allowances had relatively little impact on rents and house prices. This was partly because only a small share of households in the experiment sites received the allowances. It was also because most recipients used the money to reduce the share of their income spent on housing rather than to increase their housing consumption (see Bradbury and Downs, 1981). In other words, although the allowances were intended to be a form of housing subsidy, the recipients implicitly used them as an income supplement. More recently, an analysis of the impact of a reform of housing allowances on rents at the dwelling level in France in the early 1990s found that they did result in higher rents when an assisted tenant replaced a non-assisted one. This result "is consistent with the hypothesis that in the short run individual private landlords capture part of the subsidy" (Laferrere and Le Blanc, 2004, p 36). However, it is much more difficult to assess the long-run impact of housing allowance schemes.

In addition to the moral hazard issues over housing consumption, policy makers have also been concerned about the possible work disincentive effects of housing allowances (Priemus and Kemp, 2004; Stephens, 2005; Priemus et al, 2006). Most of this concern has focused on the 'poverty trap'. This trap can affect people who are in employment and receive income-related, in-work benefits or tax credits. The concern is that they may be deterred from increasing their earnings because the extra tax and social security contributions that they have to pay – and the withdrawal of benefits and housing allowances – on that extra gross income mean they are little or no better off in net terms (Deacon and Bradshaw, 1983). There is also concern that housing allowances may contribute to the 'unemployment trap', that is, the situation where people are little or no better off in work than they would be out of work and living on benefits (Wilcox, 1993). This can arise, for example, in situations where housing allowances are payable to people living on social security benefits but not to people who are in paid employment. Notwithstanding these structural work disincentives, there is relatively little evidence that housing allowances affect labour market behaviour in practice (see Shroder, 2002; Hulse and Randolph, 2005; Ludwig et al, 2005; Norvik and Åhrén, 2005).

Fiscal pressures

Income-related housing allowances are now one of the main means by which the advanced welfare states provide financial assistance with housing expenditure. As discussed earlier, they are seen as having significant advantages over bricks-and-mortar subsidies, particularly in an era of fiscal restraint. The perceived pressure to contain public spending in the face of increasing global economic competition (and, in the EU, the Maastricht criteria for European Monetary Union) will help to ensure that housing allowances become more rather than less important as a policy instrument compared with bricks-and-mortar subsidies.

The renewed ideological preference for markets will also help to ensure that housing allowances retain their significance. This is because income-related housing allowances help to *underpin* the market, whereas bricks-and-mortar subsidies that enable social landlords to charge below-market rents serve to *undermine* it. Hence, it can be argued that means-tested housing allowances are a less 'decommodified' form of housing support than bricks-and-mortar subsidies (see Doling, 1999). What is interesting, however, is that it is not just liberal welfare regimes such as Britain and the US that have made the shift towards means-tested housing allowances. Sweden is phasing out all bricks-and-mortar subsidies (Turner and Whitehead, 2002) and the Netherlands has abolished them (Priemus, 1995), with both countries now relying on housing allowances as the principle instrument for helping low- and moderate-income households to afford their rent. Thus, income-related housing allowances appear to be 'relatively autonomous' from welfare regime types.[5] Although they appeal to the residual approach favoured by liberal welfare states, they are also consistent with both corporatist and social democratic welfare regimes in their post-industrial manifestations.

Nevertheless, the scope and generosity of housing allowances are also affected at the margin by the economic performance of welfare states. The increased reliance on housing allowances in many countries, and the economic recession that many of them experienced in the 1990s, for example, meant that housing allowance caseloads and scheme costs rose considerably. The anticipated savings from greater reliance on allowances, therefore, did not always materialise in practice and some governments responded by introducing cutbacks in order to contain rising costs. The demand-led nature of most housing allowance schemes means that costs increase during downturns in the economic cycle (and to that extent, they have a counter-cyclical effect in the housing market). However, it is precisely during such periods that governments are generally under pressure to trim scheme costs in order to contain rising budget deficits. As Priemus (1990) points out, although housing allowances are favoured by policy makers because they cost less than bricks-and-mortar subsidies, their open-ended funding means that in practice they can prove to be expensive. Thus, there is to some extent a trade-off between bricks-and-mortar subsidies for social rented housing that can relatively easily be cash limited and are less well targeted, and housing allowances that are highly targeted but which are generally not cash limited.[6]

This book

Although there is a growing literature on housing allowances (especially in the US), there have been few comparative studies devoted to the subject (see Howenstine,

1986; Kemp, 1997; Ditch et al, 2001).[7] The aim of this book is to contribute to knowledge and understanding about housing allowances in different countries. Whereas the volumes by Howenstine (1986) and Kemp (1997) were structured around particular themes, this book is largely based on chapters about individual countries. Both approaches have advantages and disadvantages, but one benefit of a country-focused approach is that it avoids disembodying housing allowances from the context within which they operate. This is important because such schemes do not exist in isolation, but rather interact with, and are embedded within, the wider housing system as well as the social security and taxation arrangements that exist in each country.

This belief that the study of housing allowances needs to be located within the wider welfare regime and not merely the housing system, has influenced the selection of the countries to be included in this volume. The ways in which income-related assistance with housing expenditure is provided has also influenced the inclusion of particular countries. The first five countries are examples of what Esping-Andersen (1990) has defined as liberal welfare regimes. There are, nonetheless, important differences between them in relation to housing allowances (Hulse, 2003). Australia (Chapter Two) and New Zealand (Chapter Three) both have relatively small social housing sectors for which income-related rents are charged. Consequently, their housing allowance schemes apply only to private housing, though in the case of Australia only renters, while in New Zealand both private renters and owner-occupiers, can receive assistance. These two countries therefore employ a bifurcated approach to income-related housing assistance, combining income-related rents for social housing and housing allowances for the private sector.

Canada provides a useful comparison with Australia and New Zealand because, while it too has a small social housing sector for which income-related rents – referred to as 'rents geared to income' – are charged, it does not have a national (that is, federal) housing allowance scheme, though some provinces do provide them (see Chapter Four and Steele, 1984, 1998). By contrast, although the US does have a federal housing voucher programme, it is cash limited rather than demand led. Hence, as Newman points out in Chapter Five, many applicants who meet the qualifying criteria do not receive a voucher. Thus both Canada and the US are countries that have what may be described as residual housing allowance systems.

Great Britain is included not simply because the editor and the publisher are both based in that country. As I have shown elsewhere (Kemp, 1994, 1997) the British Housing Benefit scheme is relatively unusual from a comparative perspective. Britain does not have what Steele (Chapter Four) refers to as a 'classic' housing allowance programme based on the housing gap model. Instead, for many of the poorest recipients, the scheme covers all of their *eligible* rent. Hence, in these cases there is no gap between their eligible rent and their housing allowance. The British scheme embodies a residual income approach to housing allowances. It is similar to – and, indeed, evolved from – the way in which some countries

---

cover all eligible housing expenditure within their social assistance schemes. As noted above, these countries include Canada, Germany, Sweden and, in the case of owner-occupiers, Britain itself.

France (Chapter Seven) and Germany (Chapter Eight) are examples of what Esping-Andersen (1990) classified as conservative welfare regimes. Both have long-established housing allowance schemes and, indeed, were early adopters of this approach to helping households to pay for their housing. The housing allowance schemes in these two countries are available to owner-occupiers as well as private and social housing tenants. As well as housing allowances, France and Germany still provide bricks-and-mortar subsidies to housing providers and tax relief to landlords and owner-occupiers. In both countries the housing allowance schemes conform to the classic, housing gap approach.

Esping-Andersen (1990) classified the Netherlands (Chapter Nine) and Sweden (Chapter Ten) as social democratic welfare regimes. Both countries have long had housing allowance schemes, but unlike France and Germany, have turned away from bricks-and-mortar subsidies. Although both employ the classic housing gap design, in Sweden the scheme for families is unusual in that it incorporates a child benefit payment. Another difference between the two countries is that the Swedish scheme is open both to renters and owner-occupiers, while the Dutch scheme is available only to renters. Sweden has a separate income-related housing supplement for pensioners, which is not regarded as part of housing policy (Turner and Whitehead, 2002).

The transition economies of central and eastern Europe were not included in Esping-Andersen's (1990) *Three worlds of welfare capitalism*. However, as noted above, many of these countries introduced housing allowance schemes in the wake of the transition from state socialism to a market economy. It was therefore decided to include one such country – the Czech Republic – in this book (Chapter Eleven).

The chapters in this volume follow a broadly similar structure, with sections that locate housing allowances within their housing and social security context, outline the design of the scheme(s), examine the role and impact of housing allowances, and discuss current policy debates and reform pressures. The chapter on the Czech Republic by Lux and Sunega includes comparisons with several other transition economies, while Chapter Twelve compares the other countries included in this volume.

Notes

[1] An earlier version of this chapter was published in (2000) *International Social Security Review*, vol 53, no 3, pp 43–57. I am grateful to the editor, Mike Gautrey, for permission to reproduce parts of it here.

[2] Housing allowances provide an amount of benefit that is *income related*. That distinguishes them from what might be termed *income-tested* subsidies for which households must have an income below a specified threshold in order to be able to receive help, the amount of

which is *not* determined by their income (Kemp, 1997). An example of an income-tested subsidy might be a low-interest loan that is provided to low-income home buyers.

[3] To some extent, the validity of the latter criticism depends on the extent to which social housing is targeted at low-income households or is available to moderate-income people as well, something that varies considerably between different countries (Stephens et al, 2002). It is also affected by whether or not social housing rents are income-related.

[4] In practice, as Stephens (2005) has pointed out, it may be difficult to identify the point at which increased consumption becomes 'over-consumption'.

[5] Interestingly, Doling (1999) shows that, contrary to Esping-Andersen's (1990) welfare regime typology, Britain has a more decommodified housing system than Sweden or Germany.

[6] This is not the case in the US because the housing voucher programme is cash limited (see Chapter Five). On the other hand, this limits the efficacy of such schemes in tackling housing affordability problems.

[7] The *European Journal of Housing Policy* published a special issue on the topic in 2005. See also Hulse (2003) and Priemus et al (2006).

References

Ball, M., Harloe, M. and Martens, M. (1988) *Housing and social change in Europe and the USA*, London: Routledge.

Barr, N. (1999) *The economics of the welfare state* (3rd edn), London: Oxford University Press.

Beveridge, W. (1942) 'Social insurance and allied services', Cmd 6404, London: HMSO.

Bradbury, K.L. and Downs, A. (eds) (1981) *Do housing allowances work?*, Washington, DC: Brookings Institution.

Deacon, A. and Bradshaw, J. (1983) *Reserved for the poor. The means test in British social policy*, Oxford: Basil Blackwell and Martin Robertson.

Department of Social Security (1998) *New ambitions for our country*, London: The Stationery Office.

Ditch, J., Lewis, A. and Wilcox, S. (2001) *Social housing, tenure and housing allowance: An international review*, Department for Work and Pensions in-house report, London: Department for Work and Pensions.

Doling, J. (1997) *Comparative housing policy*, Basingstoke: Macmillan.

Doling, J. (1999) 'De-commodification and welfare: evaluating housing systems', *Housing, Theory and Society*, vol 16, no 4, pp 156–64.

Eardley, T., Bradshaw, J., Ditch, J., Gough, I. and Whiteford, P. (1996) *Social assistance schemes in the OECD countries, volume 1: The synthesis report*, London: The Stationery Office.

Esping-Andersen, G. (1990) *The three worlds of welfare capitalism*, Cambridge: Polity.

Gibb, K. (1995) 'A housing allowance for the UK? Preconditions for an income-related housing subsidy', *Housing Studies*, vol 10, no 4, pp 517–32.

Grigsby, W.G. and Bourassa, S.C. (2004) 'Section 8: The time for fundamental program change?', *Housing Policy Debate*, vol 15, no 4, pp 805–34.

Harloe, M. (1985) *Private rented housing in the United States and Europe*, London: Croom Helm.

Harloe, M. (1995) *The people's home? Social rented housing in Europe and America*, Oxford: Blackwell.

Hegedus, J. and Teller, N. (2005) 'Development of the housing allowance programmes in Hungary in the context of the CEE transitional countries', *European Journal of Housing Policy*, vol 5, no 2, pp 187–209.

Hills, J. (1991) *Unravelling housing finance*, Oxford: Clarendon.

Howenstine, E.J. (1986) *Housing vouchers: A comparative international analysis*, New Brunswick, NJ: Centre for Urban Policy Research, Rutgers University.

Hulse, K. (2003) 'Housing allowances and private renting in liberal welfare regimes', *Housing, Theory and Society*, vol 20, no 1, pp 28–42.

Hulse, K. and Randolph, B. (2005) 'Workforce disincentive effects of housing allowances and public housing for low income households in Australia', *European Journal of Housing Policy*, vol 5, no 2, pp 147–65.

Kemp, P.A. (1990) 'Income related assistance with housing costs: A cross-national comparison', *Urban Studies*, vol 27, pp 795–808.

Kemp, P.A. (1997) *A comparative study of housing allowances*, London: The Stationery Office.

Kemp, P.A. (2000a) 'Housing benefit and welfare retrenchment in Britain', *Journal of Social Policy*, vol 28, no 2, pp 263–79.

Kemp, P.A. (2000b) *'Shopping incentives' and housing benefit reform*, Coventry: Chartered Institute of Housing and Joseph Rowntree Foundation.

Laferrere, A. and Le Blanc, D. (2004) 'How do housing allowances affect rents? An empirical analysis of the French case', *Journal of Housing Economics*, vol 13, pp 36–67.

Leibfried, S. (1993) 'Towards a European welfare state', in C. Jones (ed) *New perspectives on the welfare state in Europe*, London: Routledge.

Ludwig, J., Duncan, G. and Pinkston, J.C. (2005) 'Housing mobility programs and economic self-sufficiency: Evidence from a randomized experiment', *Journal of Public Economics*, vol 89, pp 131–56.

Lux, M. (2003) 'Efficiency and effectiveness of housing policies in central and eastern Europe countries', *European Journal of Housing Policy*, vol 3, no 3, pp 243–65.

Lykova, T., Petrova, E., Sivaev, S. and Struyk, R. (2004) 'Participation in a decentralized housing allowance programme in a transition economy', *Housing Studies*, vol 19, no 4, pp 617–34.

Malpass, P. (1990) *Reshaping housing policy: Subsidies, rents and residualisation*, London: Routledge.

Mayo, S.K. and Barnbrock, J. (1985) 'Rental housing subsidy programs in West Germany and the United States', in K. Stahl and R.J. Struyk (eds) *US and West Germany housing markets*, New York: Springer-Verlag.

Merrett, S. (1979) *State housing in Britain*, London: Routledge & Kegan Paul.

Nordvik, V. and Åhrén, P. (2005) 'The duration of housing allowance claims and labour market disincentives: The Norwegian case', *European Journal of Housing Policy*, vol 5, no 2, pp 131–46.

Oxley, M. (1987) 'The aims and effects of housing allowances in Western Europe', in W. van Vliet (ed) *Housing markets and policies under fiscal austerity*, London: Greenwood Press.

Pierson, P. (1994) *Dismantling the welfare state? Reagan, Thatcher and the politics of retrenchment*, Princeton, NJ: Princeton University Press.

Piven, F.F. (1986) 'Cities, housing and "hyper-capitalist" regimes', Paper presented to the 'City Renewal through Partnership' Conference, May, Glasgow.

Priemus, H. (1990) 'The uncontrollability of the housing allowance', *Netherlands Journal of Housing and Environmental Research*, vol 5, no 2, pp 169–80.

Priemus, H. (1995) 'How to abolish social housing? The Dutch case', *International Journal of Urban and Regional Research*, vol 19, pp 145–55.

Priemus, H. and Kemp, P.A. (2004) 'The present and future of income-related housing support: Debates in Britain and the Netherlands', *Housing Studies*, vol 19, no 4, pp 653–68.

Priemus, H., Kemp, P.A. and Varady, D. (2006) 'Housing vouchers in the United States, Great Britain, and the Netherlands: Current issues and future perspectives', *Housing Policy Debate*, vol 16, no 3/4, pp 575–609.

Robinson, R. (1979) *Housing economics and public policy*, Basingstoke: Macmillan.

Shroder, M. (2002) 'Does housing assistance perversely affect self-sufficiency? A review essay', *Journal of Housing Economics*, vol 27, pp 381–417.

Steele, M. (1984) *Canadian housing allowances: An economic analysis*, Toronto: Toronto University Press.

Steele, M. (1998) 'Canadian housing allowances inside and outside the welfare system', *Canadian Public Policy – Analyse de Politues*, vol 24, no 2, pp 209–32.

Stephens, M. (2005) 'An assessment of the British housing benefit scheme', *European Journal of Housing Policy*, vol 5, no 2, pp 111–29.

Stephens, M., Burns, N. and MacKay, L. (2002) *Social market or safety net? British social rented housing in a European context*, Bristol: The Policy Press.

Struyk, R., Lee, L. and Puzanov, A.S. (1997) 'Monitoring Russia's experience with housing allowances', *Urban Studies*, vol 34, pp 1789–818.

Titmus, R.M. (1968) *Commitment to welfare*, London: Allen & Unwin.

Turner, B. and Elsinga, M. (2005) 'Housing allowances: Finding a balance between social justice and market incentives', *European Journal of Housing Policy*, vol 5, no 2, pp 103–9.

Turner, B. and Whitehead, C.M.E (2002) 'Reducing housing subsidy: Swedish housing policy in an international context', *Urban Studies*, vol 39, no 2, pp 201–17.

Wilcox, S. (1993) *Housing Benefit and the disincentive to work*, York: Joseph Rowntree Foundation.

Winters, S. (2005) 'Are there grounds for housing allowances in Flanders (Belgium)?', *European Journal of Housing Policy*, vol 5, no 2, pp 167–85.

—

TWO

Housing allowances and the restructuring of the Australian welfare state

Kath Hulse

Introduction

Housing allowances have become increasingly important in Australia since the early 1980s, both in terms of the number of households assisted and government expenditure. Increasing reliance by governments on housing allowances has not been the result of an explicit process of policy development. Instead, two different types of housing allowances developed gradually and incrementally within the housing assistance and income support systems. Housing allowances are specific to either the public or private rental sectors and are the product of considerable dualism in rental market structuring (Kemeny, 1995).

This chapter traces the development of both types of housing allowances and examines their role, design and impacts. It raises a number of current policy debates, including prospects for integration of the two housing allowance schemes, the implications of 'welfare-to-work' policies, the role of housing allowances in developing the not-for-profit housing sector, and issues associated with designing housing allowances for a large country with significant differences in housing sub-markets.

The context for government housing assistance in Australia

Housing in Australia is a market commodity, almost entirely in private ownership and in which access is determined primarily by ability to pay market prices. In 2001, almost seven in ten Australian households were homeowners. This high rate has changed little for 40 years but is now bolstered by the more than four in ten households who own their housing outright with no mortgage, as shown in Table 2.1. Almost three in ten Australian households rent their housing, predominantly from private landlords and real estate agents. There is also a small social housing sector comprising 5.4% of occupied private dwellings.

Australian governments use a range of policy instruments to achieve housing outcomes, including tax expenditures, supply subsidies to social housing providers and personal subsidies to households. The most significant of these in terms of

Table 2.1: Occupied private dwellings by tenure, Australia, 2001

Tenure	Number	%
Fully owned	2,810,917	41.7
Being purchased	1,872,132	27.8
Rented	1,858,324	27.6
Rent free	94,771	1.4
Other	101,255	1.5
	6,737,399	**100.0**

Source: ABS (2003, p 10, table 6).

Note: Excludes non-responses; 'rented' includes 4.7% public housing and 0.7% community housing, a total of 5.4% social housing.

dollar value are tax expenditures for homeowners, in particular, exemption of owner-occupied housing from capital gains tax. The most recent estimate for 2001 suggests that the dollar value of tax expenditures for homeowners[1] (A$21 billion) is about five times greater than direct government outlays on housing programmes (A$4.2 billion), although the different nature of assistance and data problems make such a direct comparison difficult (Wang et al, 2004, p 2).

Direct government expenditures on housing, by contrast, mainly provide assistance to renters rather than homeowners, as indicated in Table 2.2. The exception is a non-means-tested First Home Owners Grant, which was brought in to sustain housing demand following the introduction of a Goods and Services Tax in 2000. There are two separate and parallel types of direct government assistance for renters: housing allowances for private renters, embedded within the national income support system, and supply subsidies for public and community housing, within the housing assistance system.

Over the last two decades there have been three main changes to direct government expenditure programmes on housing: a withdrawal of most direct assistance programmes for home purchasers (Berry, 1999), a decrease in real expenditure on social housing (Hall and Berry, 2004), and a shift in the composition of government expenditure from supply subsidies to the providers of

Table 2.2: Direct government expenditures on housing, Australia, 2003–04

	A$ billion
Ownership	
First Home Owners Grant	0.9
Rental	
Public and community housing (Commonwealth–State Housing Agreement)	1.3
Housing allowances for private renters (Rent Assistance)	1.9
Total direct expenditure	**4.1**

Sources: Commonwealth Budget 2003–04, Budget Paper no 3, Table 11; and SCRGSP (2005, ch 16, p 5).

Note: Excludes expenditure on specific programmes for veterans and indigenous people outside the Commonwealth–State Housing Agreement.

---

social housing to personal subsidies to households who rent (Hulse, 2002). These changes reflect attempts to contain taxation levels by restricting direct expenditure programmes and to reduce direct government involvement in housing markets to a safety net for renters with low household incomes. Housing allowances have become increasingly attractive to Australian governments because they enable targeting directly to households, rather than indirectly via social housing providers, and appear to support household choice (Hulse, 2003).

Separate and parallel development: housing allowances within the income support and housing systems

Housing allowances internationally generally have both income support and housing objectives, although one or the other is usually dominant (Kemp, 1997, p`56). In Australia, housing allowances developed separately within both systems. This has largely been a product of the country's federal system of government, which determines the roles of different levels of government in income support and housing. Once established, these two types of housing allowances have been characterised by substantial 'institutional path dependence' (Esping-Andersen, 1999).

Australia has a federal system in which the federal government and six state governments have substantial powers. Local government is relatively weak by international standards, having no powers under the constitution, only those delegated by state governments. The federal government[2] is responsible for providing a safety net for people who are unable to maintain a minimum standard of living from market income, thus combining what in other federal systems like Canada and the US are effectively two tiers of income support: upper-tier income support at a federal level, and social assistance at a state or provincial level. This national system has universal coverage and those in prescribed categories (such as pensioners, people with disabilities, sole parents and unemployed people) are entitled to payments if they meet asset and income limits. Income support payments are funded by taxation, not insurance contributions, and are flat rate and not related to earnings. The system aims to provide the same level of payment to people in similar circumstances wherever they live in Australia (Whiteford and Angenent, 2002).

This national system of income support was part of the post-war settlement on the welfare state.[3] Payments were intended to cover all types of costs required for a minimum standard of living, including housing. Housing costs, which vary by sub-market, tenure type and household type, size and composition, pose problems in such a system. Successive federal governments have responded to these problems through the incremental development of a scheme for providing additional income related to housing costs within the income support system. Its origins date back to 1958 with the introduction of a flat-rate 'supplementary allowance' for single pensioners (age, invalid and widows) who faced higher costs because they could not share their rental costs, unlike couple pensioners (Kewley, 1973).

Eligibility for this housing-related payment, which subsequently became known as Rent Assistance (RA), was extended incrementally over the ensuing decades until, by the mid-1980s, almost all income support recipients were eligible. In the late 1980s, eligibility was further extended to low-income working families with dependent children in receipt of a specific family payment, as part of the federal Labor government's strategy to reduce poverty among low-income families. This was epitomised by Prime Minister Bob Hawke's famous, and ultimately unachievable, declaration in 1987 that by 1990 no Australian child would live in poverty. These changes resulted in an increasing RA caseload and expenditure, as shown in Table 2.3.

Major changes to the payment formula were made in 1982 when the flat-rate payment was converted into a more explicit housing allowance for income support recipients who rented in the private market, with new public tenants no longer able to access the payment. The new formula had a minimum rent threshold below which no assistance was payable, a maximum rate of assistance, and a taper rate of 50 cents in the dollar for payment between the threshold and the maximum. A series of further incremental changes were made in the late 1980s and early 1990s to target assistance to families with children, including maximum payment levels that varied by household type and composition. Other changes aimed to target assistance to income support recipients living in areas with higher housing costs, such as increases in the rent threshold and, in 1993, an increase in the taper rate from 50 to 75 cents in the dollar (Prosser and Leeper, 1994). The federal Coalition[4] government elected in 1996 made further changes to the scheme, including its extension to young people in receipt of an income support payment, a lower rate of payment for single people sharing accommodation, and tighter rent verification procedures to address government concerns about fraud and multiple payments of RA for the same rental property.

Quite separate from this system, another part of the post-war settlement on the welfare state was agreement by the federal government and the states on joint responsibility for housing policy. This involved the federal government providing funding via loans to the states at concessional interest rates (later a mix of loans and

Table 2.3: RA caseload and expenditure, Australia, 1986–2004

June	Income units in receipt of RA	Expenditure A$ million (constant 2004 dollars)
1986	582,869	172.0
1991	645,626	572.8
1996	893,946	1,290.1
2001	967,333	1,573.8
2004	949,698	1,953.0

Source: Department of Social Security and DFaCS, Annual Reports (various years).

Note: Constant 2004 dollars calculated using implicit price deflators provided by the Australian Bureau of Statistics; 'income unit' refers to a single person or a couple and any dependent children living with them who are aged 16 and under (or under 18 years if in full-time schooling).

---

grants, and subsequently grants) while the six state governments, and later the two territory governments, delivered programmes to provide public housing and to assist people to buy their own homes. This was codified in a series of multilateral financial treaties called the Commonwealth–State Housing Agreement (CSHA) from 1945 onwards. By the 1990s, most homeownership programmes had been phased out and the funds were used to support the social housing sector, comprised of public housing, which is owned and managed by state and territory housing authorities, and a very small community housing sector.

These arrangements included 'implicit' housing allowances in which rents are set in relation to household income (Kemp, 1997, pp 15–16). Initially most public housing tenants paid property rents set at cost (historic and dwelling specific, and then current and averaged), later moving to market-related rents and subsequently market rents. As property rents increased, and as public housing was increasingly targeted to those on the lowest incomes, the percentage of tenants paying rents based on income (called 'rebated rents') increased. In the late 1960s, this ranged from 7% to 19% across the states (Jones, 1972, pp 161–9). By 1986 it had risen to 62% of tenants across Australia and, by 2004, 88% of public housing tenants were in receipt of rent rebates (SCRGSP, 2005, table 16.4).

Supply subsidies for social housing and housing allowances (RA) for private renters developed in relative isolation from each other. State and territory governments, policy makers, practitioners and academics focused on periodic renegotiations of the CSHA, which was the centrepiece of Australian housing policy. RA was mainly of interest to federal income support administrators and not regarded as a form of housing assistance until the 1990s. Private rental was the 'forgotten sector' of Australian housing, even though research from the 1970s onwards had consistently found that most poor households lived in private rental housing (Commission of Inquiry into Poverty, 1975; National Housing Strategy, 1991).

The role and design of housing allowances

There are two defining features of RA. First, the payment is only available to people for whom the federal government accepts responsibility in terms of its income support or family assistance legislation. This excludes other groups, such as low-income earners who do not have dependent children. Second, it is a tenure-specific payment for people who rent in the private market. Home purchasers or owners and public housing tenants in receipt of income support or family assistance payments are not eligible for RA.

According to the federal government, RA 'contributes to' improvement of housing affordability and 'complements' broader income support objectives by assisting individuals and families with the additional costs associated with renting in the private housing market (DFaCS, 2005, p 102). It is essentially a non-taxable income supplement for private renters who are in receipt of income support payments or who have dependent children and receive more than the base rate of family payment.[5] Eligibility for RA is an entitlement, subject to means testing for 'primary' income support payments or defined family payments, and there is no separate test of income or assets.[6] RA is assessed, and paid, as part of an income support payment by a federal agency (Centrelink) or, in the case of families with dependent children, is attached to family payments administered by another federal agency (Office of Family Assistance).

Payment of RA is calculated at 75 cents in the dollar above a minimum rent threshold and is capped by a maximum payment level, with thresholds and maxima being set according to family size and composition, as indicated in Table 2.4. Maximum rates of RA and rent thresholds are indexed twice yearly in association with indexing of primary payments. As RA recipients start to earn income from paid work, the primary payment is withdrawn at a rate applicable to that payment. RA is the last part of the payment to be withdrawn at the applicable rate.

RA is a component of a cash transfer paid to the recipient, not to the landlord. Recipients can choose the type, size, location and rent level of their housing, within income and supply constraints, and the extent to which they allocate RA to housing costs or other expenditures. The payment formula is uniform across Australia and the design does not explicitly address regional variations in rent levels, unlike the Accommodation Supplement in New Zealand. No standards of affordability, quality or appropriateness of housing are included in the scheme.

Since RA is an entitlement, expenditure is demand driven and depends on the number of eligible households in receipt of income support payments, which in turn is affected by factors such as the level of unemployment. There is no budget item for the scheme, no waiting list and funds are not rationed, as for example with Housing Choice Vouchers in the US. Expenditure is calculated and reported upon *post hoc*; in 2003–4, expenditure on RA was A$1.953 billion. In 2004–05 expenditure on RA was A$2.086 billion or just over 1% of federal budget expenditure or 0.25% of gross domestic product, as shown in Table 2.5.

Table 2.4: Weekly rates of RA, Australia, effective from 20 September 2005 (A$)

Family situation	Maximum weekly rate of RA	Minimum weekly rent threshold	Weekly rent at which maximum rate of RA is payable
Single, no children, living alone	49.60	44.10	110.24
Single, no children, sharing	33.07	44.10	88.19
Couple, no children	46.80	71.80	134.20
Single, with 1 or 2 children	58.31	58.10	135.85
Single, with 3 or more children	65.87	58.10	145.93
Couple, with 1 or 2 children	58.31	85.96	163.71
Couple, with 3 or more children	65.87	85.96	173.79

Source: Centrelink.

—

Table 2.5: Australian federal budget estimates, 2004–05

	A$ million	As % of GDP	As % of federal budget expenditure
Estimated GDP	784,980	100.0	N/A
Federal budget revenue	193,151	24.6	N/A
Federal budget expenditure	192,306	24.5	100.0
Federal social expenditure	135,898	17.3	70.7
Federal expenditure on income support and welfare (includes RA)	82,678	10.5	43.0
Federal expenditure on housing and community services (includes federal expenditure on the CSHA)	1,671	0.2	0.9
Federal expenditure on RA	2,086	0.3	1.0

Source: Calculated from Jamrozik (2005, table 6.8, p 145).

Note: Source data are from estimates for 2004–05 contained in Commonwealth Budget Papers 2004–5; budget revenue does not include state taxes, including the Goods and Services Tax, which goes to the states; federal expenditure on RA is based on actual expenditure.

Rent rebates for public housing tenants are also tenure specific but, unlike RA, they are determined largely by state and territory housing authorities, and there is some variation in the payment formula within the multilateral CSHA and bilateral agreements between the federal government and each jurisdiction. Rent rebates for public housing tenants are regarded as a central point of housing policy and, historically, changes to formulae have been subject to approval by high levels of authority, often by state government cabinets. They are designed to enable public housing rents to be affordable to households on low incomes and, technically, are a concession on the rent chargeable on a property, usually the market rent. In practice, many public tenants are unaware of the amount of this concession (the extent of the rebate), and they are more accurately described as 'income-related rents', the term used in New Zealand, where there is a similar system (in Canada they are referred to as 'rents geared to income', see Chapter Four). State and territory 'rent rebate' schemes vary slightly but most rents, at least for incoming tenants, are now set at 25% of assessable household income, which provides a benchmark of affordability. Rents continue to be set as a percentage of income until they reach the level of market rent for the individual property.

Unlike RA, access to rent rebates is not an entitlement for households eligible for public housing but is only available to those who are allocated tenancy of public housing units. The stock of public housing in Australia is small (345,000 units or 4.7% of occupied private dwellings) and access is strictly rationed. The annual rate of new allocations declined by 42% between 1989–90 and 2003–4, from 53,100 to 30,962 households (Hulse and Burke, 2005, p 22). In this environment, most jurisdictions have further targeted their allocations to households with the greatest levels of housing and support needs. Those allocated public housing can access rent rebates and other attributes of public housing, such as relative security of tenure, but have little choice in terms of the type, size or location of their housing. If they leave public housing, for whatever reason, they lose their rent rebate.

Unlike in most other countries, the cost of rent rebates for public tenants in Australia is internally funded by state and territory housing authorities and there is no explicit arrangement to cover the 'community service obligation' involved in providing housing in which rents are set at a percentage of income. The cost of rebates is thus affected by two factors: the incomes of public tenants, which in turn have been affected by tight targeting to those on the lowest incomes, and the level of market rents, which are determined by market conditions. The cost of rent rebates, defined as the difference between market rents and rent payable by tenants, was calculated at A\$1.2 billion in 2003–4 (SCRGSP, 2005, table 16A.1). It is arguable, however, that market rents are not an applicable benchmark in the public housing sector. The sector has a social purpose, does not seek to generate a profit, and the cost of capital funds is considerably lower than in the private sector as, particularly since the 1989 CSHA, all funds have been non-repayable grants from Australian governments.

The impact of housing allowances

Who gets them?

Just under a million income units were in receipt of RA in June 2004. Recipients were predominantly of workforce age, in receipt of income support payments of one type or another, female, a single adult rather than a couple, and without dependent children, as shown in Table 2.6. A substantial minority (38%) do have dependent children, and approximately 630,000 dependent children are living with adults in receipt of RA (Hulse, 2002).

A number of researchers have attempted to convert income units in receipt of RA into households, since a household may comprise more than one income unit; for example, a family with both dependent and independent children, an extended family or a group of young people sharing. Using different methods, these estimates indicate that about 700,000 households are in receipt of RA (for example, Wulff, 2000; Wang et al, 2004). This means that an estimated 9.5% of Australia's 7.4 million households are in receipt of RA, compared with just under 300,000 households in receipt of rent rebates in public housing (or 4% of all households). Thus approximately a million households or 13.5% of all Australian households are in receipt of one or another type of housing allowance.

Both RA and rent rebates for public renters provide direct assistance to some of the country's lowest income households. Recent research for the Australian Institute of Health and Welfare suggests that more than 77% of RA expenditure is received by households with incomes in the bottom two quintiles. Rent rebates in public housing are even more targeted to those on low household incomes, with 90% of their cost going to households in the bottom two quintiles. This is in contrast to tax expenditures for homeownership whereby almost 70% of the

Table 2.6: Key characteristics of income units in receipt of RA, Australia, June 2004

Key characteristic	Number of income units	% of income units
Age		
Above workforce age (age pension)	162,602	17.1
Workforce age (all others)	787,096	82.9
Income source		
Receives income support/Family Tax Benefit	872,229	91.8
Receives Family Tax Benefit only	77,469	8.9
Gender of recipient		
Female only	588,813	62.0
Male only	303,903	32.0
Couple (female and male)	56,982	6.0
Composition of income unit		
Single, no children	512,837	54.0
Single, with children	227,928	24.0
Couple, no children	75,976	8.0
Couple, with children	132,958	14.0
Total recipients	949,698	100.0

Source: DFaCS (2004a, table 35, p 115).

Note: Definition of income unit as per Table 2.3; in income units with dependent children, payment of RA is usually attached to Family Tax Benefit payments, which go to the mother.

benefits go to households with incomes in the top two quintiles (Wang et al, 2004, pp 2, 21, 32).

Affordability

The federal government measures the impact of receipt of RA on housing affordability *post hoc* in terms of percentage of income paid in rent. Using this measure, more than two thirds (69%) of recipients would pay more than 30% of their income on rent if RA were not available. RA does decrease the percentage of income paid in rent quite substantially, although more than a third (36%) of recipients still pay over 30% of income in rent[7] after receipt of RA (DFaCS, 2004a, p 114, table 33).

Within these general figures, there is some variation in affordability outcomes for different income unit types. In particular, singles and couples without children are more likely to pay in excess of 30% of income in rent after receipt of RA than families with dependent children, as shown in Table 2.7. This is due to the design of RA which sets rent thresholds and maxima according to family type and size, and makes relatively generous family payments to people with dependent children.

These calculations treat RA as a specific housing payment (that is, rent minus RA as a percentage of income net of RA) rather than as an income supplement

Table 2.7: Recipients of RA, by income unit type and by proportion of income spent on rent after receipt of RA, Australia, June 2002

Income unit type	30% or less of income in rent	30%–50% of income in rent	More than 50% of income in rent
Single, no children	55	32	13
Couple, no children	67	24	8
Single, with 1 or 2 children	77	20	3
Single, with 3 or more children	88	11	1
Couple, with 1 or 2 children	80	15	5
Couple, with 3 or more children	92	7	1

Source: AIHW (2004, table 8, p 12).

Note: 'Single, no children' includes both those living alone and those living in shared accommodation.

(rent as a percentage of income plus RA). This assumes that all RA is offset against rent payment and gives significantly better affordability outcomes than the alternative treatment of RA as an addition to income, as illustrated in Table 2.8, which compares affordability outcomes for selected households in receipt of RA and income support in the Melbourne metropolitan area. The federal government contends that deducting RA from rent for these calculations enables a direct comparison with public housing in which rent rebates are a form of 'in-kind' assistance that can only be used to offset housing costs. RA recipients can choose

Table 2.8: Comparison of the impact of RA on affordability, using housing payment and income supplement methods, selected households in receipt of income support payment, Melbourne metropolitan area, 2005

Property type, size and rent level	Weekly rent ($)	Rent-to-income ratio without RA (%)	Rent minus RA as % of income (%)	Rent as % of income plus RA
Single person of working age, no children				
1-bedroom flat at median rent	185.0	91.5	39.2	60.1
1-bedroom flat at 75% of median rent	138.8	68.6	33.5	50.8
Couple of working age, no children				
2-bedroom flat at median rent	215.0	58.9	29.5	45.5
2-bedroom flat at 50% of median rent	161.3	44.2	25.8	37.3
Sole parent of working age plus two children				
2-bedroom house at median rent	235.0	48.8	21.3	38.3
2-bedroom house at 75% median rent	176.3	36.6	18.2	30.9

Source: Median rents from Victorian Office of Housing, Rental Report, June Quarter 2005; and Centrelink payment rates effective from 20 September 2005.

Note: Income support payment rates exclude small, specific allowances paid in certain circumstances, for example, education entry payment and pharmaceutical allowance; calculation of payments for sole parents with two children includes Family Tax Benefit A and B and assumes one child under five and one under 13 years.

---

how to spend the money but must, unlike public tenants, pay the market rent of the property.

RA is designed to provide equity between income units of the same type and size, wherever they live. The nature and type of settlement around Australia, one of the world's largest countries in terms of land area, means that private rent levels do vary considerably. Similar levels of RA deliver quite different affordability outcomes in high-rent areas, such as Sydney and other major metropolitan centres, compared to smaller state capitals, regional centres and rural Australia. In 2004, there was a difference of only A$3.60 per week between the highest average weekly RA payment in Australia's highest rent market (Sydney) and the lowest average weekly RA payment (non-metropolitan South Australia). At the same time there was an average difference in weekly rent paid by RA recipients of A$48.90 between Sydney (the highest average) and non-metropolitan Tasmania (the lowest average), as shown in Table 2.9.

The differences illustrated in Table 2.9 can largely be attributed to the effect of the maximum rates of assistance that are set by income unit size and composition but not location, in the context of different rent levels around Australia. Thus two thirds (66%) of RA recipients in New South Wales, including Sydney, received the maximum RA payment for their family type and size in 2004, compared to fewer than half (45%) of recipients in lower priced Tasmania (SCRGSP, 2005, tables 16A.58, 16A.60).

RA recipients renting in the private sector pay market rents in a sector regulated by state rather than federal legislation. No Australian state has laws that provide general controls over rent levels. Private tenants can, however, usually apply to a state tribunal or small claims court if they consider a rent increase to be excessive. Such tribunals only consider rents to be excessive if the property has deteriorated since the rent level was struck or if they are clearly above market rates. State legislation also usually places restrictions on the number of times a landlord can

Table 2.9: Impact of RA by location, Australia, 2004

	Average RA entitlement per week (A$)	Average weekly rent paid by RA recipients (A$)	Average weekly rent payable by RA recipients net of RA (A$)
Sydney	40.10	161.20	121.10
Melbourne	38.60	137.50	98.90
Brisbane	39.50	139.50	100.00
Rest of New South Wales	38.00	127.80	89.80
Rest of Victoria	37.10	120.00	82.90
Rest of Queensland	39.30	136.80	97.50
Rest of Tasmania	36.50	112.30	75.80
Rest of South Australia	36.40	117.70	81.30
Difference between highest and lowest	**3.60**	**48.90**	**45.30**

Source: Calculated from SCRGSP (2005, table 16A.58).

Note: Assumes that all RA is offset against rent payment.

increase the rent, typically no more than once every six months, and prescribes the period of notice to be given to tenants.

In contrast, rent rebate schemes operate in a highly regulated public housing sector. They are specifically designed to achieve a benchmark percentage of household income, typically 25%. While almost three quarters of tenants pay up to 25% of income on rent, almost a quarter pay 20% or less, due mainly to 'grandfathering' provisions under which rents have increased for new tenants but not for existing tenants, as illustrated in Table 2.10.

Table 2.10: Housing costs as a percentage of household income for public tenant households in receipt of rent rebates, Australia, June 2004

Public tenant households in receipt of rent rebates	% of households
Paying 20% or less in rent	24.4
Paying more than 20% and up to 25% of income in rent	73.6
Paying more than 25% and up to 30% of income in rent	1.6
Paying more than 30% of income in rent	0.4
All	**100.0**

Source: SCRGSP (2005, table 16A.75).

Note: Rent is calculated as a percentage of assessable household income, the definition of which varies between the states and territories.

While this system has been a non-negotiable component of Australian public housing policy for years, it presents two major problems. First, there is no guarantee that meeting a benchmark in terms of rent as a percentage of household income constitutes 'affordability' if households have insufficient income for other essential items after paying rent. Second, equity in treatment, defined as payment of rent based on a flat-rate percentage of household income, does not result in equity in outcomes. Public tenants with similar incomes pay the same rent irrespective of the type, size, condition, amenity and location of their housing. Since allocations to public housing are based on administrative processes and criteria, there are no price signals and no scope for households to trade off rent level with housing attributes that they may value. As these attributes may affect other costs, such as heating, cooling and public transport, after-housing costs may vary considerably.

Other housing impacts

There are no explicit objectives of RA beyond assisting in improving affordability; the quality, size and type of housing in which RA recipients live are considered a matter of individual household choice. As a result there is little information on their housing circumstances other than a survey commissioned by the federal government in 1998. This found that recipients were generally satisfied with the size of their housing, with 85% rating this as good or very good, and with its condition, rated by 63% as good or very good (Wulff, 2000, figures 3.1, 3.3).

It should be noted that these are self-assessments and that Australian housing stock is generally of good quality and amenity.

In contrast, governments regularly assess what public housing tenants think about the adequacy and appropriateness of their housing via a national survey conducted annually since 1996. A recent survey indicated that almost two thirds (64%) of respondents were satisfied with the overall condition of their home while a quarter (23%) were actively dissatisfied (Colmar Brunton Social Research, 2004, p 83). Data from state and territory housing authorities collected by the federal government as part of a jointly negotiated process of 'performance management' suggest that just under 6% of households in public housing are moderately overcrowded, defined as requiring one additional bedroom to satisfy a proxy occupancy standard (SCRGSP, 2005, table 16A.80).

The terms and conditions under which RA recipients rent their housing are, as indicated above, set by state legislation, with the federal government having no jurisdiction in this area. In 1994–5, the federal Labor government raised the issue of a national code for residential tenancy law, and federal, state and territory housing ministers agreed to commission some research on this topic. This did not progress any further as it ran into opposition based on 'states' rights', as the states have constitutional responsibility for land development and management, including regulation of residential tenancies. This means that private tenants in Australia have limited security of tenure with, at best, one-year leases, sometimes shorter. They can be asked to leave at any time for a 'just cause', such as the owners wishing to sell the property untenanted, and in some jurisdictions without a 'just cause'. This lack of security means that private tenants in receipt of RA have much higher rates of mobility than public tenants, controlling for differences in composition between the two sectors. For example, research comparing low-income lone parents in receipt of RA and renting privately with a similar group of sole parents renting public housing showed much higher rates of mobility experienced by private renters (Burke and Hulse, 2002).

Traditionally, public tenants have enjoyed considerable security of tenure, in some cases extended to children of the original tenants. Many low-income households wish to enter public housing for security of tenure as much as affordability (Burke et al, 2004). However, while security is still considerably more assured than in private rental, the public sector is slowly moving to time-limited leases. For example, in New South Wales, which has more than a third of the nation's public housing, households entering after 1 July 2006 will be offered leases ranging between two and ten years, depending on an assessment of whether their circumstances are likely to improve.

Policy debates: risks and reforms

An integrated housing allowance scheme

An important, although intermittent, policy debate in Australia has been whether the two different types of housing allowances, as previously discussed, should be integrated into one scheme; this debate has proved difficult to progress. The institutional arrangements around social housing and RA have both reflected, and reinforced, dualism in thinking about the roles of the public and private rental sectors, in a way that has created barriers to change. Politically, the 'housing lobby' have been strong supporters of social housing, particularly public housing. Many supporters of government housing assistance for low-income households have seen rent rebates for public tenants as non-negotiable but have provided at best passive support for RA, and have generated few ideas about how to improve the scheme (Hulse, 2003). Further (unlike, for example, the US), Australia has very little experience with experimentation in government social programmes. Thus there is a high degree of financial and political risk for the federal government in developing and implementing across the board reforms to RA, given that it is demand driven, based on entitlement and currently assists almost one in ten Australian households.

From 1992 to 1997, successive federal governments of both major political parties proposed to integrate the two types of assistance so that RA would be paid to public housing tenants instead of most capital funding via the CSHA. While the detail of the proposals differed, heated policy debate in the mid-1990s centred on their impact on capital funding for public and community housing and on increased rents payable by existing (and incoming) public housing tenants, rather than on the effectiveness of RA for the much larger number of private tenants. In 1997, these plans were withdrawn following failure of the federal government and the states and territories to agree on a new model (Caulfield, 2000). They did, however, agree to differentiate the roles of social housing and RA further. RA was to assist income support recipients who faced problems of affordability in private rental housing, while CSHA funds for social housing were to be targeted at households with additional needs beyond affordability, such as domestic violence, medical conditions, disability and homelessness.

Given this experience, the federal government has not attempted to reintroduce reforms to integrate the two types of housing allowances, but the issue remains on the back burner. The government has commissioned a university research centre to undertake further consultation into issues around RA and possible reform, although it is unclear whether there is any political will to attempt this when the risks of failure are considerable and there is no consensus about a preferred model.

Welfare reform

The federal coalition government, in office from 1996 to the time of writing, has developed 'welfare reform' policies that have implications for both types of housing allowances. It is using both 'carrot' and 'stick' measures to get working-age households in receipt of income support to move into paid work. Indeed, the term 'income support' is gradually disappearing from the lexicon of Australian public policy for people below the age of retirement in favour of temporary 'participation support' payments until the recipient becomes economically and socially engaged (RGWR, 2000, p 5).

Stringent work activity tests and a 'work for the dole' scheme for younger unemployed people have been in place since the mid-1990s, but recently work or training requirements have also been introduced for older people below the official retirement age, lone parents and disabled people, in conjunction with employment assistance. These are likely to affect RA recipients, almost 40% of whom receive payments due to their impairments or lone-parent status. There has been little time to evaluate the effects of these more recent changes but there is a risk that RA recipients will move into low-paid work and lose their housing assistance, but still face difficulties in paying market rents.

The federal government has also suggested simplifying income support payments for workforce-age people into a single payment, with additional allowances for factors such as disability and care of children. This recognises that there would still need to be some type of supplement for single-adult households who cannot share their living costs, particularly housing, and those with housing costs above a specified level (RGWR, 2000, p 23). If this proposal were to be introduced, housing costs, which vary by household type, size, tenure and location, would still pose the same problems as in the 1950s when the forerunner of RA was introduced.

Assistance with private rental costs for all income support recipients of workforce age is now conditional on participation in job search or training. Where there is non-compliance with activity requirements, for whatever reason, they risk losing some or all of their RA as well as their primary payment. Age pensioners, who comprise 17% of RA recipients, will be unaffected by these changes and will continue to receive the payment on an entitlement basis, if eligible. These changes will mark a move to a de facto two-tier system of income/employment support in Australia, raising the possibility that RA for age pensioners could become a separate scheme, tailored to their specific needs and circumstances. A similar development is taking place by default in Great Britain (see Chapter Six).

A further aspect of welfare reform has been federal government scrutiny of disincentives to entering paid work as a result of the design or administration of all federally funded programmes. While the interaction of the income support and taxation systems does provide substantial disincentives for households entering paid work, RA in itself makes little contribution to these effects. There is no stacking of taper rates; the only effect of RA is to add some additional income that must be withdrawn as the recipient moves into paid work. In other words, RA does not deepen the unemployment trap; it broadens it slightly. The rent rebate system, however, provides a double taper and significantly deepens the unemployment trap for public tenants (Hulse and Randolph, 2005). The federal government has, for this reason, been putting pressure on the states and territories to reduce these effects, including a compliance clause within the most recent CSHA that they risk losing a percentage of federal funding if they do not achieve increases in the number of public tenants in paid employment.

State and territory housing authorities have made some attempts to lessen the work disincentive effects of income-related rents, such as a temporary deferral of increased rents for people entering work. They are reluctant to implement more extensive measures as most are currently running an operating deficit on their rental operations (Hall and Berry, 2004). In 2004, the cost of rent rebates almost equalled total expenditures by all governments on the CSHA, such that 'new' funds for social housing were effectively absorbed by the cost of rebates for existing tenants, indicating the de facto income support role of rent rebates. State and territory housing authorities have responded to their financial problems by selling down some existing assets, often as part of redevelopment projects, thus reducing the stock of housing for which rent rebates are potentially available.

Developing the not-for-profit housing sector

Australia has a very small community housing sector, supported by capital funding provided by the CSHA. Many of the dwellings are financed and owned by state or territory housing authorities and managed by community organisations as part of a small property portfolio. There is also an emerging sector in which community organisations are developing larger portfolios, own at least some of their dwellings and are able to leverage in private finance in addition to capital funding from governments. This is often referred to as the 'affordable housing' sector, although the precise meaning of this term is still evolving.

Depending on arrangements negotiated with state and territory governments, either type of housing allowance considered in this chapter may apply to the not-for-profit sector. Some providers receive an operating subsidy from the state or territory housing authority that enables them to charge a rent based on household income as in public housing, although this type of arrangement is in decline. Others rely on their tenants accessing RA from the federal government.

There are two main means of setting rents in community housing: either tenants are charged 25% of their income including RA, or they are charged the amount of their RA plus 25% of income, so that their post-housing income is the same as if they were in public housing. These practices encapsulate the hybrid nature of RA, which is treated either as an income supplement or a specific housing payment, depending on the circumstances. In either case, a primary objective of community housing providers in setting rent is to capture the maximum rate of RA for tenants, some or all of which then gets passed through to the provider as rent revenue. Some of the larger affordable housing providers are experimenting with other models of rent setting, including discounted market rents, but all models include RA in their calculations.

This rather confusing variation in practice highlights the difficulties of developing a 'third sector' or not-for-profit housing sector in Australia in the context of strongly established divisions between public and private rental housing. Federal, state and territory governments now say that they wish to expand the not-for-profit sector, having been influenced in part by the substantial growth of housing associations in Great Britain. Planning for growth is, however, highly dependent on tenants being able to afford rents and on rent revenue being sufficient to cover operating costs. In effect, the states and territories are passing on the risk of operating deficits in rental housing to not-for-profit housing providers and, since these are capturing at least some RA from their tenants, this effectively shifts costs from the states and territories to the federal government.

These developments pose a number of risks. The federal government could at some stage in the future make tenants of community housing organisations ineligible for RA on the grounds that it already provides capital funding to these providers through the CSHA. This 'double-dipping' was the original reason for exclusion of public housing tenants from eligibility for RA in the 1980s. This would leave providers exposed in terms of rent revenue to fund their operations and in financial difficulty where they have used projected revenue streams from rents that factor in RA to leverage in additional capital funding from the private sector.

Australian governments are gradually recognising these risks and are considering new policy settings. There is renewed political interest in moving towards a more integrated rental sector with various models of financing, ownership and management being developed at a state or territory level. The politics of a federal system means that reaching agreement across all governments on these issues and respective roles and responsibilities is a slow process.

In August 2005, a joint meeting of housing, local government and planning ministers of all Australian governments agreed to a Framework for National Action on Affordable Housing. This offers the prospect of a coordinated approach to developing an affordable housing sector for low- to moderate-income households. The Framework commits to developing "mechanisms and policy initiatives that will deliver increased affordable homeownership and rental opportunities for low-moderate income households" (Housing, Local Government and Planning Ministers, 2005, p 6). Such households are defined as those earning less than A$56,219 gross per year, or about 120% of annual gross median income for Australian households. This broad definition includes households that are employed but have difficulties in accessing affordable housing, as well as those eligible for public housing and RA who have been the traditional target group of direct government assistance. The Framework commits the governments to producing a National Sector Development Plan for not-for-profit housing providers by June 2006. This will include options to 'strengthen certainty' in subsidy arrangements for not-for-profit providers, although the extent to which RA will be considered is not explicit.

Further incremental change?

The problems of the current RA system have been widely discussed, in particular, the varied affordability outcomes for recipients in different housing markets, as previously mentioned. In the mid-1990s, there was some debate about changing the RA formula to address variations in private rental markets, including maximum payment rates that varied by geographic region (for example, Industry Commission, 1993; Ecumenical Housing, 1997). This led to dissension among the states, with the smaller ones fearing that the result would be a redistribution of the quantum of federal funding towards high rent markets, particularly Sydney, Melbourne and Brisbane, and away from smaller state capitals and regional and rural Australia.

In general, the federal government has not supported such changes, raising 'constitutional issues' if RA recipients paying the same level of rent in different areas of Australia received different levels of payment, as well as the practical difficulties in defining regions for this purpose. While both of these concerns could probably be addressed, the federal government has also argued that the RA scheme enables households to choose the rent level they wish to pay. In choosing to pay higher rents, the argument runs, households get improved access to facilities, services and jobs that may enable them to reduce their other living costs, such as transport. Trading off the costs and benefits of housing consumption in this way is a matter for individual households and should not be distorted by additional RA for those who choose to pay higher rents.

An alternative view has been that the current design of RA has the effect of constraining households to live in lower rent areas, particularly in large cities such as Melbourne and Sydney. There is some evidence that RA recipients, in particular those with dependent children, are tending to concentrate in lower rent areas that have poor access to jobs, facilities and services, thus contributing to increasing socio-spatial polarisation in Australian cities (Wulff and Evans, 1999).

There appears to be little political appetite for introducing more complexity into the RA formula to make it more sensitive to regional variations in rents. In a context of budget neutrality, there would be winners and losers among the states and territories in terms of their share of RA expenditure, so they are unlikely to agree on such a change. Modelling of changes to existing parameters of RA (the rent threshold, the taper rate and maximum rates of assistance) indicates that including an explicit regional variation in the formula may not be necessary. This work suggests that changes to some of these parameters could improve housing outcomes for RA recipients in higher rent areas while keeping the simplicity of the current formula (Melhuish et al, 2004).

Conclusion

The separate and parallel development of two types of housing allowances in Australia illustrates the hybrid nature of this type of policy instrument. Housing allowances have been, on the one hand, a housing-related supplement within the income support system and, on the other, a de facto income support measure within the housing assistance system. In the Australian context, the way in which these two types of allowances developed over the years was based on clear delineation between tenures and, in particular, between two distinct rental sectors: a small and highly regulated public sector and a much larger and relatively unregulated private sector. Once established, housing allowances within each sector developed incrementally, and the politics of a federal system of government made it difficult to make fundamental changes once the two schemes had been established. This 'institutional path dependence' (see Kemp, 2000) has contributed to difficulties in developing a more integrated rental sector and, in particular, in developing a not-for-profit sector.

In recent years, the federal government's welfare reform agenda has eclipsed housing policy in changing the parameters of the income support and housing assistance systems in which housing allowances are located. There are some signs, however, of a re-emergence of a national approach to housing policy with responsible ministers from all Australian governments agreeing in mid-2005 to a Framework for National Action on Affordable Housing. This may lead to better integration of various forms of housing assistance across tenures, including across the two rental sectors. The framework provides an opportunity for governments to consider, in a more explicit and informed way, the dual roles of housing allowances in affecting both affordability for households and rent revenues and financial sustainability for housing providers.

Notes

[1] This estimate includes exemption of homeowners from capital gains tax on the sale of their home (A\$13 billion) and no tax on imputed rent for homeowners (A\$8 billion).

[2] The term 'federal government' will be used in this chapter for clarity. In practice, it has also been called at different times the 'Commonwealth government' and the 'Australian government'.

[3] Some of the system dates back to the years following Federation in 1901, when Australia was a recognised pioneer in social provision, for example, age pensions (1909), invalid pensions (1910) and maternity allowances (1911).

[4] Australia has two main political parties: the Liberal Party (which usually governs in a coalition with the National Party) and the Australian Labor Party. The coalition is the more conservative of the two.

[5] This payment is Family Tax Benefit A, which is for people with dependent children or students. It can be paid fortnightly via the Office of Family Assistance or in a lump sum via the tax system at the end of the year.

[6] There was a separate means test for RA from 1965 but this was abolished from 1987.

[7] It should be noted that these figures cannot be directly compared with data from countries such as Canada and the US where rent payments typically include utility costs, a practice that is unusual in Australia.

References

ABS (Australian Bureau of Statistics) (2003) *2001 Census housing census*, paper no 03/02, Canberra: Australian Bureau of Statistics.

AIHW (Australian Institute of Health and Welfare) (2004) *Commonwealth Rent Assistance, June 2002: A profile of recipients*, bulletin no 14, cat no AUS 45, Canberra: Australian Institute of Health and Welfare.

Berry, M. (1999) 'Unravelling the "Australian housing solution": The post-war years', *Housing, Theory and Society*, vol 16, no 3, pp 106–23.

Burke, T. and Hulse, K. (2002) *Sole parents, social wellbeing and housing assistance*, final report, Melbourne: Australian Housing and Urban Research Institute.

Burke, T., Neske, C. and Ralston, L. (2004) *Entering rental housing*, final report, Melbourne: Australian Housing and Urban Research Institute.

Caulfield, J. (2000) 'Public housing and intergovernmental reform in the 1990s', *Australian Journal of Political Science*, vol 35, no 1, pp 99–110.

Colmar Brunton Social Research (2004) *National social housing survey of public housing tenants 2003*, Canberra: Commonwealth Department of Family and Community Services.

Commission of Inquiry into Poverty (1975) *Poverty in Australia*, first main report, Canberra: Australian Government Publishing Service.

DFaCS (Department of Family and Community Service) (2004a) *Annual report 2003–04*, vol 2, Canberra: Department of Family and Community Services.

DFaCS (2004b) *Housing Assistance Act 1996 annual report 2002–2003*, Canberra: Department of Family and Community Services.

Ecumenical Housing (1997) *National housing policy: Reform and social justice*, Melbourne: Ecumenical Housing.

Esping-Andersen, G. (1999) *Social foundations of post-industrial economies*, Oxford: Oxford University Press.

Hall, J. and Berry, M. (2004) *Operating deficits and public housing: Policy options for reversing the trend*, Melbourne: Australian Housing and Urban Research Institute.

Housing, Local Government and Planning Ministers (Australia) (2005) *Framework for National Action on Affordable Housing*, approved by joint meeting of ministers, 4 August, www.nchf.org.au/downloads/naah_framework.pdf.

Hulse, K. (2002) *Demand subsidies for private renters: A comparative review*, final report, Melbourne: Australian Housing and Urban Research Institute.

Hulse, K. (2003) 'Housing allowances and private renting in liberal welfare regimes', *Housing, Theory and Society*, vol 20, no 1, pp 28–42.

Hulse, K. and Burke, T. (2005) *The changing role of allocations systems in social housing*, Melbourne: Australian Housing and Urban Research Institute.

Hulse, K. and Randolph, B. (2005) 'Workforce disincentive effects of housing allowances and public housing for low income households in Australia', *European Journal of Housing Policy*, vol 5, no 2, pp 147–66.

Industry Commission (1993) *Public housing, vol 1: Report*, report no 34, Canberra: Australian Government Publishing Service.

Jamrozik, A. (2005) *Social policy in the post-welfare state* (2nd edn), Sydney: Pearson Education.

Jones, M.A. (1972) *Housing and poverty in Australia*, Melbourne: Melbourne University Press.

Kemeny, J. (1995) *From public housing to the social market: Rental policy strategies in a comparative perspective*, London: Routledge.

Kemp, P.A. (1997) *A comparative study of housing allowances*, research report no 60, Department of Income Support, London: The Stationery Office.

Kemp, P.A. (2000) 'Housing benefit and welfare retrenchment in Britain', *Journal of Social Policy*, vol 28, no 2, pp 263–79.

Kewley, T.H. (1973) *Income support in Australia 1900–1972* (2nd edn), Sydney: Sydney University Press.

Melhuish, T., King, A. and Taylor, E. (2004) *The regional impact of commonwealth Rent Assistance*, final report, Melbourne: Australian Housing and Urban Research Institute.

National Housing Strategy (1991) *The affordability of Australian housing*, issues paper no 2, Canberra: Australian Government Publishing Service.

Prosser, B. and Leeper, G. (1994) 'Housing affordability and changes to rent assistance', *Social Security Journal*, June, pp 58–61.

RGWR (Reference Group on Welfare Reform) (2000) *Participation support for a more equitable society*, final report, Canberra: Reference Group on Welfare Reform, Department of Family and Community Services.

SCRGSP (Steering Committee for the Review of Government Service Provision) (2005) *Review of government service provision 2005*, vol 2 and 16A Housing: Attachment, Canberra: Steering Committee for the Review of Government Service Provision, Productivity Commission.

Wang, H., Wilson, D. and Yates, J. (2004) *Measuring the distributional impact of direct and indirect housing assistance*, cat no HOU 108, Canberra: Australian Institute of Health and Welfare.

Whiteford, P. and Angenent, G. (2002) *The Australian system of social protection: An overview* (2nd edn), occasional paper no 6, Canberra: Department of Family and Community Services.

Wulff, M. (2000) *The 1998 survey of Rent Assistance recipients: A report on key findings*, Canberra: Department of Family and Community Services.

Wulff, M. and Evans, S. (1999) 'The spatial impact of commonwealth Rent Assistance on Australia's low-income households', in J. Yates and M. Wulff (eds) *Australia's housing choices*, Brisbane: University of Queensland Press.

THREE

The New Zealand experience of housing allowances

David C. Thorns

Introduction

Understanding the development of housing allowances within a particular nation state requires a historical perspective and a consideration of the way in which allowances are linked to state policy and practice. Further, current policy instruments arise out of both past decisions made and contemporary debates and understandings (Lowe, 2005). The history of New Zealand housing policy since the 1950s shows it has gone through a number of stages. This chapter tracks these changes to illustrate the changing position of housing allowances and their place within the overall housing policies of successive governments.

Housing allowances in context

In the 1950s and 1960s, the dominant thrust of public policy was to extend homeownership. The belief that underlay this policy was that a home-owning society was a more stable and prosperous one. Also, as this was a time of strong population growth and inward migration, there was a need to encourage the growth of the housing stock. Thus, much of the emphasis in housing policy was around increasing the housing supply. In the 1950s and 1960s, governments were active in both land development and providing a range of supports for first-time buyers to acquire housing, with this being targeted to the purchase of new housing. This policy mix provided a range of assistance that included the capitalisation of family benefit, a weekly cash allowance for each child, which could be used as a deposit and the provision of low-interest loans to modest- and low-income earners from the State Advances Corporation.[1] In 1974, these loans were transferred to the Housing Corporation of New Zealand. The corporation was a multifunctional entity created to manage state stock, assist in the purchase of housing through the operation of lower-interest rate mortgages, to provide policy advice, and to undertake research with respect to housing affairs. The policies at this time with respect to homeownership were complemented by the provision of state social rented housing. However, the amount of such housing has always been relatively small and only briefly did this sector achieve 9% of the total tenure.

The welfare regime in place in New Zealand, from the 1930s to the 1980s, has been characterised as a wage earners welfare state (Castles, 1985). This has meant that state policies that were designed to include and engage people in society gave primacy to paid work and participation in the labour force. Wages were meant to be at a level that would enable the single-income working family to acquire a house, and, therefore, to develop a secure base from which to engage in wider community activity. The capitalisation of family benefit and first homeowner loans were therefore seen as critical to allowing New Zealanders to provide for themselves the sought after ideal of homeownership (Ferguson, 1994). Renting was seen as a second-best and far from desirable option.

To encourage supply, government support and low-interest loans were available only for the purchase of a new house and to those buying their first home. Such loans encouraged the expansion of suburban developers on greenfield sites (Perkins and Thorns, 1999). Therefore, this pattern became the typical one for urban development through the 1950s to the 1970s. By 1981 the rate of homeownership had climbed to 71%. Some variation existed between urban areas reflecting the growth pressures and housing costs. From 1981 through to 1991 the pattern in Table 3.1 indicates a moderate increase in the rate of homeownership from 71% to a peak of 74% and then a decline through to 2001.

It is important to note that there are different tenure experiences within the main ethnic groups within New Zealand. For example, there are significant differences in the tenure experiences of the European and the indigenous Māori population, especially after the urban migration of Māori to the cities, which led to a decline in ownership from 70% in the 1930s to 44% in 2001. This move resulted in a substantial increase in the tenanted Māori population and a move for many into public social housing. Table 3.2 shows that, of the more recent Asian migrants, a higher proportion of this group have become homeowners, although the rate is lower than for people of European origin. Further the rate for Pacific peoples is the lowest, with 3% in 1981 rising to 44% by 1991 and falling to 36% in 2001.

Table 3.1: Housing tenure in New Zealand, 1981–2001

	1981		1986		1991		1996		2001	
Region	Owned	Rented	Owned	Rented	Owned	Rented	Owned	Rented	Owned	Rented
Auckland urban area	72.3	28.7	73.9	26.1	72.4	27.6	68.7	31.3	63.8	34.2
Wellington urban area	66.7	34.3	70.1	29.9	70.0	30.0	67.9	32.1	64.5	35.5
Other main urban areas	74.0	26.0	75.4	24.6	75.6	24.4	71.5	28.5	68.0	32.0
Secondary urban areas	74.0	26.0	77.0	23.0	78.0	22.0	74.1	25.9	71.3	28.7
Minor urban areas	70.2	29.8	74.1	25.9	76.1	24.9	72.1	27.9	69.4	30.6
Rural centres	68.5	31.5	71.7	28.3	75.2	24.8	73.9	27.1	72.9	27.1
Other rural	65.2	37.8	75.9	24.1	70.1	29.9	71.2	28.8	76.2	25.8
New Zealand	**71.4**	**28.6**	**73.7**	**26.3**	**73.8**	**26.2**	**70.7**	**29.3**	**68.0**	**32.0**

Source: DTZ (2004, p 206).

Table 3.2: Homeownership rates by ethnic group, New Zealand, 1981–2001

	1981	1986	1991	1996	2001
Asian	64.8	69.1	62.7	61.9	58.8
European	74.2	76.4	77.1	74.1	71.9
Māori	47.9	49.2	52.0	48.0	44.0
Pacific peoples	38.8	44.5	43.7	40.2	35.5
Other ethnic groups	50.2	56.3	52.4	39.7	32.8

Source: DTZ (2004, p 230).

The mid- to late 1970s saw the beginning of a substantial shift in New Zealand's welfare policies. The changes arose out of the ending of the post-war economic boom in the developed world, the oil price shock of the early 1970s and the necessity for New Zealand to restructure its trading arrangements as a consequence of the entry of the United Kingdom into the European Economic Community. These changes to the external environment created pressures on the social welfare system and led to moves to restructure public expenditure. The housing market in the 1970s became more volatile with booms and slumps creating both winners and losers and generating increasing affordability problems. Higher demand caused by the rapidly escalating prices in the early to mid-1970s created shortages of housing, which in turn led to further price rises, in turn creating an affordability gap. Also, during the 1970s it became increasingly clear that in New Zealand, as in many other countries, in the future it would require a two-income household to purchase a house. By the late 1970s, New Zealand experienced sharp outward migration and increased unemployment, leading to a slump in house prices; the economic downturn stimulated broader restructuring, which included the shifting of resources from the welfare vote to promote a range of new economic growth projects (Thorns, 1992).

The election in 1984 of the fourth Labour government marked a time of radical restructuring to New Zealand's economy and society (Boston and Holland, 1990; Kelsey, 1995). Economic policies were changed to embrace a much more strongly competitive, liberal free-market set of practices. Significant changes took place in the tax regime with a shift from direct tax towards indirect tax, and the creation of a Goods and Services Tax (GST) (Dalziel, 2001). This tax also added to the cost of housing, as it was applied to house building and building services. Alongside economic changes were a series of reforms to the structure of government. Here, New Zealand followed the path taken in the United States under Reagan and in the United Kingdom under Thatcher. The reforms were concerned with reducing government expenditure on welfare to create improved opportunities for economic growth and innovation, and enabling the more extensive incorporation of New Zealand into the rapidly changing global world. To enter this world of freer trade, the curing of inflation through monetary policy was seen as central to the rekindling of economic growth, improving efficiency, and therefore ultimately of improving social well-being. To improve efficiency, it was seen as necessary to reform the process of government itself. This led to the corporatisation of government departments, the separation of the funding and the supply of government services and the tendering of advice, and the more extensive use of contracting out and competitive and contestable processes to achieve improved efficiency (Hazeldine, 1998; Boston et al, 1999; Dalziel, 2001).

Strong advocacy by the New Zealand Treasury for change in the delivery of housing support towards greater reliance upon a system of demand-side interventions such as housing vouchers or allowances was present at this time. In the briefing papers to the incoming governments in 1984 and 1987, a radical overhaul was advocated to replace existing policies with a single demand-side subsidy or voucher. However, no significant change in direction took place until the early 1990s. The Labour government adopted a version of business as usual with respect to housing policy. The policy followed at the time was a mixture of supply- and demand-side interventions designed to enable the continuation of homeownership as the preferred policy for low- and modest-income earners. Thus, when affordability became recognised as an increasing problem due to the interest rate increases on mortgages and price increases, a number of schemes were introduced to try and assist. The Housing Corporation, formed in 1974, continued through the 1980s to be one of the largest business organisations in New Zealand, worth over NZ$6,000 million, and although it was a multifunctional government organisation it was spared from the restructuring that took place in other such organisations. The majority of public service activities were remodelled at this time to create a clearer separation of policy advice and delivery aspects of government activity, with the latter being transferred to state-owned enterprises (SOEs) initially, and then later some were privatised (Thorns 1990).

During the mid- to late 1980s, the Housing Corporation provided around 10,000 loans annually to modest-income buyers to purchase their own housing. However, to improve the targeting of state assistance, income-related interest rates were introduced in the 1980s as part of the shift towards more targeted structures. After this change rates varied from 5% to 17%; a rebate was available when outgoings rose above 25% of gross household income. Further, the refinance, second chance and home improvement loans, available since 1973 to prevent the sale of the family home or to assist people with dependants following a marriage break-up, were increased in value and interest rates reduced. Some innovative new schemes were added to try and assist entry to homeownership at this time, including equity share and sweat equity in 1985. However, one of the key policies of the past, the capitalisation of family benefit, was abolished, and in its place a more restricted Homestart deposit and GST assistance scheme was introduced. This in part reflected the increased costs associated with the introduction of GST, which was a key part of the shift from direct to indirect taxation in the mid-1980s. GST was set initially at 10%, and then a couple of years later it rose to 12.5%, where it has remained.

Homestart was a targeted scheme to fill the deposit gap that was opening up for low- and modest-income earners. The Labour government also increased the rate of acquisition of state houses by the Housing Corporation, raising the number from 57,547 in 1984 to 56,091 by 1986 (see Table 3.3). Rental assistance – called Accommodation Benefit – for beneficiaries and low-income tenants was available in the form of a housing allowance, administered by the Department of Social Welfare. This benefit was paid as a supplement to other benefits where housing costs were high. Changes made in 1987–8 resulted in beneficiaries receiving assistance where their housing costs exceeded 25% of their income (excluding family benefit and support) and the subsidy rate was set at 50% of costs once the household had moved over the 25% threshold. The policy also brought in the same threshold levels, abatement regime and maximum rates for low-income wage and salary earners.

Table 3.3: Social rented housing units, New Zealand, 1981–2001

	1981	1986	1991	1996	2001
Housing New Zealand	56,979	56,091	63,552	52,671	52,500
Local government	16,158	16,653	15,420	14,781	14,115

Source: DTZ (2004).

In the 1980s there were three agencies involved in delivering housing assistance. The principal agency was the Housing Corporation, which administered state rentals, managed the house loan portfolio, carried out some land development, and managed tenancy legislation and tribunals. In addition, the Corporation also conducted research into housing issues and provided the government with advice on housing and urban development, running competitions, and examining alternative designs for houses, subdivisions and forms of tenure, including cooperatives. The other major players on the housing scene were the Department of Social Welfare, which administered the Accommodation Benefit, and the Department of Māori Affairs, that administered rented housing and purchase loans for Māori and Pacific households. However, such households also had access to Housing Corporation rental stock.

The role and design of housing allowances after the 1992 reforms

The debate over housing reform had been building through the 1980s. Treasury papers to the incoming government from 1984 to 1990 promoted a more market-based approach, favouring greater consumer choice. Such a position reflected the general movement of opinion within the OECD countries in favour of demand-side rather than supply-side interventions. The proposed method of support was that of income supplementation through some form of voucher or allowance scheme. This approach was seen as easier and more efficient to target to those in need than the existing income-related rent system and supplementary accommodation benefits. The Treasury also had its sights on the Housing Corporation, which, as a provider of services and accommodation, was seen as ripe for turning into a state-owned enterprise, and thus ensuring its operations would be more efficiently managed for the taxpayers.

These moves were strongly opposed by both the National Housing Commission and the Housing Corporation, as can be seen from the latter's submission to the Royal Commission on Social Policy in 1986 (Housing Corporation, 1988). In this they defended the role of the state in housing provision and rejected the adoption of a voucher-type income supplement scheme for the assistance of low-income households, on the grounds that there was evidence of continuing market failure in areas of affordability, supply, physical standards and special needs groups (such as women's refuges, emergency housing and housing for disabled people). It was argued that there was an ongoing need for government intervention within the housing market to address these areas of need. The Labour government, on the whole, supported this position and rather than turning the Corporation into an SOE, retained it as an organisation with a strong social responsibility. Changes did occur within the structure of the Corporation, with a move from a largely administrative model to a more managerial one, with the regional and divisional managers being given greater responsibility and autonomy over their areas of activity.

Prior to the election of 1990, the centre-right National Party had begun to signal its intention to reform housing. Once elected, the new government moved quickly to establish working parties to look into both the development of an Accommodation Supplement (AS) to replace existing forms of subsidy and support payments and the restructuring of the Housing Corporation. It seems, therefore, that the driving force for change was political rather than based on a careful analysis of either the existing or proposed housing environment. The result was the introduction of the 1992 Housing Restructuring Act, which brought in a radical reshaping of housing policy. This Act significantly shifted the emphasis to demand-side income supplementation via a housing allowance as the key form of housing assistance.

The National government's reform agenda was concerned about the reallocation of existing expenditure to encourage greater efficiency and a more equitably distributed government support. This concern with horizontal equity led to the new housing allowance being available across all tenures so that it could be used within the state and private rental sectors and to assist in the purchase of an owner-occupied dwelling (Waldegrave, 2002). The original Treasury papers estimated that the scheme would deliver fiscal savings of between NZ$20 and NZ$50 million a year as a result of its greater targeting. However, by the time that the scheme was launched in the 1991 budget all reference to cost savings had been removed and replaced by the claim that the reforms would be cost neutral. The overall argument that the Treasury employed was that the new benefit would assist many more people who were in housing need because it would not be as open to capture as the state housing stock had been under the existing policy of housing allocation via a points system and committees. Many state tenants were considered to have houses that were no longer appropriate to their current needs – most were thought to be too large – and thus they should be encouraged to move to smaller accommodation, thereby releasing housing for those with greater needs. However, critics of the new scheme argued that without rent controls of some kind the likelihood was that rent rises would result in more people qualifying for the supplement and lead to upward pressures upon the level of supplement, resulting in steadily rising costs (Johnston, 1993; O'Brien and Wilkes, 1993). Further, this particular relationship was exacerbated by the fact that in the same budget, which created the new housing allowance structure, other forms of state benefits were cut to create a more substantial gap between the level of benefits and incomes derived from work. This problem of the overlap of work and low incomes has been a long-running concern of policy makers to ensure that the level of benefits does not act as a disincentive to seeking employment (Higgins, 1999; Murphy, 1999).

The reforms brought in a new set of structures to deliver government housing policy and a single new measure to be the centrepiece, the Accommodation Supplement (Thorns, 2000). The allowance is a form of consumer subsidy to enhance the capacity of low-income and beneficiary households to obtain housing in either the public or private sectors. The Housing Corporation was broken up and left with a residual role to administer mortgages, until they were eventually privatised. The state's stock was transferred to a new Crown entity, Housing New Zealand (HNZ), which was required to operate on a commercial model and make a return to the government on its operation. The level of this was set in an annual performance agreement. To achieve these objectives state house rents were set to increase in three stages to market rates. Those who had rents in excess of 25% of their income would be eligible for assistance from the AS. The new AS was to be administered by Work and Income New Zealand (WINZ)[2] rather than a housing agency, as it was seen as part of the benefit system rather than a housing policy. The AS was targeted, and the amount received was linked to income and assets testing and reduced as income increased.

The impact of housing allowances

The new housing allowance was a gap scheme as it provided a subsidy to reduce the difference between the minimum contribution (25% rental and 30% ownership) of income on actual housing costs subject to the abatement regime, and regional maxima rules of the scheme. There still existed special benefits and tenure protection measures to allow people with low income and benefits to cope with the associated rise to market rents for state housing tenants. The AS replaced direct provision on 1 July 1993 and the complexity meant it had to be calculated for each household. Eligibility was restricted to low-income households with disproportionately high housing costs, defined as over 25% of renter income and 30% of owner-occupier income. The AS was designed to cease at 70% of rental

—

or mortgage outgoings. The original estimate from the Treasury was that it would be cost neutral or return a small reduction in expenditure. In the first year of operation in 1993–4 the cost was NZ$337 million and 251,500 households were assisted, most of these being beneficiaries. However, over the next five years the cost of the scheme rose rapidly to reach NZ$852 million by 2000.

The majority of people in receipt of the Accommodation Supplement in its initial years of operation were former state tenants. Data in Table 3.4 shows that the majority of those in receipt of the AS were also on benefits of one kind or another. The largest number in 1994 and 1995 were on unemployment benefits, followed by those on the Domestic Purposes Benefit.[3] These two groups also made up the majority of the Housing Corporation's tenants. In respect of type of accommodation 77% of HNZ tenants in 1995 and 74% in 1996 were in receipt of the Accommodation Supplement. Significantly, the number of boarders at 72,000 in 1994 was greater than those in HNZ tenancies. The majority of boarders (85%) are related to their landlord and 72% of them pay board to a parent or parents (Colmar Brunton, 1996, p 2). Further, the AS in both 1995 and 1996 was paid to a greater number of beneficiaries, pensioners and low-income earners who were renting rather than buying. The overall take-up rate in 1995/6 was assessed at 65%, with a much greater take-up rate (78%) amongst non-superannuation beneficiaries compared to 55% for superannuitants and 19% for non-beneficiaries. In each case, the take-up rate was much greater amongst renters than amongst homeowners (Colmar Brunton, 1996, p 3; Kemp, 1998). The rising levels of rent for properties provoked a debate over the impact of these changes upon the poverty level and the contribution made by housing to it (Stephens et al, 1995).

A key argument in favour of moving to a generic form of income supplementation across rental (public and private) and owner occupation was to achieve horizontal equity and remove discrimination between the sectors in terms of state support. The data from studies into the AS show that the majority of the money flowed into the rental sector, with limited take-up for the purchase of houses. To succeed in moving from rental to ownership required both the level of repayments to be manageable, and also the capacity to meet the deposit requirements (Murphy, 1999; Thorns, 2000).

Prior to the reforms, public rents were based on the capacity of a household to pay and had been set at a proportion of household income (25%). After the reforms, market rents were determined for the property regardless of the income of the present occupants. One of the motivations here was that of the more efficient use of the housing stock and the Treasury's belief that there was considerable mismatch between the needs of the occupants and their current housing. The example typically cited would be that of a couple living in a three-bedroom family house long after their children had left home and the 'need' for such space had ceased. The reforms were thus designed to encourage movement of such households into smaller units of accommodation, freeing up 'family houses' for those on the waiting lists (Morrison, 1993, 1995; Morrison and Murphy, 1996).[4]

Table 3.4: Accommodation Supplement by main benefit types, New Zealand, 1994–95

Main benefit	1994 (at 30 June)			1995 (at 30 June)		
	Number	Weekly value (NZ$)	Average weekly value (NZ$)[b]	Number	Weekly value (NZ$)	Average weekly value (NZ$)[c]
Unemployment[a]	92,209	2,659,068	1,499.68	89,740	2,714,540	1,573.00
Training	7,508	147,347	1,020.76	7,726	165,315	1,112.80
Sickness	20,663	708,587	1,783.08	23,708	837,554	1,837.16
Invalids	20,269	772,003	1,980.68	23,759	956,188	2,093.00
Domestic purposes	73,518	3,157,033	2,232.88	83,661	3,908,632	2,429.44
Orphans	4	181	2,353.00			
Widows	2,702	106,701	2,053.48	3,080	132,271	2,233.40
Transitional retirement	1,330	46,058	1,800.76	1,648	58,077	1,833.00
NZ superannuation	20,154	621,907	1,604.72	21,427	702,955	1,706.12
Veterans pension	309	9,260	1,558.44	316	10,144	1,669.20
No main benefit	10,869	357,560	1,710.80	11,258	405,152	1,871.48
Total	**249,535**	**8,585,705**	**1,789.32**	**266,323**	**9,890,828**	**1,931.28**

Source: NZ Department of Social Welfare, Statistical Information Report 1994, table 47, p 58, and Statistical Information Report 1995, table 53, p 54.

Notes: [a] Includes 55 plus benefit, job search allowance and independent youth benefit. [b] This column is calculated from the first two columns. [c] This column is calculated from the previous two columns.

However, the policy failed to recognise the slow rate at which the market responds to these signals. The reasons for this are numerous, but of crucial importance is the nature of private landlords in New Zealand, who are mostly owners of one or two properties, often acquired as a result of transfers on death, many of which are held for capital gain, and thus are not part of a long-term rental market. The associated question of the degree to which landlords and developers saw this as an opportunity to simply raise rents and increase profits is also hard to resolve. At the same time as the AS was being implemented, in the mid-1990s, there was also a short-term boom in the housing market, which makes separating out the impact of the AS from other price-driven increases difficult.

The new regime of support has clearly provided more people with money than the older system concentrating upon state rental housing. However, this raises the key question of whether the amounts are sufficient to offset the rises in rents brought about by the moves to market rents in the state sector and increases in the private sector as a result of an increased capacity to pay by tenants now in receipt of the AS. Data from a government-commissioned report shows that the changes have led to an increased amount of housing-related poverty, with housing costs consuming a much greater part of household income. The data show that 77% of AS recipients had only NZ$150 or less residual equivalised income per week after housing costs (Colmar Brunton, 1996, p 2).[5] This change is directly related to the shift to market rents for the house regardless of the capacity to pay of the tenants. The assumption that tenants could adjust their housing to more appropriately sized accommodation, so two people did not have to pay for a three-bedroom house, was shown to be unrealistic as there was limited supply of smaller accommodation.

Policy debates and reform

The general election of 1999 returned a Labour-led, centre-left coalition government. In the campaign, one of the pledges that Labour made was to return rents for state house tenants to an income-related basis. Therefore, in 2000 the Housing Restructuring (Income Related Rents) Amendment Act was passed. This legislation reintroduced income-related rents for state housing tenants and prevented the further sale of any more public rental stock. The allocation of state rental dwellings was to be based on need. Thus in December 2000 about 48,000 state tenants had their AS cancelled and were moved to the new regime.

In 2001, the Housing New Zealand Corporation (HNZC) was formed to replace Housing New Zealand and the remains of the old Housing Corporation. The new organisation had a broader mandate than simply managing the state rental stock. It was once again to include a policy and research capacity. This was to enable the identification of future needs and ensure that the housing sector in general was well placed to provide affordable, decent housing to New Zealand families now and in the future. However, the policy role is divided between HNZC and the Ministry of Housing, which was renamed the Department of

Building and Housing in 2004, and given a focus around regulative aspects of building and a continuing responsibility for the management of the residential tenancies legislation.[6]

The new organisation was to be a socially responsible agency and no longer had to make a profit. In the future, government would compensate the Housing New Zealand Corporation for loss of income created through the new income-related rents policy. Further, the stock of public housing was once again to rise, with the government putting in place a scheme to purchase, lease and build further public housing. The new regime of income-related rents initially aided about 40,000 state tenants (Murphy, 2003a, 2003b). The measure was a targeted one and took into account both the income of partners and any income from savings. Once tenants were over the income and assets thresholds set, rents were then adjusted to market value and assistance was similar to that provided under the AS to non-state tenants.

The AS continues to be the main source of housing support for the majority of the population and, as can be seen from Table 3.5, the amount spent through this allowance increased steadily through to 2000 when it reached NZ$852 million. The fall since that time has been due to the transfer of state tenants back to income-related rents and thus off the AS. Just as the actual dollars expended has risen over time, so has the proportion of GDP expended on the allowance. However, the amount here has only risen from 0.41% in 1994 to a maximum of 0.80% in 1999

Table 3.5: Expenditure on housing allowances as a percentage of GDP

Year	AS spending (NZ$ million)	GDP (NZ$ million)	% of GDP on AS
1994	337	82,917	0.41
1995	483	88,469	0.55
1996	551	93,966	0.59
1997	648	98,317	0.66
1998	777	100,599	0.77
1999	831	103,767	0.80
2000	852	109,938	0.77
2001	790	117,464	0.67
2002	711	125,331	0.57
2003	697	130,700	0.53
2004	691	140,512	0.49

Sources: Figures on AS spending: MSD Statistical Report (2004, table 4.4, p 101); figures on GDP: calculated for July–June years (same as AS) from 2004 Q4 GDP table 1.2 column BA, which gives inflation-adjusted (but not seasonally adjusted) GDP by quarter.

Notes: Figures start in 1994 (meaning July 1993–June 1994) because that is the first year of full AS funding; AS has been the only significant housing allowance since that time; 1998 DSW Statistics Report shows slightly different figures from 2004 MSD report.

Comment: The table shows the proportion of GDP spent on AS increasing from 1994 to a peak in 1999, then decreasing gradually from 2000 onwards. One reason for this is the introduction of income-related rents for state tenants in 2000, meaning approximately 40,000 fewer households claimed AS. Another reason is the gradual reduction in unemployment figures and number of people receiving benefits since the election of a Labour government at the end of 1999.

prior to the policy changes. After this date the proportion has slowly declined to 0.49% in 2004. However it needs to be recognised that from 2000 to 2006 New Zealand experienced a period of sustained economic growth, leading to falling unemployment and increased participation in the labour force and improved incomes. These collectively have affected the relationship of housing allowances to GDP and the number of people that are in receipt of the allowance.

The data for the numbers receiving the AS (Table 3.6) shows steady growth through to 2000 when the change back to income-related rents took place that moved people off the AS. The figures after 2001, therefore, show the impact of this policy on the AS. As numbers fall there is an increased demand for state housing, which is now cheaper, leading to the growth in waiting lists, especially in the Auckland region.

In order to explore further the way that the AS operates as a 'gap' housing allowance (Howenstine, 1986; Kemp, 1997) and illustrate the complexity that the assessment and calculation of it entails, an analysis was undertaken to try to show how the AS operates across the three largest urban areas (Auckland, Wellington, Christchurch) and the rural parts of another region. The reason for this choice of areas is that different AS maxima are available across the regions to reflect the differences in housing costs. Another major variable is that of household

Table 3.6: Number and percentage of households receiving the AS, New Zealand, 1994–2004

Year	Number of households receiving AS	Total number of households	% of total households receiving AS
1994	251,505	1,166,568	21.6
1995	266,275	1,166,568	22.8
1996	280,369	1,268,094	22.1
1997	297,134	1,268,094	23.4
1998	305,735	1,268,094	24.1
1999	313,042	1,268,094	24.7
2000	315,988	1,268,094	24.9
2001	265,882	1,344,267	19.8
2002	258,034	1,344,267	19.2
2003	251,941	1,344,267	18.7
2004	236,695	1,344,267	17.6

Sources: For number of households receiving AS 1994–97: DSW Statistics Report (1998, table 53, p 65); for number of households receiving AS 1998–99: MSD Statistical Report (2002, table 4.1, p 65); for number of households receiving AS 2000–04: MSD Statistical Report (2004, table 4.1, p 98); for figures on total number of households: 2001 Census: Families and Households, table 35, p 113. DSW Statistics Report, MSD Statistical Report and 2001 Census: Families and Households available from Statistics New Zealand (www.govt.nz).

Note: MSD Statistical Reports 2002–04 give figures for the previous five years that are consistent with each other but disagree slightly with figures given in earlier DSW Statistics Reports. Where figures disagree, the most recently published instance is given. Census figures are the only source of household numbers but are only collected every five years. It was decided not to estimate numbers for the intervening years.

composition and, in order to explore this, 17 possible household types were identified, ranging from single-person, unemployed beneficiary households under 25 through to households with varying numbers of members living at the mean and minimum wage.[7]

Table 3.7 presents a number of examples selected to illustrate how the impact of the AS varies depending on the mix of household composition, location, income and rent payments. The rent calculations are generated for the median rent and for one standard deviation below the average rent to provide a more accurate level of rent likely to be paid by those households trying to find affordable accommodation. The household types selected are first a single-person unemployed beneficiary household. The next case is that of a married unemployed beneficiary household with two children. A two-person household living on national superannuation and renting a one-bedroom dwelling is featured in the next column and, finally, the last two columns show a two-person household on the minimum wage renting a one- or two-bedroom dwelling. The assessments made here make no allowance for the quality of the accommodation.

The data show that the AS is likely to provide quite different outcomes depending on where the household is located, its composition and the level of benefits or wage they receive. The AS does affect the amount of income left after housing costs, as can be seen in the final line in Table 3.7 for each region. This shows that Auckland is the city where households have the highest housing costs after the impact of the AS is taken into account; this is followed by Wellington, Christchurch and then the non-metropolitan region. The range also shows up substantial differences. In Auckland the percentage spent on housing costs after the AS is taken into account varies from 103% (clearly single unemployed people could not afford central city accommodation) through to 39% for those on state pensions. For the calculation using the second rental figure based on one standard deviation below the mean rent, the range is lower but is still from 63% for the single beneficiary person household to 33% for the pensioner one.

In Wellington, the range is 71% through to 33%, while in Christchurch it is from 68% through to 29%, and in Manawatu from 46% through to 26%, based on the median wage. Consistently, the lowest proportion of income spent on housing costs, taking into account the AS, is by those living on National Superannuation. This in part reflects the presence of pensioner flats – though since the reforms of the early 1990s, many of these had rent increases and some local authorities have reduced the number that they own. Across the four selected regions, the figures suggests that in Auckland beneficiaries and households on the minimum or average wage would have to pay close to, and in some cases more than, their total income on median rents. Even rents at the 16th percentile would require over 70% of the income of all but a few of the household types. The situation gradually improves in the other three regions with the more rural area of Manawatu having the lowest proportion of income required to service rents.

The relation between the amount provided by the allowance and the current levels of rents and market prices for purchase has been a continuing area of debate.

Table 3.7: Examples of effects on percentage of income spent on housing after AS, New Zealand

	Unemployed		Pensioners	Wage earners	
	1 (1bdr)	8 (2bdr)	11 (1bdr)	13 (1bdr)	13 (2bdr)
Auckland renters					
Income	140.48	399.96	393.56	282.51	282.51
Median rent					
Housing costs	290	350	290	290	350
AS	145	175	135	154	160
Housing costs after AS	145	175	155	136	190
Income left after housing	–4.52	224.96	238.56	146.51	92.51
% increase on housing before AS	206	88	74	103	124
% increase on housing after AS	103	44	39	48	67
Std Dev rent					
Housing costs	200	260	200	200	260
AS	111	113	72	91	133
Housing costs after AS	89	147	128	109	127
Income left after housing	51.48	252.96	265.56	173.51	155.51
% increase on housing before AS	142	65	51	71	92
% increase on housing after AS	63	37	33	39	45
Wellington renters					
Income	140.48	399.96	393.56	282.51	282.51
Median rent					
Housing costs	200	300	200	200	300
AS	100	141	72	91	125
Housing costs after AS	100	159	128	109	175
Income left after housing	40.48	240.96	265.56	173.51	107.51
% increase on housing before AS	142	75	51	71	106
% increase on housing after AS	71	40	33	39	62
Std Dev rent					
Housing costs	140	240	140	140	240
AS	69	99	30	49	119
Housing costs after AS	71	141	110	91	121
Income left after housing	69.48	258.96	283.56	191.51	161.51
% increase on housing before AS	100	60	36	50	85
% increase on housing after AS	51	35	28	32	43
Christchurch renters					
Income	140.48	399.96	393.56	282.51	282.51
Median rent					
Housing costs	160	220	160	160	220
AS	65	85	44	63	75
Housing costs after AS	95	135	116	97	145
Income left after housing	45.48	264.96	277.56	185.51	137.51
% increase on housing before AS	114	55	41	57	78
% increase on housing after AS	68	34	29	34	51
Std Dev rent					
Housing costs	110	180	110	110	180
AS	48	57	9	28	75
Housing costs after AS	62	123	101	82	105
Income left after housing	78.48	276.96	292.56	200.51	177.51
% increase on housing before AS	78	45	28	39	64
% increase on housing after AS	44	31	26	29	37

(continued)

Table 3.7: (continued)

	Unemployed		Pensioners	Wage earners	
	1 (1bdr)	8 (2bdr)	11 (1bdr)	13 (1bdr)	13 (2bdr)
Manawatu renters					
Income	140.48	399.96	393.56	282.51	282.51
Median rent					
Housing costs	110	140	110	110	140
AS	45	29	9	28	49
Housing costs after AS	65	111	101	82	91
Income left after housing	75.48	288.96	292.56	200.51	191.51
% increase on housing before AS	78	35	28	39	50
% increase on housing after AS	46	28	26	29	32
Std Dev rent					
Housing costs	90	120	90	90	120
AS	34	15	0	14	35
Housing costs after AS	56	105	90	76	85
Income left after housing	84.48	294.96	303.56	206.51	197.51
% increase on housing before AS	64	30	23	32	42
% increase on housing after AS	40	26	23	27	30

Note: Full range used – sample only included in table here.

Household types:

1 = UB single under 25; 2 = UB single 25 and older; 3 = UB single and one child; 4 = UB single and two children; 5 = UB single and three children; 6 = UB married; 7 = UB married and one child; 8 = UB married and two children; 9 = UB married and three children; 10 = Superannuation single; 11 = Superannuation couple; 12 = Minimum wage, one person; 13 = Minimum wage, two people; 14 = Minimum wage, three people; 15 = Mean wage, one person; 16 = Mean wage, two people; 17 = Mean wage, three people; UB = Unemployment Benefit, but same rate as Sickness Benefit and DPB (Domestic Purpose Benefit); Minimum wage = NZ$9.50ph, 37.5hpw = NZ$282.51pw (after tax of 20.7%); Mean wage = NZ$554pw gross (in June 2004), NZ$439.32pw (after tax of 20.7%).

Auckland = rental properties under the heading 'Auckland Central' on the Tenancy Services market rent webpage, March–August 2005, as an example of Area 1 of the AS regional limits.

Wellington = rental properties under the heading 'Wellington' on the Tenancy Services market rent webpage, March–August 2005, as an example of Area 2 of the AS regional limits.

Christchurch = rental properties under the heading 'Christchurch' on the Tenancy Services market rent webpage, March–August 2005, as an example of Area 3 of the AS regional limits.

Manawatu = rental properties for rural areas under the heading 'Manawatu' (ie not including Palmerston North) on the Tenancy Services market rent webpage, March–August 2005, as an example of Area 4 of the AS regional limits.

Median = median rent, as calculated from Tenancy Services market rent webpage, March–August 2005, rounded to the nearest NZ$10.

Std Dev = rent at one standard deviation below the mean (ie 16th percentile), as calculated from Tenancy Services market rent webpage, March–August 2005, rounded to the nearest NZ$10.

1bdr = properties shown as having one bedroom on the Tenancy Services market rent webpage, March–August 2005, including houses, apartments, flats and rooms.

2bdr = properties shown as having two bedrooms on the Tenancy Services market rent webpage, March–August 2005, including houses, apartments, flats and rooms.

3bdr = properties shown as having three bedrooms on the Tenancy Services market rent webpage, March–August 2005, including houses, apartments, flats and rooms.

4bdr = properties shown as having four bedrooms on the Tenancy Services market rent webpage, March–August 2005, including houses, apartments, flats and rooms.

For beneficiaries with children, add Family Support of NZ$72 for first child and NZ$47 for each subsequent child to basic benefit to get income, then calculate threshold.

Threshold for renters = 25% of income, rounded down to nearest dollar.

Threshold for mortgagees = 30% of income, rounded down to nearest dollar.

Benefit rates and threshold amounts (for beneficiaries) are given on the MSD website (see www.msd,govt.nz/).

Regional limits for the AS are based on four areas and three household sizes (one, two and three or more people).

Adjustments have tended to come after political pressure has built up and have been done on an ad hoc rather than a regular basis. This has created differences in the level of affordability with the AS across regions and households and thus affects the income available to meet other expenditures after housing costs.

Since 2001, New Zealand has experienced a housing boom that has seen house prices rise much faster than rents and wages. This also affects the level and availability of rented properties that is hard to capture in the figures that are available. However, there are considerable local and regional variations in rent that (a) make it hard to draw clear conclusions and (b) highlight the difficulties of creating a satisfactory level of benefit to adequately close the affordability gap. The other impact in recent years has been fluctuations in migration particularly affecting the Auckland housing market, as it is the city to which the majority of the migrants move, at least initially.

The data in Table 3.7 illustrate the complexity and the variables that have to be taken into account in establishing both entitlement and level of allowances paid. A consequence of this appears to be the difficulty of eliminating 'poverty traps' in the operation of the allowance. The need for micro-level information also requires a considerable degree of administrative time working with individuals and families to assess their housing circumstances. Over the entire time that the system has been in place this has had an impact upon the level of uptake and has been a consistent source of criticism from housing advocacy groups (Smith and Robinson, 2005).

The other difficulty that the data show is that of the regional and local variability in levels of rents and house prices. The problem here has been that of keeping the allowance reflecting the current state of the markets. Only some form of indexation would have allowed a constant level of support but such a solution is unlikely due to the political risk to the budgeting of the cost for the allowance. Even in a more restricted form it has proved difficult for successive governments to control the amount of spending on the AS.

The tenure of those receiving the AS has remained heavily weighted towards renters (see Table 3.8). The most significant change here was as a result of the changes in policy in 2000, which drastically reduced the numbers in public housing in receipt of the AS.

Future role of housing allowances within the National Housing Strategy

The role of housing allowances within housing policy was recently reviewed as part of the development of a new National Housing Strategy. The new strategy is underpinned by a vision "that all New Zealanders will have access to affordable, sustainable, good quality housing appropriate to their needs" (New Zealand Housing Strategy, 2004, p 19). The policy identifies nine principles that will guide and influence the future. These principles range from the recognition of the pivotal role of housing to provide shelter, which is seen as a basic human

Table 3.8: Tenure of households receiving the AS, New Zealand, 1995–2004

Year	Renting privately	Renting other	Boarding	Paying a mortgage	Unspecified
1995	104,408	49,946	72,475	39,440	6
1996	111,464	54,978	70,445	43,126	8
1997	124,732	53,422	73,876	45,071	4
1998	138,834	53,261	71,163	48,468	10
1999					
2000	151,470	48,935	65,567	48,001	2,015
2001	148,500	6,505	62,151	47,104	1,622
2002	145,032	6,642	60,801	44,051	1,508
2003	142,006	5,921	61,047	41,298	1,669
2004	137,038	5,936	53,988	38,293	1,440

Source: For 1995: DSW Statistical Information Report (1995, table 52, p 53); for 1996: DSW Statistics Report (1996, table 51, p 56) (some calculation required); for 1997: DSW Statistics Report, 1997 (table 51, p 61) (some calculation required); for 1998: DSW Statistics Report (1998, table 56, p 68) (some calculation required); for 1999: MoSP Statistics Report, 1999 (table 72, p 78) (some calculation required); for 2000–04: MSD Statistical Report, 2004 (table 4.2, p 99).

Notes: 'Renting other' category includes state tenants (Housing NZ, Housing Corporation, Te Puni Kokiri), council tenants and residential home tenants; no accurate figures were available for 1994. The DSW Statistical Information Report 1994 only gave the information in graphical form, with numbers not easily estimated; no figures are given for renters in 1995 because the DSW Statistical Information Report 1995 only showed them under the headings HNZ and Other, which is different from other years. It would mean the Other figure in this table was slightly low and the Private figure slightly high, because tenants in council housing and other non-private rental housing are included in the wrong category.

Comment: The sharp reduction in the 'Renting other' category in 2001 is due to the introduction of income-related rents for state tenants in 2000, making them ineligible for the AS; the sharp increase in the 'Unspecified' category in 2000 appears to be due to a change from recording the numbers of unspecified 'tenure type' to recording the numbers of unspecified 'landlord/mortgage type'.

need, through to the fact that decent housing must be affordable and of good quality and an acknowledgement of the increasing diversity across the population. Further, the policy identifies two direct roles for the government. The first is to regulate the housing market and housing quality and the second is to improve housing assistance and affordability. Consequently, AS is to be reviewed as it "may not be the most effective form of assistance to households who rent ... it may support high rents and work against those with homeownership aspirations, although limited research has been done to date [May 2005] on this question" (New Zealand Housing Strategy, 2005, p 18). The future place of the AS within state support is thus far from clear.

The policies intended to meet the broad objectives of the strategy are to be delivered either through state rental, which as we noted earlier has been once again increasing over the past five years, or income supplementation through the AS. The government has also piloted a homeownership insurance scheme through the newly created Kiwi Bank and has provided some funding (NZ$63 million over four years) to stimulate activity by local government and other community-based social housing providers, especially Māori iwi. The strategy embraces the idea of working with third/voluntary sector partnerships and recognises that the government itself cannot be the only provider of housing services or solutions. This can be seen as a move in the direction of 'third way' or new social democratic policy ideas (Larner and Butler, 2003; Thorns, 2005).

One of the key features of the new housing strategy is an explicit recognition that housing is an instrument of social and economic policy and, as such, should have a wider range of components than simply demand-side income supplements. The document recognises changes in homeownership rates, affordability and demographic changes, particularly the pattern of household formation and the growing number of younger Māori and Pacific peoples. These latter two factors are part of the growing diversity now being seen in housing needs and requirements.

The government's housing policy identifies as one of its tasks to "actively explore the potential of a variety of interventions to deliver good housing to meet the specific needs of targeted groups and markets" (New Zealand Housing Strategy, 2004, p 17). This clearly marks a significant shift from the hands-off approach of the previous period of housing development during a more market-oriented neo-liberal phase of government and a retreat from income supplementation as the sole form of housing support.

Conclusion

This chapter has examined the last 20 years of debate and change with respect to the role of housing allowances within New Zealand's housing policy. The country is still predominantly a home-owning society, which the new National Housing Strategy strongly endorsed. However, over the period under review a major reshaping was undertaken that privileged housing allowances as the form of state assistance to address problems of affordability for beneficiary and low-income households. The results were mixed. More were in receipt of such allowances after the changes in the 1990s, but housing-related poverty also increased during the 1990s, suggesting that the level of the allowances and their take-up were inadequate on their own to address income deficiencies and supply problems. Some improvements have occurred since 1999 and the return to income-related rents has reduced the impact of housing on poverty. The impact of the AS on this is less clear and further research is needed.

The experience of the last 20 years of reforms has provided a greater recognition that single instrument solutions, though attractive to policy makers and governments, do not necessarily produce the desired outcome. Housing markets have many unusual features, which often confound the predictions and expectations of the people that create some of the policy instruments. Grounded and ongoing research and evaluation of policies is thus vital to enable sound housing policies to be generated. The National Housing Strategy does suggest that these lessons have been learnt. The future path will tell whether New Zealand will deliver on the expectations that the policy shift has generated.

—

Acknowledgement

The assistance of Simon Campbell in developing Tables 3.4 to 3.7, and with the analysis that underpins Table 3.6, is gratefully acknowledged.

Notes

[1] Family benefit/allowances could be capitalised and received as a lump sum towards home purchase for first-time homeowners and allowed up to three years' benefit to be taken in this way.

[2] WINZ was the new name for the Department of Social Welfare that was restructured at this time.

[3] Domestic Purposes Benefit is paid to lone-parent families and was introduced in the 1970s.

[4] The Minister of Housing, John Luxton, was quoted in the Wellington *Evening Post* on 25 February 1992 as saying "If the rent is too high, then shift".

[5] Equivalised income is not raw income. It differs from raw income by taking into account the economies of scale arising from a larger family size and the fact that adults cost more to maintain than children (Colmar Brunton, 1996, p 1).

[6] The department was established on 1 November 2004 when the Ministry of Housing was renamed the Department of Building and Housing, and building policy functions were added to its role. On 30 November 2004 the functions of the Building Industry Authority were added.

[7] For more details of household types, rents and data sources see notes to Table 3.7.

References

Boston, J. and Holland, M. (eds) (1990) *Fourth Labour government* (2nd edn), Auckland: Oxford University Press.

Boston, J., Dalziel, P. and St John, S. (eds) (1999) *Redesigning the welfare state in New Zealand*, Auckland: Oxford University Press.

Brodie, J. (1997) 'Meso discourses, state forms and the gendering of liberal-democratic Citizenship', *Citizenship Studies*, vol 1, no 2, pp 223–42.

Brosnan, D. (1997) 'Housing New Zealand as a case study of the Crown-Owned Enterprise model', *Public Sector*, vol 20, no 3, pp 6–9.

Campbell, S. (1999) 'Restructuring New Zealand housing policy 1990–1998: An institutional analysis', MA Sociology, Canterbury: University of Canterbury.

Campbell, S. and Thorns, D.C. (2001) 'Changes to New Zealand Housing Policy at the beginning and end of the 1990s' in S. Wilcox (ed) *Housing Finance Review 2001/2002*, London: Chartered Institute for Housing and Council of Mortgage Lenders, pp 11–17.

Castles, F.G. (1985) *The working class and welfare*, Wellington: Allen and Unwin.

Colmar Brunton (1996) *Key findings. quantitative report into the Accommodation Supplement*, Wellington: Department of Social Welfare and Ministry of Housing.

Dalziel, P. (2001) 'A Third Way for New Zealand', in A. Giddens (ed) *The global third way debate*, Cambridge: Polity Press.

DTZ New Zealand (2004) *Housing cost and affordability*, Wellington: Centre for Housing Research.

DTZ New Zealand (2004) *Changes in the structure of the housing market, Vol 1*, Wellington: Centre for Housing Research.

Ferguson, G. (1994) *Building the New Zealand dream*, Palmerston North: Dunmore Press.

Giddens, A. (ed.) (2001) *The global third way debate*, Cambridge: Polity Press.

Hazeldine, T. (1998) *Taking New Zealand seriously*, Auckland: HarperCollins.

Higgins, J. (1999) 'From welfare to workfare', in J. Boston, P. Dalziel and S. St John (eds) *Redesigning the welfare state in New Zealand*, Auckland: Oxford University Press.

Housing Corporation (1988) *Submission to the Royal Commission on Social Policy*, Wellington: Government Printer.

Howenstine, E.J. (1986) *Housing Vouchers: A comparative international analysis*, New Brunswick, NJ: Centre for Urban Policy Research, Rutgers University.

Johnston, A. (1993) *The effects of the Accommodation Supplement on the rental housing market*, Wellington: Human Rights Commission.

Kemp, P.A. (1998) *Review of housing allowances*, Wellington: Ministry of Housing.

Kemp, P.A. (1997) *A comparative study of housing allowances*, London: The Stationery Office.

Kelsey, J. (1995) *The New Zealand experiment: A world model for structural adjustment*, Auckland: Auckland University and Bridget Williams Books.

Larner, W. and Butler, M. (2003) 'Headline local partnerships in Aotearoa/New Zealand', *Research Report Local Partnerships and Governance Research Group*, Auckland: University of Auckland.

Lowe, S. (2005) *Housing policy analysis*, London: Palgrave Macmillan.

Morrison, P. (1993) 'Using SUPERMAP2 for policy analysis. Geographic implications of recent housing reforms', *NZ Population Review*, vol 19, no 1/2, May–November, pp 32–64.

Morrison, P. (1995) 'The geography of rental housing and the restructuring of housing assistance in New Zealand', *Housing Studies*, vol 10, no 1, pp 39–56.

Morrison, P. and Murphy, L. (1996) 'The geography of the housing reforms', in R. Le Heron and E. Pawson (eds) *Changing places: NZ in the nineties*, Auckland: Longman Paul.

Murphy, L. (1997) 'New Zealand's housing reforms and Accommodation Supplement experience', *Urban Policy and Research*, vol 15, no 4, pp 269–78.

Murphy, L. (1999) 'Housing policy', in J. Boston, P. Dalziel and S. St John (eds) *Redesigning the welfare state in New Zealand*, Auckland: Oxford University Press.

Murphy, L. (2003a) 'Reasserting the social in social rented housing policies: politics, housing policy and housing reforms in New Zealand', *International Journal of Urban and Regional Research*, vol 27, no 1, pp 90–101.

Murphy, L. (2003b) 'To the market and back: Housing policy and state housing in New Zealand', *Geojournal*, vol 59, no 2, pp 119–26.

National Housing Commission (1988) *Housing in New Zealand: Provision and policy at the crossroads*, Wellington: Government Printer.

New Zealand Housing Strategy (2004) *Building the future: Towards a New Zealand housing strategy (draft for discussion)*, Wellington: HNZC.

New Zealand Housing Strategy (2005) *Final policy document*, Wellington: HNZC.

O'Brien, M. and Wilkes, C. (1993) *The tragedy of the market*, Palmerston North: Dunmore Press.

Parsons, W. (1995) *Public policy: An introduction to the theory and practice of policy analysis*, Aldershot: Edward Elgar.

Perkins, H.C. and Thorns, D.C. (1999) 'House and home and their interaction with changes', in *New Zealand's urban system, households and family structures*, special issue of *Housing, Theory and Society*, vol 1, no 3.

Smith, L. and Robinson, B. (2005) *From housing to homes*, Manukau City: Salvation Army Social Policy Unit.

Stephens, R., Waldegrave, C. and Frater, P. (1995) 'Measuring poverty in New Zealand', *Social Policy Journal of New Zealand*, vol 5, December, pp 88–112.

Thorns, D.C. (1992) *Fragmenting societies?: A comparative analysis of regional and urban development*, International Library of Sociology, London: Routledge.

Thorns, D.C. (2000) 'Housing policy in the 1990s: New Zealand a decade of change', *Housing Studies*, vol 15, no 1, pp 129–38.

Thorns, D.C. (2005) 'The remaking of housing policy: The New Zealand housing strategy for the 21st century', proceedings of the APHNR Conference in Kobe, Japan, September.

Treasury (1984) *Economic management*, Wellington: Government Printer.

Treasury (1987) *Government management*, Wellington: Government Printer.

Treasury (1990) *Briefing to the incoming government*, Wellington: Government Printer.

Waldegrave, S. (2002) 'Allocating housing assistance equitably: A comparison of in-kind versus cash subsidies in New Zealand', *Social Policy Journal of New Zealand*, vol 18, pp 62–78.

FOUR

Canadian housing allowances

Marion Steele

Introduction

Housing allowances in Canada are offered by only four provinces. The absence of a national allowance should not be too surprising in a country where there is really no such thing as national policy for low-income housing. Instead there is a set of housing policies, one for each province. This has been especially true since the federal government all but vacated this area in the 1990s. It first terminated all programmes for building new social housing, as low- and mixed-income housing is called in Canada. Then it transferred the management of most existing subsidy commitments to the provinces. Even in the 1960s to the early 1980s when the federal government took an activist role, low-income housing in any province was only built if a province accepted the federal offer of funds and joined as a partner.[1] This is in line with the fact that housing is constitutionally the responsibility of the provinces – a quite different situation from that of the US states relative to their federal government – and Quebec, especially, has been sensitive to this.[2]

The Canadian provinces have differed in their take-up of federal offers. In part this is because they have widely varying housing markets. For example, some like Ontario, Alberta and British Columbia (BC) have high-rent and high-cost cities and others such as Newfoundland, Quebec and Manitoba have not. They also have varying views of their own needs and the role of governments, with, for example, Alberta generally favouring a highly restricted role, Quebec an interventionist one and other provinces, such as Ontario, a more mixed role. But all the provinces, with the notable exception of oil-rich Alberta, have less revenue-raising capacity than the federal government, despite their constitutional responsibilities. The provinces also have attached less importance than the federal government to new construction, quite naturally in view of the latter's responsibility for the macro-economy and the role of house building in maintaining full employment.

It is not too surprising in this context that some provinces have introduced housing allowances, which are cheap programmes involving no new building, although they have received no federal support. Ironically, these programmes are targeted squarely at solving a lack of housing affordability, the problem which the federal government's housing agency, Canada Mortgage and Housing Corporation (CMHC), has identified as the overwhelmingly most important housing problem. CMHC estimates that of renters who are in what it terms 'core need' – because their income is too low to allow them to obtain acceptable (physically adequate, uncrowded and affordable) housing at the rents prevailing in their local housing market – 91% are in unaffordable housing (CMHC, 2004 as revised 2005), with few in crowded or physically inadequate housing. In the 2001 Census, 26% of renters paid more than 30% of their income on rent and were in core need (CMHC, 2005). Many in core need had an especially severe affordability problem: 12% of all renters paid more than 50% of their income on rent.

The design of Canadian housing allowances is closely linked to CMHC's 30% affordability standard, and to the actual rent paid by recipients. Yet the absence of federal funding has helped keep these programmes small. They have had highly restricted eligibility everywhere except in Quebec and, since 2005, in Saskatchewan.[3] Furthermore, the experience in other provinces has not induced the largest one, Ontario, to introduce a housing allowance, and nor has it stimulated the federal government to adopt one. Paradoxically, the programmes are sometimes dismissed both because they might result in explosive expenditure and rent inflation and because they are cheap. The programmes are cheap, not just because recipient numbers are small everywhere except Quebec, but also because, in contrast to the US Housing Choice Voucher, the cost per recipient is low. Their design is far more similar to continental European housing allowances than to the US voucher.

In the next section of this chapter, the relative stagnation of these programmes over the last decade is put in the context of a virtual halt to new social housing expenditure in Canada and the expansion of quasi-universal child benefits. Following that, the role and design of allowances is explained. The payment formula explains in part the low benefit per recipient, but other aspects of design – the lack of a quality requirement and the receipt of the allowance by the tenant, first, without the landlord as an intermediary and, second, *ex post*, after the tenant has committed to and paid rent – also help explain why the payment is so low compared to the federal Rent Supplement programme. The latter, like the housing allowance, helps tenants living in private market housing, but costs many times as much per recipient. The next section examines the impact of the housing allowances. Currently housing policy in Canada is in a state of ferment, as the federal government edges back into the arena and the provinces start to recover from the ravages of the 1990s' recession and federal cuts to its transfers to them. The final section contains concluding remarks.

Housing allowances in context

Canadian housing allowances are both housing programmes, because their amount depends on rent paid (up to a defined maximum), and income assistance programmes, because the allowances are cash transfers dependent on income as well as rent. Both social housing programmes and income programmes interact with and influence housing allowances. I consider social housing first.

Social housing

Social housing is partially funded by the federal government and accounts for only 5% of Canada's 12.5 million[4] housing units, with virtually none added in the last decade. Solely provincially funded social housing, mainly in Quebec, Ontario and BC, adds a little to the total. The two major components are public housing, in which essentially all units are rented below market rates to needy households, and housing where there is an income mix. In the latter, market-rent occupants and those subsidised based on income, and paying rent geared to income (RGI), are housed in the same project and usually in the same building. Mixed-income projects are non-profit housing and non-equity cooperative housing schemes that were developed under federal–provincial programmes that started in the 1970s and terminated a decade ago (Sousa and Quarter, 2003).

The absence of federal funds for developing more social housing ended in 2001[5] with the Affordable Housing Initiative (AHI), in which the federal government, through CMHC, offered to sign agreements with each province to pay half of the capital requirements for new social housing developments. However, at that time the provinces were running large deficits, and some were slow to take up the offer. Ontario did not sign an agreement until 2005, after a change in government in that province and after the offer was amended to allow for the funding of rent supplements for needy tenants in private-market units, instead of the solely capital grants originally envisaged.

During the arid years of no new projects, demand for subsidised housing did not decline, as Canada experienced a much deeper and more prolonged recession in the 1990s than did the US or the UK, and the number of jobless rose to high levels. The recession was particularly difficult for recent immigrants (Haan, 2005), many of them visible minorities disadvantaged in the housing market. Exacerbating this, at the start of the 21st century rents rose rapidly in Toronto, Vancouver and a little later Montreal. Social housing waiting lists lengthened (Peters, 2004), and homelessness increased to become a major big-city problem as viewed by municipal authorities and business (Allan, 2004; Miller, 2004), but it did not fit into the CMHC housing problem framework, which encompassed the problems of those already in housing, not those who were without accommodation.

Housing allowances address, in small part, both the waiting list and the homelessness problems. In the case of homelessness, they help in a subtle way by assisting those heavily burdened by rent, and reducing the inflow into homelessness resulting from evictions (Lapointe et al, 2004). Housing allowances do not provide a large enough benefit to put those who are *already* homeless into private housing, but if few new people join the pool of the homeless, and the already homeless are assisted, homeless numbers will shrink.

Housing allowances should also tend to reduce that demand for social housing – as shown by the length of waiting lists – that comes from unaffordable rents. It was the affordability problem that galvanised some provincial governments into providing housing allowance programmes. The programmes for older people introduced in BC and Quebec some decades ago were explicitly motivated in part by the desire to help low-income tenants with affordability problems at a time when resources were too stretched to build much additional social housing, even with federal help. Of course, even where there is a housing allowance programme, there is still a role for social housing. It provides for households demanding a degree of security of tenure greater than that provided by private rental housing,[6] or with special needs, and it also has other rationales.

Income transfer programmes

A major reason that housing allowance benefits can be low is that for targeted types of households, the minimum income provided through federal income assistance is high enough to make rents bearable, if not affordable. This is true especially for older people, but parents are also helped, through quite generous child benefits. These supplements are indexed so that their value is not eroded by inflation. Parents with the lowest incomes receive a child benefit consisting of a basic benefit plus a supplement. The amount is greater for younger children and the amount per child declines with the number of children. For example, in 2005 it amounted to C$266 per month for one child, if under seven, C$734 for three children, two under seven, one seven to 17 (CRA, 2005).[7] The supplement portion of the child benefit declines with net family income, starting at an income of C$21,480; the initial tax-back rate is steep, for example, 12.2% for a family with one child, so that once an income of C$35,595 is reached, the supplement disappears. The tax-back of the basic benefit then starts, but its rate is much lower. In some provinces, including the largest province, Ontario, the supplement portion of the benefit is deducted from welfare cheques with the view that it is intended for working families. In most other provinces, but not Ontario, a provincially funded child benefit is added, sometimes tied to employment income.

For older people, in most cases those 65 years old and over, the federal government provides a basic universal pension of C$480 per month, which, together with a supplement for the poorest, guarantees a minimum income of C$1,050 per month for a single person, or C$1,901 for a couple. The tax-back rate ('income taper') on this supplement is 50%. The minimum income for an elderly couple is sufficiently high to make market rent affordable in small towns and most cities. However, because the federal payments do not adequately recognise the economies of scale in household spending for couples, most particularly in housing, and do not vary from place to place according to living costs, the minimum income of a single elderly person allows a less tolerable standard of living. This leads to a common problematic situation: a widow over 75 retains the apartment shared with her late husband but now pays the rent with not much more than half the original income. If she lives in a high-rent city like Vancouver or Calgary, she is apt to have little left over for food. A housing allowance in some provinces helps to remedy this situation.

While older people and working parents are entitled to benefits that have become significantly more generous in the last decade, the unemployed and those on social assistance (welfare) – sometimes the same people – have suffered severely from federal government cutbacks. During the tough times in Canada in the 1990s, and partially in response to concerns about work incentives, the federal government greatly tightened the payment of unemployment insurance benefits (and renamed the system Employment Insurance). This is particularly tough on the inhabitants of high-rent cities; unemployment insurance benefits provide more income than welfare and depend only on previous earnings; assets and other considerations are ignored. Benefits are provided in a non-intrusive way, which is in sharp contrast to the degrading process involved in applying for social assistance. The unemployment insurance system, while it provides a lower payout-to-premium ratio in most large cities – especially in growing ones, because of their relatively low unemployment rates – does not provide anything extra in consideration of the higher rents in these cities. This system is harsh on people in big cities and generous to those in stagnant or depressed, less-urbanised areas. Some notion of the effect of this on the standard of living of the unemployed can be seen from the fact that the mean rent of two-bedroom units in multiunit buildings was C$1,052 in Toronto in October, 2004, more than twice as much as in the low-growth city of Saint John, New Brunswick, and more than 50% greater than in the largest cities in the prairie provinces of Manitoba and Saskatchewan (computed from CMHC, 2005b, table 31).

At the same time that the federal government in its deficit-fighting period cut unemployment insurance benefits and eligibility, it also cut the cash transfers to the provincial governments used to fund welfare.[8] In response, most provinces slashed welfare rates in the order of 20%, and these have remained virtually unchanged in nominal terms for the last decade (National Council on Welfare, 2005). Thus welfare households and the marginally employed in cities like Toronto and Vancouver have faced the double whammy of lower incomes and rising rents without the assistance of a housing allowance.

The role and design of Canadian housing allowances

At least four types of housing subsidy in Canada have some claim to be described as a housing allowance. These will all be discussed in this section, but primacy will be given to the type with the best claim to the title: the Canadian allowance that depends both on income and rent, is intended to reduce the affordability problems of recipients who live in market housing they have chosen, is received by at least some non-welfare households, and is paid to the beneficiary, not the landlord. This is the only type of housing subsidy called a housing allowance in this chapter.

Another type of top-up to rent is the Rent Supplement. Rent supplements were introduced under this name, and partially funded, by the federal government, but this term will be used here for any subsidy under which the housing authority contracts with the landlord to pay part of the market rent; the vast majority come under the federal programme. This kind of top-up is somewhat like the US Housing Choice Voucher, but recipients have less choice than with the latter. Also, the housing authority arranges for a unit, unlike the voucher, which often depends on the ability of the potential beneficiary to negotiate with landlords.

The third type of subsidy considered is a top-up that is small for younger people, but is quite substantial for some older people; its explicit motivation is to offset property taxes, especially the education portion. The fourth type is intended not as a top-up but ideally as the whole rent; it is received by welfare recipients to fulfil the shelter component of their basic needs. For all four types of subsidy, those living in mixed-income housing (cooperatives and non-profits) are usually eligible, although, for the first two top-up payments, eligibility is restricted, reasonably, to those who are not already subsidised in the sense that they do not pay rent geared to their income.

Housing allowances

Classic housing allowances with fundamentally similar formulas exist in British Columbia, Manitoba and Quebec, and a closely related one, established in 2005, in Saskatchewan.[9] Only the programmes in BC and Quebec have a sizeable number of beneficiaries, partly because of the small populations of the remaining two provinces – Manitoba and Saskatchewan each have a population less than a quarter of the size of the population of the Toronto Census Metropolitan Area. Mean benefits are small – in the range of C$50 to somewhat more than C$100 per month – except in late 2005 in Vancouver. This is far less than the mean subsidies under other housing programmes. A quite small benefit is consistent with the focus of the programmes in improving affordability. In contrast to the US Housing Choice Voucher, the allowances are not intended to induce households to move to better housing or different neighbourhoods, but simply to reduce their rent burden. It is more appropriate to assess the amount of the allowance in terms of the food it allows a household to buy with the income freed from paying rent; in these terms, the housing allowances are substantial.

Concern about work incentives as well as child poverty is evident in the choice of eligible groups. None of the allowances goes to childless single people or couples without children, unless they are elderly – although 'elderly' is defined in Manitoba and Quebec to start at age 55 or under 55 but disabled in Manitoba and Saskatchewan. Yet most street homeless are childless and younger than 55 (Burt, 2001). Both families and older people are eligible in Manitoba, Quebec and (since 2006) BC. To qualify, families must have at least one child under 18, except in Quebec, which includes families with a child up to 21 if that child is in full-time schooling. Social assistance recipients are eligible in Quebec and Saskatchewan, but not in Manitoba or in BC. This exclusion has little effect on older people in BC because its allowance starts at age 60, the age of eligibility for federal elderly benefits for many, and close to the standard eligibility age of 65.[10]

Consistent with the affordability motivation for the allowances, the classic Canadian housing allowances (those in BC, Manitoba and Quebec)[11] pay a high percentage of the affordability gap (under constraints mentioned later), where the latter is generally defined as the difference between the rent and an affordable rent. Affordable rent is taken as 30% of income, except that in Manitoba it is taken as only 25% of income for the lowest-income recipients, rising linearly to 27.5% of income for the highest-income recipients.

An important deviation occurs in the Quebec formula, which sets a certain *minimum* rent, which is used in place of affordable rent when the latter is less than the minimum. This minimum is the rent that welfare households are expected to pay from their social assistance. It implies that the '30% of income' rule is inappropriate when income is at the welfare level; indeed the rule is nonsensical when income, as is the case of welfare payments, is determined by adding up the funds required to meet various basic needs. The minimum rent requirement also serves to limit the allowance payment when income is low; Manitoba accomplishes much the same objective by setting a maximum benefit.

Rent is taken as actual rent until a set maximum is reached, after which the allowance is based on that rather than the actual rent. Starting only in 2005 was there any variation in the maximum within a province – introduced first in Saskatchewan and later in BC. The Vancouver maximum was set at C\$90 per month higher than elsewhere in BC. The maximum rent implicitly sets a limit on the income of recipients, because when 30% of income (using BC as an example) is the same as the maximum rent, the affordability gap disappears. Quebec sets income limits that are slightly below the implicit maximum.

A more precise statement of the general formula is:

$$P = \begin{cases} a(R - bY) & \text{if} \quad R \leq R^* \\ a(R^* - bY) & \text{if} \quad R > R^* \end{cases}$$

where R^* is the set threshold rent, generally called the 'maximum'. The percentage of the gap in BC and Manitoba is variable, starting at 90% ($a = 0.90$) for the lowest-income recipients declining linearly to 60% in Manitoba and 65% in BC, while in Quebec the payment is only two thirds of the gap.

The Saskatchewan housing allowance follows the Quebec lead not only in covering welfare recipients as well as others, but also in its incorporation of a 'minimum rent' in the payment formula and its emphasis on the use of the telephone. The application starts with a telephone call, in which applicants are asked for rent and other information before they are mailed an application form.

The Saskatchewan programme departs from other housing allowances in a number of ways. First, and most important, payment is not a percentage of the affordability gap.[12] Second, the programme defines affordable rent as 35% of income, where heating costs are included in rent, rather than the conventional 30%. In Saskatchewan, the payment's relation to the rent of the recipient is a step function (so the allowance for recipients with a low enough income is a flat amount for rents between two values, rising to another flat amount for rents between the next pair of values and so on). Thus there are big differences in the response of the benefit to a dollar change in rent depending on the rent at which this change occurs. However, the dollar amounts are sufficiently small that these discontinuities may not matter.

The housing allowance payment, which depends on the recipient's rent, family type and location, is reduced by 12% of the difference between the income of the recipient and a set income. The allowances vary by family type and range from C$62 to C$113 per month. For a quite typical recipient, a lone mother with one or two children living in Regina, the capital of Saskatchewan, the reduction based on income starts at an income of C$10,800[13] per year. If her income is C$12,000 and her rent rises to C$450 from C$425, the allowance rises by C$29; that is, the allowance rises by slightly *more* than the C$25 rent increase. At a rent of C$475 per month, somewhat below the Regina CMHC Rental Survey mean for a one-bedroom apartment in 2004, there is no more response of the housing allowance to an increase in rent. In no case for this family is the 35% rent-to-income ratio requirement binding. However, for a couple with one or two children this requirement does bite. For example, a couple with one or two children, an income of C$16,000 (C$1,333 per month), and paying rent of C$465 would be eligible for a C$30 per month allowance except if the rent is less than 35% of income. Because their rent-to-income ratio is too low, they receive nothing. If they paid a rent C$2 higher they would receive an allowance of C$30 per month because the constraint no longer bites.

Harking back to the defunct New Brunswick housing allowance, the Saskatchewan one requires the housing of the recipient to pass an inspection, but the legislative requirement is merely that the programme manager must be of the opinion that the condition does not present a serious hazard to health or safety and there is no indication that there will be a list of specific requirements like those for the US voucher. Nonetheless it has been sharply condemned by Hunter and Donovan (2005) as placing some low-income tenants in the position of being denied the payment merely because of an uncooperative landlord. There does not seem to be any need for the landlord to be present at the inspection, so at least this requirement may not identify Saskatchewan recipients to their landlords, with the consequent weakening in their negotiating position. Also, recipients are strongly urged to arrange for the direct deposit of the cheque (via an automated bank transfer) so that there may not be official mail helping the landlord to discover they receive the allowance.

Rent supplement programmes

Under rent supplement programmes, a government agency negotiates with landlords and secures market rent units for a period, commonly five years. Tenants are usually drawn from social housing waiting lists and landlords sometimes have a limited right to participate in selection. Tenants pay a rent geared to their income (usually 30%) and the rent supplement, paid directly to the landlord, makes up the difference between this and market rent. Thus the formula is like the classic Canadian housing allowance formula, with the supplement filling all of the affordability gap, instead of part of it, as in the classic housing allowances. Most landlords are private, but some rent supplement units are in non-profit and cooperative projects. In those projects the market rent is, in principle, at the low end of the range of market rents.

Beneficiaries of the rent supplement do not freely choose their units and almost always must move in order to receive the subsidy. As with the US voucher, not all eligible households who apply receive this subsidy, in great contrast to housing allowances. Beneficiaries are usually drawn from social housing waiting lists. The landlord–tenant relationship is not the standard private market one, because part of the rent is paid by the housing agency directly to the landlord. The programme is not attractive to, or suitable for, small informal landlords, but instead, in the private landlord part of the programme, to property managers with large development firms (Rose, 1980). Furthermore, landlords have no motivation to give tenants discounts for long tenure in a unit, although average tenure discounts are found to be quite substantial in empirical studies. As a consequence, rents and the cost of the programme per recipient tend to be high. For example, in 2003 the rent supplement cost per recipient in Quebec in the private rental market programme partially funded by CMHC was C\$455 per month, while the cost per recipient of the Quebec housing allowance was C\$59 per month.[14] Finkel et al (2006, exhibit D-2) estimated the average subsidy per recipient of a full gap housing allowance, that is, one using almost the same formula as the rent supplement, for low-income owners and renters in 2001 at C\$92 per month; while the estimated subsidy for those paying more than 50% of income in housing costs was substantially greater, it was still less than a third of the CMHC–Quebec rent supplement.

The programme has certain advantages. One is its mix of subsidised with unsubsidised households (Rose, 1980) – although there is nothing to prevent the landlord placing the former in the least marketable units in a building or identifying them to other tenants. The programme improves resource allocation by filling vacant housing units. Housing for the homeless is available quickly without the waiting that construction of social housing entails. The other side of the coin is that when the market is tight, landlords are motivated to end the programme and subsidised tenants may have to move, because staying requires paying market rent, an impossible option if their income is still low (Sewell, 1994). The supply of rent supplement units will tend to fluctuate with market conditions, plentiful when the rental market is soft and drying up as the market tightens.

Originally, all rent supplements were funded 50% by the federal government through CMHC and 50% by the provinces, in the same way as public housing (CMHC, 1977, p 104). This is in contrast to housing allowances, which are solely provincially funded. While funding through this arrangement still dominates, some provinces including Ontario and Quebec have their own rent supplement programmes. In addition, so-called portable rent supplements exist, where the unit is chosen by the recipient, subject to housing agency approval, and recipients are free to move to another unit if they prefer it (Gallant et al, 2004). The subsidy is firmly attached to the tenant, not the unit, making it, in essence, the same as the US housing voucher.

Rent and income – conditioned refundable tax credits

Some provinces have refundable tax credits for renters (and homeowners) that are a form of top-up housing payment because they depend on rent and income. These have as their rationale compensation of low-income households for payment for local property taxes, but the formula for renters is independent of the property tax actually paid and instead depends on rent.[15] They generally are much more generous for older people (65 and over) than for younger people. For example, in Ontario, very low-income younger people in most cases receive annually C$250 plus 2% of rent minus 2% of the amount by which the income of the person (and spouse, if there is one) exceeds C$4,000. Thus the amount is tiny. For older people in Ontario the situation is different. The amount is substantial and the tax-back *starts* only at an income far above the *maximum* income for the Quebec housing allowance. Elderly renters receive in most cases C$625 plus 2% of rent; a marginal tax-back of 4% starts, for a single elderly person, only at an income of C$22,000. If rent is C$800 per month, and an elderly person has an income of C$22,000, the annual payment is C$817, the equivalent of C$68 per month.[16] This is greater than the average housing allowance for older people in Quebec. The Ontario property tax credit is clearly very poorly targeted. Property tax credits will be ignored in the remainder of this chapter.

Shelter allowances within the social assistance system

Social assistance recipients receive a shelter allowance that is calculated as a separate part of their social assistance in some provinces.[17] This allowance is merely the actual rent, plus an allowance for utilities in some provinces, up to a maximum. Two of the provinces where this system is not used, but where, instead, social assistance is a flat sum depending on the composition of the family, are Quebec and Saskatchewan, where recipients are eligible for housing allowances discussed above. The shelter allowance is often, and perhaps usually, paid directly to the landlord, not the tenant. For example, in Manitoba this happens something like 80% of the time. In provinces where allowances *can* be paid to the landlord, landlords usually insist that they be paid directly.[18] It is commonly believed that whenever the allowance is increased, landlords simply increase their rents.[19]

In Ontario and British Columbia, the maximum shelter allowance is less than 60% of mean rent in the largest and most expensive cities (Toronto and Vancouver respectively), but more than 90% of mean rent in the least expensive urban place in those provinces (Table 4.1). This implies a vast disparity in the standard of

Table 4.1: Maximum monthly welfare shelter allowances, maximum housing allowance rents and mean market rents, Canada

	Max. shelter allowance	Maximum rent, housing allowance		Two-bedroom apartment						
				Costliest urban area			Cheapest urban area		
					Ratio of max. to mean rent			Ratio of max. to mean rent	
	Small family	Costliest urban area	Cheapest area	Mean rent	Shelter allowance	Housing allowance	Mean rent	Shelter allowance	Housing allowance
	C$	C$	C$	C$	%	%	C$	%	%
Nova Scotia	600	np	np	751	80	np	593	101	np
Quebec	np	554	554	663	np	84	360	np	154
Ontario	571	np	np	1,052	54	np	617	93	np
Manitoba	430	480	480	667	64	72	na	na	na
Saskatchewan	np	471	328	605	np	78	na	np	na
British Columbia	555	755	665	986	56	77	604	92	108

Notes: np = 'no programme'; na = 'not applicable' because no CMHC data exist; 'Small family' refers to a lone mother with two children or a childless elderly couple; British Columbia's housing allowance maximum was C$575 prior to October 2005 and had been at that level since 1990; Manitoba's allowance includes utilities; amount without utilities is C$310; the mean rents of two-bedroom apartments are for October 2004 and are from CMHC's annual rental market survey, which is intended to include units in all buildings of three or more units; it is somewhat upwardly biased as an estimate of mean rents in the stock of units in all sizes of buildings; rents in the CMHC survey may or may not include utilities; 'Urban area' refers to the Census categories, metropolitan area, urban centre and urban agglomeration; in Manitoba and Saskatchewan there are no data for relevant small places.

living of recipients living in the large cities compared with that elsewhere. The Quebec and Saskatchewan systems, which combine a flat welfare amount with housing allowances, covering welfare recipients as well as working families, do not have this great disparity as a feature, partly because the 'minimum rent' in their formulae means that most people in small towns and other low-cost places will not receive an allowance. It is not surprising that in large cities social assistance recipients have great difficulty in the private rental market, often paying rents far higher than their shelter allowance. Basic social assistance including the shelter allowance, plus other benefits, often does not give welfare families in these cities a large enough income for the necessities of life. For example, the total income, including federal Child Tax Benefit, of a single welfare mother with one child was just C$14,251 in Ontario in 2004[20] but the mean annual rent of a one-bedroom apartment in Toronto was C$10,644 (CMHC, 2005, table 31), leaving C$69 per week for food and other essentials. Of course many welfare families find cheaper accommodation in basement apartments and other informal accommodation. And some are able to supplement their welfare income with income from part-time work: all provinces have earnings exemptions before welfare benefits are reduced dollar for dollar and these apply to employable as well as unemployable recipients, except in BC. But some families in Toronto and Vancouver and other expensive cities are driven to use food banks.

The impact of housing allowances

The numbers of households reached and participation rates

For many years after their beginning in the late 1970s, the classic housing allowances in Canada reached few beneficiaries. This was in part the result of their restricted eligibility and partly because programmes were in place only in a few provinces. Manitoba, which two decades ago was the only province with an allowance both for older people and families, has a small population, only 10% of the number of renters in Ontario (Table 4.2) and few recipients. Quebec established a housing allowance at about the same time, but only for older people. The big breakthrough came a decade ago when Quebec extended a modified version of the standard formula to welfare families. This was followed a few years later by a reform in which the province rolled the allowance for older people together with the allowance for families, and took the courageous step of extending coverage to families not in receipt of welfare. Quebec's Allocation Logement (AL) now reaches about 12%[21] of the province's renting households, despite the ineligibility of childless households with heads under 55, and the low maximum income level for recipient families – just 40% of median family income in Montreal.[22]

An important reason that the AL reaches a far higher proportion of families in Quebec than the housing allowances do in Manitoba is that AL goes to welfare families as well as to others. This has indirect as well as direct effects. In Quebec, a single mother landing a low-paid job that takes her off welfare continues to

Table 4.2: Estimated number of households receiving housing allowances and associated programmes, Canada

| | Top-up housing payments | | | | | Beneficiaries of housing payments as a percentage of renting households | | |
	Housing allowances (1)	Rent supplements (2)	Total, top-up payments (3)	Non-top-up housing payments (actual rent to maximum) (4)	Renting households, 2001 Census ('000) (5)	Housing allowance (%) (6)	All top-up (%) (7)	All (%) (8)
Newfoundland	np	np	1,000[a]	np	37.8	np	2.6	2.6
Nova Scotia	np	800	800	*14,500*	93.9	np	0.9	16.3
New Brunswick	np	1,708	1,708	np	65.6	np	2.6	2.6
Quebec	138,822	16,677	155,499	np	1,154.7	12.0	13.5	13.5
Ontario	np	28,000[c]	28,000[c]	273,451	1,232.7	np	2.3	24.5
Manitoba	3,140	1,870	5,010	*10,000*	118.7	2.6	4.2	12.7
Saskatchewan	2,833[c]	500	3,333	np	92.2	3.1	3.6	3.6
Alberta	np	2,312	np	np	294.9	np	0.8	0.8
British Columbia	11,894[b]	4,000	15,894	63,000	458.7	2.6	3.5	17.2
Nine provinces	156,689	56,867	213,556	*360,951*	3,549.1	4.4	6.0	16.2
Canada	156,689	57,500	214,189	*380,000*	3,576.0	4.4	6.0	16.1

Notes: np = no programme; numbers in italics are especially crude or questionable estimates; numbers refer to the fiscal year 2003–04 (which ends spring, 2004, except in Quebec, where year ends 31 December 2003) except where noted; data for top-up housing allowances were taken directly from government reports or obtained from government officials, except that the Saskatchewan housing allowance here is simply 12 times November amount; renting households include those living in social housing as well as those in private rental; Canada total includes data for the Territories and Prince Edward Island as well as for the other nine provinces; data are not strictly comparable between provinces; see also notes for Table 4.3. [a] 2002–03. [b] 2004–05. [c] 2005 (and includes estimates of take-up in 2005 of new programmes).

receive the AL she received while on welfare; if she then becomes unemployed without enough weeks of eligibility for unemployment insurance benefits and has to go back on welfare, the AL simply continues. There is not this seamlessness in Manitoba; there she would have had to apply for the Manitoba Shelter Benefit (MSB). This is far more important than many might think. There is evidence that the average length of receipt is less than a year: the average number of recipients per month in each of the last three years was less than 60% of the number who ever were recipients during the year.[23] It seems likely that many low-income families bounce between welfare, low-paid jobs, better-paid jobs or full-year employment which would take them above the MSB income maximum, and unemployment insurance. In contrast, in Quebec eligibility for AL among those not on welfare depends only on income in the previous year, and rent in September prior to the annual application date, so that if AL is received at the standard start date of October, it will be received for 12 months. In Manitoba families go off and on during the year as their status fluctuates. Estimates in Steele (2004) are that virtually all rent- and income-eligible renting families in Quebec receive AL, and the participation rate of fully eligible families in Manitoba is almost certainly well below this.

The new programme in Saskatchewan covers only families (not older people), which accounts in part for the low percentage of renters covered there as compared with Quebec (Table 4.2); in addition a significant number of renters, especially in small, declining places, have rents below the required minimum. In Quebec and Manitoba more than half of recipients are older people. In BC, only older people are covered, but the numbers shown reflect a much lower maximum income and rent than those effective in October 2005; numbers by early 2006 had risen 17%. The participation rate of eligible renting older people in BC was estimated at only about 60% for the early 1980s (Steele, 1985b) and recent estimates for older people in Quebec (Steele, 2004) are similar.

The other top-up housing payment, rent supplements, for which all types of households including singles are eligible, is received by only about a third of the number reached by classic housing allowances. The number is greatest in Ontario, not coincidentally a province with high rents and no housing allowance.

The estimated number of welfare households in the private rental market receiving a shelter allowance, calculated as the actual rent of the recipient up to a set maximum, as part of their welfare amount, is substantially larger than the number receiving top-up payments. Ontario dominates the total and more than 22% of all renters in that province receive a shelter allowance (Table 4.2). In comparing Ontario with other provinces it is important to realise that the large numbers in Ontario merely reflect its number of welfare recipients in private rental; welfare recipients in other provinces receiving a shelter component computed as a flat amount do not show up in this table. Quebec adopted the flat-amount system when it introduced housing allowances for welfare families. It was motivated in part by the wish to increase aid to welfare recipients with severe affordability problems while eliminating the temptation to landlords to increase their rent whenever the maximum rent under welfare increased. The AL was the incentive compatible solution.

Total expenditure and mean benefit

Total expenditure on classic housing allowances is tiny as a proportion of GDP (Table 4.4 overleaf) and at 4%, tiny even as a proportion of total housing subsidies (as the latter is defined in Canada). Even total top-up housing payments account for just 10% of total housing subsidies, as conventionally defined. Expenditure on the shelter component of welfare in provinces where payments are actual rents up to a maximum dwarfs top-up housing payments. Beside them the expenditure on classic housing allowances is puny indeed.

It is illuminating to contemplate the mean benefit of some of the programmes (Table 4.3). Although the mean allowance in BC in early 2006 was C$164 per month, most classic housing allowance payments are much smaller – the lowest, in Quebec, is just C$55 per month – reducing the recipient's affordability problem but not eliminating it; by design, except in Manitoba, they cannot. The allowances do lift many households from the deep need category of paying more than 50% of income for rent,[24] and help prevent the housing budget from eating up so much of income that households are forced into using food banks. In Quebec, the mean subsidy of the other top-up payment, rent supplement (both federal–provincial and solely provincial programmes), at C$244, is more than four times that of the AL; the mean rent supplement in other provinces is of the same order of magnitude. Yet the rent supplement means in Table 4.4 are misleadingly low as an indicator of the cost of expanding the programme. Many of the payments are made to social housing providers and are based on a cost-based unit charge, not market rent, minus 30% of income of the tenant. This social housing was almost entirely built 20 or 30 years ago, when construction costs were much lower, so that interest costs are low. Payments made to private landlords, which are based on market rents, are far higher. For example, under Ontario's recent, provincially funded Strong Communities Rent Supplement Programme, the mean payment to landlords per unit is C$631 per month,[25] more than twice the mean shown in Table 4.3.

Table 4.3: Mean monthly payments, housing allowances and rent supplement programmes, selected Canadian provinces

	Housing allowance (C$)	Rent supplements (C$)
Newfoundland	No programme	281
Quebec	55	244
Ontario	No programme	269
Manitoba	84	208
Saskatchewan	85	317
Alberta	No programme	346
British Columbia	126	192 (est.)

Table 4.4: Estimated expenditure on top-up and non-top-up housing payments, by province and for Canada (C$ millions)

	Top-up housing payments			Non-top-up housing payments (actual rent to maximum)	Housing subsidies (total for all programmes except non-top-up housing payments)		Grand total federal and provincial
	Housing allowances	Rent supplements	Total top-up payments		Provincial expenditure	Federal (CMHC) expenditure	
Newfoundland	np	3.4[a]	3.4	np	9.9	62.9	72.8
Nova Scotia	np	2.9	2.9	78	21.2	73.6	172.8
New Brunswick	np	3.6	3.6	np	25.5	59.9	85.4
Quebec	92.4	48.8	141.2	np	279.0	446.3	725.3
Ontario	np	90.5[c]	90.5[c]	1,277.9[d]	100.0	728.7	2,106.6
Manitoba	3.2	4.7	7.8	48.0	30.8	134.0	212.8
Saskatchewan	2.9[c]	1.9	4.8	np	21.7	162.6	184.3
Alberta	np	9.6	9.6	np	42.4	149.2	191.6
British Columbia	18.0[b]	9.2	27.2	295.5	151.4	278.8	725.7
Nine provinces	116.5	174.5	291.0	1,699.4	681.8	2,096.0	4,477.2
Canada	116.5	180.0	296.5	1,750.0	700.0	2,216.0	4,666.0
Ratio to GDP (%)	0.010	0.015	0.024	0.144			
Ratio to total (excl. non-top-up) housing subsidies (%)	4.0	6.2	10.2				
Ratio to grand total	2.5	3.9	6.4	37.5			

Notes: [a] refers to 2002–03; [b] refers to 2004–05; [c] refers to 2005 and includes estimates of the take-up in 2005 of programmes announced in 2005; [d] refers to net of deductions for National Child Benefit supplements and earned income; expenditure would be in the order of C$1.6 billion without these deductions; italicised numbers are especially crude or questionable estimates; np = no programme; total top-up payments exclude the non-monthly, and usually small, payments under property-tax credit schemes; numbers refer to the fiscal year 2003–04 (which ends spring 2004, except in Quebec, where numbers refer to the year ended 31 December 2003) except where noted; columns which sum previous columns may refer to a mix of years; data for top-up housing payments were taken directly from provincial government reports or obtained from government officials, except that the Saskatchewan housing allowance is simply 12 times November amount; italicised numbers under housing subsidies, provincial expenditure, are estimates from sources such as public accounts; non-top-up payments refer to shelter allowances for social housing allowance recipients; provinces not using the 'actual rent up to a maximum' system (and indicated in this column by np) nonetheless spend large amounts for the shelter component of social assistance payments; federal expenditure is from CMHC (2005b, table 51), and excludes the item 'research and information transfer'; Canada total includes data for the Territories and Prince Edward Island as well as for the other nine provinces; housing subsidies for all programmes may mix capital and operating subsidies; data are not strictly comparable between provinces.

No means are shown for shelter assistance payments to welfare recipients, because in the one province – Ontario – where data were obtained from public officials, the expenditure number is an understatement of expenditure fully attributable to the shelter allowance. Adding back an estimate of the deductions, the mean benefit is estimated at about C$500 per month. This is far above the mean for other subsidies shown in Table 4.3, but this subsidy is not merely a top-up. Unlike other subsidies, it is intended to account for the total housing cost of the recipient.

Impact on rent inflation and housing consumption

Early empirical investigation (Steele, 1985a) indicates that the classic housing allowances in Manitoba and BC have had no detectable effect on rent inflation or housing consumption. No current data from these provinces and Quebec overturn this general finding. Indeed, the stagnant level of mean benefits in *nominal* dollars is convincing evidence that these housing allowances have had little effect on housing consumption or on the rent setting of landlords. This is surprising to economists because the allowance formula seems to provide a powerful behavioural incentive. Subject to certain constraints, the formula implies that for a recipient with a given income, every dollar of increase in rent results in a subsidy increase of 67 cents in Quebec and as much as 90 cents in Manitoba. 'Subject to certain constraints' is very important, however, as these ensure that the rent range over which there is a high marginal subsidy is very short, so that the possible returns to responding to this incentive are minimal. Furthermore, landlords need not be aware that a tenant is in receipt of the allowance. Finally, and perhaps most important, is the *ex post* nature of the benefit; for example, in Quebec, a tenant whose rent increases on 1 July will not receive any increase in subsidy until October and there is no retroactivity.

The situation in the case of the second top-up housing payment, rent supplements, is quite different. Housing authorities negotiate rent with landlords and then the units are offered to households on the social housing waiting lists. There is apparently little room for behavioural response. Yet rent supplements are much more costly per recipient than housing allowances. Accounting for this in part is the full affordability gap design of the former in contrast to the partial gap of the latter. But the means from Finkel et al (2006) cited earlier show this explains only a small part of the difference. Another reason for the difference is that economies of scale dictate that housing authorities contract with landlords of large buildings. In addition to this and reasons mentioned earlier, there is a possible market and building effect: if landlords set aside their least marketable units for rent supplement tenants and the supply of such tenants props up the rents of marginal units, rents in the building might be higher than otherwise. A city without rent supplement units might have lower rents in the formal rental sector.

Policy debates and reform
Debates

Housing allowances have had a limited impact in Canada. There is no federal funding and allowances for families are in place only in three provinces and are meagre. A major reason for the lack of expansion has been the concern, especially at the federal level, that offering a benefit to all eligible people constitutes an open-ended commitment that might prove ruinously expensive, a view similar to that in the US in relation to housing vouchers (Priemus et al, 2006). The concern has been shown to be unwarranted by experience at the provincial level, but the federal government decided in the deficit-fighting years in the 1990s to get out of housing and that decision has inhibited ventures since then. A second reason has been a lack of advocacy from various interest groups. Landlord groups have only been sporadically interested, although the Canadian Federation of Apartment Associations has recently given support. The support of landlords is striking, given the small mean payments and direct payment of the subsidy to tenants, not landlords, in contrast to the situation with rent supplements.

An important impediment to the spread of housing allowances is the opposition of social housing and poverty advocates. They see housing allowances as benefiting landlords, as too easy to cut and as a threat to increased funding to build and renovate housing for non-profit and cooperative groups (Hulchanski, 2004). The first point is not well taken, given the evidence in Steele (1985a), except in the sense that anything that helps their tenants helps landlords. The second has considerable merit. Although only two very small programmes for older people, in low-rent and low-population provinces, have ever been cut entirely, programme funding in real terms has been allowed to decline through a policy of neglect, by omitting the annual increases needed to keep pace with inflation. This kind of situation is inherently unlikely in the case of supply-side subsidies. At an elemental level, a building once built is likely to be there for social housing occupants for decades to come. The third criticism seems an unnecessary fear; for example, while Quebec has a housing allowance programme and Ontario has not, it also spends far more per renting household on traditional housing subsidies (compare Tables 4.2 and 4.4).

Points made about housing allowance programmes by the official body of the social housing providers, the Canadian Housing and Renewal Association (CHRA), however, are not well taken. While the CHRA grudgingly accepts 'portable shelter allowances' as a low-priority possibility, it suggests that they are designed to encourage people to search for housing at below-average market rent. This is simply not the case for Canadian programmes, although it is true for the US voucher: Canadian programmes are designed simply to help people where they happen to live currently. These programmes also do not create areas of low-income households far from jobs, contrary to the CHRA (2006) predictions. It is unfortunate that the CHRA fails to recognise the needs of low-income households who do not live in social housing, whose absence in most cases from social housing waiting lists indicates their preference to live elsewhere, and yet who are impoverished by high housing costs. It is manifestly unfair that some low-income households in Toronto, Calgary and other cities receive large housing subsidies but others receive nothing.

Reform

As housing need has increased and homelessness has emerged as a major big-city problem, concern about both the fate of the homeless themselves and about their degrading effect on the quality of life in cities, has placed housing high on the agenda of business (see Hulchanski and Shapcott, 2004). Classic housing allowances are not suitable for inducing the homeless off the street. On the street and in homeless shelters they pay nothing at all for housing, desperately unsatisfactory as it is, and are able to use all their income to buy food and other necessities. Helping them to navigate the application process to get welfare, and finding them housing that leaves them with just as much income net of housing expense as they had earlier, is required. Social housing and expensive rent supplements are needed.

Recently, rent supplements have been used in a new and flexible way in Toronto to house displaced inhabitants of a homeless encampment (Gallant et al, 2004). Instead of being placed in line for an existing rent supplement unit, with the help of social workers they found other rental units and landlords. If they wanted to move after initial placement, they were allowed to do so. This choice makes the supplement like the US voucher. In fact, choice for other applicants is also greater than it was at one time. People in Toronto may choose to apply for one of many rent supplement buildings in the city. Sometimes people already living in one of these buildings may be able to receive the supplement without moving, that is, may receive it *in situ*, although the new CMHC-funded rent supplement programme in Ontario prohibits such arrangements. An innovative small pilot in Toronto, taking advantage of the current high vacancy rate, offers units to people on the Toronto waiting list for C$300 below the current market rent, with C$150 borne by the landlord, and the other half by the government. In effect, in return for filling vacant units, the landlord has to reduce the rent. Quebec's recent, provincially funded, rent supplements, like the Toronto pilot, are cheaper than the federal–provincial rent supplements.

While housing allowances are not large enough to enable the homeless to be housed, they do help staunch the flow into homelessness. Forced moves appear to have been especially great since the deep cuts in welfare incomes in the lean years of the 1990s. In fact in Toronto, the 22.1% cut in welfare shelter allowances in the autumn of 1995 was followed the next year by a 50% increase in the multiunit rental vacancy rate.

In the later 1990s and in the 2000s, provinces in less dire fiscal straits were beginning to think of making the life of welfare recipients less difficult, especially in cities where rents have risen markedly. One way to do this without the enormous welfare expenditure that scarred the provinces in the early 1990s is to target and to include constraints. The Quebec housing allowance, AL, does this by aiding welfare recipients only when they have a rent above the assumed welfare standard, and then not dollar for dollar. Furthermore, because the Quebec housing allowance also goes to working families, it reduces the work disincentives of welfare. The housing allowance in Saskatchewan does the same. Saskatchewan also varies the rent maximum by region of the province, as now does BC. This geographic sensitivity improves programme efficiency.

However, there has not been reform in housing allowances in two major areas where it is needed. First, if housing allowances are to be a continuing and dependable programme, benefits must be indexed. In the difficult times of the 1990s and early 2000s, governments allowed real benefits to decline by not increasing rent maxima as market rents rose. In BC, large increases in 2005 reversed this, but only indexing would provide continuing assurance. Quebec and Manitoba have not increased their maxima for years, although Quebec is now undertaking a review of its programmes. A second needed reform is widening eligibility. Disabled people are now eligible in Saskatchewan and Manitoba, but nowhere are childless people under 55 eligible. Yet most of the homeless are single and under 55, and much of the flow into homelessness is from this group. There is understandable reluctance to extend eligibility to childless younger people because of concern about work and other disincentives. But a cautious gradual reduction of the minimum age is called for.[26]

Conclusion

Housing allowances reduce the depth of affordability problems. They are relatively cheap because they help households with affordability problems living in many types of accommodation at low administrative cost, and with no negotiation or contact with landlords. They put income into the hands of tenants paying high rents without requiring them to move, permitting them to rent from informal as well as formal landlords and to occupy uncertified dwellings. They are horizontally equitable, going to those in social housing (if not already paying RGI), and, in Quebec, also to those in owner-occupied housing. Unlike the far more expensive rent supplements and subsidised social housing, they do not go just to a lucky few. However, they will not have a secure, dependable place in the bundle of housing programmes until two reforms take place. First, maximum rents in their formulae must be indexed, so that just as rent supplement payments to landlords rise when markets inflate, so do housing allowance payments to tenants. Second, they must be extended to welfare tenants so that they are integrated into the welfare system. This increases the size and efficiency of programmes, reducing large swings in numbers of beneficiaries, and increasing participation rates; it also reduces work disincentives for welfare recipients.

But housing allowances should not be the only low-income housing programme. They are not generous enough to move homeless people into housing, although they will help staunch the flow into homelessness. The much more expensive rent supplements need to be judiciously used. Furthermore, they cannot replace buildings managed and run by cooperatives and non-profits. The latter are required for households needing security of tenure and by those able to afford market rent but preferring to pay that rent in housing that is not privately owned.

Acknowledgements

I am very much indebted to Jill Leslie for her ingenious and relentless tracking down of provincial information and to many public officials, especially Hubert Du Nicolini of Quebec, for the insights they have shared and information they have provided. Any errors of facts or interpretations are mine alone.

Notes

[1] Some non-equity cooperative housing arrangements are an exception to this.

[2] The federal government is only able to fund housing through its constitutional right to spend in any way that 'advances peace, order and good government'.

[3] However, the Saskatchewan housing allowance is distinctly different from the 'Canadian' design, that is, the design used in Quebec, Manitoba and British Columbia.

[4] This is the number at the last census, in 2001 (CMHC, 2005a).

[5] There was also an initiative in response to homelessness, the National Supporting Communities Initiative introduced in 1999. Although not administered by the housing agency, CMHC, it funded transitory housing, including apartment buildings that are now part of the social housing stock.

[6] Most provinces have security of tenure legislation for tenants in the sense that they allow evictions ('terminations of tenancy') only for one of a specific list of reasons, the most important of which is nonpayment of rent. However, one of the reasons is the desire of the owner (or members of his or her family) to occupy the unit. With the increase in the importance in the rentals market of individual apartments owned under condominium tenure (Steele, 1993) the probability has increased of a renter being required to vacate because the apartment is sold to a would-be owner-occupier.

[7] The federally funded Alberta child benefits vary somewhat from this according to the age and number of children (CRA, 2005).

[8] Currently welfare is funded through the Canadian Health and Social Transfer, which is for health and post-secondary education as well as for social assistance. Generally, eligibility for social assistance starts at an early age, and includes all demographic categories. Benefits are substantially larger for those considered disabled or unemployable (about half the beneficiaries) than the employable. The names of programmes for the latter reflect the emphasis on encouraging recipients to find work or undertake training, for example, Ontario Works.

[9] The names of these programmes all use the word 'shelter allowance', which is also the term used in Canada (and in this chapter) for the shelter component of welfare payments. The Saskatchewan programme is called the Saskatchewan Rental Housing Supplement but is entirely distinct from the federally-funded rent supplement.

[10] There are certain restrictive provisions. For example, recipients in BC must have lived in the province for at least one year. In Quebec, there is no length of residence requirement. Owner-occupiers are eligible in Quebec, but not elsewhere; they constitute only a tiny percentage of older recipients, because most mortgages in Canada are paid off by age 55, but the incidence of owner-occupiers among large families (those with three or more children) is quite substantial (Steele, 2004).

[11] There was also, for a short period, an allowance in New Brunswick for older people (Steele, 1985a). However, the size of the minimum federal pension for older people, given the low rents in this province, means the affordability problem for older people is much less severe there than in BC.

[12] This, as well as other information, is taken from Saskatchewan (2005).

[13] Income as defined for the programme includes workmen's compensation and unemployment insurance benefits and the universal old-age pension (OAS), but as in other allowance programmes excludes the child benefit and the GST tax credit (a payment made to all low-income adults who apply).

[14] Of course the cost per recipient depends on factors in addition to market rent, including average income of recipients. Also, rent geared to income in Quebec is 25% of income, while affordable rent for the purpose of the housing allowance is 30% of income subject to a minimum rent constraint. The Quebec housing allowance does not pay 100% of the affordability gap, but just two thirds; if it did, the cost per recipient still would be only C$89 per month (assuming no feedback on rents of this parameter change and ignoring the minimum rent constraint).

[15] The almost universal rule in Canadian municipalities is that property taxes are levied on the property owner, not on tenants.

[16] More details of the rules are available at http://www.cra-arc.gc.ca/E/pbg/tf/5006-tc/5006-tc-04e.pdf, on which the description in the text is based (accessed 11 November 2005). 'Income' is net *family* income, which is the net income of the person plus spouse. Net income is gross income net of a number of deductions including pension contributions and union fees.

[17] When reference is made to provinces, the more precise reference would be 'provinces and territories', but the shorter expression is used for simplicity and because the provinces are far more important quantitatively and politically than the territories.

[18] I am indebted to Michael Mendelson, senior scholar, Caledon Institute, for this information.

[19] See Hunter and Donovan (2005). Steele (2001) gives some empirical indications of the effect, in Ontario, of increases in the social assistance housing allowance.

—

[20] This amount is the sum of basic social assistance, C$10,281, additional benefits, C$105, Ontario refundable tax credits, C$398, and two federal payments, the Child Tax Benefit and the GST credit, which were respectively C$2,911 and C$556 (National Council of Welfare, 2005, table 1.2).

[21] Because the AL goes to homeowners as well as renters, but current data giving the split are not available, the 12.0% given in the table is a small overstatement of the proportion of renting households aided.

[22] This is for a three-person family in 2001. The AL maximum is C$20,360 and median income in 2001 is C$51,680 (computed from Heisz and McLeod, 2004, table 2.1, applying their suggested factor of 1.7). The AL maximum is a higher percentage of median income for singles and two-person families.

[23] Manitoba, 2005, p 56. See also Steele (1985a) for somewhat different evidence on length of stay.

[24] The recent use of 50% in some contexts, rather than 30%, raises the issue of the appropriateness of the 30% criterion. The affordability standard implicit in the new Saskatchewan plan is indeed 35% not 30% and this higher percentage has popped up in other contexts. Steele (1985a) argues that normative and empirical reasons indicate that if 30% is the appropriate criterion for a couple, less than 30% is appropriate for a three-person family and more than 30% – perhaps as high as 40% – is appropriate for a single person. Other authors have also argued for higher rates for smaller households. This implies, since household size has fallen greatly over the last few decades, that the 30% rule should be increased if a single yardstick is to be used.

[25] This is derived from the fact that total annual funding is C$50 million, as of July 2005 for the Strong Communities Rent Supplement Programme and the number of beneficiaries is 6,600 (information received by email from the Ontario Ministry of Municipal Affairs and Housing).

[26] In late 2006, the government of BC introduced a housing allowance programme for families, called the Rental Assistance Programme. Families on welfare are not eligible and employment within the past year is required. Also in 2006, Manitoba renamed its two allowances Manitoba Shelter Benefit and extended it to the disabled non-elderly. In spring 2007, the Ontario government announced that it intended to introduce a flat rate housing allowance programme, which it estimated would serve 27,000 families. This will not cover welfare families and there is no indication that it will be indexed to consumer prices or average earnings.

References

Allan, E. (2004) 'The business case for affordable housing', in D. Hulchanski and M. Shapcott (eds) *Finding room: Policy options for a Canadian rental housing strategy*, Toronto: Centre for Urban and Community Studies.

Burt, M.R. (2001) 'Homeless families, singles, and others: Findings from the 1996 national survey of homeless assistance providers and clients', *Housing Policy Debate*, vol 12, no 4, pp 737–80.

Canadian Housing and Renewal Association, Research and Policy Committee (2006) 'Rent supplements, shelter allowances and a new approach to housing policy', discussion paper, CHRA_Rent_Sup_Final_Jan_2617NVW-1262006-5730.pdf.

CMHC (Canada Mortgage and Housing Corporation) (1977) *Canadian housing statistics, 1976*, Ottawa: CMHC.

CMHC (2004) *2001 Census housing series: Issue 3 revised: The adequacy, suitability and affordability of Canadian housing*, Ottawa: CMHC.

CMHC (2005a) *Canadian housing observer 2005*, Ottawa: CMHC.

CMHC (2005b) *Canadian housing statistics, 2004*, Ottawa: CMHC.

Finkel, M., Climaco, C., Khadduri, J. and Steele, M. (2006) *Housing allowance options for Canada final report*, prepared by Abt Associates for CMHC, Ottawa: CMHC.

Gallant, G., Brown, J. and Tremblay, J. (2004) *From tent city to housing: An evaluation of the City of Toronto's emergency homelessness pilot project*, Toronto: City of Toronto.

Haan, M. (2005) *The decline of the immigrant homeownership advantage: Life-cycle, declining fortunes and changing housing careers in Montreal, Toronto and Vancouver, 1981–2001*, Analytical Studies Branch research paper series, cat no 11F0019MIE2005238, Ottawa: Statistics Canada.

Heisz, A. and McLeod, L. (2004) *Low-income in Census metropolitan areas, 19802000*, cat no 89-613-MIE, Ottawa: Statistics Canada, Business and Labour Market Analysis Division.

Hulchanski, D. (2004) 'How did we get here? The evolution of Canada's "exclusionary" housing system', in D. Hulchanski and M. Shapcott (eds) *Finding room: Policy options for a Canadian rental housing strategy*, Toronto: Centre for Urban and Community Studies.

Hulchanski, D. and Shapcott, M. (eds) (2004) *Finding room: Policy options for a Canadian rental housing strategy*, Toronto: Centre for Urban and Community Studies.

Hunter, G. and Donovan, K. (2005) *Transitional employment allowance, flat rate utilities, rental housing supplements and poverty in Saskatchewan*, SPR Occasional Paper, Regina, Saskatchewan: Social Policy Research Unit, Faculty of Social Work, University of Regina.

Lapointe, L. in association with Novac, S. and Steele, M. (2004) *Analysis of evictions under the Tenant Protection Act in the City of Toronto: Overall rental housing market*, prepared for the City of Toronto Shelter, Housing and Support Division, Toronto: City of Toronto.

Manitoba Family Services and Housing (2005) *Annual report, 2004–2005*, Winnipeg: Department of Family Services and Housing.

Miller, M.D. (2004) 'Preface', in D. Hulchanski and M. Shapcott (eds) *Finding room: Policy options for a Canadian rental housing strategy*, Toronto: Centre for Urban and Community Studies.

National Council of Welfare (2005) *Welfare incomes 2004*, Ottawa: National Council of Welfare.

Peters, D. (2004) 'Affordable housing policy challenges in Ontario: The view from the non-profit sector', in D. Hulchanski and M. Shapcott (eds) *Finding room: Policy options for a Canadian rental housing strategy*, Toronto: Centre for Urban and Community Studies.

Rose, A. (1980) *Canadian housing policies 1935–1980*, Toronto: Butterworths.

Saskatchewan (2005) *The Rental Housing Supplement Regulations*, Chapter S-8, Reg 7, Regina: The Queen's Printer.

Sewell, J. (1994) *Houses and homes: Housing for Canadians*, Toronto: Lorimer.

Sousa, J. and Quarter, J. (2003) 'The convergence of non-equity housing models in Canada: Changes to housing policy since 1990', *Housing Policy Debate*, vol 14, no 4, pp 591–620.

Steele, M. (1985a) *Canadian housing allowances: An economic analysis*, Ontario Economic Council Research Study, Toronto: University of Toronto Press.

Steele, M. (1985b) 'Housing allowances: An assessment of the proposal for a national programme for Canada', report prepared for the Canadian Home Builders' Association.

Steele, M. (1993) 'Conversions, condominiums and capital gains: The transformation of the Ontario rental housing market', *Urban Studies*, February, pp 103–26.

Steele, M. (1998) 'Canadian housing allowances inside and outside the welfare system', *Canadian Public Policy – Analyse de Politiques*, vol 24, no 2, pp 209–32.

Steele, M. (2001) 'Housing allowances under Section 8 and in other countries: A Canadian perspective', *Urban Studies*, vol 38, no 1, pp 81–103.

Steele, M. (2004) 'Quebec's housing allowance program: A good program destined to wither away?', paper prepared for presentation to the International Housing Conference, Toronto, June.

FIVE

Housing allowances American style: the Housing Choice Voucher programme

Sandra J. Newman

Introduction

In the US, housing allowances take the form of housing vouchers. Whereas housing allowances are typically unrestricted cash transfers earmarked for housing, housing vouchers are earmarked for housing but have restrictions. Put simply, a voucher is essentially a promissory note from the government – with strings attached. It allows a low-income household to lease a physically decent private market unit that is rented for an amount considered reasonable for modest, existing, standard rental units in the housing market area, typically the county or metropolitan area.

Unlike housing allowances in most other countries included in this volume, housing vouchers in the US, along with all other forms of housing assistance, are not entitlements. As a result, roughly one quarter of eligible households receive any form of housing assistance (Fischer and Sard, 2005; US Department of Housing and Urban Development, 2005),[1] and about 9% receive vouchers (US Department of Housing and Urban Development, 2005; Fischer, 2006). Nonetheless, the housing voucher programme now serves more households – roughly 2 million – than any other means-tested form of housing assistance (Fischer, 2006).

Housing policy context

Although housing assistance programmes in the US date back at least 75 years,[2] a housing allowance-like programme was introduced only about three decades ago.[3] Prior to the 1970s, housing policy for low-income households consisted of an array of construction and finance subsidies. These included federal subsidies to build and rehabilitate housing, reduce interest rates on loans to developers of housing for low- and moderate-income households, provide mortgage insurance for low-income homeowners and rental apartment developments, and provide tax shelters to investors in low- and moderate-income housing projects (Weicher, 1980). By the early 1970s, virtually all of these housing programmes had run into serious problems. These included abandonment of federally subsidised homes, defaults in apartment subsidy programmes, scandals involving bribery of public officials in a low-income homeownership programme (Section 235), and significant social decay in some public housing developments, the most infamous of which was Pruitt-Igoe in St Louis. President Richard Nixon called for a moratorium on all housing programmes and established a taskforce to recommend a course of action for the future. One key proposal of the taskforce was a shift to a 'demand-side' subsidy, including the first iteration of today's housing voucher programme (Weicher, 1980; Grigsby and Bourassa, 2004).

The virtues touted by housing voucher promoters in the 1970s were the same as those trumpeted now. A major component of its attractiveness is its simulation of the private market, since individual households are given the wherewithal to find rental units that meet their preferences – subject to programme rules – in the regular housing market. Voucher holders can also remain in their current units if that is their choice (and, again, if programme rules are met). Programme costs are also dramatically lower than the main alternative, housing production programmes. And the concentration of very disadvantaged, often minority, households in public housing or other housing projects, and the attendant negative externalities for both residents and neighbouring areas, should be avoidable because vouchers are not a 'project-based' programme; that is, they are not tied to a particular housing development.

Social welfare context

Housing has always had an uneasy relationship with the rest of the social welfare safety net, making it the 'orphan issue' in social policy. This is understandable given that the largest government housing subsidy – the mortgage income tax deduction – benefits the middle class and the affluent, not the poor. But even housing assistance programmes for low-income individuals and families, such as housing vouchers, have always used higher income eligibility cut-offs than welfare programmes, most recently relying on a standard that is about 30% higher than the poverty line but has reached up to three times the poverty line in the heyday of subsidies to developers of low-income housing (Newman, 1999).

Partly as a result, housing programme clientele were a mixed-income group of the lower middle class and the working poor, along with the most disadvantaged. This profile began to change dramatically in the 1980s with the decision to target housing assistance more narrowly to those with very low incomes or, in the parlance of the decade, the 'truly needy'. The increasing share of housing assistance recipients who are very disadvantaged, and the fact that more than half of all housing assistance recipients receive some form of income assistance, have pushed a significant part of housing policy into the social welfare policy arena. The decision in 1998 to apply different income targeting to the two main types of housing assistance for the poor – project-based assistance, primarily public housing, and tenant-based assistance, namely, vouchers – shifts the housing voucher programme further into the social safety net.[4] Vouchers are now directed to a lower-income population, and public housing to a more mixed-income population.

One significant by-product of both the greater overlap between housing assistance and welfare programmes, as well as the evolution in public opinion concerning the goals of welfare and other social programmes for the poor, is the increased interest in the effects of housing programmes on residents' economic self-sufficiency, such as their work hours and earnings.

Housing Voucher programme design[5]

Although the Housing Voucher programme in the US[6] has undergone several changes since being implemented in its initial form in 1974, its core features are largely the same. The US Department of Housing and Urban Development (HUD), the federal agency with responsibility for federal housing programmes in the US,[7] issues a set number of rental housing assistance vouchers each year to the roughly 3,000 local housing authorities across the country. Eligible households – those with incomes at or below 80% of the housing market area median income – apply to the housing authority for acceptance into the programme. Because the programme is not an entitlement and in many parts of the country the demand for vouchers is greater than the supply, approved households are placed on a waiting list. As vouchers become available, they are issued on a first-come, first-served basis, subject to any locally established preference rules and the 1998 requirement that a minimum of 75% of new voucher users each year have incomes equal to, or less than, 30% of the area median income.

Households receiving vouchers have between 60 and 120 days to find housing that is physically adequate, based on a HUD housing quality standard or local codes, and that passes a rent reasonableness test, based on comparable units available for rent in the market area. If these criteria are satisfied – and if the landlord is willing to participate in this federal programme – the landlord enters into a lease with the household and a contract with the housing authority. The household pays the landlord 30% of its adjusted gross income for rent and utilities, while the housing authority pays the landlord the difference between this amount and the payment standard, or fair market rent, established for that housing market area.[8] The household can elect to rent a more expensive unit, but it must bear the extra cost out-of-pocket, though this additional expense cannot exceed 40% of the household's income.

Table 5.1 provides selected statistics on the housing voucher programme. Owing, in part, to its non-entitlement status, and in part to the relatively small expenditures associated with many social programmes, voucher expenditures constitute only one tenth of 1% of GDP. And owing largely to its non-entitlement status, less than 2% of US households are voucher users. Although the voucher programme has evolved into the key housing assistance programme for the poor, it represents about 34% of total housing subsidy costs. About three in 10 voucher users receive income assistance from the main cash welfare programme, Temporary Assistance for Needy Families, in addition to housing assistance, and more than 50% receive benefits from Social Security (SS), the Supplemental Security Income (SSI)

Table 5.1: Key statistics on the Housing Choice Voucher programme, US

	%
Voucher expenditures as % of GDP	0.1
Voucher expenditures as % of total housing subsidies	34
% of households using vouchers	1.7
% of voucher users with any welfare income	30
% of voucher users with any SSI/SS/pension income	51
% of unassisted renter households with rent >50% of income	14–23

Sources: Fischer (2006); US General Printing Office (2006); US Office of Management and Budget (2006); US Bureau of the Census (2006); US Department of Housing and Urban Development (2005, 2006b).

Notes: Expenditures and % of households using vouchers are for 2005, welfare and SSI/SS/pension income is for 1 April 2005 to 31 July 2006, and rent burden estimate is for 2001; total housing subsidies includes HUD housing assistance programmes and Low Income Housing Tax Credit Welfare includes cash assistance; rent burden information: the 14% comes from the US Department of Housing and Urban Development, 2005, worst-case needs report, and is based on tabulations of 2003 American Housing Survey (AHS) data for unassisted renter households with less than 50% of the area median income; the 23% comes from the Joint Centre for Housing Studies (2006) report, and is based on tabulations of 2004 American Community Survey (ACS) data of all renter households; because assisted households are expected to have lower cost burdens, on average, than unassisted households, the ACS should provide a conservative estimate. However, it is nearly two thirds higher than the AHS estimate for unassisted households. 'Unassisted renter households' are those without any form of housing assistance; GDP = gross domestic product; SSI = Supplemental Security Income for older and disabled people; SS = Social Security.

programme for older and disabled people, and from pensions. Finally, between 14% and 23% of renters who do not receive any form of housing assistance spend more than half their income on rent.

Correlates, outcomes and impacts of housing vouchers

Housing vouchers have been evaluated from three primary perspectives. The first focuses on the housing and neighbourhood quality and housing affordability achieved by voucher participants (for example, Leger and Kennedy, 1990; Devine et al, 2003; Feins and Paterson, 2005), and is based on the three US housing goals memorialised in landmark legislation: 'a decent home', 'a suitable living environment' and 'reasonable shelter costs' (US Statutes at Large, 1950; US Statutes at Large, 1969). A second yardstick shifts the focus from housing and neighbourhood effects on the voucher *household* to the *neighbourhood* in which the household is located. The main question here is the effect of voucher housing units on surrounding property values (Galster et al, 1999; Lee et al, 1999). The third and most recent perspective asks whether vouchers affect the economic self-sufficiency of participants, such as their income level, work effort, earnings and receipt of welfare (for example, Bania et al, 2003; Van Ryzin et al, 2003; Mills et al, 2006).

The empirical evidence on the achievement of these three sets of goals comes primarily from statistical analysis of observational data based on either household surveys or HUD administrative records. These include descriptive studies of voucher households in a sample of metropolitan areas (for example, Devine et al, 2003), and pre–post studies in which a voucher household's pre-programme status is compared with its status after participation, again, in selected metropolitan areas or states (for example, Leger and Kennedy, 1990; Feins and Patterson, 2005). Such studies are informative, but caution is required in interpreting results as 'causal impacts'. An important addition to this body of knowledge occurred in 2000 with the launch of the Welfare-to-Work Voucher (WtWV) experiment in six cities.[9] A sample of 8,732 families receiving, or eligible to receive, welfare were randomly assigned to either the treatment group that received housing vouchers, or to the control group that did not. The analysis has examined the impact of vouchers on neighbourhood quality and self-sufficiency effects (Mills et al, 2006).

Success rates

Before reviewing the empirical evidence for the programme's achievement of each of these goals, however, there is the prior question of the success rates in the voucher programme; that is, what fraction of households who receive vouchers are ultimately successful in leasing an apartment? Ignoring those who fail to lease a unit using the voucher could produce a misleading picture of the programme's effects.[10]

The most recent success-rate data pertain to 2000 and cover 48 large metropolitan area housing authorities (Finkel and Buron, 2001).[11] Overall, 69% of voucher recipients successfully leased a rental unit in these locations. In tight markets, the proportion dropped to 61%; in loose markets, it rose to 80%. There were no differences in success rates by race, ethnicity, gender or the disability status of household head, though very low-income households (incomes less than 30% of area median income) had higher success rates than households with incomes above 30% of area median. However, the housing and neighbourhood characteristics of those who were unsuccessful at leasing a unit have not been studied, making it impossible to assess whether those in the worst – or best – housing, neighbourhood and affordability circumstances fail to use the voucher. This information is vital for judging whether the programme is assisting those with the greatest housing needs.[12]

Housing quality

Little empirical research has been done on the housing quality effects of housing vouchers despite the fact that such 'bricks-and-mortar' impacts have historically been the key justification for housing programmes. For example, no national data are available on the fraction of voucher units that fail their annual housing quality re-inspections. And HUD does not systematically study the accuracy of housing quality inspections in the voucher programme as it does in its periodic quality-control studies of the accuracy of their methods for calculating rent contributions from housing subsidy recipients. Although the Office of the Inspector General at

HUD conducts half-yearly audits of assisted housing programmes, these data are not very useful for the question at hand because the audited housing authorities are selected mainly because they are known to have problems. As such, they are not a representative sample (US Department of Housing and Urban Development, 2006a).[13]

The only national information on the physical quality of voucher units compared with the housing units of income-eligible, but unassisted renters comes from 1993 data (McGough, 1997).[14] Table 5.2 demonstrates two features of the voucher programme, at least as of 1993: the housing units were generally in good physical condition, with only water leakage problems exceeding 10% of units. But the quality of voucher units was virtually indistinguishable from the housing units of renters who met the income eligibility criteria for housing assistance but were not receiving it.

While this simple comparison is not an adequate test of the *effects* of housing vouchers on the housing quality of its occupants, it strongly suggests that the programme has little if any impact on participants' housing quality. This may occur because of the overall soundness of the US housing stock across the income spectrum. Also, because voucher users and comparable non-users are located in similar neighbourhoods, voucher participants are not accessing the even higher-quality – and presumably higher-rent – units that may be found in other neighbourhoods. These data call to mind a key finding of the Experimental Housing Allowance Programme (EHAP) of the 1970s, one of the largest social experiments ever undertaken in terms of both scope and cost (more than US$163 million) (Hanushek and Quigley, 1981; MacLaury, 1981). EHAP found that a housing allowance had little effect on the recipient's housing quality because those in the worst housing were the least likely to participate (de Leeuw, 1981). Data on the housing conditions of the 31% of households who were unsuccessful in leasing a voucher unit in 2000, and updated data on the housing quality of

Table 5.2: Dwelling unit quality, voucher versus eligible unassisted renter units, 1993

	Vouchers[a]	Unassisted, income-eligible renters[b]
Water leakage – inside	17	16
Water leakage – outside	13	15
Rats	6	7
Open cracks/holes	9	11
Broken plaster/peeling paint	4	8
Exposed wiring	3	3
Severe problems[c]	3	4
Moderate problems[c]	6	9

Source: McGough (1997).

Notes: [a] Data also pertain to the housing certificate programme, which was still operational in 1993; [b] income eligible renters are defined as those with incomes below 50% of area median income; [c] severe problems and moderate problems pertain to the dwelling's heating, plumbing, electrical and interior, with the nature of the problem (for example, duration) determining whether it is severe or moderate.

—

eligible unassisted renters, would help to address the full housing quality effects of the voucher programme.[15]

Although the WtWV research has not studied physical housing quality effects, crowding in the housing unit, as measured by persons per room, declined significantly among the voucher treatment group compared with those in the control group (Mills et al, 2006).[16]

Evidence on two cities – Baltimore and Chicago – suggests that vouchers are not solving the housing quality problems of a substantial fraction of participants in these two very different big cities. In Baltimore, more than 50% of rental units failed the initial inspection from 2002 to 2004 (Newman, 2005), and an estimated 41% under contract failed the annual inspection in the first three months of 2004 (Armstrong and Basgal, 2004). In Chicago, 50% of units inspected each month fail, as do 30% of units re-inspected (Armstrong and Basgal, 2004).

Housing affordability

As with housing quality, there is also no current systematic information on the housing affordability effects of housing vouchers. The most recent examination of rent burdens in the programme (McClure, 2005), which used HUD administrative data for 2002, found that 62% of households pay about 30% of income for rent, the general rule of thumb for housing affordability. The 38% of households with rent burdens above 30% were primarily those with very low incomes who lived in housing market areas with a very low payment standard (or fair market rent for that area). Although the fraction of households with burdens beyond the 30% standard is large, it represents an improvement from 2000, having declined by eight percentage points in just two years.

Another analysis of HUD administrative data for 2000 for the 50 largest metropolitan areas indicates that the average rent burden among voucher users is roughly 29% (Devine et al, 2003). This cost burden estimate is dramatically lower than McClure's estimate cited previously, presumably because he excluded the roughly 73,000 households reporting zero income, and because large fluctuations in the incomes of very poor households in the voucher programme create serious problems when trying to match administrative records over time. The median housing cost burden in McClure's (2006) data is about 30%, however.

Ten years earlier than Devine et al's study, a study of 18 large urban metropolitan areas and two states reported an average rent burden of 35% (Leger and Kennedy, 1990). While these figures suggest a decline in rent burdens, they are based on different samples and are not strictly comparable. It is not known whether the decline in rent burdens between 2000 and 2002 experienced by voucher participants across the country (McClure, 2005) also pertained to the 50 largest metropolitan areas examined by Devine et al.

The only additional insights into housing affordability date back to the 1990 study. It reports that although average rents of voucher units were much higher than in the household's pre-programme unit, rent burdens dropped by 67%, from 52% of income devoted to rent to 35%, on average (Leger and Kennedy, 1990). For the one third who remained in their pre-programme units, the drop in rent burden was most dramatic: from 80% before participation to 28% after. For those who moved, the decline was less arresting but still substantial: from 60% to 39%. By 2002, fewer than 20% of households with children remained in their pre-programme units (Feins and Patterson, 2005), but how this might have affected housing cost burdens has not been reported. The rent burdens of households that were unsuccessful in using their voucher are also not known. That lower-income households are more likely to be successful at leasing a unit than higher-income households (Finkel and Buron, 2001) at least suggests a beneficial effect on affordability.

Neighbourhood quality

Data for 2000 indicate that most voucher participants live in neighbourhoods where fewer than 20% of households have incomes at or below the poverty line, while about 10% of voucher households live in very high poverty concentration neighbourhoods (greater than 40%) (Devine et al, 2003). The most recent evidence on the pre–post comparison of voucher participants' neighbourhood quality suggests that neighbourhood locations of voucher households with children are very similar to their pre-voucher neighbourhoods across a range of attributes such as the fraction of households in poverty, the unemployment rate, the fraction of minority residents, the rate of single female parents, and the high-school dropout rate (Devine et al, 2003; Feins et al, 2003; Feins and Patterson, 2005). Most indicators change by no more than one percentage point, typically in a favourable direction, although the fraction of minorities in the post-period voucher neighbourhood increases. Neither an initial move upon entering the voucher programme,[17] nor subsequent moves, alter these results, presumably because those living in the highest poverty (greater than 40%) neighbourhoods are less likely to move than those in middle-range poverty (20–39%) neighbourhoods.

Neighbourhood quality findings from the experimental WtWV are generally consistent with the pre–post studies (Patterson et al, 2004).[18] Effects on a range of neighbourhood quality indicators such as those noted above were positive, small and statistically significant at both the 15-month follow-up and again at the roughly four-year follow-up (Mills et al, 2006).

Another experiment, Moving to Opportunity (MTO), provides one additional insight. MTO tested the effects of residential moves by inner-city public housing residents to neighbourhoods with less than 10% poverty. Public housing residents in five cities were randomly assigned to one of three groups: the treatment group that received a housing voucher and was required to move to a low-poverty neighbourhood, a comparison group that received a voucher with no constraint on neighbourhood choice, and a control group. The comparison group's choices may be suggestive of the effects of housing vouchers on the neighbourhood quality of a particular subgroup: former inner-city public housing residents. In the MTO sites, these households moved from neighbourhoods with an average poverty rate of 59% to neighbourhoods with an average poverty rate of 27% – less than half the rate in their public housing neighbourhood (Orr et al, 2003).

Neighbourhood property value spillovers

Only two studies in the published literature have used systematic methods to evaluate the spillover effects of Section 8 tenant-based housing subsidies[19] on residential property values in the surrounding neighbourhood. The two studies come to different conclusions, apparently because of the particular housing markets studied, the richness of the analysis data and the methods used. In a pre–post study in Baltimore County, Maryland, for the 1991–5 period, Galster et al (1999) examined effects on the value of residential properties at 500 feet, 1,000 feet and 2,000 feet from the location of a Section 8 site pre- and post-occupancy by one or more Section 8 households.[20] They found a strongly positive impact on sales prices within 500 feet in higher-priced predominantly white census tracts (roughly 3,000 residents) where the housing price trajectory was increasing. But prices declined at all distances within 2,000 feet of Section 8 sites in lower-priced tracts having a downward housing price trajectory. Lee et al (1999) used a hedonic approach to study Section 8 certificates and vouchers during the 1989–91 period in Philadelphia, Pennsylvania. By contrast to the Baltimore County study, these authors found a small negative sales price spillover effect.

Economic self-sufficiency

The predominant finding across the five studies conducted to date on the effects of vouchers on the economic outcomes of participants (Ong, 1998; Bania et al, 2003; Van Ryzin et al, 2003; Susin, 2005; Mills et al, 2006) is that vouchers have insignificant effects on work. The results for earnings effects are more mixed.

The WtWV arguably provides the strongest evidence on the question of self-sufficiency effects of vouchers (Mills et al, 2006). Although there were statistically significant declines in work and earnings five to seven quarters after random assignment, these effects became insignificant over time and remained insignificant at the four-year follow-up. Susin (2005) reports similar findings in his carefully conducted non-experimental study using nationally representative survey data to examine the outcomes, in 2000, of individuals who were voucher users in 1996. He finds insignificant differences in earnings and work hours between voucher recipients and matched controls.

These results are not consistently mirrored in three non-experimental studies. Bania et al (2003), Ong (1998) and Van Ryzin et al (2003) each focused on a single housing market or set of markets in a single state. This approach may have the advantage of controlling market conditions (Shroder, 2002), but comparisons of individual markets is difficult. Bania et al (2003) and Van Ryzin et al (2003) find insignificant effects of vouchers on employment, while Ong (1998) finds positive effects.[21] Bania et al (2003) also find weak, negative and significant effects on earnings. It is worth noting that, in their study of voucher 'movers' in large metropolitan areas referred to earlier, Feins and Patterson (2005) report that moving was associated with small, significant declines in income and earnings, but there were no effects on welfare receipt.

State of knowledge on housing vouchers

A stylised summary of findings to date is as follows. A significant share of eligible households who apply for housing vouchers are unsuccessful in using them. Vouchers have no effect on the housing quality of participants, but they appear to reduce crowding significantly. Any positive effects they may have on neighbourhood quality are very small. Vouchers seem to have no effects on work and earnings, and the jury is out on whether vouchers have a positive or negative effect on neighbourhood property values. The one goal they seem to achieve is affordability, with average cost burdens below the 30% rule of thumb and improvements in affordability over the years. But even here, one analysis reports that a significant share of voucher households – 38% – is paying more than 31% of income in rent, and 16% have cost burdens above 40% (McClure, 2005).

This summary reads very much like a synopsis of the findings from EHAP conducted more than 30 years before. Today's housing voucher programme, like EHAP in the 1970s, is primarily addressing the goal of housing affordability, allowing participants to spend more of their household budgets on non-housing goods and services. Then, as now, some ask whether a voucher is truly a housing programme, as described next.

Current policy debates

Housing assistance for the low-income population is not a focus of national domestic policy debates. If any housing issue has captured attention in the last few years, it was the effect of the 2003–5 housing boom on middle-income households in search of housing. But housing 'policy' seldom surfaced in the popular media's coverage of this problem, and, when it did, it more often highlighted solutions such as inclusionary zoning[22] or creative financing, such as no-interest mortgages. Even when the working poor were referenced, housing vouchers as a possible policy solution were not. Within the more rarefied environment of the housing field, by contrast, debate never ends. Sard (2004) recently summarised three strands in the current debate, which range from the 'radical restructuring' end of the continuum to the 'fine-tuning' end.

The first strand is whether housing assistance should be an entitlement, similar to other components of the safety net. This is one of the most enduring topics of debate in US housing policy, rivalled only by the even longer-term conversation about supply-side versus demand-side housing subsidies. By and large, the debate about an entitlement voucher programme is less about *whether* housing should be

—

an entitlement than the specific design of the entitlement benefit.[23] Illustrative proposals include an entitlement to the working poor – both owners and renters – via the Earned Income Tax Credit,[24] with the key goal of reducing housing cost burdens (Stegman et al, 2004), and a voucher entitlement programme targeted on the poorest renters (Butler, 1989; Zigas, 1989; Olsen, 2003). One of the entitlement voucher proposals would reduce the size of the subsidy and, ultimately, eliminate all other housing programmes, using the savings to cover the costs of the entitlement (Olsen, 2003).

A second topic of debate is whether the housing voucher programme should be converted into a block grant, adjusted over time for inflation, and provided to the state or local housing authority. This would replace the current system, in which housing authorities receive a fixed amount of money regardless of actual costs, but with two important limitations. First, the authority can contract only for their authorised number of voucher units, even if they could afford to lease additional units. Thus, any dollars remaining in the account must be returned to HUD, not used to fund additional vouchers. And second, the housing authority is not informed of the amount of their budget allocation until well after the start of the fiscal year, unlike a true block grant, which is predictable because it is formula driven (for example, last year's amount, adjusted for inflation) (Armstrong and Basgal, 2004; Basgal, 2006). The purported reason for the shift to a block grant is to provide maximum flexibility to the administering entity to tailor the programme to local needs and priorities, though advocates feared it was the first step towards eliminating the federal commitment to housing for the poor. Block grant proposals were actually introduced by the Bush administration in both 2003 and 2004 but were not successful.

The third and most persistent strand focuses primarily on improving the administrative efficiency of the existing voucher programme. Included here are strategies to increase success rates and voucher utilisation (such as by increasing the maximum subsidy payment; allocating unused vouchers in one jurisdiction to other jurisdictions; and modifying inspection requirements [Sard, 2004]). Some of these proposals, however, move well beyond the single goal of administrative efficiency. For example, the recommendation to shift administration of the programme from the local to the regional level is motivated by the goal of improving access of low-income voucher households to better neighbourhoods and job opportunities (Katz and Turner, 2001; Millennial Housing Commission, 2002). Similarly, the case for simplifying rent determinations is based not only on improving efficiency and reducing errors and fraud, but also on increasing equity within the universe of participants (Armstrong and Basgal, 2004). A budget-based programme, such as under a block grant, is believed by some to offer the benefits of improved manageability, transparency, understandability and fairness (Armstrong and Basgal, 2004). The question of inspection requirements pertains not only to concerns about the accuracy and cost of inspections, but also to vertical equity. As noted earlier, the EHAP results of the 1970s showed that many of the worst-housed families did not participate in the housing allowance programme (de Leeuw, 1981), and the most recent data that exist on voucher unit quality show no difference compared with units of eligible renters without vouchers.

Conclusion

The most fundamental and timeless housing policy debate, of course, is whether there should be 'housing policy', that is, a separate system of housing subsidies for the poor. This question has gained increasing attention as the problem of physically inadequate housing has been replaced by the problem of housing affordability (for example, Weicher, 1980; Grigsby and Bourassa, 2004). The research reviewed in this chapter also strongly suggests that the key effect of the current housing voucher programme is on housing affordability. Some argue that housing affordability is an income problem, not a housing problem, and does not require a housing solution.

The response to this argument is well-known in the housing field. One of the rationales for housing subsidies is the belief that living in decent, stable and affordable housing is important to the well-being of low-income families and, ultimately, to society. If this were not the case, then families could be given cash assistance to spend as they saw fit. No developed country has chosen this 'cash-out' approach, choosing instead to regulate – to a greater or lesser extent – the quality, quantity and distribution of housing (Harsman and Quigley, 1991; Catalano and Kessell, 2003). Proposals to cash out housing assistance have been made in the US from time to time, but no serious proposal has been put forward in the last 30 years.

While cashing-out assistance has not resurfaced, basic questions about housing assistance are being asked. The combination of severe fiscal constraints on domestic programmes, coupled with a presidential administration and Congress that is ideologically averse to social programmes, have put the rationale for housing policy on the table for reconsideration. The question that is now receiving some scrutiny is whether decent, stable and affordable housing does, indeed, yield benefits to low-income families and society over and above the improvement in the housing itself (Newman, 2006). What may be most surprising is how little we know about the answer to this fundamental question. Much existing research on housing quality and crowding is correlational but has not established causation, and despite the prominent view that housing affordability is the key US housing problem at present, its effects on residents and the broader community have been largely neglected. There are some indications that a new wave of research may begin to address these questions. For example, research is now under way that will begin to close the gap on the role of affordability in the lives of children and families.[25]

A debate that may be looming on the horizon concerns the insignificant work and earnings effects of housing vouchers in the WtWV experiment (Mills et al, 2006). Taken at face value, these results counter the claims by advocates that housing assistance provides a platform for a wide range of salubrious outcomes, including self-sufficiency. But only a few years earlier, another careful study came to a different conclusion. The Jobs-Plus initiative, a quasi-experiment tested in public housing developments in six cities, reported that providing a package of services to residents that includes job training, reduced financial disincentives to work in the subsidy structure,[26] plus supportive social networks increased earnings and employment (Bloom et al, 2005). Would services have similarly beneficial effects on voucher households, where economics of agglomeration and scale are much lower? And which services are most important? Whether the debate will take up the question of combining housing and service subsidies in pursuit of the goal of self-sufficiency for participants remains to be seen.

Acknowledgements

The author gratefully acknowledges research assistance of Amy Buck and Amy Robie, valuable insights from Ophelia Basgal and Barbara Sard, and production assistance by Laura Vernon-Russell.

Notes

[1] This estimate refers to all housing assistance programmes (for example, HUD programmes, tax credits) and assumes the income eligibility cut-off is 80% of the area median income.

[2] Prior to the 1930s, the only previous piece of legislation was the 1862 Homestead Act (US Statutes at Large, 1863), which made 160 acres of land available to households willing to live on the land, build a home, make improvements and farm it for at least five years.

[3] Some believe that rent supplements and the Section 23 programme, introduced in 1965, were the first manifestations of a housing allowance approach in the US (Weicher, 1980).

[4] This tighter targeting of vouchers to the very poor was authorised by the 1998 Quality Housing and Work Responsibility Act.

[5] This description is based heavily on the cogent summaries provided by Grigsby and Bourassa (2004) and by Priemus et al (2005).

[6] The current programme is formally titled the Section 8 Housing Choice Voucher programme (Section 8 refers to the section of the housing act of which it is a part).

[7] Other agencies that also play a role in housing policy are the US Department of the Treasury, which administers all tax policy, including the mortgage interest deduction noted at the outset, the Low-Income Housing Tax Credit (a subsidy to investors in affordable housing), and the US Department of Agriculture's Rural Housing Service (formerly the Farmers' Home Administration), which runs rural housing programmes.

[8] Fair market rents are set at about the 40th percentile of rents in the housing market, and are based on units occupied in the previous 15 months.

[9] Atlanta, Georgia; Augusta, Georgia; Fresno, California; Houston, Texas; Los Angeles, California; and Spokane, Washington.

[10] If vouchers have no effects, then excluding failures would presumably not present a problem.

[11] Large metropolitan areas are those where the housing authority administers more than 800 voucher units. They represent about 60% of all vouchers.

[12] If unsuccessful households are not systematically different from eligible, unassisted renters, then the research presented below suggests that unsuccessful voucher applicants' primary housing problem is affordability. But we have no empirical evidence on whether there are differences between unsuccessful applicants and the universe of eligible, unassisted renters.

[13] An audit of the housing quality inspection involves a re-inspection of the housing unit. In the most recent audit, more than 90% of re-inspected voucher units in the authorities selected for review failed to meet housing quality standards (US Department of Housing and Urban Development, 2006b).

[14] These data come from the biennial American Housing Survey, a nationally representative survey of about 60,000 housing units, address-matched to administrative data on addresses of assisted housing units, including vouchers. The 'voucher' category also includes the predecessor certificate programme since the data are for 1993.

[15] Although the American Housing Survey provides detailed measures on housing quality, the self-reported data on housing assistance receipt is unreliable, so there is no accurate way to subtract these households from the tabulations. Calculating income eligibility with these data is also difficult.

[16] Van Ryzin and Kamber (2002, p 211) also report significantly less crowding among voucher users than comparable households in the private rental market, but urge caution that the results may be spurious because of false self-reports.

[17] Voucher recipients are allowed to remain in their pre-programme unit as long as it meets the housing quality and rent standards of the programme, and the landlord is willing to participate.

[18] Findings reported here pertain to voucher *users*, not all voucher *recipients* (including those who were ultimately unsuccessful in leasing a unit under the programme).

[19] In both studies, the tenant-based assistance examined pre-dates the current Housing Choice Voucher programme. However, these differences are unlikely to affect spillovers on neighbouring property values.

[20] The unit of observation is a property or site, which can be occupied by more than one household, not a household participating in the certificate programme.

[21] Bania et al studied Cleveland, Ohio; Van Ryzin et al studied New York City; and Ong studied several counties in southern California.

---

^{22} Primarily in the form of requirements of developers of new housing to include some fraction of 'affordable' units in their developments.

^{23} One striking piece of evidence supporting this assessment occurred at the inaugural housing research conference sponsored by the Fannie Mae Foundation in 1989, when Stuart Butler, director of Domestic Policy Studies at the Heritage Foundation, a conservative think tank, and Barry Zigas, the then president of the National Low-Income Housing Coalition, a liberal advocacy group, both publicly announced their support for a housing entitlement voucher programme, and sealed this announcement with a handshake (Butler, 1989; Zigas, 1989).

^{24} The Earned Income Tax Credit is paid to all households with labour force earnings below a set threshold.

^{25} Of note, the MacArthur Foundation has identified housing as one of its areas of future interest, and HUD's Office of Policy Development and Research has issued requests for research related to some of these questions. The affordability research is being done by the author and colleague J. Harkness.

^{26} The financial incentive reduced the extent to which rents increased when earnings, and, therefore, income, increased.

References

Armstrong, J. and Basgal, O. (2004) 'Comment on William G. Grigsby and Steven C. Bourassa's "Section 8: The Time for Fundamental Change?"', *Housing Policy Debate*, vol 15, no 4, pp 851–63.

Bania, N., Coulton, C. and Leete, L. (2003) 'Public housing assistance, public transportation and the welfare-to-work transition', *Cityscape*, vol 6, no 2, pp 7–44.

Basgal, O. (2006) email correspondence, 1 August.

Bloom, H., Riccio, J., Verma, N. and Walter, J. (2005) *Promoting work in public housing: The effectiveness of Jobs-Plus*, New York: MDRC.

Bogola, C. (2006) telephone interview with assistant director, Technical Oversight and Planning Division, HUD Office of Inspector General, 4 August.

Butler, S. (1989) 'The federal role in low-income housing', paper presented at the Fannie Mae Annual Housing Research Conference, Translating Housing Needs into Shelter: Strategies for the 1990s, Washington, DC.

Catalano, R. and Kessell, E. (2003) 'Comment: Housing policy and health', *Journal of Social Issues*, vol 59, no 3, pp 637–49.

de Leeuw, F. (1981) 'Comments of Frank de Leeuw on the Aaron Paper', in K. Bradbury and A. Downs (eds) *Do housing allowances work?*, Washington, DC: Brookings Institution.

Devine, D., Gray, R., Rubin, L. and Taghavi, L. (2003) *Housing Choice Voucher location patterns: Implications for participants and neighborhood welfare*, Washington, DC: US Department of Housing and Urban Development, Office of Policy Development and Research.

Feins, J., Patterson, R., Rodger, C. and Climaco, C. (2003) *Geographic mobility in the Housing Choice Voucher program: A study of families entering the program, 1995–2002 – revised final report*, Cambridge, MA: Abt Associates.

Feins, J. and Patterson, R. (2005) 'Geographic mobility in the Housing Choice Voucher program: A study of families entering the program, 1995–2002', *Cityscape*, vol 8, no 2, pp 21–47.

Finkel, M. and Buron, L. (2001) *Study on Section 8 voucher success rates, Volume 1: Quantitative study of success rates in metropolitan areas*, Washington, DC: US Department of Housing and Urban Development, Office of Policy Development and Research.

Fischer, W. (2006) senior policy analyst, Center for Budget and Policy Priorities, personal communication, 26 July.

Fischer, W. and Sard, B. (2005) 'Sources and methods used to estimate components of changes in Section 8 expenditures from 1996 to 2003', Washington, DC: Center for Budget and Policy Priorities, www.cbpp.org/3-16-05hous-meth. pdf, accessed 24 July 2006.

Galster, G., Tatian, P. and Smith, R. (1999) 'The impact of neighbors who use Section 8 certificates on property values', *Housing Policy Debate*, vol 10, no 4, pp 879–917.

Grigsby, W. and Bourassa, S. (2004) 'Section 8: The time for fundamental change?', *Housing Policy Debate*, vol 15, no 4, pp 805–34.

Hanushek, E. and Quigley, J. (1981) 'Consumption aspects', in K. Bradbury and A. Downs (eds) *Do housing allowances work?*, Washington, DC: Brookings Institution.

Harsman, B. and Quigley, J. (eds) (1991) *Housing markets and housing institutions: An international comparison*, Boston, MA: Kluwer Academic.

Joint Center for Housing Studies (2006) *The state of the nation's housing 2006*, Cambridge, MA: Joint Center for Housing Studies.

Katz, B. and Turner, M.A. (2001) 'Who should run the Housing Voucher program? A reform proposal', *Housing Policy Debate*, vol 12, no 2, pp 239–62.

Lee, C.-M., Culhane, D. and Wachter, S. (1999) 'The differential impacts of federally assisted housing programs on nearby property values: A Philadelphia case study', *Housing Policy Debate*, vol 10, no 1, pp 75–93.

Leger, M. and Kennedy, S. (1990) *Final comprehensive report of the freestanding housing voucher demonstration*, vol 1, Washington, DC: US Department of Housing and Urban Development, Office of Policy Development and Research.

McClure, K. (2005) 'Rent burden in the Housing Choice Voucher program', *Cityscape*, vol 8, no 2, pp 5–20.

McClure, K. (2006) email correspondence, 7 August.

McGough, D.T. (1997) *Characteristics of HUD-assisted renters and their units in 1993*, Washington, DC: US Department of Housing and Urban Development.

MacLaury, B. (1981) 'Foreword', in K. Bradbury and A. Downs (eds) *Do housing allowances work?*, Washington, DC: Brookings Institution.

Millennial Housing Commission (2002) *Meeting our nation's housing challenges*, Washington, DC: Millennial Housing Commission.

Mills, G., Gubits, D., Orr, L., Long, D., Feins, J., Kaul, B., Wood, M., Amy Jones & Associates, Cloudburst Consulting and The QED Group (2006) *Effects of Housing Choice Vouchers on welfare families: final report*, Cambridge, MA: Abt Associates.

Newman, S. (2005) *Low-end rental housing: The forgotten story in Baltimore's housing boom*, Washington, DC: Urban Institute.

Newman, S. (2006) *How housing matters: A critical summary of research and issues still to be resolved*, Baltimore, MD: Johns Hopkins University Institute for Policy Studies.

Newman, S.J. (1999) *The home front: Implications of welfare reform on housing policy*, Washington, DC: Urban Institute.

Olsen, E. (2003) 'Comment on Jill Khadduri's "Should the Housing Voucher program become a state-administered block grant?"', *Housing Policy Debate*, vol 14, no 3, pp 283–93.

Ong, P. (1998) 'Subsidized housing and work among welfare recipients', *Housing Policy Debate*, vol 9, no 4, pp 775–94.

Orr, L., Feins, J., Jacob, R., Beecroft, E., Sanbonmatsu, L., Katz, L., Liebman, J. and Kling, J. (2003) *Moving to Opportunity for Fair Housing demonstration: Interim impacts evaluation*, Washington, DC: US Department of Housing and Urban Development.

Patterson, R., Wood, M., Lam, K., Patrabansh, S., Mills, G., Sullivan, S., Amare, H. and Zandniapour, L. (2004) *Evaluation of the Welfare to Work Voucher program. Report to Congress*, Washington, DC: US Department of Housing and Urban Development.

Priemus, H., Kemp, P.A. and Varady, D. (2005) 'Housing vouchers in the United States, Great Britain, and the Netherlands: Current issues and future perspectives', *Housing Policy Debate*, vol 16, no 3/4, pp 575–609.

Sard, B. (2004) 'Comment on William G. Grigsby and Steven C. Bourassa's "Section 8: The Time for Fundamental Change?"', *Housing Policy Debate*, vol 15, no 4, pp 835–49.

Shroder, M. (2002) 'Does housing assistance perversely affect self-sufficiency? A review essay', *Journal of Housing Economics*, vol 11, no 4, pp 381–417.

Stegman, M., Davis, W.R. and Quercia, R. (2004) 'The Earned Income Tax Credit as an instrument of housing policy', *Housing Policy Debate*, vol 15, no 2, pp 203–60.

Susin, S. (2005) 'Longitudinal outcomes of subsidized housing recipients in matched survey and administrative data', *Cityscape*, vol 8, no 2, pp 189–218.

US Bureau of the Census (2006) Current Population Survey, 2005 Annual Social and Economic Supplement, Internet Table H1, at www.census.gov/population/www/socdemo/hh-fam/cps2005.html, accessed 18 July 2006.

US Department of Housing and Urban Development (2005) *Affordable housing needs: A report to Congress on the significant need for housing: Annual compilation of a worst case housing needs survey*, Washington, DC: Office of Policy Development and Research, December.

US Department of Housing and Urban Development (2006a) 'HUD office of the inspector general – Semiannual results by program office', at www.hud.gov/offices/oig/fraud/Jun06/, accessed 8 August 2006.

US Department of Housing and Urban Development (2006b) 'Resident characteristics report database', at https://pic.hud.gov/pic/RCRPublic/rcrmain.asp, accessed 25 July 2006.

US General Printing Office (2006) 'Analytical perspectives: Budget of the United States Government, fiscal year 2007', at www.whitehouse.gov/omb/budget/fy2007/pdf/spec.pdf, accessed 18 July 2006.

US Office of Management and Budget (2006) 'Budget of the United States Government, public budget database spreadsheet', at www.whitehouse.gov/omb/budget/fy2007/sheets/outlays.xls, accessed 7 February 2006.

US Statutes at Large (1863) An Act to Secure Homesteads to Actual Settlers on the Public Domain, vol 12, chapter 75, pp 392–94.

US Statutes at Large (1950) Housing Act of 1949, vol 63, chapter 338, pp 413–44.

US Statutes at Large (1969) Housing and Urban Development Act of 1968, vol 82, pp 476–611.

Van Ryzin, G. and Kamber, T. (2002) 'Subtenures and housing outcomes for low income renters in New York City', *Journal of Urban Affairs*, vol 24, no 2, pp 197–218.

Van Ryzin, G., Kaestner, R. and Main, T. (2003) 'The effects of federal and local housing programs on the transition from welfare to work: Evidence from New York City', *Cityscape*, vol 6, no 2, pp 45–72.

Weicher, J. (1980) *Housing: Federal policies and programs*, Washington, DC: American Enterprise Institute.

Zigas, B. (1989) 'The federal role in low-income housing', paper presented at the Fannie Mae Annual Housing Research Conference, Translating Housing Needs into Shelter: Strategies for the 1990s, Washington, DC.

SIX

Housing Benefit in Britain: a troubled history and uncertain future

Peter A. Kemp

Introduction

Great Britain has provided income-related assistance with housing costs since the 1930s, but it is only since the 1970s that it has assumed central importance within housing policy. It has also become a major component of social security expenditure in recent decades. At present, housing allowances in Britain take two major forms. The first is a scheme called Housing Benefit, which provides help for low-income tenants. The second is known as Income Support for Mortgage Interest and is available to home buyers who are in receipt of social assistance. Housing Benefit is by far the most important of these two schemes in terms of expenditure and the number of recipients.

During the last two decades, Housing Benefit has become the central component of government support in housing. It has also been instrumental in facilitating a major transformation in rented housing provision (Stephens, 2005). Yet it has also had a highly troubled history over the same period, with numerous problems, including both structural deficiencies and administrative difficulties. There have been several major reforms of Housing Benefit since the early 1980s and another reform is currently being piloted prior to being rolled out nationally. Tensions between housing and social security objectives have contributed to these problems (Kemp, 1994).

This chapter examines income-related housing allowances in Great Britain and focuses largely, but not exclusively, on the largest of these, Housing Benefit. The next section briefly outlines the housing market and social security policy context. Subsequent sections discuss the origins and development of Housing Benefit, the design of the current scheme, and its role and impact. The chapter then looks at Income Support for Mortgage Interest. This is followed by a discussion of the reform of Housing Benefit, the problems that reform was or is intended to address and the difficulties involved in attempting to resolve them. The chapter then discusses the impact of the new Local Housing Allowance, which is the most significant element of the reform. The final section sets out some conclusions.

Context

Although Esping-Andersen (1990) has described Britain as a 'liberal welfare regime', that characterisation is not strictly accurate. It is true that, in some respects, the British welfare state bears the hallmarks of a liberal welfare regime. For example, social housing has a residual role and the social security system makes considerable use of means testing. But the British welfare state also contains important elements of universality (for example, in relation to health care) that are more characteristic of social democratic welfare regimes (Cochrane et al, 2001). Nevertheless, since the 1980s, the welfare state in Britain has become more liberal in orientation, not least in relation to housing provision. There has been a move away from state provision of welfare services towards privatisation and the use of quasi-markets, as well as increased emphasis on user charges and means testing. Although this trend began under the Conservative governments of Margaret Thatcher and John Major, it has largely continued under the 'New Labour' governments since 1997.

Social security

The state social security system in Britain includes social insurance (contributory) benefits, means-tested social assistance, categorical (non-contributory, non-means-tested) benefits, and income-related tax credits. The principal insurance benefits cover incapacity to work (Incapacity Benefit), unemployment (*contributory* Jobseeker's Allowance) and retirement (Basic State Pension). These are supplemented by a safety net of means-tested benefits: *income-based* Jobseeker's Allowance (JSA) for people of working age who are expected to be available, and actively search, for work; Income Support for people who are not automatically expected to be available for work (mainly lone parents and people who are long-term sick or disabled but are not entitled to receive Incapacity Benefit); and the Pension Credit. Because the contributory benefits are flat rate and paid at a relatively low level (and in the case of contributory JSA, only paid for six months), many recipients are entitled to top up their income from the equivalent means-tested benefit. Consequently, the British social security system, like other liberal welfare states, relies heavily on means-tested benefits to provide social protection.

As for categorical benefits, a universal flat-rate Child Benefit is paid to all families with dependent children irrespective of their income. Meanwhile, certain disability benefits are paid to qualifying people to help them with the extra living costs associated with disability. A small Carer's Allowance is paid to informal care givers with extensive unpaid caring responsibilities, provided any earnings are below a modest level. A Child Tax Credit is payable to people with dependent children; although most families are entitled to receive it, those on relatively low incomes get the most. Finally, a Working Tax Credit is payable to low-income single people and couples as an earnings supplement; this includes a Childcare Tax Credit for families with approved forms of childcare.

As in many other advanced welfare states, the social security system has become more work focused in recent years. A range of welfare-to-work programmes for long-term unemployed and economically inactive people were introduced by the New Labour government after it was returned to office in 1997. It also introduced compulsory 'work-focused interviews', not only for the unemployed, but also for some lone parents and disabled people in receipt of social security benefits. The tax credit for people with low earnings (mentioned previously) and a national minimum wage were both introduced to help make work pay (Brewer et al, 2002).

The poverty rate is relatively high in Britain compared with many other advanced welfare states. Child poverty trebled between the late 1970s and mid-1990s. Since 1997 the New Labour government has introduced a range of measures to tackle both child and pensioner poverty. These include significant real increases in benefits for children and in the means-tested pension, which is now substantially higher than the contributory Basic State Pension. As a result of these reforms, the number of children and pensioners in poverty has begun to fall, though both remain at relatively high levels compared with many countries in western Europe (see Hills and Stewart, 2004).

Housing and housing policy

The housing market in Britain has undergone a major transformation over the past quarter-century. Firstly, there has been a significant growth in owner occupation. Surveys repeatedly show that owner occupation is the tenure of preference for the vast majority of households in Britain, even if not everyone can achieve that aspiration. The growth in owner occupation has in part been fuelled by the 'right-to-buy' policy introduced by the Conservative government in 1980, which enabled council tenants to purchase their home at a substantial discount on the market value (Jones and Murie, 2005). The owner-occupied sector increased from 58% of the housing stock in 1981 to 70% in 2004 (Table 6.1).

Second, there has been a modest revival in the fortunes of the privately rented housing sector. Although Table 6.1 shows that the share of the housing stock that was rented privately fell slightly from 11% from 1981 to 10% in 2004, comparing

Table 6.1: The housing stock by tenure, Great Britain, 1981 and 2004

Tenure	1981		2004	
	'000s	%	'000s	%
Owner-occupation	12,171	57.7	17,783	70.4
Private renting	2,340	11.1	2,626	10.4
Housing association	470	2.2	1,979	7.8
Local authority	6,115	29.0	2,886	11.4
Total	**21,094**	**100.0**	**25,274**	**100.0**

Source: UK Housing Review, at www.ukhousingreview.org.uk.

the two dates masks a fall up to 1988 followed by a small increase after rent deregulation in 1989. The significant change is that the late 1980s marked the cessation of a decline in the size of the privately rented sector that had been under way more or less continuously for the previous seven decades. Public attitudes to private renting have improved in recent years (Kemp, 2004).

Third, the number of households renting their dwelling from a local authority declined substantially in both relative and absolute terms. In 1981, local authorities were by far the largest type of landlord. At that date, as Table 6.1 shows, they owned 6.1 million dwellings, or 29% of the housing stock. Yet by 2004, they accounted for only 2.9 million dwellings, or 11% of the total. Thus in two decades the size of the local authority housing sector halved, a substantial drop by any standards. This decline was the result of several key developments, most of them driven by policy. As well as the right-to-buy policy involving the sale of individual dwellings, over a quarter of local authorities transferred all of their housing stock to newly established housing associations (Malpass, 2005). Meanwhile, some of the others sold parts of their stock to existing housing associations. Also, in the 1990s a number of local authorities, especially in the north of England and in Scotland, began to experience low housing demand in some neighbourhoods, which they have in part tackled by selective demolitions and sales of the most unpopular or unsuitable stock (Nevin and Leather, 2006). In addition, construction of new local authority dwellings more or less came to an end in the 1980s, not least because of government restrictions on capital spending (Cole and Furbey, 1994; Malpass and Murie, 1999).

Fourth, the number of dwellings owned by housing associations quadrupled, rising from 0.5 million or 2% of the stock in 1981 to 2.0 million or 8% in 2004 (Table 6.1). As well as stock transfers from local authorities, housing associations have accounted for almost all newly constructed social housing over the last few decades (Malpass, 2000).

Housing finance has also been transformed since the early 1980s. First, supply-side ('bricks-and-mortar') subsidies to local authorities and housing associations have been significantly cut back. Second, in the late 1980s housing associations were required to switch their borrowing from the public to the private sector to fund their new developments and other stock acquisitions. Meanwhile, their rents were deregulated in order to facilitate this change, though they remained as not-for-profit landlords letting accommodation at below market rents (Malpass, 2000). Third, in 1989 private sector rents were deregulated and a short-lived tax subsidy was introduced in order to stimulate a revival of investment in the privately rented sector (Crook and Kemp, 1996). Fourth, in the 1990s Conservative and Labour governments phased out mortgage interest tax relief for owner-occupiers. However, owner-occupiers remain exempt from tax on both capital gains and imputed rental income on their primary residence.

The reduction in bricks-and-mortar subsidies, the shift from local authorities to housing associations, the use of private finance to fund housing association development and rent deregulation in the private rental and housing association sectors all helped to raise rent levels. This transformation in housing finance has been facilitated by the availability of Housing Benefit, which has enabled the poorest households to afford the increased rents.

Origins and development

The first explicit attempts by the British state to influence the amount that people pay for their housing came with the First World War. In 1915, the wartime government was forced to introduce rent controls on working-class housing in the wake of rent strikes and threats of industrial action in support of them (Melling, 1980). Immediately after the war, government subsidies were introduced to enable local authorities to build housing to rent at below market levels (Bowley, 1945; Merrett, 1979). Meanwhile, rent controls were expanded in scope and extended in 1919 and 1920 to include virtually all privately rented housing (Kemp, 2004).

These interventions were initially intended to be short-term expedients to tackle what were seen as temporary war-related housing problems. In fact, both forms of intervention remained in place, in one form or another, for many decades. What they have in common is that they both involved intervention on the *supply* side to tackle the supply and pricing of rented housing. In both cases, affordability was addressed by keeping rents at below market prices, in the one case by subsidising the construction of new homes and in the other by imposing rent controls on existing privately rented accommodation. At the time, little consideration was given to the possibility of intervening on the *demand* side by introducing housing allowances.

In Britain, the origins of housing allowances lie in two separate systems of income-related help with housing expenditure (Kemp, 1992). The first was provided through the social security system and was known as 'housing additions' to social assistance benefits. The second was part of the housing finance system and was comprised of rent rebates for council tenants and rent allowances for private and housing association tenants. We shall look at the development of these two systems in turn.

Within the social security system, a housing allowance has been provided since 1943 when, for the first time, an amount for 'reasonable' housing expenditure was added to the benefit rates for means-tested social assistance. This covered (1) the full amount of the householder's rent in the case of tenants; and (2) mortgage interest payments (but not capital repayments) and an allowance for repairs and insurance in the case of owner-occupiers. This approach was carried over into the post-war scheme of means-tested social assistance established in 1948 (George, 1968).

The system of social security set up following the Second World War was strongly influenced by the proposals set out in the Beveridge Report, which had been published in 1942 to great acclaim (Harris, 1977). Beveridge (1942) recommended the introduction of a National Insurance scheme funded by contributions from employers, employees and the state. This was to be supplemented by a safety-net, means-tested National Assistance scheme for those people who had not made sufficient contributions to qualify for National Insurance (Harris, 1977). National Insurance provided flat-rate benefits, including a notional amount for housing expenditure, in return for flat-rate contributions. Meanwhile, National Assistance provided a less generous basic benefit, plus the actual rent (or mortgage interest) payable by the recipient, provided it was deemed to be reasonable. For people with high rents, the means-tested assistance scheme was more generous than the insurance benefit. National Insurance recipients with high rents were able to top up their incomes by applying for National Assistance to cover the difference (Dilnot et al, 1984).

The decision to include a specific allowance for housing expenditure within National Assistance reflected the fact that rents varied widely, both within and between areas, and the view that people on very low incomes had little choice over the amount of rent they paid (George, 1968). At this time, the great majority of recipients of National Assistance were living either in rent-controlled private housing or in council housing and paying below market rents. Although Beveridge did consider whether to include a variable amount for housing costs within his proposed National Insurance scheme, he felt it would be inconsistent with the principle of flat-rate benefits for flat-rate contributions (Beveridge, 1942; DHSS, 1985). This system of 'housing additions' to social assistance remained in place more or less untouched until the early 1980s when the Housing Benefit scheme was introduced.

Turning now to housing finance, central government has provided local authorities with capital grants to build rented dwellings at below market rents since 1919. In the 1920s, the new council houses were too expensive for the poorest tenants, even though they were heavily subsidised. This was partly because of the high cost of building materials and partly because the new homes were designed and built to higher standards than pre-war private housing (Bowley, 1945). However, in the 1930s, local authority house building was shifted towards rehousing people displaced by slum clearance schemes or who were overcrowded, which meant that many new council tenants had lower incomes than those typically housed in the previous decade. In order to ensure that the rents they charged were affordable to low-income tenants, local authorities were given discretionary power under the 1930 Housing Act to provide rent rebates or to operate income-related rent schemes (Bowley, 1945; Merrett, 1979; Malpass, 1990).[1]

Despite encouragement from central government to introduce rent rebates, few local authorities made use of their *discretionary* power until the 1960s and 1970s (Malpass, 1990). By 1970, less than 10% of council tenants were receiving a rent rebate (DHSS, 1985). A *mandatory* national scheme of Rent Rebates for council tenants and Rent Allowances for private and housing association tenants, to be administered by local authorities, was introduced by the 1972 Housing Finance Act in England and Wales and corresponding legislation in Scotland. The new scheme was intended to protect council and private tenants from the rent increases envisaged by that Act (Merrett, 1979; Malpass, 1990). Although introduced for reasons of housing policy, the Conservative government noted that Rent Rebates and Allowances would "also be an important weapon against family poverty" (DoE, 1971, p 11).[2]

Thus, by the 1970s there were two different schemes providing housing allowances for low-income households. They were introduced and designed for different purposes: one had an income maintenance focus for households getting social assistance, while the other provided protection against rent increases for low-income tenants. They were administered by different agencies under different government departments; one responsible for social security, the other for housing policy. They had different means tests, different structures and provided different levels of assistance, and they also overlapped, so that some households could apply for either benefit, though not both (Donnison, 1979).

In 1982/3, the administration of the housing component of social assistance – though only for tenants – was handed over to local authorities. The two schemes continued to run in parallel and were collectively renamed Housing Benefit – 'certificated' Housing Benefit for people receiving social assistance and 'standard' Housing Benefit for other low-income tenants – but administered by one agency (local authorities) instead of two. Meanwhile, the social security ministry took over from the environment department responsibility in central government for the Housing Benefit paid to non-social assistance recipients (it was already responsible for housing additions paid to people on social assistance). Thus local authorities were now paying Housing Benefit on behalf of the social security ministry. However, the social security ministry's local offices remained responsible for providing the now separate system of housing additions to owner-occupiers in receipt of social assistance (Kemp, 1987).

The implementation of the new administrative arrangements proved to be disastrous and, shortly afterwards, a review was set up (Kemp, 1984; Walker, 1985; Walker et al, 1987). This inquiry was then incorporated into a wider review of social assistance (DHSS, 1985; Housing Benefit Review Team, 1985) and led to reforms that were introduced in 1988 under legislation enacted in 1986. Meanwhile, as part of a wider attempt to reduce the growing social security budget, a succession of cuts in Housing Benefit was made in the 1980s. Most of these cutbacks involved an increase in the 'taper' (tax-back rate), that is, the rate at which benefit is withdrawn as income rises. The explicit intention was to focus the scheme much more tightly on the poorest tenants (Kemp, 1984).

Following the 1984/5 review of Housing Benefit and of social assistance more generally, the two housing allowance schemes for tenants were unified into a single housing benefit. The new scheme used the same means test as the reformed schemes of social assistance for people not in full-time work (now called Income Support) and the means-tested wage supplement scheme (Family Credit). At the same time, a further cut in Housing Benefit was made with the introduction of the new unified scheme (Kemp, 1987).

Thus, the Conservative governments of Mrs Thatcher introduced two major reforms of Housing Benefit, the first (in 1982/3) being largely administrative and the second (in 1988) structural in nature. It also introduced a series of cutbacks in Housing Benefit, which mainly affected tenants who were not in receipt of social assistance; people who in the pre-Housing Benefit regime would have been getting Rent Rebates and Allowances under the programme administered by the ministry responsible for housing policy. Thus, the social security ministry's 'traditional' clients were to some extent protected from the cutbacks in Housing Benefit entitlement in the 1980s.

Despite these cuts in Housing Benefit, the cost of the scheme and the number of recipients increased substantially during the late 1980s and early 1990s. These increases partly reflected the economic recession during that period, but also the transformation in housing finance and rental housing that took place over the same period (discussed previously). This transformation was predicated upon increases in rent levels in private and social housing and, consequently, an increase in expenditure on Housing Benefit. But while the new housing policy was driving the rent increases, the cost in terms of Housing Benefit was the responsibility of the social security ministry. The economic recession and a relaxed approach to government spending in the run-up to the 1992 general election led to a sharp increase in public borrowing, to which the re-elected Conservative government responded with a 'fundamental review' of public expenditure in order to search for reductions in the social security budget (Kemp, 1994). The outcome of the review was cuts in Housing Benefit for private tenants in 1996/7 and in Income Support for Mortgage Interest payments in 1995.

The New Labour government, which came to power in 1997, published a housing Green Paper in 2000, which outlined a range of problems with the Housing Benefit scheme (DETR/DSS, 2000). Although the Green Paper discussed various options for reform, structural changes seemed to have been ruled out, except in the long term (Robson, 2001). However, in 2002 the government announced proposals for a radical reform of Housing Benefit and its replacement by a Local Housing Allowance to be piloted in a number of local authority areas before being implemented nationally (DWP, 2002). This new scheme is discussed later in the chapter.

Housing Benefit design

The Housing Benefit scheme in Great Britain is administered by local authorities on behalf of the central government department responsible for social security, currently called the Department for Work and Pensions (DWP). The rules governing the scheme are determined by Act of Parliament and statutory regulations, supplemented by detailed guidance provided by the DWP. The rules are national and designed to ensure that people in similar circumstances receive the same amount of benefit wherever they live. However, local authorities do have the discretionary power to ignore income from war pensions when calculating entitlement to Housing Benefit. In addition, local authorities may make discretionary housing payments under a very small-scale scheme that is legally separate from Housing Benefit (Walker and Niner, 2003).

Housing Benefit is designed to ensure that recipients have an income, once eligible rent is deducted, that is no less than the social assistance benefit rates (Hills, 1991). It therefore does not take the form of a 'housing gap' scheme that is common in many other countries (Howenstine, 1986). The way in which Housing Benefit entitlement is calculated is relatively simple:

1. Tenants who are in receipt of one of the social assistance benefits – Income Support, income-based Jobseeker's Allowance and the Guarantee Credit component of Pension Credit – or who have an income that is not in excess of the social assistance benefit rates, are entitled to a Housing Benefit payment that is equal to 100% of their eligible rent.
2. Tenants whose income is more than the social assistance benefit rates, are entitled to a Housing Benefit payment that is equal to their eligible rent minus 65% of the difference between their net income and the social assistance benefit rates.

One consequence of (2) above is that the amount that recipients contribute to their rent is determined by the difference between their income and the social assistance benefit rates. Beyond that amount, their Housing Benefit payment increases or decreases with their eligible rent. In other words, the marginal cost of housing for people on Housing Benefit is nil (Hills, 1991). This had been the case for social assistance recipients since 1943, but the new design meant it was extended to other claimants in the 1988 reform – the year before rents were deregulated.

For private tenants, there is a complex set of administrative rules that are designed to ensure that benefit is not paid on 'unreasonable' rents. These rules limit the amount of rent that is taken into account to calculate Housing Benefit. If the rent is deemed to be unreasonably expensive or above the market value for the property, or if the accommodation is in excess of specified size criteria for different types and sizes of household, Housing Benefit is calculated on a lower amount that is deemed to be reasonable. Rent *increases* may also be restricted for benefit calculation purposes if they are deemed to be too large or too soon after the last one.

In addition to these 'unreasonable rent' rules, since 1996 rent ceilings have existed that limit the maximum amount of rent that is eligible for benefit. Rent in excess of the ceiling is ignored when entitlement to Housing Benefit is calculated. A government agency, the Rent Service, sets the rent ceilings and makes the judgements about the reasonableness of the rent. The rent ceilings are based on local areas determined by the Rent Service, of which there may be one or more in each of the 408 local authority areas in Great Britain. The Local Housing Allowance (discussed later), which is currently being tested prior to implementation nationally in 2008, removes the need for these rent restrictions.

In calculating entitlement to Housing Benefit, amounts are deducted from the eligible rent if the applicant has non-dependants such as adult children living with them. These 'non-dependant deductions' vary according to the income of the non-dependant. The assumption underlying such deductions is that non-dependants should be making a contribution to the rent, the size of which should vary according to their ability to pay. In effect, non-dependant deductions are an alternative to a household means test in a system that is based on single people and couples as the unit of eligibility for benefit.

The means test for Housing Benefit is based on the income of the applicant and partner (if any). Income is calculated after Income Tax, National Insurance contributions and certain other allowances are deducted. Rental payments from sub-tenants or lodgers are included in the applicant's income assessment. Charges in the rent for items such as heating, lighting and service charges are mostly not eligible for benefit. Hence they are deducted from the rent when Housing Benefit is calculated. Housing Benefit entitlement is immediately reassessed if income, rent, household composition or other relevant circumstances change.

In recent years, partly as a result of the Labour government's efforts to tackle pensioner poverty, the means test for pensioners has begun to vary in significant ways from the means test for other claimants. Among other things, it has become more generous (for example, in the way that savings are treated) and changed in other ways in order to remove the obstacles to pensioners claiming Housing Benefit. If this trend continues, it may soon be possible to talk about two Housing Benefit schemes, one for pensioners and one for applicants of working age. This age distinction mirrors the separation of the central government agency responsible for local offices of the DWP, which has been split into the Pensions Service for people over the state pension age and Jobcentre Plus for people of working age.

There are two forms of Housing Benefit payment. Local authority tenants receive their benefit in the form of a *rent rebate*, which is paid directly into their rent account. Private and housing association tenants receive a *rent allowance*, which may be paid to them or – if they request it or are more than eight weeks behind with their rent – sent directly to their landlord. In practice, nine out of 10 housing association tenants have their Housing Benefit paid to the landlord. Meanwhile, many private landlords require their tenants to 'request' direct payment if they are receiving Housing Benefit. Nationally, about 60% of allowances are paid to the private landlord (DWP, 2002).

The role and impact of Housing Benefit

While Housing Benefit is an important part of the social security system and plays a critical role in housing policy, the aims of the scheme have rarely been explicitly articulated. Indeed, the now-defunct Advisory Committee on Rent

Rebates and Rent Allowances (1983) noted that there had been some debate about whether housing benefits should be considered primarily as part of the income maintenance system or as an instrument of housing policy. Government statistical publications describe the scheme as being designed to help tenants who "have difficulty meeting their housing costs" (DWP, 2005, p 48), which hints at an income-maintenance role. Meanwhile, a Green Paper on Housing Benefit stated that the fundamental purpose of the scheme is "to ensure that people on low incomes have the opportunity of a decent home" (DWP, 2002, p 14), which seems to imply that it is mainly about housing policy.

Housing Benefit is certainly an important part of what Rein et al (1986) have called the welfare state 'income package'. It accounts for a substantial share of the income transfers paid to people whose main sources of income are social security benefits and tax credits. This is especially true for people who are in receipt of means-tested social security benefits, that is, income-based Jobseeker's Allowance, Income Support and the Guarantee Credit component of the Pension Credit.[3] For people renting their accommodation, these three social assistance benefits are all based on the assumption that housing expenditures will be covered entirely by Housing Benefit. Thus, Housing Benefit makes a significant contribution to income maintenance.

Housing Benefit also plays an important role in the housing finance system for rented accommodation. In the first place, it enables low-income tenants to afford their rental obligations. Secondly, it has become an increasingly important pillar in the British housing subsidy system. As Table 6.2 shows, the share of total housing subsidies accounted for by Housing Benefit has increased from 33% in 1990/1 to 87% in 2002/3. General subsidies that keep social housing rents below market levels have been substantially cut back in both real and nominal terms, while mortgage interest tax relief has been phased out completely.[4]

Expenditure on Housing Benefit increased – in 2004/5 prices – from £6.9bn in the financial year 1991/2 to £13.9bn in 1996/7, a rise of 56% in real terms

Table 6.2: Housing subsidies by subsidy category, Great Britain, 1990/91 and 2002/03

	1990/91		2002/03	
	£ million	%	£ million	%
General subsidies[a]	3,665	22	1,895	13
Housing allowances[b]	5,686	33	12,954	87
Tax expenditures[c]	7,705	45	0	0
Total	**17,056**	**100**	**14,849**	**100**

Source: Calculated from UK Housing Finance Review online table 2.6.1.

Notes: [a] includes the value of discounts to council tenants buying their home under the right-to-buy legislation; [b] Housing Benefit and mortgage interest payments to home buyers receiving social assistance; [c] mortgage interest tax relief to owner-occupiers and tax relief to investors in Business Expansion Scheme rental housing companies. Excludes mortgage interest tax relief to private landlords. Owner-occupiers are exempt from tax on capital gains and imputed rental income.

in just five years. This growth in expenditure reflected not only the increase in rents discussed previously but also growth in the number of people claiming social security benefits. Thereafter, as unemployment – and, to a lesser extent, the numbers of lone parents claiming Income Support – decreased, expenditure on Housing Benefit fell slightly in real terms, reaching £12.6bn in 2003/4. By this time, expenditure on Housing Benefit accounted for 1.1% of GDP and 2.7% of general government expenditure.

Since the 1988 reform, the Housing Benefit caseload has fluctuated at around 4 million (Figure 6.1). In May 2005, there were 3,957,000 recipients, which represents 15.7% of all households in Britain. Some 45% of these recipients were renting from local authorities, 35% were renting from housing associations and 20% were renting from private landlords (Table 6.3). According to the Survey of English Housing, in 2003/4 three out of five social housing tenants and one in five private tenants were in receipt of Housing Benefit.

Figure 6.1: Housing Benefit recipients, Great Britain, 1988–2006

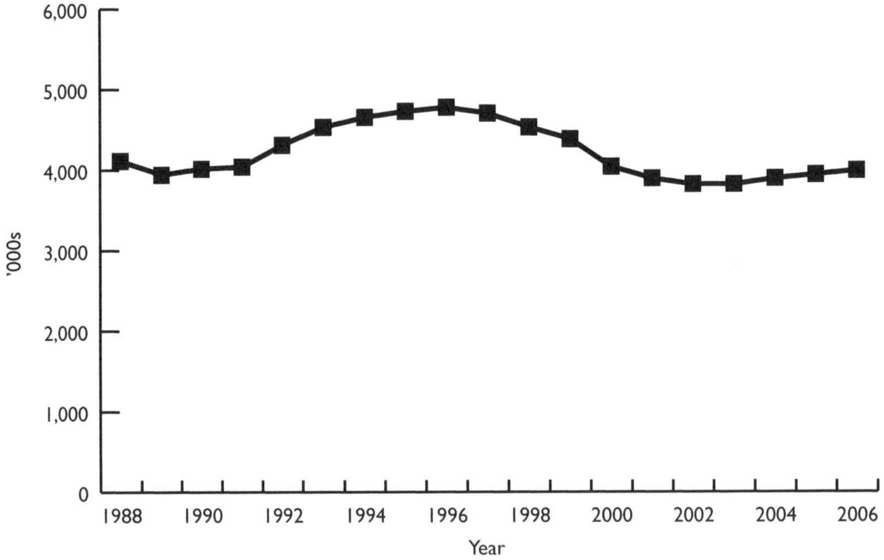

Source: DWP Housing Benefit and Council Tax Benefit Statistics (various years).

Table 6.3: Housing Benefit recipients by tenure, Great Britain, May 2005

Tenure	'000s	%
Local authority	1,790	45
Housing association	1,377	35
Private rented	790	20
All	3,957	100

Source: DWP Housing Benefit and Council Tax Benefit Quarterly Summary Statistics, London, November 2005, table 1.1.

One further sign of the importance of Housing Benefit in the housing finance system is the share of rental income that is covered by payments to tenants under the programme. A very approximate estimate of the contribution of Housing Benefit to rents within each of the three rental tenures may be made by computing the total Housing Benefit paid (mean Housing Benefit multiplied by the number of recipients) as a percentage of the total rent payable (mean rent multiplied by the number of tenants). These calculations were made using data from the 2003/4 Survey of English Housing (www.communities.gov.uk). This suggests that about a third (34%) of the total rent bill in England was covered by Housing Benefit. It accounted for 59% of the total rent due in the local authority sector, 53% in the housing association sector and 13% in the private rental sector (Table 6.4).

Thus, Housing Benefit is not just of critical importance to tenants in receipt of it; it is also an important contributor to their landlords' rental income stream, especially in social housing. Cuts in Housing Benefit will consequently have an adverse impact, not only directly on the recipients, but also indirectly on their landlords (Kemp, 1994). For this reason, landlords, and the banks that lend mortgages to them, have tended to be wary or critical of proposals to cut or reform Housing Benefit (Kemp, 2000a).

The majority of Housing Benefit recipients are economically inactive. For example, in May 2004 DWP statistics indicated that only 1% of recipients in Britain were unemployed and 10% were in paid work. Lone parents, disabled people and retired people accounted for almost all of the remainder (Table 6.5).

Table 6.4: Estimated contribution of Housing Benefit to rent in England, 2003/04

Tenure	Housing Benefit as a % of rent
Local authority	59
Housing association	53
Private rented	13
All	34

Source: Own calculations from Survey of English Housing data.

Table 6.5: Housing Benefit recipients by client group, Great Britain, May 2004

Client group[a]	'000s	%
Aged 60 or older	1,600	42
Disabled	931	25
Lone parents	846	22
Unemployed	20	1
Others	378	10
Total	**3,773**	**100**

Source: DWP Housing Benefit and Council Tax Benefit Quarterly Summary Statistics, November 2005, table 3.3.

Note: [a] These are the DWP client group descriptions.

About seven out of 10 recipients were also in receipt of one of the three main means-tested benefits: Income Support, income-based Jobseeker's Allowance and the Guarantee Credit component of the Pension Credit.

Housing Benefit has important distributional impacts, the shape of which reflect the fact that it is an income-related programme. Using micro-data from the Family Expenditure Survey, Gibbs and Kemp (1993) showed that receipt of Housing Benefit is heavily concentrated on households in the bottom three income deciles. Likewise, the Office of National Statistics has shown that, when calculated as a share of total income aggregated across all households, Housing Benefit is focused on the lower end of the income distribution. Among the non-retired population, for instance, 86% of Housing Benefit in 2003/4 was going to households in the bottom two income quintiles (Jones, 2006). Thus, Housing Benefit is highly targeted on low-income households (Stephens, 2005).

The take-up of Housing Benefit is relatively high among people who are both eligible and entitled to receive it. The official estimates distinguish between caseload take-up and expenditure take-up (a distinction that is important because take-up tends to be lower among those with relatively small entitlements). These suggest that between 84% and 90% of people who are entitled to Housing Benefit were receiving it in 2003/4. Meanwhile, expenditure take-up was between 88% and 93% (DWP, 2006b). Take-up is known to be particularly low among tenants in paid work. This partly reflects the fact that many people in work do not realise that they are eligible to apply for Housing Benefit (Ford et al, 1996) but also because some are put off by the delays and other problems with the administration of the scheme.

Housing Benefit has an impact upon rent-to-income ratios, though exact figures are not available. Table 6.6 shows rent as a percentage of income before and after Housing Benefit, averaged across *all* households (that is, including non-recipients). It indicates that rent-to-income ratios are approximately halved by Housing Benefit among social housing tenants and reduced by about a tenth among private tenants (Stephens, 2005). These data underestimate the impact of Housing Benefit because they are averaged across each sector as a whole, not just people who are recipients. This is especially true for private tenants, a much smaller proportion of whom are on Housing Benefit than is the case for social housing tenants.[5]

Table 6.6: Rents as a percentage of income before and after Housing Benefit in England, 2001/02[a]

	Local authority	Housing association	Privately rented
Before Housing Benefit	26.2	30.9	25.3
After Housing Benefit	12.8	15.7	22.8

Source: Stephens (2005, tables 1 and 2).

Note: [a] Averaged across all tenants in each tenure.

———

The impact of Housing Benefit on affordability among private tenants is attenuated by the fact that it is calculated on *eligible* rents.[6] The evidence suggests that a considerable proportion of private tenants have their Housing Benefit calculated on a rent that is less than they are due to pay their landlord. In 1999 about 70% of private tenants in England and Wales claiming Housing Benefit had their entitlement restricted because their rent was deemed to be unreasonably high or was in excess of the local rent ceiling or both (Kemp et al, 2002).[7] Research suggests that these rent restrictions cause financial hardship to many of the Housing Benefit recipients affected by them (McLaverty and Kemp, 1998; London Research Centre, 1999; Kemp and Rugg, 2001).

Low-income homeowners

As with tenants, since 1943 a housing allowance has been paid to owner-occupiers who are buying their home and are in receipt of social assistance. This covers mortgage interest payments and certain other housing-related expenses, but not repayments of capital (that is, the money borrowed). However, unlike Housing Benefit, this help with mortgage interest payments has never been made available to low-income home buyers who are *not* in receipt of social assistance benefits.

Prior to the introduction of Housing Benefit in 1982/3, the amounts that were added to social assistance payments in respect of rent and mortgage interest were referred to as 'housing additions'. They are now usually referred to as Income Support for Mortgage Interest – ISMI – but in fact there is no official name for this benefit. One government Green Paper referred to the payments as "benefit help with mortgage interest" (DETR/DWP, 2000), perhaps because it is not just home buyers in receipt of Income Support that receive them; they are also paid to people getting the two other social assistance payments, income-based Jobseeker's Allowance and the Guarantee Credit component of the Pension Credit. For this reason, they are referred to here as 'mortgage interest payments' (MIP).

For many years, mortgage interest payments within the social assistance scheme were calculated on the recipient's actual interest payments and covered them in full unless the home was deemed to be unnecessarily large or in an unnecessarily expensive area. In practice, it was very rare for payment to be restricted (Ford and Griffiths, 1994). This system remained intact until 1987, when the amount of mortgage interest covered by social assistance was reduced to 50% for the first 16 weeks of a claim (100% thereafter). At the same time, a new rule was introduced whereby benefit could be restricted if the cost of the dwelling was deemed to be unreasonably high in relation to other suitable accommodation in the area. This rule brought MIP into line with the restrictions on unreasonable rents that then applied within the Housing Benefit scheme. The limited evidence available suggests that this new restriction was also used only rarely, in part because it was considered too costly and complicated to administer (Oldman and Kemp, 1996) as it required social security staff to collect evidence on local house prices and make judgements about which accommodation should be considered suitable in any one case.

In 1992 MIP ceased to be paid to the claimant and was henceforth paid direct to the claimant's mortgage lender. Before that, it had only been paid direct to the lender if the claimant proved unable or unwilling to pay the mortgage interest to their lender themselves. Prior to this change, benefit was paid direct to the lender in respect of less than 0.2% of MIP recipients. This reform was the product of lobbying by the trade organisation representing mortgage lenders, in response to concerns that many borrowers were not using their MIP to pay their mortgage interest. This occurred in the midst of the economic recession of the late 1980s and early 1990s, during which mortgage arrears and possessions had risen rapidly to an all-time high. In response to this concession by the government, the mortgage lenders promised to limit the number of people against whom possession action for arrears was being taken (Murphy et al, 1994).

In 1993, in response to media stories about benefit being paid to unemployed homeowners with large mortgages, a ceiling was introduced for the first time on the amount of mortgage interest that was covered by new claims for MIP. The ceiling was initially set as the interest payable on the first £150,000 of a mortgage, but this was reduced in two steps to £100,000 in 1995. It is a national ceiling and takes no account of the substantial differences in house prices within and between localities and regions (Oldman and Kemp, 1996). Nor has the ceiling been raised since then, despite very substantial increases in house prices over the past decade.

Further cutbacks to MIP were introduced in October 1995. These reductions were introduced as part of a drive to reduce public expenditure in the wake of the economic recession of the late 1980s and early 1990s, an escalating public sector borrowing requirement, and a sharp increase in the number of recipients and cost of MIP (see Figure 6.2). As well as aiming to reduce expenditure, this new cut also had an explicit ideological objective of shifting responsibility from the state to the individual. Instead of relying on MIP, home buyers were expected to make their own provision against the risk of unemployment or sickness by taking out mortgage payment protection insurance or similar products (Ford and Kempson, 1997; Whitehead and Holmans, 1999). The main change was that, for new claimants under 60 years old, there was now a 39-week waiting period during which they would receive no help with their mortgage interest. It was instead assumed that home buyers either had mortgage payment protection insurance or sufficient savings to cover them during this waiting period. However, new claimants aged 60 and over were to receive their full mortgage interest from the date of their claim. A number of other changes were introduced at the same time, of which the most important was that mortgage interest was now to be calculated on a standard rate rather than the claimant's actual rate of interest (unless it was less than 5%, in which case the actual rate was used).

Analysis of the impact of this reform suggested that possession action for mortgage arrears may have become more likely to increase when unemployment

Figure 6.2: Mortgage interest payments to social assistance recipients, Great Britain, 1980–2004

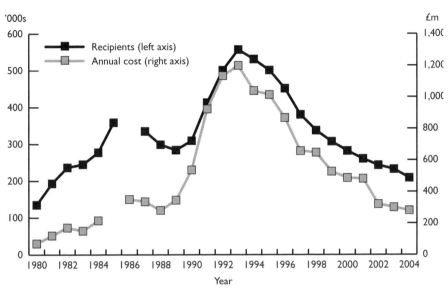

Source: UK Housing Finance online, table 110.

rises (Kemp and Pryce, 2002). This is hardly a surprising result as, among people aged below 60, the mortgage safety net is now only available after a considerable waiting period. However, since 1993 the economy has grown every year and unemployment has fallen (although there has more recently been a modest increase). Thus, as various authors have pointed out, the system introduced in October 1995 has not yet been tested by economic recession. Perhaps for that reason, there is little political pressure to reform MIP (Gibb, 2001). Largely because of the decline in unemployment, as well as the introduction of the nine-month waiting period, the number of recipients of MIP fell from an all-time peak of 555,000 in 1993 to 209,000 in 2004, a decrease of 62% in 11 years (Figure 6.2). Meanwhile, take-up of mortgage payment protection insurance is 36% of new mortgages and 22% of all borrowers (Ford et al, 2004); figures that are well below the 55% required to sustain homeownership, according to Whitehead and Holmans (1999).

One of the criticisms often levelled against Housing Benefit is that, unlike tenants, owner-occupiers who are not on means-tested social security benefits are not eligible to apply (Wilcox, 1998; Gibb, 2001). In the past, this exclusion was arguably justified by the fact that owner-occupiers buying their home received mortgage interest tax relief. However, this subsidy was phased out in the 1990s. Another argument is that, because of the long-term real increase in house prices, owner occupation is an investment, and not just a consumption good, and, therefore, not one that should be subsidised through Housing Benefit.

Yet critics point out that, because of the growth in low-income homeownership, owner-occupiers now account for half the poor in Britain (Burrows et al, 2000). Even so, some of these poor homeowners are older people who have paid off their mortgage.

Housing Benefit reform

Problems with Housing Benefit

When it was introduced in 1988, the unified Housing Benefit was widely welcomed as major step forward. In practice, however, the scheme has encountered widespread difficulties. A succession of reports have highlighted numerous problems with the way that Housing Benefit is designed and administered (for example, Kemp, 1998, 2000b; Social Security Select Committee, 2000; Hills, 2001). These problems are so extensive that there is space here to consider only the most important ones.

First, the administration of Housing Benefit is beset with problems, with a substantial minority of local authorities unable to process benefit claims within a 14-day target. For claimants, these delays can result in financial hardship and negatively affect their relationship with the landlord if they are living in private rental housing. In extreme cases, delays in the processing of claims may result in eviction if the tenant is unable to pay the rent while waiting for their claim to be processed (Audit Commission, 2002).

Second, the 100% subsidy of rent for those on social assistance, combined with the 100% marginal rate of benefit for all recipients (whose rent is not deemed to be excessive), is believed by policy makers to be an important problem with Housing Benefit. This is because, at the margin, it insulates people on Housing Benefit from price signals (Hills, 1991). Consequently, it gives them little financial incentive to shop around when looking for accommodation (Kemp, 2000b). By eliminating price signals in this way, it also potentially reduces the likelihood of achieving an efficient allocation of the housing stock (Hills, 1991; Gibb, 1995).

Third, the Housing Benefit scheme lacks transparency. The rules governing the scheme are highly complex, which makes it difficult, time consuming and costly to administer. Moreover, over time Housing Benefit has tended to suffer from what might be termed 'complexity creep'. This occurs in two main ways: new, often highly complex, rules are introduced or existing ones are amended in response to queries that arise when some previously unconsidered issue occurs in claimant circumstances. Also, amendments to aspects of the rules governing Housing Benefit get made frequently in response to changes in either the 'parent benefits' of Income Support, Jobseeker's Allowance and Pension Credit or the Working Tax Credit and Child Tax Credit. As a result of both these factors, Housing Benefit has tended to become more complex over time.

Fourth, the lack of transparency in Housing Benefit is particularly a problem for private tenants who have deregulated tenancies. Because of the need to have complicated administrative rules to prevent over-consumption as a result of the lack of a shopping incentive, private tenants on Housing Benefit often do not know how much money they will be awarded and, consequently, what rent they can afford. Indeed, because of delays in processing claims, it is often some time after a lease has been signed that private tenants find out how much of their rent will be considered eligible for Housing Benefit (Kemp, 2000b). Those caught out by these rules are left with shortfalls that they have to make up out of the income intended for their non-housing living expenses. Research has found that, by the time the Housing Benefit claim has been processed, there is little scope for tenants to go back to the landlord and negotiate a lower rent (McLaverty and Kemp, 1998; London Research Centre, 1999).

Fifth, the poor administration of the scheme is believed to act as a disincentive for claimants to leave benefit and take up paid employment. For example, in 2001/2, it was taking three weeks on average for Housing Benefit entitlement to be adjusted following a change of circumstances (DWP, 2002). This can make it financially risky for unemployed claimants to take up employment (while continuing to claim Housing Benefit) if the job is a short-term one. These frictional work disincentives are potentially exacerbated by the sharp rate of benefit withdrawal as income rises (referred to as the 'taper'), which may make some employed claimants reluctant to work more hours. The income taper in the British scheme is steeper than in the housing allowance schemes in most other countries (Kemp, 1997; Stephens et al, 2002). When combined with additional income tax and social security contributions (National Insurance), and reduced social assistance and tax credits, the effective marginal tax rate for Housing Benefit recipients can be very high and in some cases over 90% (Wilcox, 1993), as shown in Table 6.7. These very high marginal deduction rates in effect create a 'poverty trap' for people in receipt of means-tested benefits (Deacon and Bradshaw, 1983).

Sixth, Housing Benefit has a relatively high level of fraud and error. At any one time, approximately one in six recipients may be receiving the wrong amount of

Table 6.7: The poverty trap: cumulative deductions from each £1 of additional pay, UK

	With tax credits	Without tax credits
Marginal gross earnings	£1.00	£1.00
Less:		
Income Tax	22p	22p
National Insurance	11p	11p
Tax credits	37p	
Net income	30p	67p
Housing Benefit	19.5p	43.5p
Council Tax Benefit	6p	13.5p
Net disposable income	4.5p	10p

Source: Wilcox (2006).

Note: 2005/06 tax and benefit rates. Assumes the standard rate of income tax and the tax credit taper above the first income threshold.

benefit because of official error, claimant error or fraud. The high level of error reflects the complexity of the scheme. Fraud in particular is a major concern for the Labour government (DWP, 2002). One response to the perceived high level of fraud and error has been to introduce stringent checks to verify that claimants are being paid the right amount of benefit, but this has helped to make the administration of the scheme still more complicated and time consuming.

Reforms

These problems with Housing Benefit were more or less ignored by the Conservative governments after the 1988 reform, but eventually, after some hesitation, the New Labour government introduced a programme of reform to tackle them (DWP, 2002). This programme has two main aspects. First, the government introduced a raft of relatively minor reforms that were designed to improve the administration of the scheme and remove obstacles that deter recipients from moving off welfare and into paid employment. These reforms appear to be having some impact and, among other things, the average number of days that it takes to process applications has begun to fall (DWP, 2006a).

Second, in November 2002 the Labour government announced that it would introduce a radical reform of Housing Benefit involving a new Local Housing Allowance for *private* tenants. At the time of writing, the new scheme for private tenants is being tested in 18 'pathfinder' local authority areas prior to being implemented nationally in 2008. The Local Housing Allowance (LHA) scheme removes the necessity for the complex rules on 'unreasonable' private sector rents (discussed earlier). The main feature of the LHA is that entitlement is no longer calculated on the claimant's eligible rent. Instead, within each local market area, there is a standard allowance, which varies only by household size and composition.

However, it is important to note that non-dependant deductions and the means test still apply under the LHA. Thus, claimants whose income is at or below the social assistance benefit rates receive the full standard allowance, but for those with an income above that level the allowance tapers out at the same rate (that is, 65% of net income) as in the existing Housing Benefit scheme. Thus, although the determination of rent is greatly simplified, the complexities concerning income assessment, household composition and most changes of circumstances, still apply in the LHA.

In the pathfinder scheme, recipients living in accommodation with a rent that is less than the LHA can keep the difference; while those renting a home that is more expensive have to pay the excess out of their own income. The design of the LHA is therefore such that the marginal cost of housing for recipients is 100%. To that extent, LHA recipients have a financial incentive to shop around when looking for accommodation. If the recipient moves to somewhere more expensive, they have to pay the full amount of the increase out of their own pocket. However, where the LHA is more than the rent, the government is proposing to limit the maximum gain to £15 per week when the scheme is rolled out nationally (DWP, 2006a). This proposed limit is partly intended to ensure that work incentives are not undermined for the minority of recipients of the LHA who make large gains and partly to contain the anticipated increase in the cost of Housing Benefit when the new scheme goes nationwide in 2008.

The LHA is normally paid to the tenant rather than the landlord. It is only paid directly to the landlord where the claimant is eight or more weeks in arrears with their rent or is deemed to be 'vulnerable' and unable to manage their financial affairs. Although the LHA represents a radical departure from previous Housing Benefit designs, most of the debate has focused on the fact that it would be paid to claimants rather than directly to landlords. The poverty lobby and organisations representing landlords and their mortgage lenders argued that, if the LHA is paid to the claimant rather than directly to the landlord, the money will be spent on other things; and that, consequently, rent arrears and evictions will increase and landlords' income streams will be placed in jeopardy (Kemp, 2006).

The rationale for the LHA reform is to 'build choice and responsibility' into Housing Benefit. The government hopes that the design of the LHA will encourage recipients to make trade-offs between quality and price when looking for accommodation in the rental housing market. The much simpler system will also be far more transparent than the old one. It is hoped that knowing how much allowance they will get in advance, and having it paid to them instead of their landlord, will empower recipients and encourage them to take responsibility for their budgeting and rent payment obligations (DWP, 2002). These objectives therefore seek in part to address the moral hazard problems of the existing Housing Benefit scheme. They also attempt to build on the 'rights and responsibilities' agenda that has informed many of New Labour's other reforms of the welfare state (Dwyer, 1998). Tenants on Housing Benefit are expected to become active and responsible consumers in the marketplace, armed with their Local Housing Allowance rather than being passive recipients of Housing Benefit that is paid on their behalf directly to the landlord.

The government hopes that the LHA will also help to improve administration. As it will no longer be necessary to refer rents to the Rent Service to check that they are not unreasonable, it should be possible for the Local Housing Allowance to be processed and paid more quickly than is the case with the present scheme. But while improving administration is an important objective in its own right, it is mainly seen as a means to encourage more claimants to move from welfare to work. The government hopes that recipients will be less worried that taking a job will result in lengthy disruption to the payment of their Housing Benefit (DWP, 2002). (The impact of the LHA pilot reform is discussed in the next section.)

The government initially hoped to extend the LHA to social housing in due course, but this proposal has now been dropped, at least for the time being (DWP, 2006a). This change of plan was made because it proved difficult to design a flat-rate scheme that was compatible with the way tenancies are allocated and rents are set in that part of the housing market (see Kemp, 2006). Unlike the private rental market, where rents and access are determined by the interaction of supply and demand, in the social housing sector both prices and tenancies are administered by officials following rules. Tenancies are allocated on the basis of assessed need, not ability to pay. Consequently, Housing Benefit recipients in social housing are not currently in a position to shop around for accommodation. It will be difficult to introduce a housing allowance scheme that relies on the operation of a market when an administered system, rather than a market, is in place (Kemp, 2000b). Making social housing more market-like in order to facilitate the introduction of an LHA would raise fundamental questions about the nature of this tenure, including the extent to which it is primarily focused on helping those people who are in most need. However, the Labour government still intends to move towards the payment of Housing Benefit to the claimant instead of the landlord in the social housing sector (DWP, 2006a).

Impact of the LHA

At the time of writing, the official evaluation of the LHA in the pathfinder areas is not complete and it may be too early to make a definitive assessment of its impact. However, the results published so far, together with other research evidence, make it possible to draw some provisional conclusions.

First, the proportion of recipients that were personally receiving their benefit (instead of it being paid directly to the landlord) had increased, from about half prior to the LHA pilot to about nine out of 10 after its introduction (Roberts et al, 2006). However, this substantial increase in payment to the claimant had not resulted in a significant rise in rent arrears. Thus, the evaluation team concluded that "non-payment of rent does not appear, after 15 months of the LHA, to be a problem affecting a large number of claimants and their landlords" (Walker, 2005, p 4). Hence, despite the fears expressed by landlords, lenders and consumer groups, it seems that the great majority of LHA recipients were successfully paying their rent and not falling into (a higher level of) rent arrears. Meanwhile, although there were some initial teething problems (Citizens' Advice, 2005), the nine local authorities where the LHA was being evaluated were managing to identify 'vulnerable' recipients who were not able to manage their affairs and for whom direct payment to the landlord remained appropriate.

Second, concerns that the loss of direct payments and increased rent arrears would encourage landlords to stop letting their accommodation to recipients do not appear to have materialised. Although some landlords had withdrawn, or said they would withdraw, from letting accommodation to recipients, in practice the decreases were not substantial (Rhodes and Rugg, 2006). Moreover, there was little evidence to suggest that homelessness had increased among recipients in the nine areas included in the official evaluation (Walker, 2006). Likewise, an assessment of the impact of the LHA in four of the pathfinder areas by the housing pressure group Shelter (2006) also found that homelessness had not increased. In fact, the official evaluation found that, because homeless people could still have their benefit paid directly to the landlord, the ability of organisations assisting them to find accommodation had been increased compared with the situation before the LHA was introduced in the pathfinder areas. In other words, because most other claimants had their LHA paid to them, homeless people had become a more attractive client group to some private landlords (Walker, 2006).

Third, after 15 months, the evaluation found little evidence that the LHA had much influenced whether or not recipients had moved or were likely to move house. In addition, there was no evidence that significant numbers of recipients had moved into smaller accommodation in order to maximise the excess of their LHA over their contractual rent. However, more recipients than before were judged to be living in accommodation that was 'appropriate' in terms of size. The evidence suggested that factors other than just the amount of benefit they receive affect recipients' decisions to move and their choice of accommodation (Roberts et al, 2006). This finding is consistent with previous research on the effects of benefit on housing decisions (Kemp et al, 1994). In practice, therefore, the impact of the LHA on the willingness of recipients to shop around when looking for accommodation may be less marked than the government had originally hoped.

Fourth, most recipients were better off financially under the LHA than they had been under the previous Housing Benefit scheme. Over half of LHA recipients had an excess of benefit over their rent. The high proportion of recipients gaining in this way reflects the fact that, in the pathfinders, the LHA payment was set at the rent *ceilings* used for calculating Housing Benefit for private tenants under the previous scheme. For the same reason, under the LHA a smaller proportion of recipients than before had a 'shortfall' between their contractual rent and their eligible rent for benefit calculation purposes. Further, among those recipients that continued to have one, the average amount of the shortfall was smaller under the LHA than the previous Housing Benefit scheme (Roberts et al, 2006).

Fifth, although in the 'pathfinder' areas the average *eligible* rent had increased, contractual rents had not, when compared with the comparison areas in the evaluation (Roberts et al, 2006). This is important because there had been concern that the more generous level of the LHA compared with the previous scheme would encourage landlords to increase rents. An evaluation of the LHA conducted by Shelter also found that the LHA had not resulted in rent inflation within the four pathfinder areas included in their study when compared with four comparison areas (Shelter, 2006).

Finally, there was no evidence that the introduction of the LHA had had a significant effect in practice upon work incentives (Roberts et al, 2006), even though this was a major motivation behind the government's decision to pilot the reform. However, compared with national trends there had been a modest reduction in the time taken to process benefit claims. In addition, the evaluation confirmed that the LHA represented an improvement in clarity and transparency for recipients and their landlords compared with the previous Housing Benefit scheme in relation to the amount of benefit that private tenants receive (Walker, 2006).

In summary, the impact of the LHA has been relatively modest. The LHA has not had the disastrous impact that its critics argued it would have, for example, in relation to rent arrears and homelessness as a result of paying benefit to tenants instead of landlords. Equally, while it has had clear benefits for many recipients, particularly in relation to financial gains, these have been relatively modest overall. Meanwhile, some of the government's hoped-for outcomes, such as improved work incentives, have not yet materialised. However, the impact of many reforms is often neither quite as beneficial as the advocates hope, nor as deleterious as the opponents claim, will be the case. This is hardly surprising as both proponents and critics are almost obliged to exaggerate the likely effects in order to mobilise support either for or against contentious reforms. Nevertheless, the evidence so far suggests that the LHA represents an important, but not particularly marked, improvement on the previous Housing Benefit scheme for private tenants.

Conclusion

Housing Benefit in Britain is an important policy instrument, both in terms of income maintenance and its contribution to the housing finance system. Nevertheless, since it was introduced in 1982/3, the scheme has endured a problematic history. The initial introduction of the scheme was described by *The Times* newspaper as the "biggest administrative fiasco in the history of the welfare state".[8] Although the reform that quickly followed on from that experience was widely welcomed, in practice the scheme has attracted sustained criticism, not only because of structural flaws in its design, but also because of problems with its administration.

These enduring problems were largely ignored by central government during the 1990s, but after some hesitation the Labour government began to introduce reforms that aimed to tackle them. The new Local Housing Allowance represents a radical reform of Housing Benefit for private tenants. Nevertheless, it is only a partial solution: it addresses some of the design and administrative problems of the scheme, but leaves many others untouched. It largely eliminates the complexities and perverse incentive effects surrounding the determination of the eligible rent for Housing Benefit in relation to private tenants, but it fails to tackle the problems that arise from the assessment of income and household composition, especially in relation to changes of circumstances. These problems may be politically harder to solve because they are likely to involve difficult trade-offs between the cost of the scheme and the number of losers that may result from reform (Kemp, 2000a). The administrative reforms that have recently been introduced have helped to speed up the processing of claims, but overall performance remains poor and is unlikely to improve substantially without further, radical change.

Notes

[1] In addition, council dwellings were built to lower standards in the 1930s compared with the 1920s (Merrett, 1979).

[2] As well as Rent Rebates and Allowances, the Conservative government under Prime Minister Edward Heath also introduced a means-tested, in-work benefit known as Family Income Supplement for families with a breadwinner in low-paid employment (Deacon and Bradshaw, 1983). It was renamed Family Credit in 1988, which was in turn replaced by a Working Families Tax Credit in 1999 and the Working Tax Credit in 2003.

[3] The Guarantee Credit component of the Pension Credit (PC) is the social assistance scheme for people above the state pension age. It was previously known as the Minimum Income Guarantee and, before that, as Income Support. The other component of the PC is the Savings Credit, which is payable to households (not just those on social assistance) who have a small amount of savings.

[4] These estimates of subsidy are calculated using public expenditure definitions. Calculations by Steve Wilcox (2005) suggest that, when defined in economic terms as the difference between the rents people pay and what they would have paid if the rent was set at market levels, general subsidies to council housing are broadly similar to the amount of money spent on Housing Benefit.

[5] In addition, these figures are estimates of the *nominal* rather than the *effective* incidence of Housing Benefit on rent-to-income ratios. The usefulness of rent-to-income ratios as a measure of affordability has also been questioned (see Bramley, 2006).

[6] These restrictions in eligible rents do not affect the amount that the landlord charges the tenant, except indirectly by constraining the amount of rent that the latter can afford to pay.

[7] It is likely that the proportion of recipients affected by these rent restrictions has declined since 1999 and present indications are that it is more like 50%.

[8] As Paul Spicker (2005) has pointed out, that was written before the Child Support Agency was introduced, which has also had a highly problematic implementation.

References

Advisory Committee on Rent Rebates and Rent Allowances (1983) *Report no 3 '(final report). January 1977 to March 1983*, London: HMSO.

Audit Commission (2002) *Learning from inspection: Housing benefit administration*, London: Audit Commission.

Beveridge, W. (1942) *Social insurance and allied services*, London: HMSO.

Bowley, M. (1945) *Housing and the state 1919–1944*, London: George Allen and Unwin.

Bramley, G. (2006) 'Affordability comes of age', in P. Malpass and L. Cairncross (eds) *Building on the past: Visions of housing futures*, Bristol: The Policy Press.

Brewer, M., Clark, T. and Wakefield, M. (2002) 'Social security in the UK under New Labour: What did the Third Way mean for welfare reform?', *Fiscal Studies*, vol 23, no 4, pp 505–37.

Burrows, R., Ford, J. and Wilcox, S. (2000) 'Half the poor? Policy responses to the growth of low-income home-ownership', in S. Wilcox (ed.) *Housing finance review 2000/2001*, Coventry and London: Chartered Institute of Housing/Council of Mortgage Lenders.

Citizens' Advice (2005) *Early days: CAB evidence on the Local Housing Allowance*, London: Citizens' Advice.

Cochrane, A., Clarke, J. and Gewirtz, S. (2001) *Comparing welfare states* (2nd edn), London: Sage.

Cole, I. and Furbey, R. (1994) *The eclipse of council housing*, London: Routledge.

Crook, A.D.H. and Kemp, P.A. (1996) 'The revival of private rented housing in Britain', *Housing Studies*, vol 11, pp 51–68.

Deacon, A. and Bradshaw, J. (1983) *Reserved for the poor: The means test in British social policy*, Oxford: Basil Blackwell and Martin Robertson.

DETR/DSS (Department for Environment, Transport and the Regions/Department of Social Security) (2000) *Quality and choice: A decent home for all*, Green Paper, London: Department for Environment, Transport and the Regions and Department of Social Security.

DHSS (Department of Health and Social Security) (1985) *Reform of social security, Volume 3: Background papers*, London: HMSO.

Dilnot, A.W., Kay, J.A. and Morris, C.N. (1984) *The reform of social security*, Oxford: Clarendon.

DoE (Department of the Environment) (1971) *Fair deal for housing*, London: HMSO.

Donnison, D. (1979) 'Benefit of simplicity', *Roof*, March/April, p 68.

DWP (Department for Work and Pensions) (2002) *Building choice and responsibility: A radical agenda for Housing Benefit*, Green Paper, London: Department for Work and Pensions.

DWP (2005) *Work and pensions statistics 2004*, London: Department for Work and Pensions.

DWP (2006a) *A new deal for welfare: Empowering people to work: Consultation report*, London: The Stationery Office.

DWP (2006b) *Income related benefits: Estimates of take-up in 2003/2004*, London: Department for Work and Pensions.

Dwyer, P. (1998) 'Conditional citizens? Welfare rights and responsibilities in the late 1990s', *Critical Social Policy*, vol 18, no 4, pp 519–43.

Esping-Andersen, G. (1990) *The three worlds of welfare capitalism*, Cambridge: Polity.

Ford, J., Burrows, R., Quilgars, D. and Rhodes, D. (2004) 'Mortgage insurance: Its role in the mortgage safety-net', *Housing Finance*, Spring, pp 34–45.

Ford, J. and Griffiths, A. (1994) 'Preventing mortgage arrears: a shrinking safety net', *Benefits*, no 10, pp 15–19.

Ford, J. and Kempson, E. (1997) *Bridging the gap? Safety nets for mortgage borrowers*, York: Centre for Housing Policy, University of York.

Ford, J., Kempson, E. and England, J. (1996) *Into work? The impact of housing costs and the benefit system on people's decision to work*, York: Joseph Rowntree Foundation.

George, V. (1968) *Social security: Beveridge and after*, London: Routledge & Kegan Paul.

Gibb, K. (1995) 'A housing allowance for the UK? Preconditions for an income-related housing subsidy', *Housing Studies*, vol 10, no 4, pp 517–43.

Gibb, K. (2001) 'Helping with housing costs? Unravelling the political economy of personal subsidy', in D. Cowan and A. Marsh (eds) *Two steps forward: Housing policy into the new millennium*, Bristol: The Policy Press.

Gibbs, I. and Kemp, P.A. (1993) 'Housing benefit and income redistribution', *Urban Studies*, vol 30, no 1, pp 63–72.

Harris, J. (1977) *William Beveridge: A biography*, Oxford: Oxford University Press.

Hills, J. (1991) *Unravelling housing finance*, Oxford: Clarendon.

Hills, J. (2001) 'Inclusion or exclusion? The role of housing subsidies', *Urban Studies*, vol 38, no 11, pp 1887–902.

Hills, J. and Stewart, K. (eds) (2004) *A more equal society? New Labour, poverty, inequality and exclusion*, Bristol: The Policy Press.

Housing Benefit Review Team (1985) *Housing benefit review: Report of the Review team*, London: HMSO.

Howenstine, E.J. (1986) *Housing vouchers: A comparative analysis*, New Brunswick, NJ: Rutgers University, Centre for Urban Policy Research.

Jones, C. and Murie, A. (2005) *The right to buy*, Oxford: Blackwell.

Jones, F. (2006) 'The effects of taxes and benefits on household income, 2004/05', *Economic Trends*, no 630, May, pp 53–98.

Kemp, P.A. (1984) *The cost of chaos: A survey of the housing benefit scheme*, London: SHAC.

Kemp, P.A. (1987) 'The reform of housing benefit', *Social Policy & Administration*, vol 21, no 2, pp 171–86.

Kemp, P.A (1992) *Housing benefit: An appraisal*, London: HMSO.

Kemp, P.A (1994) 'Housing allowances and the fiscal crisis of the welfare state', *Housing Studies*, vol 9, no 4, pp 531–42.

Kemp, P.A. (1997) *A comparative study of housing allowances*, London: Department of Social Security.

Kemp, P.A (1998) *Housing benefit: Time for reform*, York: Joseph Rowntree Foundation.

Kemp, P.A (2000a) 'Housing benefit and welfare retrenchment in Britain', *Journal of Social Policy*, vol 28, no 2, pp 263–79.

Kemp, P.A (2000b) *'Shopping incentives' and housing benefit reform*, Coventry and York: Chartered Institute of Housing and Joseph Rowntree Foundation.

Kemp, P.A. (2004) *Private renting in transition*, Coventry: Chartered Institute of Housing.

Kemp, P.A. (2006) 'Housing benefit: Great Britain in comparative perspective', *Public Finance and Management*, vol 6, no 1, pp 65–87.

Kemp, P.A. and McLaverty, P. (1998) 'Private tenants and "perverse incentives" in the housing benefit scheme', *Government and Policy: Environment and Planning C*, vol 16, no 4, pp 395–409.

Kemp, P.A., Oldman, C., Rugg, J. and Williams, T. (1994) *The effects of benefit on housing decisions*, Department of Social Security research report no 26, London: HMSO.

Kemp, P.A. and Pryce, G. (2002) *Evaluating the mortgage safety net*, London: Council of Mortgage Lenders.

Kemp, P.A. and Rugg, J. (2001) 'Young people, housing benefit and the risk society', *Social Policy and Administration*, vol 35, no 6, pp 688–700.

Kemp, P.A., Wilcox, S. and Rhodes, D. (2002) *Housing benefit reform: Next steps*, York: Joseph Rowntree Foundation.

Kempson, E., Quilgars, D. and Ford, J. (1999) *Unsafe safety nets*, York: Centre for Housing Policy, University of York.

London Research Centre (1999) *Housing benefit and the private rented sector*, London: Department of the Environment.

McLaverty, P. and Kemp, P.A. (1998) 'Housing benefit and tenant coping strategies in the private rental housing market', *Environment and Planning A*, vol 29, pp 355–66.

Malpass, P. (1990) *Reshaping housing policy: Subsidies, rents and residualisation*, London: Routledge.

Malpass, P. (2000) *Housing associations and housing policy*, Basingstoke: Macmillan.

Malpass, P. (2005) *Housing and the welfare state*, Basingstoke: Palgave.

Malpass, P. and Murie, A. (1999) *Housing policy and practice* (5th edn), Basingstoke: Macmillan.

Melling, J. (ed) (1980) *Housing, social policy and the state*, London: Croom Helm.

Merrett, S. (1979) *State housing in Britain*, London: Routledge and Kegan Paul.

Murie, A. (2006) 'Moving with the times: Changing frameworks for housing research and policy', in P. Malpass and L. Cairncross (eds) *Building on the past: Visions of housing futures*, Bristol: The Policy Press.

Murphy, D., Taylor, S. and Whitworth, J. (1994) *An evaluation of the mortgage interest direct payment scheme*, London: Department for Social Security.

Nevin, B. and Leather, P. (2006) 'Understanding the drivers of housing market change in Britain's post-industrial cities', in P. Malpass and L. Cairncross (eds) *Building on the past: Visions of housing futures*, Bristol: The Policy Press.

Oldman, C. and Kemp, P.A. (1996) *Income support for mortgage interest: An assessment of current issues and future prospects*, London: Council of Mortgage Lenders.

Rein, M., Rainwater, L. and Schwartz, J. (1986) *Income packaging in the welfare state: A comparative study of family income*, Oxford: Clarendon.

Rhodes, D. and Rugg, J. (2006) *Local Housing Allowance final evaluation: The survey evidence of landlords and agents experience in the nine pathfinder areas*, Department for Work and Pensions' Local Housing Allowance Evaluation Report 11, Leeds: Corporate Document Services.

Roberts, S., Beckhelling, J., Phung, V-H., National Centre for Social Research, Boreham, R., Anderson, T. and Li, N. (2006) *Living with the LHA: Claimants experiences after 15 months of the LHA in the nine pathfinder areas*, Department for Work and Pensions' Local Housing Allowance Evaluation Report 9, Leeds: Corporate Document Services.

Robson, P. (2001) 'Housing benefit', in D. Cowan and A. Marsh (eds) *Two steps forward: Housing policy into the new millennium*, Bristol: The Policy Press.

Shelter (2006) *The path to success? Shelter's research on housing benefit reform: The final report*, London: Shelter.

Social Security Select Committee (2000) *Housing benefit: Session 1999-2000, sixth report*, London: Stationery Office.

Spicker, P. (2005) 'Five types of complexity', *Benefits*, vol 13, no 42, issue 1, pp 5–9.

Stephens, M. (2005) 'An assessment of the British housing benefit system', *European Journal of Housing Policy*, vol 5, no 2, pp 111–29.

Stephens, M., Burns, N. and MacKay, L. (2002) *Social market or safety net? British social rented housing in a European context*, Bristol: The Policy Press.

UK Housing Review online, www.ukhousingreview.org.uk.

Walker, B. (2005) *15 months on: An interim evaluation of running the LHA in the nine pathfinder areas*, Department for Work and Pensions' Local Housing Allowance Evaluation Report 8, Leeds: Corporate Document Services.

Walker, B. (2006) *Local Housing Allowance final evaluation: Implementation and delivery in the nine pathfinder areas*, Department for Work and Pensions' Local Housing Allowance Evaluation Report 10, Leeds: Corporate Document Services.

Walker, B. and Niner, P. (2003) *Review of discretionary housing payments*, In-house Report no 127, London: Department for Work and Pensions.

Walker, R. (1985) *Housing benefit: The experience of administration*, London: Housing Centre Trust.

Walker, R., Hedges, A. and Massey, S. (1987) *Housing benefit: Discussion about reform*, London: Housing Centre Trust.

Whitehead, C. and Holmans, A. (1999) *Why mortgage payment protection insurance? Principles and evidence*, London: Council of Mortgage Lenders.

Wilcox, S. (1993) *Housing benefit and the disincentive to work*, York: Joseph Rowntree Foundation.

Wilcox, S. (1998) *Unfinished business: Housing costs and the reform of housing benefits*, Coventry: Chartered Institute of Housing.

Wilcox, S. (ed.) (2005) *UK Housing Review 2005/06*, Coventry: Chartered Institute of Housing and Council of Mortgage Lenders.

Wilcox, S. (2006) personal communication to the author, 27 August 2006.

SEVEN

Housing allowances in France

Madhu Satsangi

Introduction

For most of the past 60 years, France has had two housing allowance regimes, one for market-priced housing and one linked to the country's intricate system of housing capital subsidies. Neither allowance regime has paid 100% of housing costs. How has this system evolved? What are its market impacts and distributional consequences? This chapter presents a review of the main features of the French system of income-related housing allowances; it identifies the context of that system in the country's welfare state and then looks at the design of the system and how it is intended to operate. The third main section looks at the key impacts of housing allowances in France. The chapter then discusses evidence for the failings of the system and the concluding section summarises the main points discussed.

France's population is estimated to have been 62.2 million in mid-2004, some 5.5 million higher than 20 years earlier (INSEE, 2005). Its population density is less than that of many of its European neighbours and about a quarter of the population lives in rural areas (a similar number to those in the three main metropolitan regions centring on Paris, Lyon and Marseille/Aix-en-Provence). The mean age of the country's population is currently estimated at between 39 and 40, about four years older than at the end of the Second World War and seven years older than at the start of the last century (INSEE, 2005). Around one person in 10 living in France was not born in the country, with about half of these having been naturalised as French citizens. About a quarter of France's 24 million households are couples without children, about a third are couples with children and slightly fewer than one in three are comprised of a single person. There are around 2 million lone-parent families.

Figure 7.1a shows how average disposable incomes have changed over the past 30 years in real terms. From 1970 to 1990 there was rapid and then slightly more modest growth with real falls until 1997, followed by renewed growth (to the 2002 mean of €27,300 and median of €24,000).[1] Unsurprisingly, disposable incomes are higher for non-pensioner households than for pensioners (€30,000 compared to €21,500 at the mean), with households headed by a person aged 40–49 the most well-off (mean €34,000). However, households with a reference person aged under 30 fared, on average, only roughly as well as pensioners (all data sourced as Figure 7.1a).[2]

Figure 7.1: Three decades of household income growth in France

(a) All households, 1970–2002

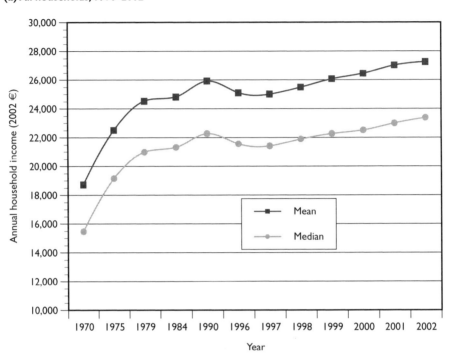

Source: Enquêtes Revenus Fiscaux, 1970, 1975, 1979, 1984, 1990, and 1996 to 2002,
www.insee.fr/fr/ffc/chifcle_fiche.asp?ref_id=NATSOS04202&tab_id=45.

Commentaries for the 1980s and 1990s tend to suggest that there were increasing inequalities in earned incomes in those decades (for example, Chambaz et al, 1999). One dimension of this is seen in housing tenure. Figure 7.1b looks at cross-sectional sample survey data for tenant households only in the same period as Figure 7.1a. Apart from a hump in the early to mid-1990s for the upper two deciles, the trend lines are rather flatter as a group than for the country as a whole. The data suggest that in real terms, earnings for the poorest quarter of tenant households are effectively the same as they were 30 years ago and that low- to middle-income tenant households earn less in real terms than they did in the early 1970s. Given general price inflation, the clear implication is that poverty amongst France's renters has increased considerably. This outcome is likely to reflect broad economic change, processes of differential tenure selection and the fortunes of those who have become renters.

Table 7.1 looks at housing tenure change over the past 20 years. Most notable here are the relatively rapid increases in the proportion (and absolute number) of households owning their home outright and the growth until 1996, albeit more modest, in the proportion of households in social housing (habitations à loyer

Figure 7.1:Three decades of household income growth in France

(b)Tenant households, 1973–2002

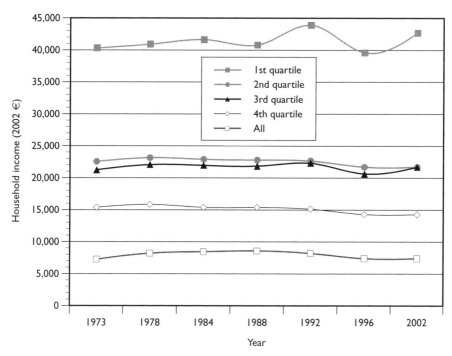

Source: Fack (2005, annexe 1, p 37).

Table 7.1:Tenure change in housing, France, 1984–2002

Tenure (% of households)	1984	1988	1992	1996	2002
Owner-occupiers	**50.7**	**53.6**	**53.8**	**54.3**	**56.0**
Outright	26.3	27.4	30.3	32.1	35.0
With a loan	24.4	26.1	23.5	22.2	21.0
Tenants	**39.0**	**37.2**	**37.7**	**38.1**	**37.9**
Habitations à loyer modéré	14.6	15.0	15.3	15.7	15.6
Other social housing	1.9	2.0	1.8	1.9	1.6
Controlled rent (1948 Act)	3.5	2.5	2.0	1.4	1.0
Market rent	19.0	17.7	18.6	19.1	19.7
Other tenures	**10.4**	**9.1**	**8.4**	**7.6**	**6.1**
Furnished rented housing tenants, sub-tenants	1.9	1.5	1.5	1.6	1.6
Agricultural tenancy	0.6	0.4	0.2	0.2	0.3
Rent free	7.9	7.2	6.7	5.8	4.2
Number of households (thousands)	**20,364**	**21,256**	**22,131**	**23,286**	**24,525**

Source: INSEE, Enquêtes logement, www.insee.fr/fr/ffc/chifcle_fiche.asp?ref_id=NATTEF05235&tab_id=95.

Note: Data are for households and their main residences, that is, they exclude second/holiday homes and vacant houses.

modéré, HLM). Figure 7.2 looks at data for 1988 and 2002 alone and compares the housing tenure distributions of households on low incomes (those with less than half the median, adjusted for household composition) with the country as a whole. Over 14 years, homeownership (mainly outright) clearly became less common amongst low-income households, and renting (particularly in the social rental sector) much more so.

Figure 7.2: Tenure and household income, France, 1988 and 2002

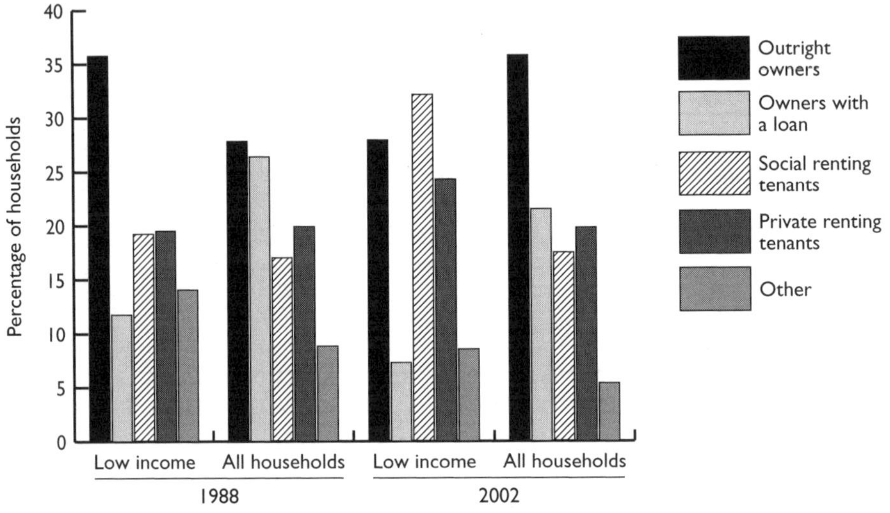

Source: Driant and Rieg (2004, table 1).

Social welfare in France

As Spicker (1997) has noted, there is a general preference in France to talk of a system of social protection rather than of a welfare state. This can be linked to a key feature identified by Barbier and Théret (2000, pp 3–4), namely a historical tendency to create new schemes and benefits continuously to cover uninsured risk or new categories of the population rather than applying a single scheme to the whole population. They argue that the fragmentation that results, alongside its basis on social insurance principles, funding through employees' and employers' contributions and relative independence from the state, testify to the system being 'Bismarckian'. At the same time, however, the fact that the identification of specific needs has provoked new targeted benefits arguably shows the pursuit of universality. For Barbier and Théret (2000) this, alongside unity being pursued through a label of 'sécurité sociale',[3] complementarity, financial coherence and similar administrations and uniformity through ceilings for calculating contributions, tailors the system to 'Beveridgean' objectives.

Compared to many European Union (EU) or OECD countries, France spends a large percentage of its national income on social protection. Using the definition of public social expenditure[4] of the OECD (2005), it has been estimated that, in 2002, France spent 31% of GDP in social protection (Abramovici, 2005). This compared with 28% for the 15 older EU countries (with 21% for the OECD). Country-by-country, France's level of spending was closer to regimes typically viewed as highly welfarist (for example Sweden or Denmark, at 32% and 30% respectively) or corporatist (for example Germany at 30%) than to some of its other geographic neighbours (for example Italy at 26%, and Spain at 20%). In the early 1970s, however, the proportion of GDP going to social protection in France was only about half this figure. Barbier and Théret (2000) suggest that three periods can be distinguished:

1. The years 1974–83 saw a significant increase in the ratio caused by increasingly weak economic growth, rapid increases in unemployment and high inflation. From 1974, unemployment insurance benefits were increased, family benefits from 1981 and the retirement age was reduced in 1982. In nominal terms, expenditure on social benefits increased by 16% per annum.
2. The years 1984–93 saw annual increases in benefit spend of 6%. A series of measures contained and reduced expenditure. The first half of the period saw improvement in economic growth rates, the second renewed deterioration.
3. From 1994, the social spending share first stabilised and then declined as structural reforms have taken root.

An important characteristic of the French social protection system is that, in comparison to other EU countries, a high proportion of revenue is derived from employer and employee contributions. These are flat-rate levies made on all income sources: wages, benefits and earnings from capital. Through the 1980s and 1990s, contributions accounted for over three quarters of total revenue (the rest deriving from general taxation) and the rate of levy on employees (Cotisation Sociale Generalisée, CSG) saw some sharp increases. From the mid-1990s there were, however, an increasing number of exemptions from payment for both particular groups of worker and for (particularly small) businesses. These were made in response to the adverse labour market consequences of the levy, and the consequence was that the late 1990s saw a gradual shift away from contributions towards general taxation (Abramovici, 1999). More recent data testify to the continuance of this trend (see Table 7.2).

In all EU countries, pensions and health care account for the majority of social protection expenditure. Over at least the past two decades, France has allocated around three quarters of spending on these two areas. The increasing absolute amounts and shares of expenditure that they attract largely testify to the country's ageing society and outweigh shifts due to economic volatility. They also outweigh the results of policies of deliberate restraint, occasioned by government concern about budgetary deficit. Beyond efficiency gains, it is arguably harder to restrain

Table 7.2: Financing structure of social protection, France, 1990–2003

Element (cash sums in € billion)	1990	1995	2001	2002	2003
Social protection benefits	267.9	342.9	419.6	443.3	465.0
Management costs	11.4	14.4	17.5	18.6	18.5
Other costs	2.3	5.2	4.8	5.5	5.5
Total expenditure	**281.7**	**362.5**	**441.9**	**467.4**	**489.0**
Employer and employee contributions	227.4	266.7	300.9	312.6	323.2
Taxation	8.9	25.7	87.2	89.2	91.4
Other public contributions	39.7	51.0	49.9	53.1	53.7
Other income	10.1	12.6	12.9	12.6	12.7
Total income	**286.0**	**356.0**	**450.9**	**467.6**	**481.1**
Balance (income – expenditure)	**4.4**	**–6.5**	**9.0**	**0.2**	**–7.9**

Source: Ministère de la Santé et de la Protection Sociale, author's adaptation of data from www.insee.fr/fr/ffc/chifcle_fiche.asp?ref_id=NATFPS04612&tab_id=218.

health and pension spending than it is to restrict spending on other social benefits (to be discussed later).

Leaving housing allowances aside, France's principal social welfare benefits are outlined next. Whilst those who have made adequate CSG contributions are more generously treated, there is a safety net formed by a series of benefits. At the end of the 1990s, it was estimated that almost 6 million people (that is about 10% of the population) were reliant on the safety net (Zoyem, 1999):

- **Unemployment insurance**. Recipients have to be actively seeking work, have paid the CSG continually for at least four of the previous eight months and not have left their previous job of their own volition. Benefits are time limited: the greater the length of CSG payment, the greater the period covered. The benefit paid is the sum of a fixed amount (around €10 per day) and a proportion of the ceiling for social security payments (known as the salaire journalier de référence or 'reference salary', around €28,000 per annum in 2005). The proportion (maximum 75%) is at its highest initially and decreases as the length of claim increases (to 40%).
- **Unemployment assistance**. This is a safety-net benefit set up in the 1980s for unemployed people who had exhausted their rights to unemployment insurance. The claimant has to have been in work for at least five years in the 10 years prior to the job loss for which unemployment insurance was first paid. The amount of benefit is limited to the fixed amount above, though a higher rate is paid to those aged 55 or above. France also has a specific 'inclusion allowance', originally intended as a subsidiary unemployment benefit for those people who have made inadequate social contributions to qualify for unemployment insurance/assistance.

- **Minimum wage**. Also dating from the 1980s, this guarantees a minimum income to anyone aged 25 or above (though the age criterion does not apply to pregnant women or people with a dependent child). The benefit is designed to bring income (including any housing allowance) up to a floor. It is paid on condition that the recipient agrees to undertake training or job placements under a social inclusion contract ('contrat d'insertion'). In 2005, a single person would be entitled to around €420 per month, a couple to one and a half times that sum. There are allowances for children on top of these amounts.
- **Family benefits**. These are paid to all families, irrespective of means, with two or more children under the age of 20. At the time of writing, the minimal amount is around €120 per month, with older children being treated more generously. (In addition to this principal benefit, there are numerous grants paid in specific circumstances: the education allowance, the back-to-school allowance, the adoption allowance and the special education allowance.)
- **Childcare benefits**. These are means-tested benefits, paid to parents with a child or children aged under six, employing a childcare worker. Both parents have to be in work. In 2005, maximal grants were around €150 per month.
- **Lone-parent benefit**. Paid to a person bringing up a child or children alone or to an expectant mother, this benefit guarantees a minimal income of (in 2005) around €500 per month.
- **Disabled adult allowance**. This is a benefit paid to disabled persons of limited means who have no entitlement to old age or disability benefit (discussed later).
- **Invalidity benefit**. This was created in the 1930s and is paid to people over 60 who have a permanent disability that reduces their work capacity to a third.
- **Supplementary pension**. Introduced in the 1950s, this is intended to bring the incomes of older people up to the level of the minimum non-contributory old age pension.
- **Widows'/widowers' allowance**. This was introduced in 1980 to give a minimal income to the surviving partner of someone with contributory social insurance cover.

(Zoyem, 1999; OECD, 2004; CAF, 2005)

Figure 7.3 categorises different elements of social welfare spending and compares France's expenditures to the mean for the 15 older EU countries (EU15). (The EU15 refers to the 15 countries that comprised the European Union before it expanded.) The French pattern is generally similar to that of these other member states, though expenditures on family and childcare benefits are slightly higher and those on health care and disability slightly lower. It is notable that in 10 of the 15 countries (including France), unemployment benefits and health care and disability spending saw rapid rates of growth in 2003 (generally repeating what had happened in 2002).

Figure 7.3: Expenditure shares of social welfare benefits, France and the EU, 2001

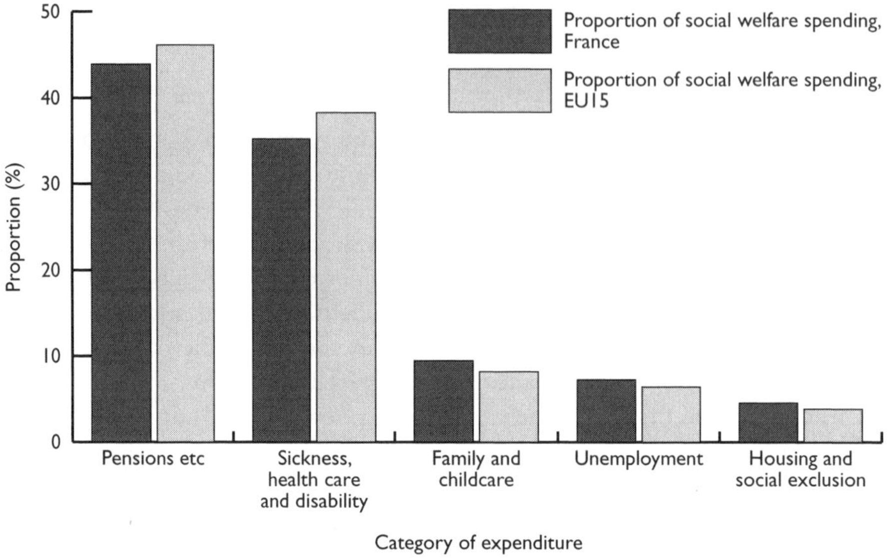

Source: Abramovici (2005).

The housing allowance regime

The data in Figure 7.3 show that income-related housing allowances take a very modest share of France's total expenditures on social protection and spend is small in relation to GDP (continually under 1% from 1981 to 1998) (Barbier and Théret, 2000). That still means, nevertheless, significant annual expenditures of around €15 billion, with over 6 million households (approximately one in every four) receiving help. Figure 7.4 compares the number of recipients of housing allowances to other protection benefits from 1990 to 2003. The number of people receiving pensions (including supplementary pensions) is significantly higher than those for any of the other categories. It also showed continuous growth during the 1990s and early years of this century. Apart from a dip in 1998, the numbers receiving family benefits stayed fairly flat over the period. The minimum wage was received by rather more people in the late 1990s than other years and the number of adults with a disability allowance saw modest growth. The number of people receiving housing allowances grew sharply from 1990 to 1995 and then stayed relatively flat. This trend, however, masks differences between the set of allowances.

Before discussing these, the origins and rationales of housing allowances need to be examined, and the discussion extends my previous work (Satsangi, 1998; see also Kemp, 1990). The system grew from 1948 when the Rent Act consolidated and sought to loosen a series of pre-war rent controls (of varying targets and extents, emanating in the late 19th century). Simultaneously, the government

Figure 7.4: Recipients of social protection benefit, France, 1990–2003

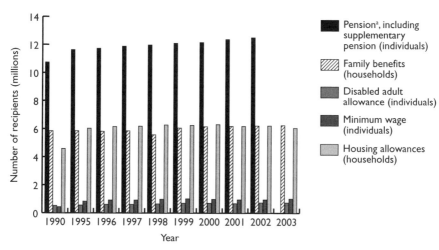

Source: Ministère de la Santé et de la Protection Sociale, author's adaptation of data from www.insee.fr/fr/ffc/chifcle_fiche.asp?ref_id=NATFPS04611&tab_id=244; Ministère des Transports, de l'Équipement, du Tourisme et de la Mer, 2005; Compte du Logement, 2003, www.statistiques.equipement.gouv.fr/IMG/xls/A340_cle578f43-1.xls.
Notes: [a]No pensioner data for 2003; counts are in December of each year.

introduced the Aide au Logement à Caractère Familiale (subsequently renamed the Allocation de Logement Familale or ALF). As the name implies, this was paid to families: originally to those with dependent children, subsequently to those with dependent older relatives and to childless couples married for five years or fewer. It was designed to allow families to be housed decently[5] without having to devote too much of their budget to housing. The scope of allowances was widened significantly in 1971, with the introduction of the Aide au Logement à Caractère Social (subsequently renamed the Allocation de Logement Sociale or ALS). Potential clients could now be single pensioners or pensioner couples, employed persons under 25 or disabled adults. When, in the 1980s, the social protection benefits of the minimum wage and unemployment assistance were introduced, their recipients became entitled to the ALS. Both renters and purchasing owners are eligible for the ALF or ALS, though residents of houses built with one of a series of subsidised loans are excluded. Those households are eligible to a parallel allowance, the Aide Personnalisée au Logement (or APL, introduced in 1977). Tenants entitled to the ALF or ALS receive the benefit themselves whereas the APL for eligible tenants is paid directly to their landlord (see also Lafarrère and le Blanc, 2002). The importance of history is affirmed by considering that, even now, the ALS and ALF are treated as *family* benefits, with the APL alone considered a specific *housing* benefit (Fack, 2005).

Figure 7.5 looks at trends in the number of households receiving allowances, first according to the type of allowance and second according to tenure. The total number of housing allowance recipients grew through the 1980s, but at a

Figure 7.5: Recipients of housing allowances, France, 1984–2003

(a) Allowance regime

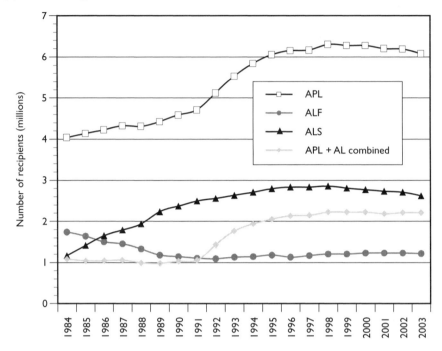

(b) Tenure

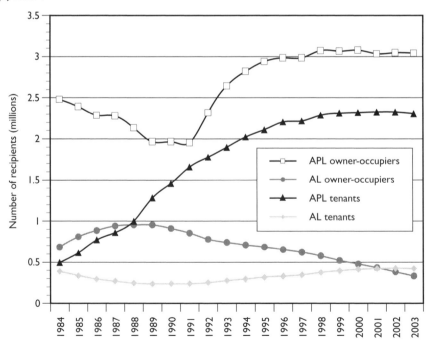

Figure 7.5: Recipients of housing allowances, France, 1984–2003 (contd)

(c) Spread within tenure

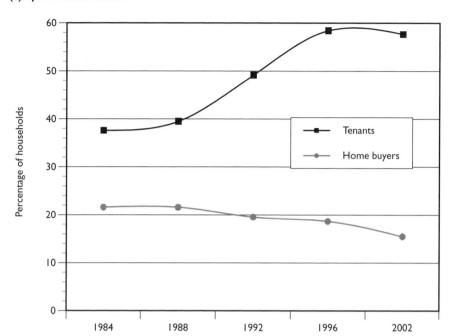

Source: Compte du Logement, www.statistiques.equipement.gouv.fr/IMG/xls/A340_cle578f43-1.xls; Lincot and Rieg (2003, table 8).

rate much more modest than in the early to mid-1990s when the recession bit. As was seen previously, the mid-1990s saw an abatement in the rate of increase, with some decline in the early years of the 21st century. Figure 7.5a also shows, however, that the global trend is effectively a composite of the (dominant) trend in subsidised housing (the APL) and the ALS, that is, 'non-traditional family' household types living in unsubsidised housing.

Much more than ever before, the housing allowances go to tenants rather than homeowners (Figure 7.5b). The chart shows continual growth in the number of tenants of subsidised housing receiving an allowance and this was particularly sharp in the early 1990s. Although it started a little later, that sharp increase was also seen for tenants of unsubsidised housing, though the favourable economy of the mid- to late 1980s is reflected in falls in the number of recipients. For homeowners buying unsubsidised housing the pattern is of gentle decline in receipt followed by gentle increase. In subsidised housing, the pattern initially follows that of tenants and then goes into sharp descent from the 1990s. The last point is unexpected given the fate of the national economy and relates rather more to explicit policy decisions to reduce capital subsidies for homeownership (discussed later). Figure 7.5c looks at the proportion of households receiving either the ALF/ALS or APL according to whether they were tenants or buying their own home. For tenants, the proportion peaked in 1996 at little under 60%, having risen from slightly under 40%, for house purchasers, a gentle logarithmic decline can be seen, although only a little under one buyer in five received an allowance in 2002.

From the mid–1970s onwards, personal housing allowances assumed greater importance in French housing policy. This was because France, like many other European countries at that time, increasingly questioned the housing capital subsidies that had been dominant since the end of the Second World War (Kemp, 1990). The main bricks-and-mortar subsidies used have been the Prêt Locatif Aidé (PLA, subsidised rental loan) available principally to the organisations that provide HLM; the Prêt Aidé à l'Accession à la Propriété (PAP, subsidised ownership) for low- to modest-income households to access homeownership; and rehabilitation grants for owners and landlords (Satsangi, 1998). These *aides à la Pierre* (bricks-and-mortar subsidies) had allowed large-scale construction and had resolved the housing shortages of the post-war and baby-boom eras and helped the repair and improvement of older housing. Two particular criticisms of them were that they were technically inefficient in an economic sense; they were not going to those who needed them the most. It was also argued that they were inefficient; their administration was too costly. Broadly, the housing question was seen less in terms of financing house building, and more in terms of the solvency of particular households. The break-up of the traditional family had reduced the resources of poorer households and made individuals more vulnerable in the face of disability or illness, unemployment was appearing more and more often. Instead of poor people more typically being older and rural – owning decaying houses but income poor – they were younger, salaried and urban. Furthermore, large-scale social rental housing schemes were increasingly seen as areas of concentrated anti-social behaviour (Lafarrère and le Blanc, 2002).

It was argued that personal housing allowances could resolve these new problems: they would be better targeted on those who needed them and leaving an individual free to choose their housing would avoid the creation of ghettoes. As in other countries, however, the question remains as to whether it was the changing shape of poverty and the housing question or the weaknesses of bricks-and-mortar subsidies in comparison to personal housing allowances that led to the redirection of subsidy. Subsidy is discussed here in an accounting sense, as the sums paid by government to consumers/producers of housing. This should be distinguished from the true economic sense of subsidy, that is, the difference between the price paid per unit of housing service by the consumer and the price that would prevail in a free market. France does not levy imputed rental income on homeowners and has tax relief for home buyers' mortgages that is subject to a ceiling at around the median income level. Driant and Jacquot (2005) show that accounting for imputed rental income accentuates labour market inequalities, but they do not estimate the total scale of revenue foregone.

The only recent calculation of the scale of mortgage interest tax relief was made in the mid-1990s. Its growth and the balance between allowances and capital subsidies from the mid-1980s is shown in Figure 7.6. From a position of approximate budgetary parity, housing allowances first overtook capital subsidies and then accelerated away as bricks-and-mortar subsidies were reduced. Between 1984 and 1995, the total amount paid in capital subsidy fell by 30%: that through the PLA was halved and that through the PAP fell by 20%. From 1996, PAP saw some regrowth after it was made available at 0% interest.[6] For homeowners, the direct consumption 'subsidy' of mortgage interest tax relief has clearly been rather less important than in other EU countries.

Louvot's (1998) analysis of expenditure trends shows that for housing allowances budgetary growth is partly explained by increases in the number of people meeting the criteria for receipt and partly by deliberate extension to the eligibility criteria. To the pressure of underlying structural causes of expenditure growth (socio-economic and demographic) was added, in 1991, that of an explicit policy decision to make the means test the sole rationing criterion for access to a housing allowance. Thus, households of types previously excluded added their weight; Lafarrère and le Blanc (2002) argue that the number of students was the most significant extension. The extension was undertaken in phases: first for Paris and the Ile de France, then for larger provincial cities (those with at least 100,000 residents in 1992) and for the rest of the country a year later. The end

Figure 7.6: Expenditure on housing subsidies, France, 1984–2003

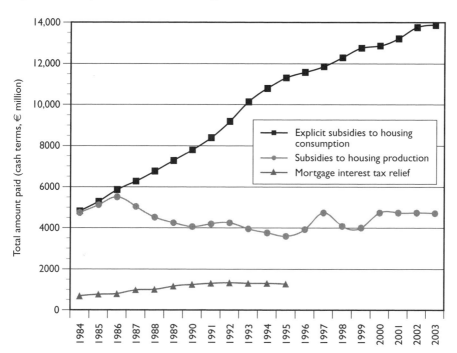

Source: Compte du Logement, www.statistiques.equipement.gouv.fr/IMG/xls/A311_cle5835e7-1.xls; Commissariat Général du Plan, 2001, *Financement du Logement*, Paris: la Documentation Française, table 4.

of the last century and start of this have seen stabilisation in allowance spread and expenditure.

The reason for this is seen largely in the other key expenditure element: change in the amount of allowance due to house price/rent inflation. Until 1997, the essential relationship in the design of the allowance system was:

$$A = k(I, S) \, [\min(L, L_p(G, S)) - L_o(I, S) + C(I, S)]$$

where:

A is the allowance payable;

k is a coefficient which increases with increases in household size and decreases with increases in household income (discussed further below);

I is the income of the household;

S is the size of the household;

L is the rent/mortgage paid by the household;

L_p is the rent/mortgage ceiling for allowance payments for households of that size which also varies according to geographic zone. L_p is highest in zone 1 (Paris and its suburbs), lower in zone 2 (the Ile de France region beyond zone 1, provincial metropolitan regions with more than 100,000 residents, Corsica and the Départements d'Outre-Mer) and lowest in zone 3 (the rest of the country);

G is the geographic zone;

L_o is the minimal rent/mortgage payment, a percentage of the rent/mortgage that increases with household income; and

C is the service charge paid by the household.

(Laferrère and le Blanc, 2002, p 6)

Decisions taken on what *k* should be, on the minimal rent payment and on rent ceilings have clearly therefore been important. Afsa (2001) notes that historically *k* ranged from 0 to a maximum value of 0.95 or 0.9, depending on whether the household was entitled to an APL (the higher percentage) or ALF/ALS, though they were equalised at 0.9 in 2000/01. (The coefficient is reduced by 10% for each additional €1,500 earned.) L_p was also more generous for the APL than for the ALF or ALS. Simply from looking at the maximal value for *k*, it can be seen that France does not allow for any household to have 100% of its rent met through a housing allowance. Laferrère and le Blanc (2002) note that the combined effect of the ceiling on *k* and of L_o is to give an effective value for *k* of between 0.45 and 9.

In 1997, the equation for calculating APL was, in Fack's (2005) argument, simplified to show more clearly how much of their own resources households were paying for their housing. In 2001, this was extended to the ALF and ALS with the form of:

$$A = L + C - P_p$$

where P_p is 'personal participation', that is, the sum payable by the household (other terms as equation 1).

At first sight, this equation is, indeed, rather more straightforward than equation 1, principally as there are fewer terms with the k and L_o elements having been 'combined' into P_p. Fack notes that the total amount of the allowance increases with the amount spent on housing and the size of the household and decreases with household income, but the paper does not clarify how P_p is determined.

In fact, there has been no removal of rent/payment ceilings nor any reduction in the number of variables considered. The amount payable by a household is given by the equation:

$$P_p = 0.085 \times (L + C) + (T_f + T_l).(R - R_o)$$

where:

T_f is a variable reflecting the number of dependants in the household;
T_l is a variable related to the rent paid;
R is household income after earnings disregards; and
R_o is an income floor
(other terms as equations 1 and 2).

(Jacquot, 2000, p 128)

There are two constraints applied to this calculation: that if R is less than R_o, P_p is given a value of zero; in all other cases, P_p has a minimum of 175 francs per month (approximately €12, with benefits etc at 2001 levels). From 2002, R_o was to be fixed so that a person receiving support to reach the minimum wage and a person in a job paying the minimum wage would have the same income net of housing allowances and other (principally family) benefits. The relevant equation was:

$R_o = 0.72 \times$ [RMI ceiling – family benefits – housing component of RMI]

(Jacquot, 2000, p 128)

Of greater significance than the (largely presentational) change, however, is the unification of the values of k for the different allowances. The logic for this was seen in evidence on the way in which allowances were impacting and this is considered in the following section.

The impact of housing allowances

The previous discussion has shown that the main objective of the French housing allowance regime is to enable households to access a decent standard of housing without devoting too large a share of income to it. To what extent has this been achieved?

A contextual issue, first of all, is the fact that housing standards have generally increased over the past 30 years. In 2002, nine out of every 10 main residences had a toilet, bath and central heating, but in 1973 only 44% had met that same standard. In 2002, one in 10 houses was considered overcrowded (at least one room too few for the size/composition of the household); this was half the figure from three decades earlier (Lincot and Rieg, 2003). For those on low incomes (definition as for Figure 7.2), however, a fifth of those with two people or more lived in overcrowded conditions and 7% did not even have housing that met minimal sanitation standards (running water, inside toilet and shower or bath) (Driant and Rieg, 2004). This suggests that there are grounds for doubting whether the restriction of allowance payments to occupiers of housing of at least minimal standard is always rigorously enforced.

Successive governments in France have made no official clarification of what an excessive share of income devoted to housing might be considered to be.[7] But the broad picture is clearly that housing allowances ease affordability constraints. Table 7.3 looks at data from four cross-sectional surveys on housing costs-to-income ratios pre- and post-housing allowances according to tenure. It shows reductions in ratios, deeper for tenants than house purchasers and deeper in the HLM than elsewhere. In net terms for all tenures, housing costs have taken a progressively greater share of incomes over time. The net figure in rental housing in 2002 of 16% of income going on housing might be judged to be quite favourable in comparative terms. Given the evidence on the tenure distribution of low-income households (Figure 7.2), it *might* also be seen as equitable that net cost-to-income ratios are lowest in the HLM.

A second broad conclusion from the evidence is that in rental housing at least, housing allowances are strongly progressive. This is the predictable consequence of income rationing and of subsidy withdrawal as incomes rise. Table 7.4 looks at data for renting households on income (adjusted for household composition), rent payments and gross and net cost-to-income ratios. The most dramatic impact of allowances is seen lower down the income distribution. Allowances do not avoid housing costs being regressive however: net cost-to-income ratios fall as income rises, albeit much less sharply than pre-allowances. Analysis by the Ministère des

Table 7.3: Gross and net housing affordability ratios, France, 1988-2002

	1988		1992		1996		2002	
Tenure	Gross[a]	Net[b]	Gross	Net	Gross	Net	Gross	Net
House buyer	17.6	16.2	18.0	17.0	18.8	17.8	18.2	17.6
Tenant	15.3	12.8	17.1	14.3	19.6	15.9	20.2	16.4
HLM	13.3	9.3	14.8	10.7	17.3	12.1	17.7	12.6
Market rent	16.9	15.3	19.3	17.0	22.0	18.9	22.2	19.2
Controlled rent (1948 Act)	13.8	12.4	14.5	12.5	15.6	13.1	15.2	13.0

Source: Adapted from Lincot and Rieg (2003, tables 16 and 17).

Notes: [a] rent or mortgage payment/gross income (including family benefits); [b] rent or mortgage payment – housing allowance; gross income (including family benefits).

Table 7.4: Rents and allowances for tenant households, France, 2002

Income per equivalent adult (€)	Monthly rent (€)	Gross housing cost-to-income ratio (%)	Net housing cost-to-income ratio (%)	Share of tenant households (%)
Under 6,000	271	43.9	18.3	9.9
6,000–8,000	287	30.8	16.2	11.5
8,000–10,000	301	24.2	15.9	12.2
10,000–12,000	298	20.8	16.8	13.1
12,000–15,000	329	18.7	17.0	16.4
Over 15,000	435	15.0	14.8	37.0
All	349	18.6	14.9	100.0

Source: Ministère des Transports, de l'Équipement, du Tourisme et de la Mer (2005, table 4).

Notes: Tenants of unfurnished housing; excludes students and those housed free; ratios calculated as Table 7.3.

Transports, de l'Équipement, du Tourisme et de la Mer (2005) also qualifies the judgement above on tenure. The mean net ratio of 18.3% amongst the poorest households rises to almost a quarter when they rent from a private landlord.

Driant and Rieg (2005) also point out that certain sorts of low-income household are faced with paying relatively high shares of their income on housing costs. In particular, this applies to single people below retirement age and households comprising one or more pensioners or non-retired people over the age of 65. Lone-parent families and jobless couples have considerably lower ratios (Table 7.5).

These data are drawn from the national housing study of 2002, which, as will be recalled, post-dates the equalisation of housing allowances. A longer historical sweep is shown in Figure 7.7, with APL allowances rather more generous than the ALF or ALS throughout.

Such a situation might be seen as equitable if, in comparison to ALF/ALS recipients, those drawing an APL had lower incomes or were faced with higher housing costs or both of these. In fact, the reverse was the case (Table 7.6). Wider evidence showed that there were no significant differences in quality or house size between the private sector (where tenants were eligible for an ALF/ALS) and the social renting sector (where tenants were eligible for an APL). As noted previously, the government's response was to equalise coefficients; it also made uniform the rent ceilings – at the more generous levels. It was estimated that 4.8 million allowance recipients would be affected by the reform at an initial cost of 6.5 billion francs. One recipient in four would gain over 200 francs per month, one in three between 50 and 200 francs. It was also predicted that the maximum marginal tax rate that a household would face would be 38% for childless couples (in zone 2) (Jacquot, 2000, p 128).

Table 7.5: Low-income households' housing tenure, costs and affordability, France, 2002

Type of household	Tenure (%)					Tenants' mean rent (€ per month)	Net housing cost-to-income ratio (%)
	Tenants excluding social renting	Social renting	Outright owners	Home buyers	Other tenure		
Person(s) aged under 65, non-retired	40	28	13	3	16	260	26
Pensioner(s)/single person aged 65 or over	14	17	57	3	10	270	21
Couples, at least 1 person in work	25	31	17	20	6	338	17
Single-parent family, reference person aged under 50	29	56	5	5	4	334	11
Non-retired couples, neither person in work	27	50	13	Unknown	Unknown	315	10
Other	16	38	29	Unknown	Unknown	313	19
All low-income households	**24**	**32**	**28**	**7**	**9**	**304**	**16**

Source: Driant and Rieg (2004, table 4).

Figure 7.7: Mean monthly housing allowances, France, 1984–2001

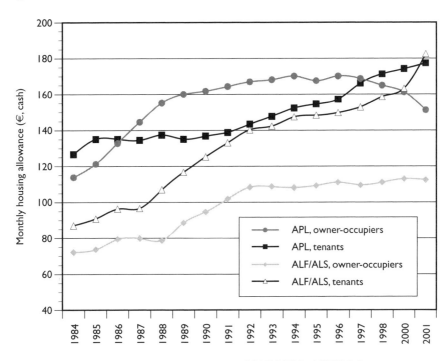

Source: Compte du Logement, www.statistiques.equipement.gouv.fr/IMG/xls/A340_cle578f43-1.xls.
Note: Data unavailable for 1999, trend-line shown.

Table 7.6: Rents, incomes and housing allowances, France, 1999

	Mean monthly rent (francs)	Mean monthly revenue (francs)	Mean monthly housing allowance (francs)	Allowance rent (%)	Number of recipients ('000s)
ALF/ALS	2,074	29,100	1,011	48.7	2,533
APL	1,653	35,924	1,137	68.8	2,044
All tenants	1,886	32,148	1,067	56.6	4,578

Source: Adapted from Jacquot (2000, table 1).

Notes: Revenue, including family benefits, after allowing for earnings.

Adverse impacts of the housing allowance regime

Concern over the high marginal tax rates that can accompany means-tested benefits has been a feature of debate around housing allowances in many countries. A key issue is whether they effectively undermine policies to reduce unemployment by acting as a disincentive to take up work, particularly low-paid work. Analysis by Afsa (2001) suggests that the French allowance system is not prone to this problem; other things being equal, housing allowance recipients in

1997/8 receiving support through the minimum wage guarantee were more likely to take up (more) work than those who were not receiving a housing allowance. The analysis suggested the result was due to the fact that the allowance does not cover a tenant's full rent and as the benefit calculation has a delayed reaction to changes in income; means assessments are undertaken annually or on change of tenancy. It is pointed out that the results are not wholly conclusive: in order to be so, longitudinal data on housing and employment careers would be needed.

A further concern in some countries has been with upmarketing: that is, the possibility of an over-consumption of housing enabled by housing allowances (Hills, 1991). There is little reference to this issue in France. Indeed, in principle, it can be seen that the combined effect of L_o and L_p in equation 1 (the pre-2001 system) and of P_p and rent ceilings in equation 2 (post-2001) should be to remove the scope for upmarketing.

There is, however, scope for (literally) rent-seeking behaviour amongst private landlords: renting to a low-income household encourages rent to be raised to the appropriate ceiling. Whilst 100% of the household's *rent payment* is not covered, *increases in rent up to the ceiling* are fully covered.

There has been general concern in France about the extent to which housing allowances fuel inflation by being capitalised into house prices or rents. Lafarrère and le Blanc (2002) look at cross-sectional market sector rent data, including the benefit status of tenants, from 1984 to 1993 and at panel data from 1993 to 1997. Taking account of housing quality, location and other attributes, their analysis shows that allowances are partially capitalised into rent increases, although it does not estimate the scale. Fack (2005) looks at a longer time span of both panel and cross-sectional data. Her analysis shows that benefit receipt has had a significant role in rent inflation amongst low-income households, with between 50% and 80% of the ALF/ALS received absorbed by rent increases. To a small extent, damage is mitigated by considering that the quality of housing consumed improved to a greater than expected degree. Nevertheless, supply inelasticity largely explains an overall adverse effect. Data from the Ministère des Transports, de l'Équipement, du Tourisme et de la Mer (2005) confirm that in the 1991–2005 period, rent increases in both the market and the HLM sectors have tended to be rather greater than either price increases in general or increases in construction costs.

Conclusion

This chapter has reviewed the development, principal features and key impacts of the French system of means-tested housing allowances. The chapter placed these in their housing system, social welfare and macro-economic contexts. For the majority of the post-war period, France has had a dual housing allowance system, linked to its housing capital subsidy systems. Whilst housing allowances do not take up a big share of welfare budgets, they are clearly important to meeting an equity objective for housing policy. Though evidence is limited, the French system seems less prone to adverse labour market consequences than that of other countries. There is, however, concern about the inflationary impact of housing allowances. The country does not seem currently to have any appetite for further housing allowance reform, although questions may arise in the medium term as to whether rent inflation can be tackled without penalising some groups of low-income households that are relatively disadvantaged at present.

Notes

[1] In 2003, France's economy grew only marginally (0.8% increase in GDP) with 2004 being significantly better (2.3%) (Friez and Mordant, 2005). There are no current data on resultant household income changes.

[2] Guillemin and le Roux (2002) analyse the close relationship between a household's disposable income and living standard in a similar period, see also Herpin and Verger (1999).

[3] Note that this does *not* equate to 'social security' as generally understood elsewhere.

[4] The OECD's definition is as follows: public social expenditure comprises cash benefits, direct 'in-kind' provision of goods and services, and tax breaks with social purposes. To be considered 'social', benefits have to address one or more social goals. Benefits may be targeted at low-income households, but they may also be for older, disabled, sick, unemployed or young persons. Programmes regulating the provision of social benefits have to involve: a) redistribution of resources across households, or b) compulsory participation. Social benefits are regarded as public when general government (that is central, state and local governments, including social security funds) controls relevant financial flows.

[5] There should, in principle, be a check on the condition of the house to ensure that it meets statutory minima.

[6] Gobillon and le Blanc (2005) noted that this was of questionable technical efficiency.

[7] There is no visible sign of the debate seen in other countries as to whether cost-to-income ratios or residual incomes are better measures of affordability (Hancock, 1993).

References

Abramovici, G. (1999) 'Social Security', translated chapter from INSEE, *Données sociales*, Paris: INSEE, available at www.insee.fr/en/ffc/docs_ffc/ds9959.html.

Abramovici, G. (2005) 'Social protection in the European Union', *Eurostat Statistics in Focus*, no 14, available at http://europa.eu.int/comm/eurostat/.

Afsa, C. (2001) 'Aide au logement et emploi', *Economie et Statistique*, no 346–7, pp 123–36.

Barbier, J.-C. and Théret, B. (2000) 'The French social protection system: Path dependencies and societal coherence', paper presented to the International Social Security Association Research Conference, Social Security in the Global Village, Helsinki, September, available at www.issa.int/pdf/helsinki2000/topic1/2barbier.pdf.

CAF (Caisse d'Allocations Familiales) (2005) 'Allocations familiales', available at www.caf.fr/catalogue/.

Chambaz, C., Guillaumat-Taillet, F. and Houriez, J.-M. (1999) 'Household income and assets', translated chapter from INSEE, *Données sociales*, Paris: INSEE, available at www.insee.fr/en/ffc/docs_ffc/ds9945.html.

Driant, J.-C. and Jacquot, A. (2005) 'Loyers imputes et inégalités de niveau de vie', *Economie et Statistique*, no 381–2, pp 177–206.

Driant, J.-C. and Rieg, C. (2004) 'Les conditions de logement des ménages à bas revenus', *INSEE Première*, no 950.

Fack, G. (2005) 'Pourquoi les ménages à bas revenus paient-ils des loyers de plus en plus élevés? L'incidence des aides au logement en France (1973–2002)', *Economie et Statistique*, no 381–2, pp 17–40.

Friez, A. and Mordant, G. (2005) 'Les comptes de la nation en 2004: Une reprise tirée par la demande', *INSEE Première*, no 1017.

Gobillon, L. and le Blanc, D. (2005) 'Quelques effets economiques du prêt à taux zéro', *Economie et Statistique*, no 381–2, pp 63–89.

Guillemin, O. and le Roux, V. (2002) *The standard of living of French households from 1970 to 1999*, Paris: INSEE, available at www.insee.fr/en/ffc/docs_ffc/DS065en.pdf.

Hancock, K. (1993) 'Can't pay, won't pay or economic principles of affordability', *Urban Studies*, vol 30, no 1, pp 127–45.

Herpin, N. and Verger, D. (1999) 'Ways of life and consumption in France from 1980 to 1996', translated chapter from INSEE, *Données sociales*, Paris: INSEE, available at www.insee.fr/en/ffc/docs_ffc/ds9948.html.

Hills, J. (1991) *Unravelling housing finance*, Oxford: Clarendon.

INSEE (Institut National de la Statistique et des Etudes Economiques) (2005) *Tableaux de l'economie Française, 2005–2006*, Paris: INSEE, available at www.insee.fr/fr/ffc/accueil_ffc.asp?theme=8&souspop=.

Jacquot, A. (2000) 'La réforme des aides au logement dans le secteur locatif', *Recherches et Prévisions*, no 62, pp 125–9.

Kemp, P.A. (1990) 'Income-related assistance with housing costs: A cross-national comparison', *Urban Studies*, vol 27, pp 795–808.

Lafarrère, A. and le Blanc, D. (2002) 'Comment les aides au logement affectent-elles les loyers?', *Economie et Statistique*, no 351, pp 3–30.

Lincot, L. and Rieg, C. (2003) 'Les conditions de logement des ménages en 2002, enquête logement 2002', *INSEE Résultats Société*, no 20.

Louvot, C. (1998) 'Les dépenses de logement de 1984 à 1996', *INSEE Première*, no 688.

Ministère des Transports, de l'Équipement, du Tourisme et de la Mer (2005) 'Depuis 2002, la hausse des loyers reste soutenue', press release, available at www.statistiques.equipement.gouv.fr/IMG/pdf/Loyers2004_cle7be2b4.pdf.

OECD (Organisation for Economic Co-operation and Development) (2004) *Chapitre pays prestations et salaires, France 2002*, Paris: OECD, available at www.oecd.org/dataoecd/2/59/34004444.pdf.

OECD (2005) *OECD factbook, 2005*, Paris: OECD, available at http://stats.oecd.org/wbos/viewhtml.aspx?QueryName=2&QueryType=View&Lang=en.

Satsangi, M. (1998) 'Private rented housing in France', *Netherlands Journal of Housing and the Built Environment*, vol 13, no 3, pp 301–26.

Spicker, P. (1997) 'Exclusion and citizenship in France', in M. Mullard and S. Lee (eds) *The politics of social policy in Europe*, Cheltenham: Elgar.

Zoyem, J.-P. (1999) 'The social minima: Eight assistance benefits in the French system of social protection', translated chapter from INSEE, *Données sociales*, Paris: INSEE, available at www.insee.fr/en/ffc/docs_ffc/ds9959.html.

EIGHT

Housing allowances in Germany

Stefan Kofner

Introduction

The social policy dimension of housing is characterised by society's (shifting) idea of the acceptable minimum level of adequate housing in terms of quality and quantity. Housing policy aims to enable everyone to realise these basic housing standards independent of their personal income and other prevailing circumstances (for example the local rent level, number of children). Housing allowances – *Wohngeld* in German – come into play whenever income is insufficient to enable the household to obtain accommodation that meets a minimum housing standard. As a tied income transfer, it is an incentive towards a higher individual housing consumption.

Wohngeld is not, of course, the only policy instrument for encouraging households to obtain housing that meets a minimum standard. Social housing can have the same effect by setting social rents below market rents and reserving the dwellings for the most needy groups. Even general rent ceilings may have a comparable effect, though they have harmful consequences for other housing policy goals.

While most housing economists and policy makers are opposed to general rent ceilings – if not in every case, then at least in an equilibrium market situation – housing allowances have not attracted as much criticism over the decades. Quite different from the often mismanaged and costly social housing programmes, housing allowances are widely seen in Germany as a relatively market-conforming instrument of social policy (eg Albers, 1982, p 204; Stern, 2001, p 81) with the ability to act as a substitute for an important part of the social housing programmes.

Housing allowances in context

In Germany, both tenants and homeowners are eligible to claim Wohngeld if they fulfil the qualifications. The role of Wohngeld in German housing policy has been very important. In 2004, 3.5 out of 39.1 million households received €5.2 billion of Wohngeld transfers (see Figure 8.1). This expenditure on Wohngeld corresponds to 0.24% of the German GDP and to around 27% of total housing subsidies excluding tax relief. In total, 9.0% of all households received a housing allowance in 2004. However, due to radical change in target group definition,

Figure 8.1: Expenditure on Wohngeld, West Germany

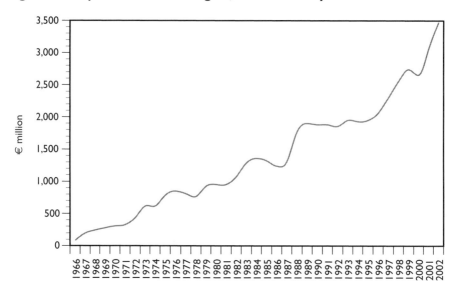

Source: Wohngeld- und Mietenbericht (2002, p 27).

the cost and caseload of Wohngeld fell dramatically in 2005 (see Figure 8.1). By the end of that year, the number of recipients was only 780,660 (a drop of 78% in one year) or 2% of all households. Meanwhile, expenditure had fallen to €1.2 billion (−76%).

The amount of Wohngeld to which households are entitled is a complex function of household size, individual and market rent and individual income. To that extent, it is an efficient programme (Eekhoff, 1987, p 407; GEWOS, 1990, p 355) that some see as a general model for an efficient approach to social policy. The mission of Wohngeld as an income transfer is to ensure that recipients can attain a certain standard of adequate housing conditions relatively independently of their financial situation in terms of household size, pre-benefit rent burden and disposable income. The implicit assumption is that, with Wohngeld, people can afford better housing than is possible without the transfer. Needless to say, however, recipients do not spend the whole transfer on additional housing consumption. An important part of the housing allowance is used to reduce households' absolute rental burden, that is, it is spent on purposes other than housing – which might be an aim in itself (distributional justification).[1]

People can claim Wohngeld irrespective of whether their dwelling is owned or rented and whether they live in private or social housing. But because social housing has rent ceilings, this tends to lower the amount of Wohngeld that needs to be paid to recipients living in this tenure.

Wohngeld was an important part of the German social security system and of German housing policy. However, since 1 January 2005 the target group for Wohngeld has been defined much more narrowly than it was before. People living on welfare – including the new *Arbeitslosengeld II* (stage two unemployment benefit) – no longer receive Wohngeld. Instead, their housing allowance is integrated with their unemployment assistance (that is, it is paid as a part of Arbeitslosengeld II [ALG II]) according to their basic housing needs. These changes were introduced to put more pressure on unemployed people to accept a job. Wohngeld is now more or less limited to the working poor and the short-term jobless. Even among these target groups, Wohngeld is losing ground since they have the option to claim ALG II instead. In 2005, 3.7 million households (9.4%) received ALG II housing benefit. Expenditure was €12.1 billion or 0.54% of GDP and the average payment was €275, compared with €132 for Wohngeld.

A short history of Wohngeld

The liberal period: no role for housing allowances

The historical development of housing allowances in Germany mirrors the change in German housing policy from the liberal laissez-faire approach of the 19th century to the social welfare state of today. Despite the housing shortages and poor housing conditions in most of the industrialising German cities at the beginning of the 20th century, the tenancy laws of the time included no element of tenant protection and no price ceilings. Freedom of contract was universal and the clauses in the German civil code were not regarded as obligatory by contemporary jurists.

Contemporary critics such as the members of the *Bodenformbewegung* (land reform movement) had a rather radical approach to the severe housing problems of their time. One of their most important demands was taxation of the landlords' capital gains. The capital gains tax was meant to limit the ever-rising land prices (and rents) in the growing industrial cities by dampening down land speculation. Surprisingly enough, their demand was fulfilled by many local governments: rapidly growing cities like Cologne, Frankfurt am Main and Gelsenkirchen introduced some kind of capital gains taxation at the beginning of the 20th century (Pergande, 1973, pp 41–2).

The pauperised period: housing allowances as help in times of need

The tenancy laws (the civil code) were not touched in an interventionist way before the final phase of the First World War. What happened after the war as a reaction to the country's growing housing shortage was a rapid descent into a state-controlled housing sector (*Wohnungszwangswirtschaft*) with typical elements such as rent controls, protection against 'unfair' dismissal, and rationing of the housing stock by establishing an agency monopoly of the local housing offices (*Wohnungsämter*). With modifications, this state-controlled regime lasted until the late 1960s in Western Germany. East Germans also had a state-controlled housing regime until German reunification in 1990.

Against this background of permanent housing shortage and rent controls, it is not surprising that little need was felt for an income transfer to provide tenants with more purchasing power. In the controlled housing sector[2] it might even have been counterproductive to introduce housing allowances on a broad scale. In an environment with administered rents, housing allowances do have a redistributive effect but they do not have much influence on rent levels (as these are fixed) or on housing supply (no incentive to invest) and consumption. Hence the role of housing allowances was rather limited in Germany until the 1950s. They were focused on low-income households who were not able to pay rising social rents. Housing allowances were widely regarded as a part of social welfare.

However, some first steps of emancipation towards an independent transfer system were being made as early as the 1920s. Housing allowances appeared for the very first time in Germany in the aftermath of the hyperinflation of the year 1923. The resurrection of the *Friedensmiete* (peace rent) from 1 July 1914 in a pauperised environment implicated sensible losses in disposable income for the groups most hit by the distributive effects of the hyperinflation. Pensioners and jobless people unable to pay their rent could rely on general social welfare. In four states (Baden, Hessen, Mecklenburg-Schwerin and Mecklenburg-Strelitz) the social welfare system already included special housing benefits. But the bulk of the states, including the largest ones (such as Prussia, Bavaria and Saxony) tried to help the poor and needy tenants by introducing pass-through tax exemptions from the so-called *Hauszinssteuer* (interest rate tax) – a tax introduced in order to skim the landlords' gains from the devaluation of their mortgage credits in the inflationary period. This was a costly and unjust solution since the Hauszinssteuer depended on the debt ratio and was only levied from buildings constructed before July 1918.

The dictatorial period: conservation of an unsatisfactory status quo

Apart from the pass-through tax exemptions of Hauszinssteuer, some communities paid housing benefits as the need arose (Führer, 1995, pp 172–4). For example, in the budget of the town of Munich 50,000 Reichsmark were allocated for *Mietbeihilfen* (housing benefit) in the fiscal year 1936/7 (Haerendel, 1999, p 362). In Munich, the municipality sometimes also took over rent arrears (486 cases in fiscal year 1936/7) (see Haerendel, 1999, pp 364–6).

Since the Nazi government wanted to abandon the Hauszinssteuer by demanding a single capitalised payment from landlords, they needed a substitute for the pass-through tax exemptions. In 1938 communities were forced by a legal ordinance to pay Mietbeihilfen exactly compensating the tenants' losses from the abandonment of the tax exemption. Tenants who became in need later could not claim this transfer. The beneficiaries were mostly jobless people and pensioners; their number fell from 943,081 in 1938 to 447,900 in 1941 (Führer, 1995, pp 233–5).[3]

The cutback period: housing allowances as a compensation for rising rents

When housing allowances appeared in the federal law gazette for the first time they were denominated as *Beihilfen* under the 1955 Erstes Bundesmietengesetz (first federal rental law).[4] This law stipulated substantial augmentations of the administered rents (up to 25%, depending on the dwelling's facilities).The financial aid was reserved for low-income households and limited to three years. The housing benefits of Erstes Bundesmietengesetz were meant as a compensation for the augmentation of the administered rent level (GEWOS, 1990, p 99), but because of the low income ceiling and perceived stigma on the part of the eligible tenants, this scheme had little practical impact (Führer, 1995, p 274).

In the 1950s, housing allowances also began to play a minor role in the 'social segment' of the housing market (*Sozialer Wohnungsbau*). This was an important part of the West German housing market of that time and these state-subsidised dwellings dominated housing construction in the 1950s (Kofner, 2003, p 251).[5] The need for housing allowances in the social housing sector arose from the fact that the price regime in social housing was changed from the *Richtsatzmiete* introduced in 1950[6] (more or less an administered rent, but with some degree of quality differentiation) to the *Kostenmiete* (cost recovery rent) in 1956.[7] With the new cost recovery rent, the running capital and management costs determined the rent level including the possibility of increase, for example, if interest rates rose. The government hence lost an important part of its influence on social rents, as the former Richtsatzmiete had left the state governments in control.

The *Miet- oder Lastenbeihilfen* (allowances for rent payments or homeowners' charges) were introduced in order to cut off the effects of rising social housing rents on the rental burden above a certain percentage rate (between 10% and 18%, depending on annual household income). It is important to note that, for the first time in German history, homeowners could claim for housing allowances too, even though the Lastenbeihilfen were only initially accessible for owners of social homes.[8] This was a consequence of the priority given to homeownership even in the social housing sector stipulated in the 1956 Zweites Wohnungsbaugesetz (GEWOS, 1990, p 99).

The immediate practical relevance of the Miet- oder Lastenbeihilfen stipulated in Zweites Wohnungsbaugesetz should not be overestimated. They were only introduced in three states: Lower Saxony, North Rhine-Westphalia and Hamburg (Führer, 1995, pp 287–9), but the further development of social housing in Germany was characterised by the coexistence of housing allowances and direct subsidies with an ever-increasing importance of the personal subsidy.

Housing allowances made their way back on the policy agenda at the end of the 1950s when the government's plans for reducing the red tape in the administered sector became more and more tangible. The 1960 Abbaugesetz law aimed at gradually cutting back the elements of the controlled housing sector.The role of housing allowances in this project was to ensure a bearable rental burden even for low-income households before and – more importantly – after the release of the dwellings into the free housing market. For a family with two children, rental burdens of between 14% and 18% of annual income were perceived to be socially acceptable. It should be stressed that the scope of the housing allowances was still limited in terms of duration and target group. Only tenants in the admittedly large administered and social sectors could demand Miet- oder Lastenbeihilfen.

The policy approach of the time was to get rid of the special laws forming the controlled housing sector (that is, the dismissal protection of Mieterschutzgesetz, the rent controls of Bundesmietengesetze and the agency monopoly of Wohnraumbewirtschaftungsgesetz), but the vision of the future policy model of the housing market had changed since the end of the 19th century. The new vision of the 'liberalised' housing market included some basic tenant protection measures in the civil code (for example, the so-called *Sozialklausel* under which tenants could contest a dismissal in cases of hardship) and housing allowances to cope with the expected rent increases after the release of the dwellings into the free housing market. The allowances introduced with the Abbaugesetz were not necessarily permanent (GEWOS, 1990, p 101); initially, they were aimed at easing the transition phase of the housing sector. A certain degree of tenant protection and housing allowances were widely seen as preconditions for the political enforceability of the necessary liberalisation of the housing sector (Führer, 1995, p 301).

The legislation on housing allowances became quite complex after 1960 (for details see Pergande, 1973, p 185; GEWOS, 1990, pp 146–8). Different laws were applicable in 'white counties' (with liberalised housing markets) and 'black counties' (with still controlled housing markets). In the white counties, all tenants were eligible for Wohngeld, both in the social and in the liberalised market segment. The rules were consolidated in the 1965 Erstes Wohngeldgesetz law (Wagner, 1995, p 100).

Everyone – all kinds of tenants and homeowners – was now eligible for housing allowances if they fulfilled the criteria stipulated in the new law. The ones meeting the criteria had a legal (that is, enforceable) claim on Wohngeld. This benefit has to be applied for at the local Wohngeld agency (Wohngeldgesetz, §3). The agency (which is a part of local government, in most cases under the authority of the social welfare office) notifies the claimant after having checked the fulfilment of the criteria. Wohngeld is normally paid for a year, after which the application has to be renewed.[9]

The aims of Wohngeld were still modest: 'to ensure economically a basic provisioning with housing space in order to avoid social hardship'. The acceptable rental burden was still dependent on the annual household income. The rental burden after transfer to be achieved was now fixed between 12% and 22% of annual income. The allowable rent was limited in terms of square metres and price per square metre.[10]

The modern period: housing allowances in the social welfare state

Zweites Wohngeldgesetz of 1970 was more ambitious in terms of economic and social feasibility: 'to ensure economically adequate and family-oriented housing'. Clearly enough, from now on more than a basic provisioning of the poor and needy was envisaged by housing policy makers. Another target of the reform of 1970 was to ease the administration of the scheme (Wörz, 1999, p 47; GEWOS, 1990, p 348); the new law introduced *Wohngeldtabellen* (tables) showing directly the amount of the transfer. Three factors played a role in determining how much Wohngeld a household could claim:

- the number of family members in the household;[11]
- the total annual family income; and
- the amount of rent or mortgage payment that qualifies for support.

The tables have been designed so that the higher the family income, the lower the Wohngeld transfer will be; the higher the rent, the higher Wohngeld will be; and the larger the household, the higher the transfer will be (and vice versa).[12]

The administration and the beneficiaries have to cope with a large set of Wohngeld tables; there is a set of tables for each household size, but the same tables are applicable for tenants and owners. Table 8.1 shows an example for a household of four people. The income classes (monthly income) are shown in the first column. The table header contains the rental classes. For example, a couple with two children having a monthly income of €1,000 and a monthly rent of €400[13] receives a housing allowance of €174 per month. Their net rental payment amounts thus to €226.

It is important to note that Wohngeld is not a dynamic, automatically uprated benefit. The tables are an annex of the Wohngeldgesetz. This means that parliamentary action is needed to change the law whenever a change in the benefit levels seems necessary. A thorough analysis of the numbers in Table 8.1 shows that the transfer is not resistant to inflation and rising rents. If all prices, annual income and the rent in our example above, rise at the same pace (say 10%) our exemple household will earn €1,100, spend €440 on rent and receive €171 in Wohngeld. The net rental payment would amount to €269, leaving them with €831 to spend for other consumption purposes, but they would need €851.40 in order to keep the purchasing power of their income. Thus there is only partial compensation for inflation. The same goes for rent increases; if only the rent rises by 10% our model household will receive €198 of Wohngeld and the net payment goes up from €226 to €242. As an incentive to rent at a reasonable price, this might be acceptable. On the other hand, the tables need to be adjusted if there are overall rent increases large enough to put pressure on the federal parliament (Nolte and Voß, 1997, p 19 et seq).

Table 8.1: Excerpt from Wohngeld table for a household of four, Germany, 1 January 2007

Monthly total family income (€)	With an allowable rent of €								
	380– 390	390– 400	400– 410	410– 420	420– 430	430– 440	440– 450	450– 460	460– 470
900–910	186	192	199	205	212	218	225	231	237
910–920	184	190	196	203	209	216	222	228	235
920–930	181	187	194	200	207	213	219	226	232
930–940	179	185	191	198	204	210	217	223	229
940–950	176	183	189	195	201	208	214	220	226
950–960	174	180	186	193	199	205	211	217	224
960–970	171	178	184	190	196	202	209	215	221
970–980	169	175	181	187	194	200	206	212	218
980–990	167	173	179	185	191	197	203	209	215
990–1,000	164	170	176	182	188	194	201	207	213
1,000–1,010	162	168	174	180	186	192	198	204	210
1,010–1,020	159	165	171	177	183	189	195	201	207
1,020–1,030	157	163	169	175	181	187	192	198	204
1,030–1,040	154	160	166	172	178	184	190	196	202
1,040–1,050	152	158	164	169	175	181	187	193	199
1,050–1,060	149	155	161	167	173	178	184	190	196
1,060–1,070	147	153	158	164	170	176	182	187	193
1,070–1,080	144	150	156	162	167	173	179	185	190
1,080–1,090	142	148	153	159	165	170	176	182	188
1,090–1,100	139	145	151	156	162	168	173	179	185
1,100–1,110	137	142	148	154	159	165	171	176	182
1,110–1,120	134	140	146	151	157	162	168	174	179
1,120–1,130	132	137	143	149	154	160	165	171	176
1,130–1,140	129	135	140	146	151	157	162	168	173
1,140–1,150	127	132	138	143	149	154	160	165	171

The basic structure of the table system has not changed up to the present time. Nonetheless, the legislative machine churned out a stream of amendment laws over the years (for details see Wörz, 1999, pp 82–5), with different objectives:

- adaptions of the benefit to increased rents and incomes;
- adaptions of the benefit to budget constraints;
- changes in the system of allowable deductions (for example for single parents) for the calculation of the annual household income;
- improvements of the benefits for large families; and
- differentiated calculation of rent ceilings according to the different rental levels in the communities.

In 1991, the Wohngeld scheme was subdivided. First, the established benefit was labelled *Tabellenwohngeld* (table housing allowances) and was later renamed *Allgemeines Wohngeld* (general housing allowance). Second, a specialised transfer system called *Pauschalwohngeld* (lump-sum housing allowances) – later renamed

Besonderes Wohngeld (special housing allowance) – was installed for recipients of social asssistance benefits such as *Sozialhilfe* (social welfare) and *Kriegsopferfürsorge* (welfare for war victims). This subdivision aimed at easing the calculation of housing allowances for these groups. The amount of the lump sum was dependent on the dwelling's domicile state and on the county's rent level (between 41.3% and 53% of the recognised housing costs) (see Klueß, 2000, p 255). However, social assistance recipients could opt for table housing allowances instead; lump-sum housing allowances were not given to owners. From 1 January 2005 this subdivision ceased to exist; housing assistance for benefit recipients is now integrated into the respective transfer system (discussed below).

Calculating Wohngeld: a task for specialists

Income definition

For the purpose of calculating entitlement to Wohngeld, annual family income includes all taxable revenues of all household members (including, for example, salaries, interest on savings and rental income) and some non-taxable revenues (such as premiums for night shifts). Eligible expenses are deductible, but not between different types of revenue, that is, it is not possible to lower the total family income by deducting losses made in one revenue type (such as 'income from rent and lease') from profits belonging to another type of revenue (say, from self-employed work). Expenses for tax and social security are covered by lump-sum deductions from income. Further lump-sum exemptions can be made by disabled persons and other groups, such as people paying alimony. Child allowances – *Kindergeld* – do not count as income for the purpose of calculating entitlement to Wohngeld (but in Arbeitslosengeld II they do).

Only claimants with an annual assessable family income below certain income ceilings will receive Wohngeld. The ceilings differ with the age of the dwelling and the 'rental stages'[14] reflecting the different rent levels in different communities. The younger the dwelling and the higher the local rent level (as mirrored in the rent stages), the higher the income ceiling. Table 8.2 shows the income ceilings

Table 8.2: Income ceilings for dwellings constructed after 1991 in a community with rental stage VI, Germany, 2007

Number of family members in the household	Income ceilings (€)	Gross income before lump sum deduction of 30% (€)
1	830	1,185
2	1,140	1,628
3	1,390	1,985
4	1,830	2,614
5	2,100	2,999
6	2,370	3,385
7	2,630	3,757
8	2,900	4,142

for dwellings constructed after 1991 in a community where rental stage VI is applicable.

The need level defined by Arbeitslosengeld II also differs with the local rent level. In general, it is more or less in line with the income ceilings of Wohngeld.[15] Hence the incentive to switch from Wohngeld to Arbeitslosengeld II cannot be attributed to different income ceilings alone. On the other hand, the bulk of Wohngeld recipients have the option to switch to Arbeitslosengeld II.

Rent definition

The definition of rent used to calculate entitlement to Wohngeld is based on the tenant's contractual rent. It also includes so-called 'cold' extra costs (but not costs for heating and warm water). For the calculation of the 'allowable rent' (the rent concept used in the Wohngeld tables) this rent is compared with rent ceilings, which vary according to the number of household members, local rental stage and the age of the dwellings (see Table 8.4).

The applicable rental stages (*Mietenstufen*) are enumerated community by community in another list. Table 8.3 shows a few examples. If the contractual rent (including 'cold' extra costs) is higher than the relevant rent ceiling, the amount of the rent ceiling is used to calculate entitlement in the Wohngeld table. Since the rent ceilings are far below typical rent levels, there is a strong incentive for recipients of Wohngeld to rent cheap dwellings. For example, in Munich the applicable rent ceiling for a dwelling for three built after 1991 is €540 whereas a market rent for a three-room flat with 70 square metres would be around €800 in this city. Arbeitslosengeld II, on the other hand, would almost cover even this rent level (the relevant rent ceiling for Munich being €760.80). It is no wonder, therefore, that low-income households have started to switch to Arbeitslosengeld II for help with their housing costs. An example of how Wohngeld is calculated for tenants in shown in the appendix to this chapter.

Table 8.3: Examples of rental stages[a]

Town	Rental stage
Warburg	I
Bamberg	II
Karlsruhe	III
Lübeck	IV
Cologne	V
Frankfurt am Main, Munich	VI

[a]In force since January 2002

Allowances for homeowners

Except for the rent, the amount of benefit for homeowners is determined by the same factors as are used in calculating Wohngeld entitlement for tenants (number

Table 8.4: The rent ceilings used in Wohngeld, Germany, 2007 (€)

Number of household members	Rental stage of community	For dwellings ready for occupancy			
		Up to 31 December 1965		From 1 January 1966 to 31 December 1991	From 1 January 1992
		Other dwellings	Dwellings with central heating and bath		
I	I	160	200	215	265
	II	170	210	230	280
	III	180	225	245	300
	IV	195	245	265	325
	V	210	260	285	350
	VI	225	280	305	370
2	I	215	265	290	320
	II	225	285	310	345
	III	240	300	330	365
	IV	260	325	355	395
	V	280	350	380	425
	VI	300	375	405	456
3	I	255	320	345	385
	II	270	340	365	410
	III	290	360	390	435
	IV	310	390	420	470
	V	335	420	455	505
	VI	360	445	485	540
4	I	295	370	400	445
	II	315	395	425	475
	III	335	420	455	505
	IV	360	455	490	545
	V	390	485	525	590
	VI	415	520	565	630
5	I	335	420	455	510
	II	360	450	485	545
	III	380	480	520	580
	IV	415	515	560	625
	V	445	555	600	670
	VI	475	595	640	715
Additional household member	I	40	50	55	60
	II	45	55	60	65
	III	45	60	65	70
	IV	50	65	70	75
	V	55	70	75	80
	VI	60	75	80	90

of household members, total annual family income, amount of mortgage payments and management costs), thus the same Wohngeld tables are used as for the tenants. The rules for the definition of the household members and the calculation of the relevant family income are also the same. Even income ceilings, rent ceilings and rental stages are used for tenants and homeowners alike.

Eligible mortgage expenditure includes all kinds of actual payments associated with the mortgage, including interest, principal, bank fees, fees for loan guarantees and ground rent payments where applicable. Eligible management costs include maintenance, extra costs and administrative outgoings (for example in a condominium). For reasons of administrative simplicity, maintenance and extra costs are taken into account with a lump sum of €20 per square metre. General subsidies for homeowners like *Eigenheimzulage* and *Baukindergeld* are deducted when calculating allowable expenditure. The total charge (*Belastung*) will be calculated in the so-called *Wohngeld-Lastenberechnung*.[16] The appendix shows an example of how housing allowances are calculated for homeowners.

Housing assistance for social security benefit recipients

Arbeitslosengeld II (unemployment benefit II)

In Germany, there were on average 4.5 million jobless people during 2006. In total, 10.8% of the workforce was unemployed in that year. It is becoming more and more costly to meet the housing needs of the unemployed people since they get a higher per capita subsidy than the (usually employed) recipients of Wohngeld.

On 1 January 2005, the old subdivision of housing allowances into lump–sum allowances for social security recipients and table allowances for other recipients ceased to exist. Housing benefits for social security recipients are now integrated into the respective benefit scheme (Arbeitslosengeld II, ALG II), which also serves needy low–income households. What we have now is a large intersection between the target groups of Wohngeld and ALG II.

These changes were part of the controversial 'Hartz reforms' of the German labour market. With the fourth package of reform laws ('Hartz IV') all employable people were moved away from social welfare. They now have the same status as the former recipients of *Arbeitslosenhilfe* (the former second stage of unemployment benefits). Instead of a combination of social welfare and Wohngeld, all employable people can now claim ALG II, which includes housing assistance as an integrated subsidy. As a result, Germany now has a two–step transfer system (Arbeitslosengeld and Arbeitslosengeld II) for the unemployed instead of the former three–step system (Arbeitslosengeld, Arbeitslosenhilfe, Sozialhilfe).

Unemployed people who have been working for at least 12 months in a job and have made social insurance contributions in the three years before they lost their job, can claim Arbeitslosengeld at the federal labour agency. This benefit is earnings related: benefit recipients are paid around 60% of their last net income (67% for jobless people with children) usually for 12 months.[17] On top of that, lower-income households receiving Arbeitslosengeld can also claim Wohngeld or ALG II.

The new ALG II normally follows on from Arbeitslosengeld. In November 2006, 5.3 million people were receiving ALG II – more than anybody had expected[18] – whereas the number of people living on Sozialhilfe was only 175,000 (comprised of more or less the non-employable people with insufficient income). The amount of ALG II paid to claimants is not comparable with the earnings-related Arbeitslosengeld, it aims to cover the basic physical and sociocultural needs of a human being ('need determination') and is flat rate in that the amount of benefit paid is the same if the needs are the same. ALG II includes the following benefits:

• *Unterkunftskosten* (housing benefit);
• *Regelleistung* (standard benefit) for all costs of living except housing; and
• other benefits (eg for pregnant women and lone parents, one-off benefits and loans, social insurance contributions, reintegration payments and payments for public interest work).

Standard benefit

The estimated needs of the people are shown as monthly lump sums in Table 8.5 and an example illustrating how they are calculated is shown in the appendix to this chapter. The need of the ALG II claimants is determined by the empirically measured consumption behaviour of single person households with a low income (lowest fifth) who do not receive social transfers. The measured expenditures are subject to normative percentage deductions, for example, 50% for tobacco, 100% for alcohol, 20% for shoes, 58% for leisure, entertainment and culture, and 70% for services. All in all, 35% of the expenditures of the reference group (€526) is ignored. Apart from that, the composition of the reference group is not methodologically convincing (they are chiefly old widows). Another problem of this approach to need determination is that it ignores interregional differences in the costs of living. The net result is that most of the ALG II recipients without additional income live close to the poverty line or even below it.

Table 8.5: Arbeitslosengeld II: lump sums for standard benefit, Germany, 1 January 2007

	€
Head of the household	345
Two persons over 18	311
Another person over 18	276
Person over 14	276
Person under 14	207

Housing benefit

The basic rent for a flat including 'cold' extra costs will be covered by housing benefit as well as heating costs, provided that the size and the rent for the flat are 'adequate' (subject to ceilings, see below). The costs for electricity and hot water are not included, however.

Because of the patchy administrative structure of Arbeitslosengeld II – local Arbeitsgemeinschaften (ARGE) in most communities (joint ventures of local employment agencies and local authorities) and in some communities or counties, the autonomous administration[19] – and the lack of federal regulation in this field, there are no uniform rules for dwelling size and rent ceilings. The ceilings differ in fact from town to town and from county to county, reflecting the different housing market situations. Since the communities have to pay the larger part of the housing benefits themselves (68.2%) they have an incentive not to be too generous. For the size ceilings, non-binding numbers were handed out by the Bundesministerium für Wirtschaft und Arbeit (Federal Ministry for Economics and Labour) that is responsible for the scheme:

* less than 45 to 50 square metres for one person;
* less than 60 square metres or two rooms for two persons;
* less than 75 square metres or three rooms for three persons;
* less than 85 to 90 square metres or four rooms for four persons;
* an additional 10 square metres or one additional room for each additional person up to a maximum of 120 square metres.

In practice, local authorities decide what counts as 'adequate housing' under the conditions of the local housing market. Table 8.6 gives an overview of the applicable rent ceilings for a household of three (including cold extra costs) for a variety of East and West German towns. The far-right column shows the market rent level according to the RDM-Preisspiegel[20] (cold extra costs are included with a lump sum of €1.20 per month and per square metre).

Among the chosen communities, Gelsenkirchen, Pirna, Chemnitz und Zittau have relatively generous arrangements. Meanwhile, cities like Cologne and Düsseldorf have set restrictive rent ceilings that, combined with high costs of living, provide an incentive to move away for recipients of Arbeitslosengeld II. If the Arbeitslosengeld II recipient is a homeowner, housing benefit covers the following costs (in many cases subject to ceilings):

* mortgage interest payments;
* real property tax;
* building insurance premium;
* building lease; and
* extra costs, excluding electricity and hot water.

Table 8.6: Examples of Arbeitslosengeld II rent ceilings, Germany, 2005

Town	Rent ceiling (€ per month)	Notes	Average rent for a flat of 70m² with 3 rooms according to RDM-Preisspiegel (€)
Munich	760.80		749.00–836.50
Hamburg	499.00	Rental stage 3	Between 560 and 749, depending on the age of the dwelling
Cologne	495.00		518.00–693.00
Düsseldorf	480.00		504.00–714.00
Oldenburg	434.60		518.60–539.00
Gelsenkirchen	346.00–404.00		294.00–434.00
Pirna	390.00–470.00	Depending on the age of the dwelling	364.00–399.00
Chemnitz	435.00 in stock; 382.50 in case of removal		364.00–469.00
Zittau	340.00–365.00	Depending on the age of the dwelling	308.00–406.00
Neubrandenburg	360.00		388.50–511.00

Fees for infrastructure connection and principal payments are not included. Owner-occupiers may apply for their maintenance costs to be covered. Homeowners with a high remainder of their debt might be able to meet their mortgage repayments at least for some years while other homeowners with a low remainder might be forced to sell their homes. There is a ceiling of 130 square metres independent of the household size.

Treatment of inadequate housing

An apartment that is larger than the size ceilings for the relevant household size is deemed to be 'unsuitable'[21] unless the rent is no higher than for a suitably sized flat. It is thus possible to get full reimbursement for a flat deemed to be too large, but only if the rent is cheap enough. Applicants whose flat is more expensive than the price ceilings allow, need to trim their housing costs, for example, by moving to a cheaper flat or renting out part of their home. The administration will compensate for an unreasonable rent for no longer than six months.[22] Self-organised removal costs and the deposit on the new flat will usually be covered. If someone does not want to move out, they have to cover the difference between their rent and an adequate rent.

The policy approach to enforced removals into cheaper dwellings differs from town to town. Some communities use differentiated approaches, for example, chronological order of the demands for removal depending on the degree of violation of the rent ceilings, larger tolerances for existing rental contracts, for dwellings in quarters with a low density of ALG II recipients, and for special target groups. It is important to note that these policies are neither uniform nor stable or even settled. The communities are currently in a trial and error phase. They might change to a more restrictive regime if rents or budget deficits rise significantly. Given the fact that the numbers depend also on the labour market situation, it is impossible at present to forecast how many households will be forced to leave their homes.

The question of whether or not an owned home is too big (or too expensive) is chiefly a matter of the poverty test. It is possible that the administration will demand the sale of the house of the homeowner. If the achievable price is lower than 90% of the current value of the home, it need not be sold.

Sozialhilfe (social welfare)

After the transfer of all employable people in need to Arbeitslosengeld II, only a relatively small group (around 175,000) is still in receipt of social welfare. The two most important transfers in the social welfare system are:

- subsistence aid (*Hilfe zum Lebensunterhalt*); and
- basic support of older people and people with reduced earning capacity (*Grundsicherung im Alter und bei Erwerbsminderung*).

There are only minor differences between these two benefits: the target group and the application procedure. Like ALG II, subsistence aid and basic support aim to cover the basic physical and sociocultural needs of people with insufficient income; the difference is the non-employability of the target group. The benefit is need determined; the physical needs include adequate housing and heating costs. Income, other transfers (eg pensions, child allowances, alimony) and the personal assets of the claimants are taken into account. Relatives are also obliged to give help. Subsistence aid is meant only as a last resort and includes the following elements:

- regular amount (*Regelsatz*) for each person living in the household;
- housing and heating benefit.

The rules for housing and heating benefits are more or less the same as for ALG II recipients. Only 'adequate' housing and heating costs will be fully covered. One-off payments can be granted for the initial equipment of the flat, for rental deposits and – in cases of impending homelessness – for rent arrears.

The impact of housing allowances

The impact of Wohngeld

The impact of Wohngeld is limited by the relatively low take-up rate (estimates suggest that only about 40% to 50% of entitled households receive it). Even among households with a very low income, about one third do not claim the housing allowance to which they are entitled (Hauser and Hübinger, 1993, p 149 et seq). The average Wohngeld payment per recipient is €132 per month (Table 8.7).

Table 8.7: Average monthly housing allowances per recipient, Germany, 1991–2001

Year	Table allowances			Lump-sum allowances
	Total	Tenants	Owners	
1991	64	62	80	103
1992	64	61	82	109
1993	66	64	77	119
1994	67	66	79	127
1995	71	70	81	134
1996	77	76	87	140
1997	80	79	90	144
1998	82	81	94	146
1999	84	83	96	148
2000	84	83	96	149
2001	102	101	115	162

Source: Wohngeld- und Mietenbericht (2002, p 32).

Wohngeld is a subsidy chiefly for the working poor and people outside the productive process (eg unemployed persons, pensioners). The share of the active labour force in the total number of the recipients of table housing allowances was only around 30% in Western Germany and around 22% in Eastern Germany in 2001 (see Table 8.8), the difference reflecting the different labour market situation in each of the two parts of the country. Most of the working recipients were blue-collar employees. The shares of white-collar employees and self-employed persons were low and the share of civil servants was negligible. Only a very small part of the active labour force relied on Wohngeld (around 1.4%). In 2005, Wohngeld lost much of its clientele to the new ALG II.

The impact of Wohngeld on the supply side of the housing market depends on the market situation and on housing regulations. In an equilibrium housing market situation without rent controls, the introduction or augmentation of housing allowances will raise rents and rates of return and thus generate incentives for new supply. The size of this effect is a function of the elasticity of housing supply. In a shortage situation, rents will increase even more. In a situation with excess supply, housing allowances will stabilise demand and rents but not necessarily induce additional supply.

The combination of housing allowances with rent controls tends to cause economic problems. The extra demand created by housing allowances will be suppressed in a controlled environment, that is, there will be no rationing inside the housing stock because rents are not allowed to rise. Presumably, housing allowances will be used chiefly for other consumption purposes then. They might also encourage the development of black markets in housing.

The impact of Arbeitslosengeld II

The German finance minister, Peer Steinbrück, has described ALG II as the "biggest budget risk" (*Frankfurter Allgemeine Zeitung*, 19 May 2006). Because of its ever-rising cost (€37.1 billion in 2005, of which €12.1 billion was for housing benefits), ALG II was put at the centre of German political debate. A great deal of the cost increases can be attributed to rising expenditures for housing.

On the one hand, the housing industry has benefited from the introduction of ALG II. This new benefit has provided incentives for additional household formation (young people leaving their parents' homes) and many of the employed recipients of ALG II have more purchasing power for housing now. On the other hand, the former recipients of Arbeitslosengeld or Arbeitslosenhilfe mostly have lost purchasing power. Also, the latter might be forced to move into a cheaper flat, which might result in a degradation of the tenant mix for some housing organisations. The follow-up costs of enforced segregation would be considerable for the housing industry and also for the communities. A one-sided tenant mix will always result in an unequal distribution of chances in life.

The impact of ALG II on social segregation depends on the ratio between rent ceilings and market rents. Many communities use uniform rent ceilings for the

Table 8.8: Social position of recipients of table housing allowances, Germany, 1998–2001

	Share of all Wohngeld recipients (%)							
	West Germany				East Germany			
Social position	1998	1999	2000	2001	1998	1999	2000	2001
Total labour force of which:	28.6	29.0	29.2	29.8	24.4	22.8	21.7	21.6
Labourers	21.7	21.8	21.8	21.7	15.8	14.7	13.8	13.4
White-collar employees	5.4	5.8	6.0	6.8	6.5	6.3	6.1	6.3
Civil servants	0.3	0.3	0.2	0.2	0.1	0.1	0.1	0.1
Self-employed	1.2	1.1	1.1	1.1	1.9	1.8	1.7	1.8
Jobless	28.2	26.8	26.4	26.3	43.7	44.5	44.7	42.8
Non-active population of which:	43.2	44.1	44.4	43.9	32.0	32.6	33.6	35.6
Pensioners	28.9	28.7	30.1	28.6	23.1	23.0	22.5	23.7
Students	2.8	2.6	2.5	2.2	1.5	1.6	1.7	1.7
Other	11.5	12.8	11.8	13.2	7.4	8.1	9.3	10.2
Total number ('000s) reporting:	**977**	**937**	**891**	**1,144**	**609**	**603**	**607**	**684**
Social welfare recipients	15.4	16.2	16.2	16.7	2.6	3.1	3.7	6.3
Recipients of welfare for war victims	0.1	0.2	0.2	0.2	0.2	0.2	0.2	0.0
Total	**15.5**	**16.4**	**16.4**	**16.9**	**2.8**	**3.3**	**3.9**	**6.4**

Source: Wohngeld- und Mietenbericht (2002, p 33).

whole urban area. This undifferentiated approach tends to force recipients to leave the better addresses, and in these cases negative effects on the tenant mix and on housing quality of the affected tenants are unavoidable. Existing tendencies of social segregation are thereby reinforced. The lower the uniform rent ceilings are set, the more rapidly the recipients will be segregated from other people.

Experts believe that housing costs will be at the centre of the political debate about the communities' cost burden from unemployment and poverty in the future. However, lowering the rent ceilings would increase demand in the low-quality segment of the housing market, which would in turn raise rents, housing costs and rent ceilings. Rising rents for low-quality dwellings will also hamper the chances of homeless people for reintegration.

The impact of ALG II on migration behaviour is ambiguous. The lump-sum standard benefit provides an incentive to move to regions with low costs of living, but these regions often have high unemployment rates, too. Also, soft location factors play a role in the migration decision. But if communities with low costs of living offer generous rent ceilings they might attract unemployed people from high-cost regions anyway.

For several reasons, the importance (and the cost) of ALG II is likely to rise still further in the future. Given the ever-shrinking market share of social housing, the subject-related subsidies will get less relief in the form of low rents. Another aspect is the pauperisation of growing numbers of the population, which might perpetuate in the future. Last but not least, ALG II is a substitute for other social transfers like Arbeitslosenhilfe and Sozialhilfe, Wohngeld and Arbeitslosengeld. More transfer recipients might switch from Wohngeld (as soon as they have realised that they could get more from ALG II) and from Arbeitslosengeld (if long-term unemployment rises even more).

Policy debates and reform

It is not possible to give a complete review of all topics of the reform debate about housing allowances in Germany here. Instead the focus will be on certain strategic aspects of the debate that are most likely to be important for the long-term role of the housing transfers in social housing policy and in the wider system of social security. Most important for the further development of the housing transfer system is the division of labour, both between the different federal levels and between the different instruments of social housing policy. Another important issue is the non-dynamic character of Wohngeld (that is, the fact that the tables are not indexed to inflation or earnings).

Wohngeld

Discontinuous adaptation

A lasting impact of a social policy instrument on people's behaviour is a question of trust in continuity. The discontinuous adaptation of the German Wohngeld tables is a severe problem in this respect. Compared with other instruments of social policy like social welfare and unemployment benefits, the development of Wohngeld has been decidedly more discontinuous. As a non-dynamic transfer, Wohngeld is vulnerable to benefit cuts by 'non-decision-making' (Wörz, 1999, p 52; cf Kemp, 2000, pp 53–4).[23]

The experience is always the same. After an adaptation, the number of recipients rises dramatically. Subsequently, their number will fall until the next adaptation. Börsch-Supan (1993, p 29) has calculated using data from the Sozioökonomisches Panel that between 1984 and 1990 less than 2% of the total number of households that received Wohngeld in any of the seven years received it in all years. The vast majority of recipients thus seem to be involuntary 'Wohngeld hoppers'. The discontinuous adaptation of the Wohngeld tables surely impairs the effect of setting incentives for more housing consumption inside the target group (Jaedicke, 1996, p 203).

The rationale behind the Wohngeld adaptations seems to be the business/budget cycle, not need determination. In Figure 8.2 the thick arrows mark expansive changes in the Wohngeld legislation and the thin arrows contractive ones.

Figure 8.2: Wohngeld expenditures and credit balance of federal and state budgets, Germany 1970–89

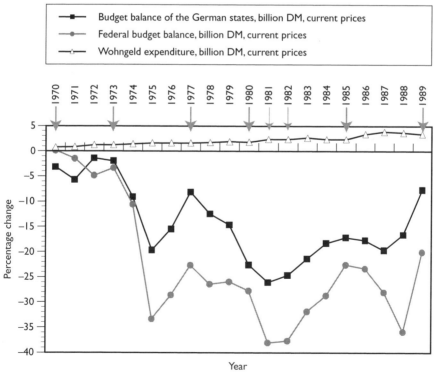

Source: Wörz, 1999, p 59.

The lawmaker is only generous in times of budget relaxation. The impact of the budget cycle is evident in all cases except for the legislative change of 1980 (a year of federal elections). From the point of view of the recipients an anticyclical variation of the transfer would definitely make more sense.

Assignment and financial responsibility in the federal state

The housing transfers are a typical example of the deficiencies of the German federal system. Wohngeld payments are financed fifty-fifty by the federal and the state budget. The legislative competence is at the federal level while the administration is carried out by the communities. Since social transfers do not generate any spillover, an efficient solution would be to assign all competences (legislation, finance and administration) to the communities. Such an assignment would ensure administrative costs as low as possible[24] and a transfer system as close as possible to the preferences of the citizens (Huber, 2001, p 18). The counter-argument is the proverbial 'uniform living conditions', the idea behind which is to ensure the same standard of housing everywhere – at any cost.

For Wohngeld recipients, the rental stages that determine the applicable rent ceilings surely make a contribution to the levelling of interregional differences of rents after taking the allowance into account. The majority of the members of Expertenkommission Wohnungspolitik had pleaded for the abandonment of this regional component because of the incentives it created to move into the big cities (1995, p 230 et seq), although the expert they had charged with an empirical analysis of the matter could not find evidence for such behaviour (Börsch-Supan, 1995, p 23). The regional differences are significant even after receipt of the housing allowance. A higher rent will, *ceteris paribus*, lead to a higher rental burden – before and after the allowance (GEWOS, 1990, p 354 et seq).

ALG II is in most cases co-administered by the federal state (Bundesagentur für Arbeit) and the communities. The legislative competence is at the federal level. The standard benefit is financed in full by the federal state. The housing benefit is currently financed chiefly by the respective community that covers 68.2% of the total expenses; the rest is financed by the federal state (see Sozialgesetzbuch II, §46). The new co-administration has encountered severe start-up problems, but it is too early to give a final judgement. The primary financial responsibility of the federal state for ALG II has created incentives at the community level to declare as many recipients of social welfare as employable as is possible (since they have to finance social welfare payments in full).

Even though there might be an economic case for assigning legislation and finance of the 'social' housing transfers to the communities too, for the moment this is just wishful thinking. It seems that German society is not ready to accept more interregional differences and nor is it imaginable that a complete municipalisation of housing allowances could be attained without a general revision of the assignment of revenues, expenses and legislative and administrative

---

competences in the federal state, which would result in an extensive separation of the federal levels.

Relationship with social housing programmes

A great deal of the German housing debate ever since the extreme post-war housing shortage was cleared in the 1960s centred on the question of balancing the investment subsidies of the social housing programmes with the individual transfers of the developing Wohngeld system. The general justification for Wohngeld was more or less undisputed in academic and political debates, whereas the costly social housing programmes were attacked by their opponents repeatedly over the decades (see, for example, Expertenkommission Wohnungspolitik, 1995; Stern, 2001, pp 69–70, 78). Over the years, the individual approach gained more and more ground, not only in terms of budget allocations. But the question of the relationship between Wohngeld and object-related (supply-side) subsidies is not finally solved.

As everywhere, the German social housing programmes are targeted on the fulfilment of the housing needs of poor and socially excluded households. A special market segment was created for them where access is subject to income ceilings and in most cases to other eligibility criteria. By this means, needy households are protected against the competition of more affluent ones. Also, they benefit from the programme-inherent rent ceilings. The approach of the German social housing programmes is an indirect one: the chosen investors receive interest subsidies for their housing projects and in return they have to accept rent ceilings and the occupancy right of the community. It is important to know that social dwellings lose their special status as soon as the last euro of subsidised credit is paid back.

Quite different from the large building programmes of the 1950s and 1960s, the current ones are modest in almost every respect: a narrow definition of the target group, low completion numbers, shorter duration, less subsidy per dwelling (and hence social rents closer to market levels), and a focus on the existing housing stock rather than new construction (for example modernisation programmes). These tendencies are a consequence of the relaxed housing market situation in most regions and the large budget deficits that force the governments to trim down expenses for social housing.

Social housing nowadays is rather decentralised. The programmes are designed by the state governments and they make every effort to take regional differences into account. Even though social housing is co-financed by the federal government, some states like Saxony and Berlin have almost or completely given up social housing programmes due to large vacancies or budget problems. In other states like North Rhine-Westphalia social housing still plays an important role.

Important differences exist between Wohngeld and social housing (Schellhaaß/ Schulz, 1987, pp 28, 35). For example, there is a legal claim for Wohngeld (that is, it is an entitlement programme) but not for a social dwelling. Also, Wohngeld recipients have a choice from all kinds of dwellings (as long as they are not discriminated against, and subject to their overall budget constraint), which households eligible for social housing do not have. Since there is a permanent shortage of social dwellings in most communities, applicants' freedom of choice is in fact almost non-existent; they need to take more or less what is offered to them. The free choice is a big advantage of Wohngeld over social housing. It is definitely more efficient because it limits mismatching. Also, it tends to inhibit the formation of social ghettoes. This is of particular importance in times when social housing programmes usually have a very narrow target group. Last but not least, object-related subsidies are simply more costly than transfers in cash directly given to households in need.[25]

Should the desirable relationship between Wohngeld and social housing thus obey the following simple rule in every case: 'As much social housing as necessary – as much Wohngeld as possible'? The answer is, it depends: there is a better case for social housing programmes where there is a (current or foreseeable) housing shortage. Housing shortages (general and partial) tend to undermine the effect of housing allowances; in a shortage situation, discrimination and not purchasing power rules. For the most part, Wohngeld will then have the effect of further lifting rents (Riege, 1993, p 41) – if rent price rules admit it. Communities that have built enough social dwellings in due time can count themselves lucky in such a market situation. Hence there is a case for a counter-cyclical variation of social housing subsidies.[26]

The social housing programmes tend to lower the Wohngeld claim since their programme-inherent rent ceilings reduce the absolute rental burden of the household compared with market rent levels. On the other hand, Wohngeld makes dwellings rented from the free market less expensive, especially for low-income households. Wohngeld hence makes social dwellings less competitive, tends to decrease social rents and thus to increase state subsidies for social housing. It might even contribute to the development of social ghettoes in the cities.

In the context of income-dependent social housing programmes, Wohngeld does not make too much sense. In these programmes, it is considered as income and thus raises the household's income-dependent social rent. If social housing programmes are not income dependent (which especially applies to the large stock of older social dwellings) the Wohngeld transfer helps to fine-tune the programme effects in terms of affordability, efficiency and distributional justice, without being able to level out all programme-inherent inefficiencies (Schellhaaß and Schulz, 1987, p 29). Finally, Wohngeld is a means to absorb the effect that a release of social dwellings into the free market has on rent levels (Stern, 2001, p 83 et seq). In view of a dramatically shrinking social housing sector in Germany this is of particular importance.

Even liberal German economists do not count on Wohngeld alone to ensure adequate housing for the poor. They concede that the government also needs some kind of instrument to influence housing allocation in favour of discriminated groups (Stern, 2001, p 85). The disputed question is how narrowly to define the target group eligible for social dwellings. The German legislator opted for a rather narrow definition in 2001. According to section 1 of the new Wohnraumförderungsgesetz, the target group of social housing are "households unable to provide themselves with adequate housing at the free market". This corresponds closely to the target group definition of Wohngeld: "to ensure economically adequate and family-oriented housing". In fact, the target group definition of Wohngeld has widened over time whereas the one for social housing has got narrower.

Interestingly enough, the income ceilings for social housing are considerably higher than for Wohngeld. This makes sense because in social housing additional eligibility criteria like the following are widely used:

- current housing situation of the applicant;
- personal situation of the applicant (pregnant, lone parent, many children, disabled, young couple); and
- financial situation of the applicant.

Also, sometimes social housing programmes are exclusively reserved for a certain target group. The wider income ceilings in social housing leave some scope for helping households that have an access problem but a slightly higher income than housing allowance recipients.

The relationship between the two instruments can be described as follows: Wohngeld refers primarily to the economic ability of a household to procure adequate housing. Social housing programmes, on the other hand, give the administration ample scope for focusing exactly on the households with the most pressing housing access problems (Eichener and Heinze, 1994, p 28; Nolte and Voß, 1997, p 22). This seems to be a reasonable division of labour at first sight. However, an even clearer division of labour between Wohngeld and social housing is imaginable.

An important policy question is whether or not the rent ceilings in the social housing programmes are necessary at all. Even their inherent income ceilings are questionable. Social housing could be more or less reduced to a barter of modest capital subsidies against the community's right to occupy a dwelling at a market rent. The problem of economic affordability would then be completely assigned to the Wohngeld system. Presumably, this would be a more efficient arrangement.

While the general division of labour between the two instruments is widely accepted the desirable size of the social housing sector remains a matter of dispute. Some economists do not want more than a 'task force' (Schneider and Kornemann, 1977, p 87; Biedenkopf and Miegel, 1978, p 84), while others favour "a relatively large stock of dwellings with public occupancy rights" (Eichener and Heinze, 1994, p 29) and still others argue for a share of 20% for the social dwellings in the total housing stock (Pfeiffer, 1993, p 47).

Meritorisation and income redistribution: is Wohngeld overcharged?

The basic problem of Wohngeld as a housing policy instrument is its inherent conflict of objectives. There is a complete antinomy between the goal of bringing down the rental burden and the goal of pushing up housing consumption, if we rely solely on Wohngeld (Börsch-Supan, 1995, p 36).[27] Every re-allocation of a euro of Wohngeld received in favour of additional housing consumption instead of other purposes will push up the relative rental burden after transfer and vice versa.

The theory of economic policy tells us that we need two policy instruments in order to pursue two conflicting economic policy goals. The other instrument at hand is obviously social housing. With cleverly designed social housing programmes it is possible, in theory, to allocate exactly the minimum volume and quality of housing consumption to every household that housing policy aims at. Wohngeld, on the other hand, would be able to trim down the rental burden to the targeted level.

The important message here is that not only social housing without housing allowances, but also housing allowances without social housing, is a waste of money. Housing policy does not have any control of the way housing allowances are spent by the recipients. The distribution is of greater importance here than the average. Some households will use the additional money chiefly to push up their housing consumption and others will try to bring down their rental burden at almost any cost. As a matter of fact, it is impossible for housing policy to bring up housing consumption of some households and to lower the rental burden of others with housing allowances alone.

The fine art of social housing policy is to coordinate social housing with housing allowances perfectly in order to make a spot landing at the desired consumption level and relative rental burden. We do not need witchcraft and wizardry for this task. The instrument is already at hand: income-dependent social housing programmes with an income-dependent contractual rent (see Kofner, 2004, pp 129–31). The superiority of these integrated programmes is indisputable. Income-dependent social housing is the only efficient way to ensure the general rule of the principle "same housing quality and same income that implies the same rent" – and hence the same rental burden (Kofner, 1999, p 89). Housing allowances are an integrated part of the income-dependent programmes since the contractual rent is a function of the family income. Another important advantage of income-dependency is its inherent bias towards a balanced tenant mix.

The new housing policy should aim at a reservoir of income-dependent social dwellings large enough to fulfil the housing needs of all households either with inadequate housing consumption or with a pre-transfer relative rental burden above the one society is willing to accept (say 25%). It should even be large enough to ensure the eligible household's freedom of choice. This arrangement will be less costly than the more or less uncoordinated coexistence of social housing programmes and Wohngeld. The remaining question is whether the state is capable of executing this kind of optimal social policy; liberal economists will have an opinion here different to that of socially spirited economists.

Arbeitslosengeld II

The reform agenda of ALG II is dominated by the need to cut costs to prevent public deficits geting out of control. Against this background the need determination of the transfer is out of the question. The legislator has already taken measures against fraud; the most effective cost-cutting measure is to bring down long-term unemployment, but it is not easy to reduce rigidified unemployment anyway.

Another problem to tackle is the incentives to work. The claims of families with children can be higher than the earned income of a worker with a low qualification level. It is questionable, however, whether this problem can be solved by lowering the standard benefit or leaving the employed recipients of the transfer more of their earned income. The standard benefit is already close to the breadline and a generous treatment of earned income provides incentives to avoid full-time employment. It seems that sufficient incentives to work can only be provided by sanctions, including public interest work.

There is also no easy solution to the problem of social segregation. Choices are limited here by the trade-off between cost-efficiency and a balanced tenant mix. An obvious shortcoming is the total lack of coordination between Wohngeld and ALG II. The employed part of the target group of ALG II can opt between the two transfers. The integration of the two transfer systems would offer a solution here.

Appendix

Example 1: Wohngeld for tenants

It might be helpful to illustrate the way that Wohngeld is calculated by using an example. The Müller family from Karlsruhe (two adults, two children) is living in a flat constructed in 1968 with a bath and central heating. Their monthly rent amounts to: €420 + €80 cold extra costs + €80 heating costs = €580.

Income: Mrs Müller is the only person with an income in the family. Her gross salary is €1,650. She pays income tax and all kinds of social security premiums. Mrs Müller can make a lump-sum deduction of €76.66 per month for relevant expenses in the income tax code (for example for travel to work costs). Her relevant monthly income after a lump-sum deduction of 30% for tax and social security contributions is €1,101.34 – well below the relevant income ceiling.

Allowable rent: The heating costs need to be ignored. We now need to compare the relevant rent amount of €500 with the relevant rent ceiling: only €455 according to Table 8.4 (in Karlsruhe, rental stage III is applicable).

Wohngeld: According to Table 8.1, the Müller family can claim €176 Wohngeld per month. For them it would not make sense to switch to ALG II because with this social security benefit they could only claim €92 per month. But for families with a lower income than the Müllers' it would be worthwhile to do so.

Example 2: Wohngeld for homeowners

The Schulze family from Karlsruhe is made up of a couple with three children and a mother-in-law (six persons). They are living in a home of 130 square metres constructed in 1972, with a bath and central heating. Their monthly charge amounts to:

	€
+ Interest payments	325.00
+ Principal	300.00
+ Ground lease	175.00
+ Lump sum for maintenance and extra costs	216.66
+ Land tax	15.00
− Eigenheimzulage	304.16
= Total charge	**727.50**

Mr Schulze's gross salary (subject to income tax and social security premiums) is €1,750. The mother-in-law is receiving a statutory pension of €500 per month and pays her own contribution for social insurance but no income tax.

Income:

	Husband	Mother-in-law
Gross income without child allowances[a] (€)	1,750.00	500.00
Lump sum for causally expenses (€)	76.67	8.50
Lump sum for tax and social insurance (€)	502.00	49.15
Relevant monthly income (€)	1,171.33	442.35

Note: [a] Child allowances for their three children total €462 (€154 for each child).

Allowable charges: We now need to compare the total monthly charge of €727.50 with the relevant rent/charge ceiling: only €585 according to Table 8.3 (in Karlsruhe rental stage III is applicable).

Lastenzuschuß calculation: According to the relevant Wohngeld table for a household of six with a relevant income of €1,613.68 and an allowable charge of €585 the Schulze family can claim for €172 of Lastenzuschuß per month.

Example 3: ALG II standard benefit

A jobless single mother with a four-year-old daughter receiving Kindergeld (child allowance) and alimony and a job paying €300 per month:

Need:
€345.00 standard benefit mother
+ €207.00 standard benefit child
+ €124.20 extra benefit for single parents (36% of the mother's standard benefit)
+ €350.00 housing benefit and heating costs (est.)
= €1,026.20 total need

ALG II claim:
€1,026.20 need
− €175.00 alimony
− €154.00 Kindergeld
− €160.00 Euro imputed earned income
= €537.20 claim

Household income:
€537.20 ALG II
+ €175.00 alimony
+ €154.00 Kindergeld
+ €300.00 earned income
= €1,166.20 monthly income

Notes

[1] Barnbrock and Mayo (1981) have calculated a share of 55% for additional housing consumption out of Wohngeld which seems to be pretty much comparable to other similar countries. The estimation of Börsch-Supan (1995, pp 24–8), derived from the superior panel data source of Sozioökonomisches Panel (between 20% and 31%), is more in line with estimations for other countries.

[2] In the Weimar Republic this segment comprised more or less the dwellings constructed before 1 July 1918. In the years of dictatorship the controlled housing sector was gradually expanded. Finally it included almost the complete housing stock. In the Federal Republic the controlled sector comprised all dwellings constructed until 20 June 1948. All in all the era of controlled housing lasted around 50 years for the dwellings constructed before 1918, in Eastern Germany it lasted a human's life span (around 75 years).

[3] Needless to say Jewish German citizens received no housing allowances (see Kornemann, n.d., p 28).

[4] BGBl I, p 458. See also Pergande, 1973, p 184.

[5] Landlords in the social housing segment had to accept price controls, and the choice of tenants was not free either. For an overview of the development of the social housing sector see Kühne-Büning and Kofner, 2005.

[6] See 24 April 1950, Erstes Wohnungsbaugesetz, §17, BGBl I, p 83.

[7] See 27 June 1956, Zweites Wohnungsbaugesetz, §72, BGBl I, p 523.

[8] The states could choose between allowances and capital subsidies as means of subsidising homeowners in need (see GEWOS, 1990, p 99). Until the 1965 Erstes Wohngeldgesetz (see below), the charge allowances were only given if the need situation was not the homeowner's fault.

[9] For details see Jürgensen, 2003, p 6 and pp 110–16. The yearly income check surely causes high administration costs. On the other hand it is a precondition for the efficiency of the Wohngeld transfer since it limits the misallocation of subsidies (Jaedicke, 1996, p 202).

[10] The price ceilings were widely criticised as insufficient (GEWOS, 1990, p 347).

[11] Family members who are temporarily not living at home, for example when they are in hospital, undergoing military or civil service or studying away from home, are still considered members of the household. For details see Jürgensen, 2003, pp 29–38.

[12] See also Stern, 2001, p 79.

[13] The rent definition includes only 'cold' extra costs, that is, heating costs are excluded from the definition. This definition does not hamper the incentives to save energy. We assume for the moment that the effective rent is below the relevant rent ceiling.

[14] The rental stages are announced officially. The allocation of the different communities to the different rental stages is not done arbitrarily by the administration; it has to follow the rules stipulated in §8 of the federal Wohngeld law. The stages reflect the deviations of the local rent levels from the federal average. The rental stages also determine the level of the allowable rent for the calculation of the Wohngeld claim.

[15] There are minor differences anyway, for example the housing benefit of Arbeitslosengeld II is defined by the local administrations (and not centrally set). The need defined by Arbeitslosengeld II also depends on the age of the family members.

[16] For details see § 6–8 Wohngeldgesetz.

[17] From 1 February 2006, jobless people aged over 55 receive Arbeitslosengeld for 18 months. For the ones becoming unemployed earlier there were generous transition arrangements, for example unemployed persons older than 57 could receive Arbeitslosengeld for 32 months.

[18] The Federal Ministry for Economics and Labour had expected only 3.2 million ALG II recipients. The consequences of this forecast error for the federal budget are dramatic; compared with the estimates, the federal budget expenses for the new transfer have more than doubled to around €26 billion in the fiscal year 2005. The reasons for this inconceivable cost overrun are diverse and have to be investigated by the government; the causes could be fraud, lower shame barriers for the claimants or additional household formations. Also the federal government had massively underestimated the number of employed recipients (more than 1 million recipients already).

[19] This administrative chaos is the result of a compromise typical of the German constitutional practice of involving the Bundesrat into the law making process – the

federal government was in favour of the ARGE model, whereas the opposition-dominated Bundesrat was backing autonomous administration by local government.

[20] RDM (Ring Deutscher Makler) is an organisation of real estate agents.

[21] In Western Germany around 30% and in Eastern Germany around 20% of the dwellings are too large. On average they have 14 to 10 square metres more than is adequate.

[22] An excess of up to 10% will usually be tolerated.

[23] The German Wohngeldgesetz uses an instrument of institutionalised agenda setting (Georgakis, 2004, p 6 et seq), the so-called Wohngeld- und Mietenberichte (reports on housing allowances and rent development) to be presented by the federal government every two years. But it apparently did not have much influence on the policy agenda, for example, before the amendment of 2001 Wohngeld was not adapted for 10 years.

[24] The last time the federal government published data on the administrative costs of the Wohngeld transfer was in 1994. The share was 7.0% of transfers paid out in Western and 8.9% in Eastern Germany (Stern, 2001, p 81). The share of administrative costs seems to have risen since then (Wohngeld- und Mietenbericht, 2002, p 53).

[25] In 1983 Barnbrock had calculated that for a given absolute reduction of the individual rental burden with object-related subsidies, three times more money is necessary than with Wohngeld. This ratio has surely fallen since then because the newer social housing programmes are more efficient in any respect (for example income-dependency, income checks, price ceilings, subsidies per square metre).

[26] Argument fully developed in Kofner (1999). Nachtkamp advocates additional social dwellings in the case of non-anticipated immigration waves (1991, p 116).

[27] Economists not willing to accept the concept of housing as a merit good do not accept the goal of pushing up housing consumption either and hence plead for the abandonment of Wohngeld in favour of an unrestricted transfer in cash. The case for a merit good with excess benefits is, however, not weak in the case of housing for the poor (Falk, 1998, p 123).

References

Albers, W. (1982) *Soziale Sicherung – Konstruktionen für die Zukunft*, Bonn: Verlag Bonn aktuell.

Barnbrock, J. (1983) 'Individual- und Objektförderung in der Bundesrepublik Deutschland', in *Auftrag des Bundesministeriums für Raumordnung*, Bonn: Bauwesen und Städtebau.

Barnbrock, J. and Mayo, S. (1981) 'Wohngeld und sozialer Wohnungsbau – Auswirkungen auf ausgewählten Wohnungsmärkten', in *Auftrag des Bundesministeriums für Raumordnung*, Bonn: Bauwesen und Städtebau.

Biedenkopf, K. and Miegel, M. (1978) *Wohnungsbau am Wendepunkt. Wohnungspolitik in der sozialen Marktwirtschaft*, Stuttgart: Bonnaktuell.

Börsch-Supan, A. (1995) 'Wohngeld und Wohnverhalten', in *Expertenkommission Wohnungspolitik – Materialband*, Bonn: Bundesministeriums für Raumordnung, Bauwesen und Städtebau.

Bundeministerium für Verkehr, Bau- und Wohnungswesen (2005) Wohngeld 2005, Ratschläge und Hinweise.

Bundesministerium für Gesundheit und Soziale Sicherung (2005) Übersicht über das Sozialrecht, Ausgabe 2005.

Eekhoff, J. (1987) *Wohnungs- und Bodenmarkt*, Tübingen: Mohr.

Eichener, V. and Heinze, R. (1994) 'Dilemmata der sozialen Wohnungspolitik', *WIS-Bericht*, vol 4, no 94.

Expertenkommission Wohnungspolitik (1995) *Wohnungspolitik auf dem Prüfstand*, Tübingen: Mohr.

Expertenkommission Wohnungspolitik (1995) *Materialband*, edited by Bundesministerium für Raumordnung, Bauwesen und Städtebau, Bonn: Bundesministeriums für Raumordnung, Bauwesen und Städtebau.

Falk, W. (1998) *Wohnen im Lebenslauf*, Amsterdam: G+B Verlag Fakultas.

Führer, K. (1995) *Mieter, Hausbesitzer, Staat und Wohnungsmarkt*, Stuttgart: Franz Steiner Verlag.

Georgakis, N. (2004) 'Wohngeld', in Schader-Stiftung (ed) *Wohnungspolitik in Deutschland*, Darmstadt: Positionen, Akteure, Instrumente.

GEWOS Institut für Stadt-, Regional- und Wohnforschung (1990) *Wohnungspolitik nach dem Zweiten Weltkrieg, Gutachten im Auftrag des Bundesministers für Raumordnung*, Bonn: Bauwesen und Städtebau.

Haerendel, U. (1999) *Kommunale Wohnungspolitik im Dritten Reich: Siedlungsideologie, Kleinhausbau und 'Wohnraumarisierung' am Beispiel Münchens*, Munich: Oldenbourg Verlag.

Hauser, R. and Hübinger, W. (1993) *Arme unter uns. Teil 1: Ergebnisse und Konsequenzen der Caritas-Armutsuntersuchung*, (1st edn), Freiburg im Breisgau: Deutscher Caritasverband.

Huber, B. (2001) 'Projekt Föderalismusreform: Die Mischfinanzierungen im deutschen Föderalismus – Ökonomische Probleme und Reformmöglichkeiten', e.V working paper no 48, Sankt Augustin: Konrad-Adenauer-Stiftung.

Jaedicke, W. (1996) 'Wirkungen wohnungspolitischer Instrumente', in H. Jenkis (ed) *Kompendium der Wohnungswirtschaft* (3rd edn), Munich: Oldenbourg Verlag.

Jürgensen, A. (2003) *Der Anspruch auf Wohngeld, Beck-Rechtsberater im Deutschen*, Munich: Taschenbuch Verlag.

Kemp, P.A. (2000) 'The role and design of income-related housing allowances', *International Social Security Review*, vol 53, no 3, pp 43–57.

Klueß, S. (2000) 'Das Wohngeld in Frankfurt am Main', *Frankfurter Statistische Berichte*, vol 2, no 3.

Kofner, S. (1999) 'Der Stabilisierungsauftrag des sozialen Wohnungsbaus', *Wohnungswirtschaft und Mietrecht*, vol 52, pp 71–90.

Kofner, S. (2003) 'Die Formation der deutschen Wohnungspolitik nach dem Zweiten Weltkrieg – Teil I', *Deutsche Wohnungswirtschaft*, vol 55, no 10, pp 246–51.

Kofner, S. (2004) *Wohnungsmarkt und Wohnungswirtschaft*, Munich: Oldenbourg Verlag.

Kornemann, R. (n.d.) 'Double murder: The "Aryanisation" of property and the forced rehousing of tenants as a prelude to the massacre of the Jews', available at http://www.ns-wohnungspolitik-gegen-juden.de/.

Kühne-Büning, L. and Kofner, S. (2005) 'Vom ersten und zweiten Wohnungsbaugesetz zum Wohnraumförderungsgesetz 2002', in L. Kühne-Büning and J.H.B. Heuer (eds) *Grundlagen der Wohnungs- und Immobilienwirtschaft* (4th edn), Frankfurt am main: Fritz Knapp Verlag.

Nachtkamp, H. (1991) 'Subvention und steuerliche Sonderregelungen für die Wohnungswirtschaft als finanz- und sozialpolitisches Problem', in H. Jenkis (ed.), *Kompendium der Wohnungswirtschaft*, Munich, Oldenbourg Verlag.

Nolte, R. and Voß, O. (1997) *Nachfrage- und Angebotswirkungen des Wohngeldes*, Münster: Institut für Siedlungs- und Wohnungswesen.

Neumann, L. and Schaper, K. (1998) *Die Sozialordnung der Bundesrepublik Deutschland* (4th edn), Bonn: Bundeszentrale für politische Bildung.

Pergande, H. (1973) 'Die Gesetzgebung auf dem Gebiete des Wohnungswesens und des Städtebaus', in Deutsche Bau- und Bodenbank (ed.) *50 Jahre im Dienste der Bau- und Wohnungswirtschaft*, Bonn-Badhotesberg: Deutsche Bau- und Bodenbank.

Pfeiffer, U. (1993) *Wohnen für alle. Ein Beitrag zur Diskussion des Wohnungsproblems in Deutschland*, Bonn: Friedrich-Ebert-Stiftung.

Riege, M. (1993) 'Der soziale Wohnungsbau. Sein Beitrag und seine Grenzen für eine soziale Wohnungspolitik', *Aus Politik und Zeitgeschichte*, no B8–9/93, pp 32–42.

Schader-Stiftung (ed) (2004) *Wohnungspolitik in Deutschland*, Darmstadt: Positionen, Akteure, Instrumente.

Schellhaaß, H. and Schulz, E. (1987) *Soziale Sicherung des Wohnens: Strategien für die Zukunft*, Berlin: Ed. Sigma.

Schneider, H. and Kornemann, R. (1977) *Soziale Wohnungsmarktwirtschaft*, Bonn: Eichholz.

Schwerz, G. (2001) *Wohngeldgesetz. Kommentar mit Durchführungs- und Ergänzungsvorschriften* (3rd edn), Baden-Baden: Nomos.

Stern, V. (2001) *Wohnungsbauförderung auf dem Prüfstand*, Berlin: Bräuer-Institut des Bundes der Steuerzahler.

Wagner, G. (1995) *Sozialstaat gegen Wohnungsnot*, Paderborn: Schöningh.

Wörz, M. (1999) 'Entwicklungsverläufe ausgewählter sozialstaatlicher Programme in der Bundesrepublik Deutschland von 1960–1989', Magisterarbeit an der Fakultät für Verwaltungswissenschaft der Universität Konstanz.

Wohngeld- und Mietenbericht (2002) Bundestagsdrucksache no 15/2200, 11 December.

Wohngeldgesetz (WGG) (2005) in der Fassung der Bekanntmachung 7 July, BGBl I, p 2029.

NINE

Housing allowances in the Netherlands: the struggle for budgetary controllability

Hugo Priemus and Marja Elsinga

Introduction

After the Second World War, bricks-and-mortar subsidies and rent control were introduced to ensure rented housing remained affordable in the Netherlands. The social rented sector was the main instrument for national government to stimulate housing production and safeguard affordable housing. In recent decades, a gradual shift has taken place from subsidised rents to personal subsidies for households: housing allowances. The shift from subsidised rents towards market-based rental is still ongoing and the housing allowance scheme has developed into the core instrument in Dutch housing policy (about 56% of the national housing budget). This shift did not take place without comment and has given rise to many lively debates.

The central theme in this chapter is: how does the housing allowance scheme operate in the Netherlands, balancing between the goals of affordability and housing quality and the need to control public budgets? The following questions are examined:

- How have housing allowances developed within Dutch housing policy?
- How has the Dutch housing allowance scheme developed since 1975?
- What are the dilemmas in designing the housing allowance scheme?
- What are the future challenges?

The next section deals with the role of housing allowances in Dutch housing policy and sketches how housing allowances captured a prominent place in this policy. The following section discusses the development of housing allowances and the affordability of housing in the period from 1975 to 2002. The chapter then describes a number of problems and the political answers in the Netherlands. The subsequent section outlines developments and current dilemmas and the chapter ends with a number of conclusions and recommendations.

Housing allowances and housing policy

The duty to provide housing is enshrined in the Dutch Constitution. The policy to make housing affordable constitutes an important dimension of this duty. In this section we provide a historical overview of this policy and show that, over time, housing allowances have played a steadily more important role in Dutch housing policy.

After the Second World War, social rented housing was heavily subsidised and financed with government loans. An important reason for this was that the rents had been frozen since 1940 as part of the government's wage policy. As a result of this stringent rent policy, the construction of new houses was not an attractive financial proposition and subsidies were needed to stimulate housing production. Since the government determined the conditions under which subsidies were granted, it gained greater control over the housing association sector (Van der Schaar, 1987).

There was much discussion during the 1960s on the desirability of the liberalisation of social housing and how this could be brought about. This led to equalisation of bricks-and-mortar subsidies for the social and commercial rented sectors, while the housing associations were encouraged to take out loans on the capital market. These capital market loans were mostly guaranteed by local governments, but government loans were also provided.

The rent policy was also overhauled in the 1960s. Until then, rents had been strictly regulated and a big gap could be observed between old low-rent housing and new high-rent housing. As a result, there was little residential mobility on the rented market; this stagnation was regarded as undesirable. For this reason, it became possible in 1967 to raise the rent of accommodation that fell vacant to 'the average rent of subsidised newly built housing'. This standard was not considered to be specific enough, however, and a need was felt for an objective quality criterion that could serve as a basis for determining rents when rents were harmonised (Van der Schaar, 1987, p 128).

In the 1960s, there was a general feeling that government spending was spiralling out of control and that the housing market was becoming too distorted (Commissie-Alozerij, 1964; De Haan, 1969). The main policy line that the government chose was that of liberalisation: a freer rental pricing mechanism, leading to higher rents and simultaneous dismantling of bricks-and-mortar subsidies. To make this possible, the Netherlands, taking its cue from such countries as West Germany (where Wohngeld had been introduced – see Chapter Eight), also warmed to the idea of income-related housing support; housing allowances, in other words. The political right was positive about this approach because housing allowances seemed to be a necessary condition for following the road of liberalisation. The political left, after some initial hesitation, was positive because this support was really targeted at low-income households and promised a non-stigmatising housing policy (Priemus, 1984). This led in 1970 to the introduction of housing allowances aimed at making sure that housing remained affordable while allowing rents to be raised to market levels. In the beginning, housing allowances were intended as a temporary measure designed to give tenants time to get used to the higher rents. However, two oil crises put the affordability of housing back on the political agenda, and both the bricks-and-mortar subsidies and housing allowances were maintained.

The 1980s brought a new tendency towards liberalisation of the rental sector, this time via the introduction of the housing valuation system in rent policy. This system was intended to meet the need for an objective quality criterion as the basis for determining rent levels. The quality of a dwelling was expressed in points, and a maximum rent price was fixed per point. The possibility was also created of exempting dwellings with more than a certain number of quality points from rent regulation. The top end of the market, comprised of the most luxurious and expensive dwellings (which only accounted for a few per cent of the total rented market), could be liberalised and was thus no longer subject to rent regulations. This change in the rent regulations enabled landlords to adopt a more market-oriented rent policy.

The Guarantee Fund for Social Housing (Dutch abbreviation WSW) was also formed in the 1980s. Initially intended for the financing of housing renovation, this fund eventually replaced local government guarantees. It currently guarantees most of the housing loans of the social housing associations.

An important step towards complete financial independence of the housing associations was taken in the 1990s, via the 'grossing and balancing' operation of 1995 (Priemus, 1995). This operation implied the total disappearance of bricks-and-mortar subsidies for the construction and management of social rented housing. At the same time, rent policy became less tight. Associations were allowed to introduce more differentiation in the annual rent rises, while the government set the maximum rent rise per dwelling and the average rent rise per housing association (Elsinga et al, 2005). Rent regulation still exists and rents in the social rental sector are below market rents. During the last decade the protection of housing affordability shifted more from rent policy towards housing allowances. Housing allowances clearly became the core instrument in the policy to safeguard housing affordability. In Table 9.1 we present a summary of these changes.

Table 9.1: Financial instruments in the social rented sector, Netherlands, 1945–2005

	Government loans	Bricks-and-mortar subsidies	Government guarantees	Rent regulation	Housing allowance
1945	++	+++		+++	
1960s	+	+++	+	+++	
1970s	+	++	+	++	+
1980s	+	+	+	++	++
1990s			++	+	+++
2005			++	+	+++

Source: Van der Schaar (1987), table compiled by authors (OTB).

Notes: +++: dominant role; ++: substantial role; +: minor role.

We may conclude that, from 1975, housing allowances developed from a marginal measure into the core instrument of housing policy in the Netherlands, replacing bricks-and-mortar subsidies. In the same period government loans were abolished and rent regulation became more liberalised.

Developments in the Dutch housing allowances scheme 1975–2005

The modest housing allowance scheme that was cautiously introduced in 1970 was soon expanded in 1975 to create a general housing allowance scheme, applicable to the entire rented sector (Lucassen and Priemus, 1977; Priemus, 1986). In 1986 it was enshrined in the Housing Allowance Act (Tweede Kamer, 1997). Right from the start, certain basic principles were definitely laid down. First of all, the allowance is an entitlement (irrespective of the size of the available public budget) for households with a below-average income living in a relatively expensive rented home. Second, since 1975 the scheme has applied to all rented housing, both social housing (accounting for about 80% of the Dutch rented housing stock) and commercial rented housing (accounting for the remaining 20% of the rented stock). Third, the housing allowance is always granted for one year. So every eligible person can apply for the subsidy once per year. Fourth, the size of the housing allowance depends primarily on the amount of the rent and household income. Broadly speaking: the higher the rent and the lower the income, the higher the allowance granted. Several other criteria were subsequently added, such as the size of the household and the age of the head of the household (65 or younger).

Over the years, the scheme has been repeatedly adjusted, particularly in times of economic hardship and periods of budgetary tightening, as in the beginning of the 1980s (Van der Schaar, 1994; Priemus, 1998; Boelhouwer and Haffner, 2002). These two circumstances, incidentally, often coincide in an affluent welfare state like the Netherlands. Until the mid-1980s the scheme was based on basic rent ratios. This, however, undermined the budget flexibility of the government, which was eager to bring the national budget under control (Van der Schaar et al, 1998). After that year the state took as its primary guideline the household's remaining income after deduction of the net housing expenditures. This improved the controllability of the expenditures. In 1997 the rented housing allowance scheme was greatly extended, giving tenants on the lowest incomes more choice and thus also promoting income differentiation in large, new-build developments (Tweede Kamer, 1997).

Politicians have constantly intended to raise the rents to the level of market-based rents while simultaneously wanting to compensate the low-income groups by means of the housing allowance. Affordability was the chief aim of the scheme. In 1997 a further objective was added to this: the promotion of social mix within neighbourhoods in order to prevent segregation. Housing allowances were generically increased to ensure that the new-built neighbourhoods and the new housing in the urban renewal areas could also be afforded by low-income groups. The target group for the housing allowance comprises about 30% of Dutch households. Figure 9.1 shows the share of rent that is covered, Table 9.2 gives an overview of the maximum income and assets in 2003, broken down by age and number of persons.

Figure 9.1: The Netherlands housing allowance system: share of the rent that is covered by the housing allowance within the relevant limits

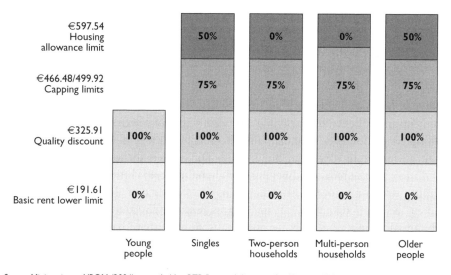

Source: Ministerie van VROM (2004), compiled by OTB Research Institute for Housing, Urban and Mobility Studies, Delf University of Technology.

Table 9.2: Maximum income and assets for housing allowance, Netherlands, 2004

	Taxable income 2003 (€)	Assets 2003 (€)
Younger than 65		
Single	18,700	20,300
Multi-person	25,075	37,600
Older than 65		
Single	16,625	34,725
Multi-person	21,675	48,050

Source: Ministerie van VROM (2004).

Determining the amount of housing allowance

The amount of housing allowance to which tenants are entitled is determined as follows. First of all, there is a basic rent, this is the minimum amount of rent that everyone must pay themselves. This basic rent also forms the starting point for social security payments; when the level of social security benefit is calculated it is assumed that the basic rent is paid by the households. The rent allowance is therefore extra. The basic rent is income dependent and was fixed at €192 in 2004 for the lowest-income households, including those on social security. This sum equates with the National Institute for Budget Information (NIBUD) figures on average housing costs for the lowest-income groups (NIBUD, 2004).

The basic rent has a so-called quality discount limit. The difference between the basic rent and the quality discount limit is subsidised at 100% for all groups. For young people up to the age of 23, this quality discount limit is also the maximum rent limit. In other words, this group receives no allowance whatsoever if the occupants live in a home with a rent over €326. For the other groups, there is a capping limit that differs for small and large households. The difference between the capping limit and the quality discount limit is subsidised at 75%. Finally, there is also a maximum rent limit for these groups. The difference between this maximum and the capping limit is not subsidised. One exception in this connection applies to older people, for whom 50% of the difference is subsidised. No housing allowance is available for housing with a rent above the maximum limit. An example is worked out in Table 9.3, which shows that the allowance increases with the rent of a dwelling. For a tenant there is little difference between a house with a rent of €200 or €400: in the former case the tenant pays €192 and in the latter case €211. With a gross rent of €500, the net rent becomes substantially higher because the quality discount starts to have greater influence (Elsinga, 2005).

The amount of rent allowance to which tenants are entitled is based on their taxable income in the previous year and is reviewed annually. Changes in the household income during the year do not lead to interim revisions of recipients' housing allowance entitlement. Households can, however, apply for a safety-net system, but only when their income falls by over 20%. They are then awarded a top-up allowance to bridge the gap until the following review date (Ministerie van VROM, 2004).

Research has shown that about 25% to 30% of entitled tenants fail to apply for an allowance (for example, Lucassen and Priemus, 1997). The reasons for this

Table 9.3: Example of housing allowance, Netherlands, 2004 (calculated for multi-person household on income benefit)

	€ per month	
Gross rent	**Subsidy**	**Net rent**
200	8	192
300	108	192
400	189	211
500	239	261
600	0	600

Source: Elsinga (2005).

are that people think they are not entitled because their rent is too low or their income is too high, that they will only receive a small amount, or that they find the application procedure too complicated. This lack of take-up largely concerns households who would only receive a modest allowance (Ministerie van VROM, 2000). It was also found that 21% of housing allowance recipients are receiving a lower amount than they are entitled to. After research had shown that the non-take-up of housing allowances served to increase poverty, policy was developed to boost the take-up rate (Tweede Kamer, 1998). Important elements here were improved public information and a simplified system that was introduced with the 1997 Rental Subsidy Act. An evaluation in 2000 revealed that the non-take-up rate had been reduced to 15–35% (Ministerie van VROM, 2000).

Table 9.4 shows how the number of housing allowance recipients increased between two and a half to three times between 1975 and 2001. Partly due to inflation, the average allowance rose much more strongly: the nominal amount in 2001 was almost 40 times higher than in 1975. As a consequence, the public budget for housing allowances exploded between 1975 and 2001: the budget in 2001 (not adjusted for inflation) is about a hundred times larger than in 1975. The share of housing allowances in GDP increased from 0.15% in 1975 to 0.35% in 2001 (see Table 9.4). As is clear from Table 9.4, expenditure on housing allowance rose between 1975 and 1985. This is attributable, on the one hand, to the fact that the programme had expanded since its inception and, on the other, to the economic recession in the early 1980s, which made a dent in the budget and necessitated economies. Even so, expenditure rose steeply. Between 1985 and 1995, expenditure was fairly constant, but at the end of the 1990s an upturn occurred, almost certainly tied in with changes implemented in 1997. Recently, a downturn can be observed.

The share of the social rented sector in the Netherlands is gradually declining, falling from 41% in 1975 to 35% in 2003 (Ministerie van VROM, 2004). Meanwhile, the share of tenants receiving housing allowances increased from 12.9% in 1975 to 31.1% in 2001. This percentage is still increasing as a result of the growing share of homeownership and the selective transformation of better-off households from tenants to homeowners. Thanks to the housing allowance, the net rent-to-income ratios of households receiving an allowance have been significantly reduced from 25.7% to 17.7% in 1981 and from 36.3% to 23.5% in 2002.

The average rent-to-income ratio for all tenants increased from 17.0% in 1981 to 27.8% in 2002. In the past 20 years, tenants have seen their net rents increase much more strongly than their incomes. Though housing allowances have over the years led to a strong rent ratio reduction (from 8.0 percentage points in 1981 to 12.8 percentage points in 2002), the remaining net rent ratio has increased substantially over that period. While more and more households are claiming housing allowances, the rent ratios have risen sharply (see Figure 9.2). This can in the first place be attributed to the choice made back in the 1970s to change over to more market-driven rents and to guarantee affordability via the housing

Table 9.4: Housing allowances, tenants, amounts and public budgets, Netherlands, 1975–2003 (selected years)

	1975	1980	1985	1990	1995	2000	2001	2003
	1975/76	1980/81	1985/86	1990/91	1995/96	200/01	2001/02	
Housing allowances								
(1) Number of recipients[a]	348,320	455,864	777,692	953,000	922,300	991,622	962,817	
(2) Average amount per household[a]	fl.974	fl.1,380	fl.1,729	€1,044	€1,260	€1,728	€1,622	
(3) Total amount of housing allowances (x million)[a]	fl.339.9	fl.628.9	fl.1,345.6	€807.3	€997.9	€1,551.4	€1,561.7	
(4) % share of housing allowances in GDP	0.15	0.18	0.31	0.33	0.33	0.39	0.35	
Stock of rented dwellings								
(5a) Number of dwellings[b]	2,694,614	2,809,976	3,033,305	3,168,153	3,189,469	3,119,397	3,097,670	
(5b) % share of rented dwellings in the housing stock[b]	62.9	59.2	57.3	54.6	51.5	47.3	46.6	
(6) % share of rented dwellings with housing allowances	12.9	16.2	25.6	30.1	28.9	31.8	31.1	
National housing budget								
(8a) Total (x million)[c]	fl.4,979.0	fl.10,099.0	fl.16,738.0	fl.14,687.4	fl.45,706.8[d]	€3,952.2		€3,504.0
(8b) % share of housing budget in national public budget	7.6	8.8	9.5	7.9	19.7	2.8		2.6
National public budget[c]	fl.65,218.0	fl.114,893.0	fl.176,124.0	fl.186,029.4	fl.231,950.1	€140,636.3		€136,658.4

Source: Ministerie van VROM.

Notes: [a] 1975, 1980, 1985 Ministerie van VROM, profile of the recipients of individual housing allowance, HIS-records; 1990, 1995, 2000 VROM, 2004 Housing Figures. €1 = about fl.2.2; [b] ABF Research – SysWov; [c] 1975–82 appendix 8.b; 1980, 1985 – estimated outcomes, 1990, 1995, 2000, 2003 – actual outcomes; [d] exceptional outlay due to the impact of the 'grossing and balancing' operation (see text).

Figure 9.2: Rent ratios before and after housing allowance, Netherlands, 1981–2002 (selected years)

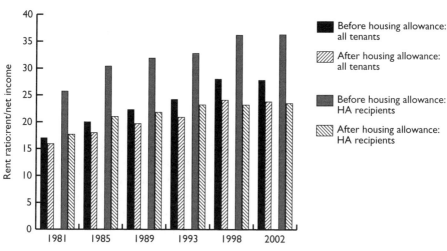

Source: Statistics Netherlands, Housing Demand Survey, 1981–2002.

allowance. Table 9.4 shows that the rents have risen sharply in recent decades, particularly after the 'grossing and balancing' operation in the early 1990s. A second explanation is that the rented sector is increasingly used by low-income groups, so that the average income has fallen (see Table 9.4). These developments, which are still ongoing, are putting more and more pressure on the housing allowance budget.

Implementation: from the Housing Ministry to the tax authorities

Traditionally, tenants can apply for housing allowances through two channels: the landlord or the municipality. Most of the tenants in the commercial rental sector preferred to apply via the municipality as they wished to protect their privacy from their landlords. In the social rental sector, the majority of tenants applied via the landlord, who then received the allowance direct. This formula is referred to as 'rent moderation'. Until 2004, landlords received payment from the Housing Ministry in return for the role they played in housing allowance applications.

It has recently been decided to transfer the implementation of the housing allowance scheme from the Housing Ministry to the tax authorities. Under the 2005 Act for the Adjustment of the General Act on Income-Related Schemes (AWIR) this took place from 1 September 2005 (VNG, 2005). This changeover is tied in with a transformation from old-style tax authorities (which only collected tax) to new-style tax authorities, which will also pay out the allowances for rent, care and child benefit. The aim of the transformation is to improve administrative efficiency and especially to gain better, more direct control of the information provided by applicants. When the AWIR came into effect, the term 'housing allowance' was replaced by 'rent supplement'. The state secretary for finance is now primarily accountable for the management of the rent supplement and the maintenance of law – and hence also for the policy to combat fraud and abuse and reports in the management report of the tax authorities.

As politicians have interpreted these changes largely as technical adjustments, there has not been much controversy or debate. The politically controversial aspects of the transfer of Housing Ministry tasks to the tax authorities have been overshadowed by the cuts in housing allowance that were introduced in 2004. Even though the housing allowance will be implemented by the tax authorities, the Housing Ministry remains responsible for the development of the housing allowance policy. The AWIR has meanwhile been approved by parliament and provides for the harmonisation of the housing allowance, the health care allowance and child benefit. The scheme is designed to create more transparency and a more effective reduction of the poverty trap. At first sight, it appears to be a merely technical operation, that is, the transfer of the implementation of the scheme. A closer look, however, reveals that the move also involves some genuine changes. One important change is that the safety–net system has been abolished. The underlying function of the safety net has thus implicitly been shifted to the municipal authorities, who are responsible for income benefit schemes and for people who need special support after a drop in income.

In the Housing Ministry's budget of €3.4 billion for 2006, €1.9 billion is earmarked for rent supplements. This is roughly 56% of the ministry's total budget, making it by far the largest item of expenditure (Ministerie van VROM, 2005). The coalition agreement of the second Balkenende government (2004) stipulates that spending on the 'housing allowance' item must be reduced by €250 million per year (indexed). Landlords, particularly the housing associations, are to make a contribution towards the affordability of housing. The aforementioned amounts will return to the Housing Ministry's budget as income. As part of the gradual liberalisation of the rent policy (referred to as the 'modernisation of rent policy') the housing minister and the umbrella landlord organisations have agreed that the landlords will also pay part of the extra housing allowance expenditures that result from the higher rent increases (Boerefijn, 2003; Priemus, 2004a, 2004b). This measure took effect in 2006 (Ministerie van VROM, 2005, p 20) but it is not yet clear whether this is only a temporary contribution.

We can thus conclude that, despite interim adjustments, housing allowances have increased relatively strongly, both in absolute and in relative terms. More than half of the Housing Ministry's budget is now taken up by housing allowances. The problem of funding the extra housing allowance expenditures appears to have been shifted from the Housing Ministry to the landlords, particularly the housing associations. Whether this is a sustainable solution is open to question. We will return to this in the following sections.

Dilemmas in designing the housing allowance scheme

Since 1995, housing allowances have almost entirely replaced bricks-and-mortar subsidies. Since that year, housing allowances have constituted a rapidly increasing part of the Housing Ministry's budget; in 2006 it consumed a share of 56% (Ministerie van VROM, 2005). So after 1995 the Housing Ministry's budget has been greatly depleted and has become highly sensitive to expenditures on housing allowances that, due to their open-ended nature, are difficult to control. From time to time, the Ministry of Finance levels sharp criticism at the housing allowance scheme, precisely because the expenditures are so hard to control.

If rents increase above inflation (due to adjustments of the rent to the present-day quality, due to renovation, due to a move to a more expensive rented home, or due to the replacement of older by new rented homes) and if household incomes fall (for example, because the head of a household or partner loses their job, or because of benefit cuts), then – under the current housing allowance scheme – the housing allowances will increase without the Housing Minister being able to do anything about it. The only remedy is to scale down the scheme, which would be an unpopular measure, particularly in times when the economy is struggling. Thus, precisely when the housing allowance should prove its value for low-income groups, the scheme fails to operate optimally.

The responsibility for keeping the expenditures controllable

When the 1997 Housing Allowance Act was introduced, an attempt was made to give the local parties greater responsibility for implementing the Act. Landlords and municipalities were given a share of the responsibility for controlling the housing allowance expenditures. Housing associations were expected to pursue a rental and investment policy that would keep the housing allowances paid to their tenants below a certain ceiling. If they failed to do so, they would incur a penalty in the form of a financial contribution to the ministry. However, when in 2001 the first financial contributions were imposed on the associations that had exceeded the ceiling, the associations took the matter to court. The Supreme Court ruled in 2002 that there was no legal basis for imposing a penalty as the ministry had failed to define what type of behaviour would be liable to a penalty (Rechtbank Rotterdam, 2002). This provisionally brought the shared responsibility for social landlords to an end.

The introduction of the new Act in 1997 also made local authorities co-responsible for controlling housing allowance expenditures. In granting housing permits, local authorities must ensure that not more than 4% of housing allowance recipients are housed in a rented home with a rent above the capping limit (see Figure 9.1). This scheme is currently proving workable so that local authorities share responsibility for controlling housing allowances through their housing allocation policy.

As noted earlier, housing allowances were originally introduced to promote a shift towards more market-based rents without hitting the lowest-paid groups. In March 2005 the minister sent a rent policy letter to parliament, which stated that the relaxation of the rent policy would be accompanied by the allocation of a share of the responsibility for controlling housing allowance expenditures to the housing associations. The letter proposed giving all landlords the opportunity to liberalise 25% of their rental housing stock in phases: in the short term there would be room for extra rent increases and in the long term rents would be completely liberalised, provided that certain criteria were met. In exchange, the housing associations would pay part of the housing allowance (€250 million in 2004, indexed thereafter) and would charge a reduced rent to housing allowance recipients. Commercial landlords would also get more freedom in the rented market, but their willingness to pay a share of the housing allowance was low to non-existent; it would take a legal regulation to force them to cooperate.

Thus there would appear to be an unholy alliance: the Housing Ministry rids itself of a large budgetary problem, the ministry hardly needs to make any further cuts on items other than the housing allowance, and the landlords have more freedom. What the effects of this new policy would have been was unclear, but the expectation is that tenants would have been the big losers. Rents would have increased and tenants without a housing allowance would receive no compensation for these increases. The recipients of housing allowances would be more dependent on the rent policy of the landlord and would also have less freedom of choice. Finally, perverse incentives would once again be introduced into the system: landlords would have an interest in minimising the number of housing allowance recipients among their tenants and hence the residential mobility for housing allowance recipients would be impeded.

However, in February 2007 the new coalition government abandoned the rent liberalisation policy. Instead, rents were to increase in line with inflation. This new political move illustrates the lack of continuity in Dutch housing policy.

Table 9.5 shows that the Dutch housing associations are in excellent financial health and are actually getting richer by the year. Hence housing associations will have no problems paying part of the extra housing allowance; certainly not if, in exchange, they are permitted to charge substantial rent increases. However, wealth in the social rental sector is not equally distributed and for the less well-off housing associations this contribution to the cost of housing allowances can be a financial burden.

Poverty trap and efficiency

Various evaluation studies of the housing allowance scheme have been carried out. These studies (SCP, 1981; Van Fulpen, 1985) repeatedly found that housing allowances are the most efficient type of subsidy. The housing allowance is efficient because it is income independent and consequently only reaches those who need it. However, as in Great Britain (Priemus and Kemp, 2004), the housing allowance

Table 9.5: Assets of housing associations, Netherlands, 1995–2003 (€ millions)

	1995	1996	1997	1998	1999	2000	2001	2002	2003
Number of dwellings ('000s)	2,432	2,442	2,410	2,434	2,437	2,439	2,440	2,432	2,421
Equity excluding revaluation reserve	6,428	6,642	6,715	7,219	8,080	8,743			
Revaluation reserve	226	287	494	644	570	603	713	740	783
Equalisation account	3,717	3,319	2,793	2,304	1,839	1,429			
Provisions	4,215	4,191	4,208	4,258	4,201	4,132			
Less: intangible fixed assets	515	471	395	320	136	90			
Capital and reserves book value	13,844	13,681	13,320	13,461	13,984	14,214	14,451	15,052	15,782
Capital and reserves based on book value per dwelling[a]	5,693	5,603	5,527	5,530	5,738	5,828	5,923	6,189	6,519
Going concern value					79,830	79,909	80,855	83,925	86,656
Book value					65,352	65,960	66,021	67,246	68,223
Profitability value correction					2,290	1,367	–390	–1,321	–2,657
Capital and reserves company based on going concern value					26,742	27,399	29,675	33,052	36,872
Capital and reserves based on going concern value per dwelling[a]					10,973	11,234	12,162	13,590	15,230

Sources: Annual Housing Association Financial Supervision Reports, 1995–2003; CFV (Central Fund for Social Housing); Ministerie van VROM (www.cfv.nl).

Comment: The data for 1995 and 1996 include the municipal housing companies. At year-end 1996 this concerned about 18,000 dwellings.

a Not in € millions.

in the Netherlands greatly aggravates the poverty trap (that is, when household income increases, the positive net effect is largely neutralised by a reduction in the housing allowance). The reduction of the poverty trap remains a high priority for the Housing Ministry.

Due to the poverty trap, to which the housing allowance makes a strong contribution (Allers, 2002), the head of the household and/or the partner lack a financial incentive to seek additional income. In other words, there is a danger that housing allowances may encourage beneficiaries to be lazy both in the housing market and in the labour market. Numerous calculations show that there is a serious poverty trap in the Netherlands (Van Steen, 2004) but whether this discourages households from working (more) is open to question. The results of empirical research are contradictory. In the social rental sector in Britain (Ford et al, 1996) and Australia (Hulse and Randolph, 2005) about a quarter of tenants calculate whether working (more) is beneficial to them; others decide to accept work without hesitation. In the private rental sector in Australia, the housing allowance plays no role in labour market decisions. And, finally, Nordvik and Åhrén (2005) show that, after a short period, housing allowance recipients in Norway generally no longer need to claim housing allowance. Similar empirical research has not yet been carried out in the Netherlands. The poverty trap is not relevant to over 40% of the housing allowance recipients as these people are over 65.

Moral hazard and fraud

In general, housing allowance schemes are expected to have a price-raising effect. After all, the demand for housing is steadily increasing while the supply on the housing market is typically slow to respond, which means there is a big chance of rising rental prices. This is evident from studies in, for example, France and the US (Susin, 2002; Laferèrre and le Blanc, 2004). A deliberate deal may also be made where the landlord raises the rent so that the tenant receives more housing allowance on the understanding that the two parties will then share the resulting 'profit' (Kemp, 2000). Rent regulation is an instrument that can limit these effects, so the existence of rent regulation in the Netherlands may explain why this subject has never been explicitly studied in that country.

In addition, the housing allowance scheme is sensitive to fraud by tenants. Recent research has found that around 10% of housing allowance recipients enjoyed income that had not been declared to the tax department (see Table 9.6). Another finding showed that 5% of the housing allowance recipients conceal part of their assets from the tax authorities (Van Gils et al, 2004). All in all, these practices cost a substantial amount of money, which has prompted the minister to pursue a policy aimed at the active detection of housing allowance fraud. According to Priemus (2004a, 2004b) the increasing incidence of fraud among housing allowance recipients is partly attributable to the introduction of automatic renewal applications, which have made it all too easy to claim and to receive housing allowance.

Table 9.6: Estimated scale of violation of housing allowance rules, Netherlands, 2004 (n = 1,238)

	%	Number
Rules relating to the housing situation:		
Do more people actually live at this address than are registered with the municipality?	3.6	30,448
Do you let out rooms in your home without informing the municipality and the Housing Ministry?	1.4	11,841
Rule relating to statement of income:		
Have you or any other members of your household failed to declare income to the tax authorities in the past two years?	10.2	86,270
Rule relating to the statement of assets:		
Do you or any other members of your household have assets that are not known to the tax authorities?	6.1	51,593
Do you possess any assets abroad, such as a second home or a savings or investment account, that are not visible to the tax authorities?	5.2	43,981
When the means-testing date is approaching, do you withdraw money from your savings or investment accounts to remain below the upper means-testing limit?	2.4	20,299
Social circle:		
Do you know anyone who in your opinion receives housing allowance without being entitled to it?	12.6	106,569

Source: Van Gils et al (2004).

Note: It is not possible to add up the percentages of the various violations to obtain a single all-encompassing measure for the scale of violation.

Accessibility and over-consumption

Housing allowances not only produce a negative incentive on the labour market, but also on the housing market. Towards the end of the 1990s, this sparked a debate about over-consumption in Britain (Kemp, 2000; Priemus and Kemp, 2004). In the Netherlands, the amount of housing allowance depends on the size of the rent, as described above. This gives tenants who receive housing allowance an incentive to move to a more expensive home. This effect, incidentally, is actually an explicit aim of the housing policy. The intention was to keep housing affordable, even in areas with higher rents such as growth centres and new-build developments in urban renewal areas, as described in the 1997 Rent Subsidy Act. The aspiration to achieve higher housing consumption was an explicit part of the Dutch housing policy (Ministerie van VROM, 2001). A cautious attempt was made by state secretary Remkes (1998–2002) to make the amount of housing allowance dependent on the rent levels in the region (and therefore not on the actual rent of the occupied dwelling) in line with the US model of housing vouchers (see Chapter Five). But this met with an early political death in the Netherlands (SEV, 1999; Conijn and Elsinga, 2000; Van der Bos, 2003; Priemus et al, 2006).

Despite the many discussions and spending cuts, the housing allowance scheme can count on broad support from both the left and right of the political spectrum and has never been seriously called into question. Though over-consumption is not inconceivable in the Netherlands, it has not yet become a political issue and has so far not been researched.

Future challenges

This section presents a number of future challenges for income-related housing support in the Netherlands.

Housing policy, social policy or income policy?

The housing allowance scheme is an important instrument in the Netherlands for guaranteeing that people with the lowest incomes can afford a home of sufficient quality. Apart from securing affordability, the successive housing allowance schemes have also played an important role in the policy to improve housing quality and thus to increase housing consumption. The most recent Housing Allowances Act is a good example of this ambition. It is, however, questionable whether such a quality incentive is compatible with the relations in the housing market and even whether it is necessary given the quality of the Dutch housing stock. Now that the quality of the housing stock is reasonably assured by the quality policy, it would seem logical to strengthen the direct benefit principle in the housing allowance scheme and, consequently, make the tenant pay more for higher quality. This implies a scheme where the amount of housing allowance depends principally on the income and less on the size of the rent. Such a system also puts a brake on over-consumption and makes the housing allowance expenditures easier to control (see the discussion of housing vouchers in Chapter Twelve).

This choice would make housing allowances less an instrument of housing policy and more a form of broad income support (Grigsby and Bourassa, 2003). The fact that the housing allowance is being increasingly concentrated on the lowest incomes suggests that the policy is steadily moving in the direction of income policy in any case. After all, to the recipients, housing allowance is often only one, albeit a substantial, part of the income support they receive. It is important to coordinate the various schemes as closely as possible, both to give these vulnerable groups the best deal and to prevent them falling into the poverty trap. The best way of doing this is to make a single ministry responsible for the various schemes and related policies. In this light, the Netherlands should seriously consider entrusting the housing allowance scheme to the Ministry of Social Affairs, as indeed has already been done in such countries as Britain and Sweden. Oddly enough, this idea has not yet been taken up in the political debate in the Netherlands.

Relationship between rent policy and rent subsidy

The fact that the housing allowance is increasingly becoming an income policy instrument does not make close coordination with the housing policy any less important. The rent policy is particularly vital to keep housing allowances affordable in the future. After all, liberalisation of rents was expected to have great consequences for housing allowance expenditure. Though the shift towards market-based rents could count on broad political support, the housing allowances scheme remains indispensable in a tight housing market like that of the Netherlands. Without rent regulation, housing allowance expenditures would in all probability increase to an undesirably high level while non-housing allowance recipients are likely to be confronted with affordability problems. Rent regulation can go hand in hand with the shift to market-based rents and must be principally aimed at countering scarcity profits, particularly in tight housing markets. In view of the social task of housing associations, it seems acceptable to expect these landlords to pursue an affordability policy. As for commercial landlords, measures aimed at countering scarcity profits in the lower rental segment until structural shortages are eliminated should be sufficient to prevent them from charging excessive rents. As long as a relationship exists between rent policy and housing allowances, a certain degree of rent regulation will remain necessary to achieve better control of housing allowance expenditures. If housing allowances were to be decoupled from the actual rent and linked to the average rent levels per region, there would be more freedom in the rent policy to be pursued.

Central versus local responsibility for the housing allowance

In the foregoing we have described how efforts are being undertaken to place part of the responsibility for the housing allowances with housing associations and municipalities. In 2005 this led to an agreement where associations have undertaken to make a contribution towards the housing allowance and also moderate the rents for housing allowance recipients. Municipalities also carry responsibility for the allocation of social housing. In addition, a tendency can be discerned towards decentralisation of income support like social security, in combination with an increasing financial responsibility for local authorities. Combining this with the broadly supported political wish to counter the segregation of low-income groups, we can come to no other conclusion than that it is undesirable to place a growing degree of responsibility for housing allowances with local parties. Such a decentralisation gives municipalities and associations an incentive to avoid allocating housing to housing allowance recipients. The degree to which housing allowance recipients are welcome will then depend strongly on the political colour of the local council and the social profile of the directors of the housing associations. These undesirable relationships form yet another argument for decoupling the size of the housing allowance from the amount of rent paid for the dwelling in question and to direct the housing allowance to those households at risk of having to pay very high housing costs. For equity reasons, this support should be made available to both tenants and owner-occupiers with a low income.

Transparency of the scheme

The housing allowance scheme has been developed over many years; new objectives were added over time and differences between households were taken into account as far as possible. This has led to a rather complex scheme as described previously. It is not immediately evident to tenants what amount of housing allowance they can expect to receive for a certain type of house. The complexity was made even greater by the fact that many tenants received their allowance through the landlord. With such a system, tenants may have no idea of the full rent of their house, let alone know what the financial consequences are of moving to a different home.

More transparency is necessary, in our opinion, as more clarity for the tenant can have positive effects on various fronts. More simplicity and transparency can be expected to reduce the non-take-up rate. The complicated and tedious paperwork is one of the reasons why eligible households fail to apply for a housing allowance. Simplification could also help to fight fraud. Greater simplicity could also help to prevent errors being made in the calculation of allowance entitlement. Finally, more transparency and simplicity would ensure that people would look more closely at the (net) rent-to-quality ratio when choosing a home. The decoupling of housing allowance entitlement from the amount of rent is one way of simplifying the system.

Conclusion

Housing allowances in the Netherlands have evolved from a temporary bridging measure in the 1970s to a core instrument of the housing policy today. Due to the dismantlement of bricks-and-mortar subsidies, housing allowances became the central pillar in the government policy aimed at fulfilling the constitutional duty to provide affordable housing. In the Netherlands, the housing allowance scheme is not only an instrument for assuring affordable housing, but also an instrument for increasing housing quality and stimulating the consumption of housing. In the process of designing this instrument and the various reviews over time, the Netherlands has encountered several dilemmas that are inherent in such a scheme and which call for further political choices.

The first dilemma is that of the constitutional duty to provide housing, which basically calls for an open-ended scheme and that of the controllability of government expenditures. This dilemma becomes painfully visible in times of recession, precisely when tenants most need their housing allowance while the government is simultaneously under pressure to control its expenditures.

A second dilemma is that of the efficiency of the scheme versus the disincentives on the housing market and the labour market (moral hazard). The better the scheme is geared to the incomes of the beneficiaries, the more efficient it will be. This, however, goes hand in hand with the incentive not to earn more and/or the incentive to look for cheaper housing.

A third dilemma is that of the accessibility of housing (of higher quality) versus the risk of over-consumption of housing services. By making the housing allowance dependent on the rent, the housing market is made more accessible. However, such a system also invites over-consumption as tenants hardly feel it in their wallet or purse when they move to a more expensive house.

A fourth dilemma is that of central versus local responsibility. A centralised scheme carries the risk that local parties will exploit the scheme as this has no negative financial consequences for themselves. Local responsibility, however, gives an incentive to control costs and thus gives rise to a reluctance to pay out the allowance and, hence, to exclude households who are entitled to such an allowance.

These dilemmas call for political choices that must be made with an eye for the context and which will therefore differ from one country to the next. Looking at the Netherlands, we have identified the following choices that need to be made to adapt the Dutch housing allowance scheme to the needs of the future:

- **Less rent dependent:** quality is at a basic level, strengthen profit principle, control state expenditures. The amount of housing allowance can be linked to the general rent level in the region.
- **Centralised control:** prevent exclusion of housing allowance recipients, countering segregation and promoting social inclusion deserve a high priority. This implies that local councils and associations must not have a financial stake in the (implementation of) the housing allowance scheme.
- **Shift of policy responsibility from Ministry of Housing to the Ministry of Social Affairs:** primarily aimed at income support and limitation of the poverty trap.
- **Simplicity throughout:** understandable for the tenant, simple and faster administration and reduction of fraud.

Acknowledgements

The authors thank Gust Mariën (OTB) for providing the statistical data for Tables 9.3 and 9.4, and Arjen Wolters for providing Table 9.5.

References

Allers, M.A. (2002) 'Aanpak armoedeval: wie durft?' ('Tackling the poverty trap: who dares?'), *ESB*, 17 May, pp 388–9.

Boelhouwer, P. and Haffner, M. (2002) *Subjectsubsidiëring in de huursector onder de loep (Personal subsidy schemes in the rented sector under the microscope)*, The Hague/Utrecht: DGW/Nethur Partnership.

Boerefijn, P. (2003) 'Meer keuze door eerlijke huurprijzen' ('More choice through honest rental pricing'), *Tijdschrift voor de Volkshuisvesting*, vol 9, no 5, pp 11–14.

Commissie-Alozerij (1964) 'Rapport inzake invoering van een individuele huurbepaling' ('Report on the introduction of an individual rent provision'), *Stedebouw en Volkshuisvesting*, vol 41, pp 267–79.

Conijn, J.B.S. and Elsinga, M.G. (2000) *Een verkenning van de toepassingsmogelijkheden van woonvouchers in Nederland (An exploration of the applications of housing vouchers in the Netherlands)*, Delft: OTB.

de Haan, G. (1969) 'Stenen voor brood. Enkele kanttekeningen en vragen bij een stelsel van subjectieve huursubsidies' ('Stones for bread. A few comments and questions on a system of personal housing allowances'), *Stedebouw en Volkshuisvesting*, vol 46, pp 378–88.

Elsinga, M. (2005) 'Politique de la location et subside locatif aux Pays-Bas', in N. Bernard and W. van Mieghem (eds) *La crise du logement a Bruxelles: Probleme d'acces et/ou de penurie*, Brussels: Etablissements Emile Bruylant, S.A.

Elsinga, M., Haffner, M. and van der Heijden, H. (2005) 'A unitary rental sector in the Netherlands? Theoretical exploration and empirical evidence', paper presented at the ENHR conference Housing in Europe: New Challenges & Innovation as in Tomorrow's Cities, Reykjavik.

Ford, J., Kempson, E. and England, J. (1996) *Into Work? The impact of housing costs and the benefit system on people's decisions to work*, York: Joseph Rowntree Foundation.

Grisgby, W.G. and Bourassa, S.C. (2003) 'Trying to understand low-income housing subsidies: Lessons from the United States', *Urban Studies*, vol 40, no 5/6, pp 973–92.

Hulse, K. and Randolph, R. (2005) 'Workforce disincentive effects of housing allowances and public housing for low income households in Australia', *European Journal of Housing Policy*, vol 5, no 2, pp 147–66.

Kemp, P.A. (2000) *'Shopping incentives' and housing benefit reform*, Coventry: Chartered Institute of Housing and Joseph Rowntree Foundation.

Laferrère A. and le Blanc, D. (2004) 'How do housing allowances affect rents? An empirical analysis of the French case', *Journal of Housing Economics*, vol 13, pp 36–67.

Lucassen, C.T.J. and Priemus, H. (1977) *Individuele huursubsidie, evaluatie van een instrument van volkshuisvestingsbeleid (Housing allowances. Evaluation of a social housing policy instrument)*, The Hague: Staatsuitgeverij.

Ministerie van VROM (2000) *Brief VROM-rapportage niet-gebruik huursubsidie (Letter on Housing Ministry's report on the non-take-up of housing allowances)*, The Hague: Ministerie van VROM.

Ministerie van VROM (2001) *Mensen, wensen, wonen. Wonen in de 21ᵉ eeuw (What people want, where people live. Housing in the 21st century)*, The Hague: Ministerie van VROM.

Ministerie van VROM (2004) *Wegwijzer huursubsidie (Housing allowance guide)*, The Hague: Ministerie van VROM.

Ministerie van VROM (2006) *Begroting 2006 (Budget 2006)*, The Hague: Sdu Uitgevers.

NIBUD (National Institute for Budget Information) (2004) *Budget handboek: Gegevens omtrent inkomen, uitgaven en bestedingspatronen van particuliere huishoudens (Budget guidebook: Data on income, expenses and patterns of spending of individual households)*, Utrecht: NIBUD.

Nordvik, V. and Åhrén, P. (2005) 'Analysing efficiency and effects of housing allowance systems – The Norwegian case', *European Journal of Housing Policy*, vol 5, no 2, pp 131–46.

Priemus, H. (1984) *Housing allowances in the Netherlands. Product of a conservative or progressive ideology?*, Delft: Delft University Press.

Priemus, H. (1986) 'Housing allowances in the Netherlands', in P.A. Kemp (ed) *The future of housing benefits*, Glasgow: Centre for Housing Research, University of Glasgow.

Priemus, H. (1995) 'How to abolish social housing? The Dutch case', *International Journal of Urban and Regional Research*, vol 19, pp 145–55.

Priemus, H. (1998) 'Improving or endangering housing policies? Recent changes in the Dutch housing allowance scheme', *International Journal of Urban and Regional Research*, vol 22, no 2, pp 319–30.

Priemus, H. (2004a) 'Dutch housing allowances: social housing at risk', *International Journal of Urban and Regional Research*, vol 28, no 3, pp 706–12.

Priemus, H. (2004b) 'Kwetsbare individuele huursubsidiëring' ('Vulnerable individual housing allowance'), *Rooilijn*, vol 37, no 2, pp 76–80.

Priemus, H. and Kemp, P.A. (2004) 'The present and future of income-related housing support. Debates in Britain and the Netherlands', *Housing Studies*, vol 19, no 4, pp 653–68.

Priemus, H., Kemp, P.A. and Varady, D.P. (2006) 'Housing vouchers in the USA, Great Britain and the Netherlands. Current issues and perspectives for the future', *Housing Policy Debate*, vol 16, no 3/4, pp 575–609.

Rechtbank Rotterdam (2002) LJN: AE0156, WET 00/2672-LUG.

SCP (Sociaal en Cultureel Planbureau) (1981) *Profijt van de overheid in 1977 (Taking advantage of the government in 1977)*, The Hague: Staatsuitgeverij.

SEV (Stuurgroep Experimenten Volkshuisvesting) (1999) *Woonvoucher, een verkenning (Housing voucher, an exploration)*, Rotterdam: SEV.

Susin, S. (2002) 'Rent vouchers and the price of low income housing', *Journal of Public Economics*, vol 83, pp 109–52.

Tweede Kamer (1997) *Nieuwe regels over het verstrekken van huursubsidies (Huursubsidiewet); Memorie van Toelichting vergaderjaar 1996–1997 (New rules on the granting of housing allowances [Housing Allowances Act], explanatory memorandum parliamentary year 1996–7)*, 25090, no 3.

Tweede Kamer (1998) *Niet-gebruik van de individuele huursubsidie, brief van de staatssecretaris van VROM, vergaderjaar 1997–1998 (Non-take-up of individual housing allowances, letter from the housing state secretary)*, 25 831, no 4.

van Gils, G.P., van der Heijden, H. and Laudy, O. (2004) *Beleving en overtreding van regels van de Huursubsidiewet (Perception and violation of Housing Allowances Act)*, The Hague: Ministerie van VROM.

van der Bos, A. (2003) *Housing vouchers, de toekomst van de huursubsidie?* (Housing vouchers, the future of housing allowances), Delft: OTB.

van der Schaar, J. (1987) 'Groei en bloei van het Nederlandse volkshuisvestingsbeleid' ('Growth and flowering of the Dutch housing policy'), PhD thesis, Delft: Delft University Press.

van der Schaar, J. (1994) *IHS in perspectief: de toekomst van de individuele huursubsidie (Housing allowance in perspective: The future of the individual housing allowance)*, Amsterdam: RIGO Research en Advies.

van der Schaar, J., Leidelmeijer, K., Zandstra, A. and van Heuven, J. (1998) *Normhuur(quotes) IHS: varianten en doorrekening (IHS standard rent [ratios]: variants and detailed calculations)*, Amsterdam: RIGO Research en Advies.

van Fulpen, H. (1985) *Volkshuisvesting in demografisch en economisch perspectief (Housing in demographic and economic perspective)*, The Hague: Staatsuitgeverij.

van Steen, G. (2004) 'Huursubsidie en marginale druk. Een vergelijking tussen Nederland, Groot-Brittannië en Duitsland' ('Housing allowance and marginal pressure. A comparison between the Netherlands, Great Britain and Germany'), *Tijdschrift voor de Volkshuisvesting*, vol 10, no 5, pp 36–41.

VNG (Vereniging Nederlandse Gemeenten) (2005) *Invoering AWIR (Introduction of AWIR)*, The Hague: VNG.

TEN

Housing allowance systems in Sweden

Per Åhrén

Introduction

Government support for housing expenditure has a long tradition in Sweden. In 1936 a means-tested housing expenditure support was introduced for families with at least three children. The support was combined with an investment support to the housing where these families lived. Originally, only rented housing was eligible. Housing expenditure support to pensioners was introduced later. In 1946 the government decided to introduce a special means-tested local government housing expenditure supplement, in addition to the existing general housing expenditure supplement, which was an addition to the general pension. The local government housing expenditure supplement was not compulsory for the local governments, but an option. Today there are three housing allowance systems in Sweden: one for households with children, one for young households and one for pensioners.

The importance of housing allowances in Sweden is shown in Table 10.1. As is clear from the table, there was a dramatic decrease in the total expenditure on housing allowances as a percentage of GDP between 1995 and 2004. The number of housing allowance recipients also decreased, from 991,000 to 632,000 during the period from 1995 to 2003, the reasons for which are discussed later in the chapter. Due to changes in other housing subsidy systems, however, expenditure on housing allowances calculated as a percentage of all housing subsidies (excluding subsidies through the tax system) increased over this period, rising from 29% in 1995 to 88% in 2004. The main explanation for the latter is the phasing-out of the guaranteed interest subsidies for investment in and renovation of housing that took place between 1992 and 2000. The guarantee system was expensive for

Table 10.1: Overview of the development of housing allowances, Sweden, 1990–2004

	1990	1995	2000	2002	2003	2004
Expenditure as a % of GDP	0.66	1.11	0.66	0.61	0.58	0.57
Expenditure as a % of housing subsidies	18	29	73	87	89	88
Number of households ('000s)	–	991	685	646	632	–
Percentage of all households	–	28	23	20	20	–

Source: Åhrén (2004) and own calculation.

the state, partly due to the design of the system where the government took the whole interest risk and partly because the system applied to almost all housing production. From 2002, only a tax-compensating interest subsidy is paid to rented and cooperative housing that matches owner-occupiers' tax relief for interest payments.

Table 10.2 shows the percentage of different types of households that received housing allowances in 2002. Lone parents and pensioners are the largest group of recipients with 82% and 23% respectively of the total population getting a housing allowance. The housing allowance scheme for families with children has evolved mainly into a support to lone parents. Only 9% of families with children – which was the main target group historically – received support in 2002. When looking at the composition of housing allowance recipients in 2002 it is clear that families with children are a fairly small group compared to lone parents and pensioners.

Table 10.2: Main types of household receiving housing allowances as a percentage of all households, by type and as a percentage of households receiving housing allowances, Sweden, 2002

	% of all households	% of households receiving allowances
Lone parents	82	22
Singles, non-pensioners	4	7
Families with children	9	10
Pensioners	23	61

Source: Åhrén (2004).

The different systems of housing allowances will be dealt with separately in the following text as they differ with regard to aims and rules. In the first section there is a short summary of the main developments in the respective systems. The second part discusses the present housing allowance in its wider context. The third section discusses the role and design of housing allowances. Next there is a discussion on the impact of housing allowances, followed by a section dealing with policy debates and reform. In the last part conclusions are drawn from the discussion.

The development of housing allowances

The development of housing allowances in Sweden is closely connected with the situation on the housing market, the distribution of income and the existence of poverty. It also depends on housing policy and the balance between different housing policy instruments as well as the development of social security (including pensions) systems. A description of the major developments in the housing allowances systems will follow in order to enhance the understanding of the present systems.

Households with children

The oldest housing allowance system in Sweden is the one for households with children. It was introduced in 1936 as one of the first government economic policies directed towards housing. The aim was partly a social policy for housing, and partly an economic policy to stimulate investment in housing and to decrease unemployment. The allowances were called 'family grants'. Only families with at least three children living in rented apartments were eligible and there was no income ceiling. The need for a grant was based on an individual assessment and depended on the income of the household and their need for accommodation. The grants were combined with financial support to the property where the grant recipients lived. Certain minimum requirements for the apartments in relation to floor space and equipment were set, as well as maximum floor space. In 1938 the family grants were extended to owner occupation.

In 1948 the family grant was exchanged for 'housing allowances for families with children'. Families with at least two children living in housing that was built after the introduction of the new allowances, irrespective of tenure and form of financing, were eligible. It was also stated that, once the supply of housing with an acceptable standard and an acceptable income level among low-income households had been reached, the allowances could become a part of a general allowance for families with children.

In 1969 the family grants were exchanged for 'housing allowances'. The aim was to support households with children in general and to increase the demand for, and facilitate the production of, a sufficient number of dwellings, with an emphasis on larger dwellings than before. The system had now changed. It consisted of three parts: one amount depended on the number of children, an additional amount was dependent on certain conditions of housing standards and the other was dependent on housing expenditure. The total amount payable depended on the household's income and decreased with increase in income.

The general characteristics of this system were kept in place for another 20 years, albeit with some exceptions. The minimum housing standard for the housing allowance was criticised on the grounds that it prevented many households from being eligible because they could not afford to increase their housing standard. As a result, the minimum standard was abolished in 1972. The only remaining condition for eligibility connected to the dwelling was that the dwelling should be independently held by the household.

In 1974, low-income households without children became eligible for housing allowances, but subject to housing expenditure ceilings. They were eligible until 1986, became eligible again in 1991 in connection with the tax reform of 1990–1 and remained eligible until 1997. The reason for discontinuing the allowances to this group was that the cost of administration was too high and that the allowances only covered a small part of their housing expenditure (Prop, 1986/87:93, p 19). Non-resident parents, where the other parent has custody of the children, have continuously been eligible for allowances.

In 1997[1] some major changes were introduced with the aims of substantially reducing expenditure by the government on housing allowances, preventing overuse of the scheme and strengthening the control of payments:

- Preliminary allowances were paid, based on the household's estimate of the income for the following 12 months. The earlier system for payments was based on assessed taxable income using two-year-old income figures. The final allowances are calculated once the assessed taxable income for the year in question is finalised. Differences between preliminary and final allowances are paid out or required to be paid back.
- Separate income limits for adults, which was aiming at encouraging all adults in a household to work.
- Different rules for calculation of the eligible housing expenditure[2] for rented and owner-occupied dwellings. Only the real interest on housing loans is included in eligible housing expenditure.
- Restrictions on eligible floor space for allowances. The expenditure for floor space in excess of limits, depending on the number of children, was no longer included in the calculation of allowances.

The development of government expenditure on housing allowances for non-pensioners is shown in Table 10.3. Here we can see that there was a sharp increase in expenditure on housing allowances from 1990 to 1995. Thereafter there was a marked decline in expenditure and in the number of recipients. Initially, these

Table 10.3: Development of public expenditure for housing allowances to non-pensioners and number of households, Sweden, 1990–2005

Year	Total expenditure SEK billion	Total number of households ('000s)	Households with children ('000s)	Others ('000s)
1990	3,160	–	–	–
1991	5,065	328	285	43
1992	5,928	360	306	61
1993	7,164	441	346	95
1994	8,669	538	406	132
1995	9,220	576	428	148[b]
1996	8,373	471	403	68
1997	6,195	365	309	56
1998	5,749	338	283	55
1999	4,936	304	255	49
2000	4,283	268	227	41
2001	4,069	238	204	34
2002	3,892	224	191	33
2003	3,223	213	179	34
2004	3,614	214	176	37
2005[a]	3,506	–	–	–

Source: Statistics Sweden (2005).

Notes: [a] Estimate; [b] includes 58,100 households age 29+ without children.

decreases were the result of major changes in the system that aimed to reduce expenditure. Thereafter, they were largely due to the fact that, since 1997, the income limits and housing expenditure bands have not been adjusted in line with increases in incomes and housing expenditures (Enqvist, 2003).

In 2004, more than 20% of households with children received housing allowances. At that date, 66% of housing allowance recipients were lone parents, 17% were cohabiting adults with children, and 17% were households (aged 18 to 28) without children. Table 10.4 shows the impact and importance of housing allowances by measuring the housing expenditure-to-income ratio for two household types in the period from 1994 to 2002. As can be seen from the table, housing allowances have a major impact on the expenditure-to-income ratio.

Households without children and without old age pensions

Housing allowances to households without children who were not in receipt of old age pensions were introduced for the first time in 1974. This group has been periodically entitled to housing allowances, but only for modest amounts. This allowance was discontinued in 1997, based on the argument that there were few recipients and the average allowance was small.

Young households aged 18 to 28 years have been entitled to housing allowances continuously since 1988. In that year, a local government housing allowance was introduced by the government (with 50% of the funding coming from the central state) as part of a package to increase the supply of accommodation for young people. One reason for the introduction of allowances for this group was the fact that young households often had problems with affordability because of low and unstable incomes. Another reason was that the increase in households receiving social support was largest in this age group (Prop, 1986/87:93). There were special rules for this group of households, with lower coverage of housing expenditure and lower income limits than those in the system for households with children.

Housing supplement for old age pensioners

In 1946 the government introduced a local government housing allowance. This allowance was an addition to the general old age pension, which included a support for housing expenditure. It was up to the local governments to decide about the rules for the supplement. The local governments financed the supplement themselves. In the beginning, only rented dwellings built after 1945 with certain types of state support were eligible.

In 1952 the rules for the supplement were changed and expenditure was now to be shared between the central and local government. At the same time, the support for housing expenditure included in the old age pension was abolished. In connection with the introduction of a law on a general insurance, including a law on old age pensions, the supplement was changed and a special 'wife

Table 10.4: Housing expenditure to gross income, before and after housing allowances, Sweden, 1994–2002 (all households with allowances)

Household type	1994	1995	1996	1997	1998	1999	2000	2001	2002
Single parent									
Gross expenditure %	47	46	46	44	44	43	42	41	41
Net expenditure %	27	27	27	26	26	26	26	26	26
Difference	20	20	19	18	18	17	16	16	15
Average gross income, SEK	185,388	186,816	184,860	149,460	138,420	131,424	126,252	124,068	120,828
Cohabiting adults									
Gross expenditure %	34	34	35	39	43	45	47	49	50
Net expenditure %	25	25	25	27	29	30	31	32	33
Difference	9	9	10	12	14	15	16	17	18
Average gross income, SEK	185,388	186,816	184,860	149,460	138,420	131,424	126,252	124,068	120,828

Source: Own calculation based on data from National Board of Housing, Building and Planning.

addition' was introduced. In 1962, local authorities were obliged to pay housing supplement to pensioners.

In 1988 state grants to finance the housing supplement partially were introduced, under certain conditions regarding the calculation of the supplement. All tenures were now eligible for the supplement. In 1995 the housing supplement to pensioners replaced the local government housing supplement. In the new system, the rules on the coverage of housing expenditure were to be the same for the whole country. In the earlier system, the coverage was up to the local governments to decide, but this was now considered to be unacceptable.

Table 10.5 gives an overview of the development of total expenditure on the housing supplement for pensioners, and the number of recipients, between 1990 and 2004. From 1995 onwards there was a stabilisation in expenditure and a decrease in the number of recipients. The latter was mainly due to increases in income, above all as a result of the gradual development of a new system for general pensions, so that an increasing number of pensioners had an income above the income limits for the supplement. Table 10.6 shows that the supplement to

Table 10.5: Total expenditure on housing supplement to pensioners, Sweden, 1990–2005

Year	Total expenditure (SEK billion)	Number of households ('000s)
1990	6,164	548
1991	7,702	559
1992	8,137	549
1993	9,750	593
1994	10,929	608
1995	10,440	563
1996	9,923	538
1997	9,544	503
1998	9,591	490
1999	9,970	474
2000	9,641	458
2001	10,420	456
2002	10,514	455
2003	10,979	447
2004	10,947	
2005[a]	7,522	

Source: Statistics Sweden (2005).

Note: [a] Estimate.

Table 10.6: Housing expenditure for pensioners as a percentage of income before and after housing supplement, Sweden, 2002

	Housing expenditure as a % of income, before supplement	Housing expenditure as a % of income, after supplement
Pensioners	54	41

Source: Calculation by National Social Insurance Board (2004).

pensioners, on average, lowers housing expenditure as a percentage of income by an estimated 13 percentage points, from 54% to 41%.

Housing allowances and supplement in context

Housing finance and other housing policy issues

There are no special housing finance means today that are directed towards households with children. In general, the Swedish parliament has been reluctant to introduce financing and subsidies for purchase of existing dwellings, based on the fear of pushing up prices in the market. However, there has been a long discussion about norms for overcrowding. For households with children in receipt of housing allowances, the goal was set in 1987 to increase the part of the housing allowances that depended on housing expenditure so that families with children would get the opportunity to live in newly produced dwellings where every child could have their own room (Enqvist, 2003). In accordance with this decision, the expenditure ceiling was successively increased until 1996. The norm for overcrowding has not been changed to date (norm three) but there are different opinions about which norm is the ruling one (discussed later).

There are also housing policy instruments that are directed to pensioners. Grants are given to households in general and often to pensioners to adjust the dwelling to their special needs. These grants can be used, for example, to remove barriers to entry for wheelchairs or to ensure that all necessary functions in the dwelling (such as a toilet or washing facilities) can be located on the same floor.

The housing supplement can be considered as a policy instrument to enable pensioners to remain in their dwellings, which is a main policy aim for this group. There are two reasons for this. First, most pensioners want to remain in their own home as long as possible. Second, in many cases this is also less expensive for society, when the alternative would be to move households to some form of institution that provides residential or nursing care, which usually is very costly.

Social insurance and pension systems

All households are entitled to social assistance benefits payments under certain conditions. Social assistance may cover housing expenditure and then comes on top of housing allowances. This assistance is means tested.

Financial support for families with children consists of different types of support, one of which is general and the rest depend on the family situation. The general support is comprised of the child allowance, which is paid to all children under the age of 17 living in Sweden. A child supplement is given to families with more than two children. In addition, financial assistance is paid to children living with a lone parent and whose non-resident parent cannot fulfil the obligation to pay for child support.

None of the supports, except for housing allowances, is explicitly connected to housing and housing expenditure. However, the National Board of Housing,

Building and Planning has analysed the connection between general social insurance and housing allowances. Based on the assumption that households eligible for social assistance are also entitled to housing allowances, they find that 40% of lone parents and 80% of cohabiting parents receiving housing allowances also received social insurance payments in 2002.

Retirement pensions consist of the income/supplementary pension, the premium pension and the guarantee pension. The guarantee pension was introduced in 2003. Its aim is to guarantee all persons over the age of 64 living in Sweden a reasonable living standard through social insurance. For example, it aims to help people who have not received enough protection through the pension system because they have not lived long enough in Sweden to be entitled to an adequate pension. Previously, such people had to depend on social assistance. Around 13,000 people were receiving support in 2003, approximately half of whom received old age pension or housing supplement. In December 2004 around 11,000 people were receiving this pension, about one third of whom were born in Sweden.

The role and design of housing allowance systems

Households with children

Over the years, housing allowances for households with children have had the aims of increasing their housing standard, decreasing overcrowding, evening out expenditure differences between regions and between newer and older dwellings with equal standards, and in general strengthening the ability of financially weak households to sustain their accommodation. The goal for this system has developed between two paths: support to housing and general consumption support (SOU, 2001:24, p 132).

The following goals have been set for today's housing allowances for households with children; "to give low-income households the possibility of having access to good accommodation with enough space. The allowances is part of the policy area 'Economic policy for families' which primarily aims at giving economic security to families with children during the period of high burden of dependency" (SOU, 2001:24, p 131).

For households with children, housing allowance entitlement depends on:

- number of persons in the household: married or cohabiting couples and children under the age of 18;
- income of the household: the household's income from employment and self-employment, income from capital and some other income;[3]
- housing expenditure:
    - rented apartments: rent including heating as well as the fees that are included in the rent;
    - cooperative housing: yearly fee to the cooperative including heating and other fees plus part of the interest expenditure on loans where the apartment is used as collateral;

  – owner occupation: property tax, 70% of leasehold fee, heating and other
    running expenses calculated according to a special formula, 70% of real
    interest on housing loans;[4]
* floor space: eligible floor space depends on number of children.[5] However, there
  is a guarantee level of housing expenditure for the calculation of allowances,
  where the guarantee level is limited to the actual expenditure;[6] and
* Calculation of income:
  – estimated taxable income for the calendar year;
  – net income from capital;
  – income from abroad;
  – 80% of student grants; and
  – 15% of net economic wealth in excess of SEK100,000 is added to the income.
    Assessed value of the household's dwelling as well as the loans for it does not
    affect the income addition.

Other conditions for eligibility are that the claimant must have lived in Sweden
for at least one year and have their own, independent accommodation – that is,
be an owner-occupier or tenant – and be registered in that accommodation.

The housing allowance (HA) consists of two parts, one of which is a support
for housing expenditure and the other is a special support for children living at
home. The allowance is calculated as follows, using the example of households
with one child:[7]

$$HA = ((0.75 \times (SEK24,000 < \text{housing expenditure} \leq SEK36,000))$$
$$+ ((0.5 \times (SEK36,001 < \text{housing expenditure} < SEK63,600))$$
$$+ \text{child allowance} (= 1 \times SEK7,200) - 0.2 \times ((\text{income} - SEK117,000)$$
$$\text{for lone parent or } 0.2 \times (\text{income} - SEK58,500 \text{ per parent for parents}))$$

The above shows that, for a household with one child, no housing allowance
is given for low housing expenditure, defined as less than SEK24,000. Housing
expenditure up to SEK36,000 is covered at 75% in the HA; and housing
expenditure in excess of SEK36,000 up to an expenditure ceiling of SEK63,600
is covered at 50%. Income over a certain amount reduces the allowances. Finally,
there is an allowance per child. This system of calculation results in maximum
allowances and incomes that different household types may have in order to
receive housing allowances, which are shown in Table 10.7.

Housing allowances are paid to the claimant. The rationale for this is that the
claimants should know the gross amount of their housing expenditure as well as
the amount of support they get from the state. However, in special circumstances,
the allowance may be paid to a third party, such as the social assistance authority.
Allowance entitlement of less than SEK1,200 per year is not paid out. The law on
housing allowances includes a general paragraph that states that an application for
housing allowances can be rejected or the amount decreased if it is evident that
the applicant is not in need of assistance. This may be because of the household's

Table 10.7: Maximum housing allowances and income by household type, Sweden, 2005

Household type	Maximum allowance (SEK)	Maximum income per year (SEK)
Lone parent, one child	30,000	261,000
Lone parent, two children	36,600	301,500
Cohabiting parents, both low income, one child	30,000	261,000
Cohabiting parents, both low income, two children	36,600	301,500
Cohabiting parents, one low income, one child	30,000	202,500
Cohabiting parents, one low income, two children	36,600	243,000

Source: Swedish Social Insurance Administration (2005).

economic wealth or because the household has a very high standard of living despite having a low taxable income.

A summary of the outcome of the housing allowance rules is shown in Table 10.8 for the year 2004. It indicates that there is a low average income among households in receipt of housing allowances. The allowances decrease the expenditure on housing, measured as a percentage of gross income, from 42% to 28%. For parents living with their children, there is a reduction from 53% to 34%.

Table 10.9 shows that the great majority of households in receipt of housing allowances lived in rented housing in 2004. One explanation could be that

Table 10.8: Housing allowances for households including children, Sweden, 2004

	Yearly average (SEK)	
	Lone parents	Cohabiting parents
Number of households	121,251	33,991
Income	141,057	118,810
Housing expenditure	59,844	63,108
Housing allowance	20,664	22,200
Net housing expenditure	39,180	40,908

Source: Swedish Social Insurance Administration (2005).

Table 10.9: Housing allowance recipients with children, by tenure, Sweden, 2004

	Tenure (%)			
Household type	Rented	Cooperative	Owner-occupied	Other
Lone parent	86	9	4	1
Cohabiting adults	91	5	3	1

Source: Swedish Social Insurance Administration (2005).

the average income of households in rented housing is lower than those in owner-occupied and cooperative housing. Another fact that contributes to the concentration of recipients in rented housing is that low-income households in need of accommodation are often located by the local social authorities in the non-profit rented sector, which is controlled by the local government.

Young households

Young households containing someone aged between 18 and 28 years, including students, are eligible for housing allowances in order to enable them to occupy decent quality dwellings. The allowances are primarily a protection against high housing expenditure as a proportion of income. For this group, the same rules apply for the calculation of income and housing expenditure as for households with children, but the allowances are lower. The allowance is calculated as follows:

$$HA = 0.75 \times (SEK21,600 < \text{housing expenditure} > SEK31,201)$$
$$+ 0.5 \times (SEK31,200 < \text{expenditure} > SEK43,200)$$
$$- 1/3 \times (\text{income} - SEK41,000 \text{ for single person or income} -$$
$$SEK58,000 \text{ for couples})$$

Table 10.10 gives some statistics for young households in receipt of housing allowances. It shows that few households receive this housing allowance, their taxable income is very low, and the allowance covers 22% of their housing expenses on average.

Table 10.10: Young households with housing allowances, Sweden, 2004

Number of households	37,958
Average yearly income, SEK	29,104
Average yearly housing expenditure, SEK	38,892
Average yearly housing allowance, SEK	8,604

Source: Swedish Social Insurance Administration (2005).

Pensioners

There are two types of housing allowance for pensioners. The main one is the housing supplement. There is also a system of allowances known as the special housing supplement. The aim of the housing supplement is to give pensioners the possibility of obtaining and keeping a decent standard, or newly completed, dwelling. The general housing supplement for pensioners is dependent on income and housing expenditure as well as certain other benefits. People that are eligible for the supplement are those with:

• full retirement pension;

- sickness compensation or activity compensation;
- widow's pension;
- special survivor's pension;
- wife supplement;
- pension or disability benefit from another EEA country.

In order to be eligible for the supplement, pensioners must be occupying a permanent dwelling located in Sweden. All types of dwellings and tenures are eligible, even nursing homes, old people's homes, service flats, accommodation in camping lodges, and accommodation occupied by lodgers.

Housing expenditure that is eligible for the general pensioner housing supplement is as follows:

- rented housing: rent including heating charges;
- tenant-owned apartments and cooperative housing: annual charges including heating and 70% of the interest expenses on loans for purchase and repair if the tenant-owned apartment was provided as collateral for the loan;
- owner occupation:
  - 70% of the interest expenses on property loan after any interest subsidy has been deducted;
  - 70% of the site leasehold charge;
  - property tax;
  - heating (according to standard); and
  - other running costs (according to standard) such as water, sewerage and refuse collection.

Eligible income is calculated in accordance with tax law rules. Income from employment, business activity and capital are considered as eligible income. Certain tax-free incomes may also be included in the calculation of the income on which the allowance is based. When calculating income, a supplement is made for the assets owned by a spouse. In the case of married couples, their incomes are added together. One component of the income is included at the whole amount, for year 1 (Y1), while other sources of income are only included at 80% for year 2 (Y2) (weighting). The whole amount is taken up for:

- income-based retirement pension, premium pension;
- guarantee pension and survivor's pension;
- sickness compensation and activity compensation;
- foreign pension or invalidity benefit;
- income from capital; and
- asset supplement.

The asset supplement is based on the valuation of assets according to the State Income Tax Act and includes real estate with the exception of the claimant's permanent home, bank deposits and cash in excess of SEK25,000. The supplement is calculated as 15% of total assets exceeding SEK100,000 for single persons and SEK200,000 for spouses. Other income, for instance, occupational pensions is weighted and taken up at only 80%. An exempt amount is thereafter to be deduced from the income. For persons with any form of pension, the exempt amount is equivalent to 2.17 price base amounts[8] for unmarried persons and 1.935 price base amounts for married persons. The amount that remains after deduction of the exempt amount is the household's 'reduction income', which affects the calculation of the housing supplement. The supplement is usually granted for a period of 12 months. It is calculated as follows:

$$\text{Housing supplement} = 0.91 \times (\text{housing expenditure below the expenditure ceiling})^9 - (0.62 \times Y1 + 0.5 \times Y2)$$

The special housing supplement is paid out as an addition to the household's income if, after paying for housing, its income is lower than is deemed to be reasonable. The reasonable income level is calculated as 1.294 times the price base amount for a single and 1.084 for a married person. The maximum housing expenditure for this supplement is SEK70,440 per year.

The impact of housing allowances

There are no extensive studies of the effect of housing allowances on the housing consumption of households in Sweden. However, an analysis conducted for the inquiry into families' economic situation concluded that the Swedish system of housing allowances appears to increase the demand for housing (Enström and Turner, 2001, p 412). The analyses on which housing allowance reforms have been based have focused on the formal, static effects of changed rules on changes in net housing expenditure for different household types and tenures, in addition to the effects on government spending.

The major changes in the housing allowances systems, such as the 1997 reform, disregarded the consequences for housing consumption. The most obvious problem, for example with introducing a limitation on eligible floor space in order to cut subsidies, is precisely the consequences for household housing consumption. In theory, households will respond by adjusting their housing consumption to a lower level if they live in a dwelling with large 'excess' space, for which the housing allowance was cut. An adjustment in housing space consumption presupposes that the household has the option to decrease it by moving to a smaller dwelling. The Swedish housing market consists in general of larger owner-occupied dwellings and smaller rented dwellings. In order to decrease the housing consumption, households might have to move from owner occupation to a rented apartment, if that choice exists at all on the local housing market. The consequence of changes in housing allowances systems, such as cuts to reduce programme expenditure, could thus be in conflict with housing policy goals.

———

The distributional effect of housing allowances is not under dispute. In a housing market with rent control, such as the Swedish one, the problem of inflationary pressure resulting from housing allowances is negligible, that is, the formal and final incidence coincide. With strict ceilings for housing expenditure, income ceilings and allowances that are decreasing with income above a certain level, it is clear that low-income households are favoured. The income effect of housing allowances on housing consumption[10] is not clear to date.

Policy debates and reform

Housing allowances for households with children

In recent years, the policy debate and reforms undertaken in Sweden have focused on two questions: the problem of rising expenditure and whether housing allowances are primarily an instrument of housing policy or of family policy.

The development of government expenditure on housing allowances since 1990 was shown in Table 10.1. The rising trend in the early 1990s was reversed from 1996; indeed, expenditure on housing allowances decreased by over 50% in the period from 1996 to 2001. The major changes in the housing allowance rules described above were not connected to housing policy in general; and nor were the consequences for recipients analysed.

The increase in expenditure on housing allowances in the early 1990s was largely due to a major tax reform, the main aims of which were to improve economic efficiency and at the same time achieve the government's aim for income distribution. The tax base was broadened and the direct taxation of income was lowered. For the housing sector, the reform meant that housing investment and property management ceased to be exempt from value added tax. In order to improve the income distribution, changes in housing allowances and child allowances were made.

The tax reform resulted in large increases in rents. The average rent, for example, increased from SEK24,100 in 1989 to SEK44,000 in 1995, with the largest increases being at the beginning of the period. Also, expenditure for homeowners increased through a decrease in the value of interest deductions for taxation by 17 percentage points. Part of the increase in government expenditure on housing allowances was aimed at protecting economically weak households from large increases in housing expenditure.

The sharp increases in expenditure on housing allowances as well as in the number of recipients between 1992 and 1995 were the result of a change in the income base for the calculation of the allowances in combination with an economic recession (Enqvist, 2003). The growth in expenditure worried the government and it appointed an inquiry to look into what could be done about this development. Based on the inquiry's recommendations, major changes were made in the system and these resulted in considerable decreases in expenditure. However, neglect of the consequences for allowance recipients made the National Board for Planning, Building and Housing start an analysis of the housing policy consequences in 2003. In a memorandum, the board analysed the effect of separate income limits for couples, which were supposed to increase incentives to work or to increase income. This analysis was based on a simulation of the change in income limits for the year 1996 (which was the latest available income data necessary for the analysis).

In the summary of the report it was concluded that the estimated savings on the government budget would have been exceeded by 40%. In addition:

> In excess of 55,000 households with very low income, normal to high housing expenditure, low payment capacity and a large support burden for the family, would have received large reductions in their allowances if the new income limits had been introduced already in 1996. Many would have had their housing allowances reduced with more than SEK900 per month.

> A reduction of housing allowances for families with very low income and normal to high housing expenditure ought to have the effect that the potential to afford a dwelling with reasonable standard would be lower. (Enqvist, 2003, p 59)

In 2000 the government initiated an inquiry into the combined effects of the general child allowance, child allowance for children with separated parents, and housing allowances. The main aim was to "try if the support to families can be made more general, that is, with decreased marginal effects, but with unchanged or increased distributional accuracy" (SOU, 2001:24, p 13). The analysis showed that families with many children, in receipt of housing allowances, have the lowest incomes, measured by household disposable income adjusted for household size and composition. It was also shown that income decreases with the number of children. Statistics also showed that low-income households have housing expenditures that are less than SEK39,900 per year.

The analysis by the inquiry team ends with the conclusion that, considering the good housing standard of households with children, there is no longer a need for a support that directs the consumption towards housing. The housing allowances cannot solve today's housing problems. Instead, the second development path of the allowances towards a more general support should be fulfilled. One should try to avoid ingredients of consumption steering and instead let the families themselves decide which priorities they want to make within their consumption space. A support to families with children should thus be considered that is not dependent on means testing in order to avoid the high marginal effects of today's system.

As a supplement to the above analysis, the National Social Insurance Board[11] and the National Authority for Planning, Building and Housing were both commissioned by the government to analyse the housing standard for families with children with and without housing allowances as well as presenting the net housing expenditure for households with housing allowances and to compare that expenditure to disposable income. The National Social Insurance Board came to the conclusion that only 7% of households in receipt of housing allowances were overcrowded according to norm two[12] and that there was less overcrowding in 2002 compared with 1991 or 1995:[13]

> The preliminary conclusion which can be drawn (from the analysis) is that the housing allowances primarily are an economic support to financially weak households with children. Its effect on housing standard seems to be limited. However, the possibility cannot be excluded that the housing allowances are important for the above households in the weakest financial situation. (National Social Insurance Board, 2004, p 34)

The National Board of Housing, Building and Planning concluded in their parallel analysis that the percentage of overcrowding had gone up from 33% in 1995 to 47% in 2002 according to norm three.[14] Between 1995 and 2002 the total number of housing allowance recipients decreased from 354,000 to 166,000. The largest change in overcrowding happened between 1996 and 1997, when it increased from 36% to 42%. For couples with children, it increased from 40% to 52%, with a decrease in the number of households from 66,000 to 52,000. For lone parents the increase was four percentage points from 32%, with an absolute increase in the number of households from 56,000 to 59,000.

The National Board of Housing, Building and Planning strongly criticised the analysis of the National Social Insurance Board and the recommendations made by the Ministry of Social Affairs in a report that was later used as the basis for a proposition to parliament:

> The report on reformed housing allowances has weaknesses, partly because there is a lack of analysis and discussion of the consequences of the proposal from a housing policy perspective and partly because it is not shown to which extent and for which household groups there is an increase in the distributional accuracy, despite the fact that the proposal aims at increasing the distributional accuracy for economically exposed families. All research so far confirms that the housing allowances have and have had a high distributional accuracy. (National Board of Housing, Building and Planning, 2005, p 1)[15]

The National Social Insurance Board thus concluded that overcrowding among families with children had decreased and was now around 7%. It is not clear, however, according to the National Board of Housing, Building and Planning, that the calculations are based on an old definition of overcrowding (norm two) and not the one in use for housing allowances (norm three). Based on the analysis made by the inquiry into families' economic situation, the government proposed in March 2005 to change housing allowances. The aim of the allowances is partly connected to housing policy, partly to policy for families:

> The housing policy goal is that all shall have the preconditions to live in good dwellings at a reasonable cost and in a stimulating and safe sustainable environment in the long run. As an economic support to families the housing allowance has as its goal to, within the framework for the general welfare, decrease the differences in economic conditions between families with and without children. (Prop 2004/5:112, p 13)

The government proposed increasing distributional accuracy by increasing the allowances, giving the largest relative increase to families with many children. This is done by increasing the support that is a function of the number of children in a household. The support is increased by SEK4,200 to 11,400 per year for families with one child. The equivalent for a family with two children is an increase by SEK5,100 to 15,900 per year. The high expenditure part of the housing allowances is abolished and the new system covers 50% of the housing expenditure between the present two housing expenditure bands, thus putting these bands together to make one band. No household is supposed to have its housing allowance decreased by the above changes.

A new type of allowance for non-resident parents with right of access, called relations allowance, is proposed. Parents with the custody of, or access to, dependent children who sometimes stay with them, will be given an allowance of SEK3,600 per year for one child, SEK4,500 for two and SEK5,400 for three or more children. The allowance is restricted to rented and cooperative dwellings. The present rules for housing allowances for non-resident parents with right of access cover part of the housing expenses but not the special allowance, based on the number of children. The new allowance compensates for the decrease in coverage of housing expenses described above and is paid in addition to the existing allowances for this household type.

The parliament decided that the proposed changes in the allowances would be effective from 2006. One interesting point to note is that despite the fact that one of the government's starting points for the revision of the housing allowances was the concern about high marginal effects of the system, the outcome was that "the existing marginal effects remain at somewhat higher incomes than before" (Prop 2004/05, p 31).

In the summer of 2005 an analysis and proposals for a new housing finance system were presented to the government. These included a short section on housing allowances for families with children. However, expenditure on housing allowances was not included in the figures for public support to housing, with the following explanation:

> Housing allowances are part of the policy area of economic family policy. Because practically all families with children have at least the housing expenditure the support system presupposes, the housing allowances for families with children have become income-dependent

child allowances. Therefore are they not part of the summary of public housing support. (Miljö-och samhällsbyggnadsdepartementet, 2005, p 188)

However, the statistics from 2000 contradict this argument. The percentage of households receiving housing allowances and having housing expenditures that exceeded the expenditure ceilings amounted to 15% up to 19%, depending on the type of household (SOU, 2001, p 24). The government plans to present a general review of the housing allowances with the aim of analysing how well the system fulfils its goals.

Housing supplement for pensioners

There is little political discussion about the pensioners' housing supplement. In recent years, the main discussion has centred on the income basis for means testing and the connection between the development of pensions and the housing supplement. According to an analysis made by the National Social Insurance Board, an estimated 28% of eligible households did not apply for the supplement in 2002. In excess of 34% of people on sickness or activity support and survivor's pension did not apply, despite being entitled to a housing allowance.

Conclusion

In recent years, housing allowances have become the most important economic instrument for housing policy in Sweden, thereby following the international trend towards concentrating subsidies to housing on housing allowances (Kemp, 1997). A major strength of the Swedish housing allowance and support systems is that all tenures are eligible. This corresponds well with the main housing policy that the government should be neutral when it comes to tenure, and that it should be up to households to choose between different tenures.

However, a major problem with the allowances is to be able to show that they are important for supporting the consumption of housing. The earlier development of the system shows that there has been a good understanding of the relation between consumption subsidies and the situation on the housing market. In recent years, the emphasis on the development of the system is connected to income distribution – that is, the second goal of the allowances – where it has been fairly simple to show the efficiency of the system.

Some changes in the system have clearly increased their efficiency. Housing allowance is a liquidity support. Until 1996, the means test was based on assessed taxable income (for example, a two-year-old income) and present housing expenditure. Given that household income was fairly stable it seemed to make sense to assess it in that way. But with fluctuating income, the liquidity support goal loses its meaning. The change to estimated future income as the basis for means testing is a clear improvement in efficiency.

Meanwhile, the rules for calculating housing expenditure changed. Since 1997 only the real interest on housing loans has been included in eligible housing expenditure. "The government consider that it is not reasonable that housing allowances are given to the part of the interest which is a compensation for inflation, because this means that the housing allowances subsidise a building up of wealth" (Prop 1995/6:186, p 32). The government meant that a three-percentage point decrease in the nominal interest rate would be the proper level for this reduction at the time. Adjustments to this figure could be made if there were major changes in inflation, but this is an example of mixing financial with economic concepts. The rationale behind this change was to make savings on the government's budget.

Another example of mixing up arguments is that housing allowances should not cover amortisation of housing loans. For a long time, amortisation has not been included in housing expenditure, based on the argument that amortisation is saving that increases the household's wealth and, therefore, is not a cost. However, amortisation *is* an item of expenditure.

When it comes to the development of the allowance system in general, one would assume that, for example, deciding on reasonable housing consumption for different household types and incomes should be the starting point. However, reasonable housing consumption, as well as expenditure-to-income ratios, are indirectly defined by rules for the allowances. As the rules, for example in relation to rent ceilings, are not differentiated by location, this also means that households living in 'low-cost' local government areas are favoured in comparison to other local governments. At present, quite a large percentage of households have housing expenditures that exceed the expenditure ceilings.

The connection between housing allowances and social insurance payments has been neglected in the discussion about the development of the allowance system. A fundamental issue to discuss would be in which form support to housing consumption should be given. In principle there is a big difference between a housing allowance that is a right to receive under certain conditions and social assistance that is mainly based on individual assessment of need for support. When it comes to income supplement for pensioners, it is clear that the system is part of the income distribution policy that enables households to remain in their dwelling after retirement and cope with larger increases in housing expenditure or decreases in income. The supplement is then mainly a 'safety net'.

A fundamental question related to the balance between types of housing subsidies is connected to the supply of housing. In general, it is argued that housing allowances do not influence the supply of housing, only the distribution of existing housing between households with low incomes. However, if there is a shortage of housing for low-income households there might be need also for subsidies for supply of this type of housing.

Notes

[1] The change took effect on 4 July 1996, but the main effect occurred from 1997.

[2] The housing allowances are supposed to be a liquidity support, that is to help the household to pay for their housing expenditure (Åhrén, 1988). In all official documents connected to allowances the word 'cost' is used. As will be described later, the economists' distinction between 'expenditure' and 'cost' is crucial in understanding the development of the system. Therefore the term 'expenditure' is used in the text unless it is evident that the proper term is 'cost'.

[3] For example, income from abroad, 80% of student grants, tax-free grants in excess of SEK36,000 per year. Fifteen per cent of wealth in excess of SEK100,000 will be added to the income (the tax assessed value of owned accommodation in which the household lives, is exempt).

[4] A 3 percentage point deduction in the nominal interest rate is made, based on the argument that owner-occupied housing is an economic wealth that increases in value at the same time as there is some inflation (Prop 1995/6:186, p 32).

[5] One child; maximum floor space: 80m^2, additional children up to five, 20m^2 per child.

[6] For households with children there is a guarantee level when calculating the housing expenditure. The household may calculate an eligible housing expenditure up to the guarantee level if the restriction on floor space would result in a lower eligible expenditure. If, however, the real total expenditure is lower than the guarantee level then the real expenditure would become the basis for calculating the allowances. The guarantee level per month is SEK3,000 for one child, and for additional children is SEK300 per child, up to five children.

[7] The housing expenditure ceilings increase with an increase in the number of children, up to three children. For a two-child family the ranges are: $0.75 \times$ (SEK24,000 < housing expenditure < SEK39,600) + $0.05 \times$ (SEK39,601 < housing expenditure < SEK70,800). The child allowance is SEK7,200 for one child and an additional SEK3,600 per child for the second and third children.

[8] The price base amount for 2005 is SEK39,400.

[9] SEK56,040 per year.

[10] The income elasticity of households receiving allowances for housing is unknown, but is most likely small.

[11] The board responsible for the administration of housing allowances. In 2005 it was renamed Swedish Social Insurance Administration.

[12] According to norm two, households are overcrowded if there are more than two persons per room, not including the kitchen and living room.

[13] It is, however, admitted that the analysis is cross-sectional and not longitudinal. Therefore it is impossible to conclude anything about the development of a specific household's situation over time.

[14] According to norm three, each child should have their own bedroom, one bedroom for the parents, kitchen and living room not included.

[15] Letter to the Ministry of Social Affairs 'Statement on reformed housing allowances', dated 21 January 2005.

References

Åhrén, P. (1988) *Bostadssubventioner och bostadskostnader i Norden (Housing subsidies and housing costs in the Nordic countries)*, Copenhagen: Nordisk Ministerråd.

Åhrén, P. (1990) *Bostadsbidragen I Norden. En jämförande analys av system och effecter (Housing allowances in the Nordic countries. A comparative analysis of systems and effects)*, NBO, vol 90, no 1, Copenhagen: Nordisk Ministerråd.

Åhrén, P. (2004) 'Housing allowances', in M. Lujanen (ed.) *Housing and housing policy in the Nordic countries*, Nord 2004, vol 7, Copenhagen: Nordic Council of Ministers.

Enström, C. and Turner, B. (2001) 'Bostadsbidrag och prisbildning. En kunskapsöversikt I' ('Housing allowances and price formation. A review of literature'), in SOU *Ur fattigdomsfällan. Slutbetänkande av Familjeutredningen (Out of the poverty trap. Final report from the Government Inquiry on Families)*, Stockholm: Fritzes.

Enström Öst, C. (2005) 'Benefit cuts and Children's Housing Situation. Evidence from the Swedish housing allowance reform', mimeo, Uppsala University, Institute for Housing and Urban Research.

Enqvist, C. (2003) 'Bostadsstandard m. m. för barnfamiljer med bostadsbidrag', ('Housing standard for families with children receiving housing allowances'), mimeo, Karlskrona: Boverket.

Howenstine, J. (1986) *Housing vouchers: A comparative international analysis*, New Brunswick, NJ: Centre for Urban Policy Research, Rutgers University.

Kemp, P.A. (1997) *A comparative study of housing allowances*, Department of Social Security, research report no 60, London: HMSO.

Miljö-och samhällsbyggnadsdepartementet (2005) 'Rapport om ny bostadsfinansiering' ('Report on new housing finance, Ministry of Environment and Infrastructure'), Ds 2005:39, Stockholm.

National Social Insurance Board (1999) 'Bostadsbidrag till barnfamiljer och ungdomar − effecter och resultat av de nya reglerna för år 1997' ('Housing allowances to families with children and to youth − effects and results of the new rules for 1997'), RFV Anser 1999:6, Stockholm: National Social Insurance Board.

National Social Insurance Board (2004) *Statistics on housing allowances and housing supplement*, Stockholm: National Social Insurance Board.

Prop 1986/7:93 *Regeringens proposition om bostäder åt unga (Government proposition on dwellings for young households)*, Stockholm.

Prop 1995/6:186 *Regeringens proposition om nya regler för bostadsbidrag* (*Government proposition on new rules for housing allowances*), Stockholm.

Prop 2004/5:112 *Regeringens proposition Ändrade regler för bostadsbidrag* (*Government proposition on changed rules for housing allowances*), Stockholm.

Riksrevisionsverket (1996) 'Bostadsbidrag – effektivitetsrevision av ett socialpolitiskt instrumen' ('Housing allowances – audit report on the efficiency of a social policy instrument'), RRV 1996:3, Stockholm.

SOU (1964:41) *Bostadsstöd till pensionärer. Förslag från bostadsförbättringsutredningen* (*Housing support for pensioners. Proposal by the Government Inquiry on Improvements in Housing*), Stockholm: Ivar Häggströms Tryckeri.

SOU (1967:52) *Barnbidrag och familjetillägg. Familjepolitiska kommitté* (*Child allowances and additional support for families. Government Inquiry on Policies for Families*), Stockholm: Esselte.

SOU (1975:51) *Bostadsförsörjning och bostadsbidrag. Slutbetänkande av boende- och bostadsfinansieringsutredninge* (*Housing supply and housing allowances. Final report from the Government Inquiry on Housing and Housing Finance*), Stockholm: Göteborgs offsettryckeri.

SOU (1992:21) *Bostadsstöd till pensionärer. Betänkande av KBT-utredninge* (*Housing supplement to pensioners. Report from KBT Inquiry*), Stockholm: Fritzes.

SOU (1995:133) *Bostadsbidragen – effektivare inkomstprövning – besparingar. Betänkande av bostadsbidragsutredningen '95* (*Housing allowances – a more efficient means testing by income – savings. Report from the Government Inquiry on Housing Allowances 1995*), Stockholm: Fritzes.

SOU (1999:52) *Inkomstprövning av bostadstillägg till pensionärer. Betänkande av BTP-utredninge* (*Income testing of housing supplements to pensioners. Report from Government Inquiry*), Stockholm: Fritzes.

SOU (2001:24) *Ur fattigdomsfällan. Slutbetänkande av Familjeutredninge* (*Out of the poverty trap. Final report from the Government Inquiry on Families*), Stockholm: Fritzes.

Statistics Sweden (2005) *Statistical yearbook for housing and building*, Stockholm: Statistics Sweden.

Swedish Social Insurance Administration (2005) *Statistics on housing allowances and housing supplement*, Stockholm: Swedish Social Insurance Administration.

ELEVEN

Housing allowances in the Czech Republic in comparative perspective

Martin Lux and Petr Sunega

Introduction

The aim of this chapter is to describe the development and functioning of housing allowances in the Czech Republic. After a short introductory description of the Czech housing system and policy, an evaluation of the allowance model is provided in two steps: first, by measuring the effectiveness of the allowance; and, second, by comparing the Czech model with the approaches applied in other transitional countries.

Under the communist regime, housing in the Czech Republic was subject to tight state control. With the exception of family houses, the entire privately owned housing stock was nationalised; subsequently, the creation of new housing cooperatives was allowed. Housing cooperatives were subjected to state administration and all rents were controlled by the state. Housing production was mostly shaped by the state, and as a result of the extensive housing construction programme financed from the state budget, the share of state rental flats in the total housing stock grew rapidly. The physical and aesthetic quality of these new flats, however, was very poor, with large concrete housing estates creating a new urban landscape. State housing policy in this period was based on the principle that a flat is such an important good in the life of a person, that the increase in construction, maintenance and management costs should not be reflected in household expenditures or rent increases. In the case of state dwellings, the rent was fixed at the level of 1964 prices through legal regulation. This necessarily resulted in the continually growing volumes of state subsidies for housing construction as well as for the operation, management and maintenance of the existing housing stock. The extensive, state-funded construction, management and maintenance costs of state rental flats were increasingly confronted with limited public resources and, consequently, other tenures (mainly cooperative housing and homeownership) gained in importance.

The 'stabilisation of cooperative housing construction' initiative was organised by housing cooperatives. The construction costs were covered using cooperative membership fees (on average approximately 18% of the total construction costs), state subsidies (on average approximately 56% of the total construction costs) and low-interest state bank credits with a 3% interest rate and 30-year maturity (on average approximately 26% of the total construction costs). However, the housing cooperative system during the period of the development of socialism acquired an altogether different character: pre-war housing cooperatives were merged into cooperative 'giants', the regulatory influence of the state and central authorities grew immensely and the statutes of the cooperatives became uniform by law. The 'nationalisation' of the cooperative movement resulted in the total disappearance of the original meaning of the cooperative system as 'self-help', independent entities. Individual housing construction for homeownership primarily included the construction of family houses, their extensions and outbuildings and, to a limited extent, the construction of residential houses with individually owned flats. Individual construction was mostly funded using the resources of the constructors themselves, and was supplemented with loans provided by state banks with up to 30-year maturity and a 2.7% interest rate.

Housing policy changes during transition

The subsidies for both new and existing state rental dwellings practically disappeared soon after the change of the regime in 1990 and this led to a sharp decrease in housing construction volumes. Many blocks of flats that had been expropriated by the communist regime have been returned to their previous owners or their descendants by so-called property restitution. However, the majority of former state dwellings were transferred from state to municipal ownership (1991) and municipalities acquired the right to sell public housing. No law gave unlimited purchase rights to tenants, neither did it set forth any method of price calculation by which the municipal council should offer the sale of flats to the tenants (unlike the 'right-to-buy' policy used in Great Britain). It was entirely left to the consideration of the municipal council to determine the price and the dwelling stock for privatisation. Thanks to the chaotic course of privatisation, many municipal rental flats were paradoxically 'saved' from privatisation (unlike the situation in Hungary or Bulgaria) and rental housing still forms a substantial part of the Czech housing stock. Table 11.1 shows the changes in tenure structure between 1991 and 2001.

The fundamental objective of the so-called 1992 Transformation Act in relation to cooperative housing was to increase the proprietary rights of cooperative members. Unlike municipal housing occupants, members of housing cooperatives living in cooperative flats acquired the right to 'sell' their flat on the open market (in fact, to sell their share in the housing cooperative) for a market price and particularly the right to a free transfer of a cooperative flat to their full ownership. Cooperative housing therefore became virtually part of the owner-occupied sector.

The Czech central government decided to maintain the system of state regulation of rents (the so-called 'first-generation rent control system') not only in transferred municipal rental dwellings, but also in private rental flats and in houses returned to the previous (pre-communist) owners. In practice, private

Table 11.1: Tenure structure, Czech Republic, 1991–2001

	1991		2001	
	No	**%**	**No**	**%**
In own family houses	1,367,027	36.9	1,371,684	35.8
In own flat	31,164	0.8	421,654	11.0
In rental housing	1,465,231	39.5	1,092,950	28.6
In cooperative housing	697,829	18.8	548,812	14.3
In tenant cooperatives[a]	–	–	103,216	2.7
In other tenure	144,430	3.9	289,362	7.6
Total	**3,705,681**	**100.0**	**3,827,678**	**100.0**

Source: Census 1991, 2001, Czech Statistical Office (www.czso.cz).

Note: [a] Tenant cooperatives are established for the purpose of house privatisation in former municipal houses.

owners could not even increase the rent to a level sufficient to cover necessary maintenance costs. Nevertheless, no public revenue subsidies were introduced to enable private or municipal landlords to cover the difference between low regulated rents and the costs of maintenance. Legislation passed in 1993 allowed a free market rent to be set if the tenant was not a citizen of the Czech Republic, if the flat had been vacant before renting, or if a privately owned family house was rented. Gradual rent deregulation for running rental contracts was launched at the beginning of the 1990s. The maximum price of a monthly rent has been increased in view of the quality of a flat (four categories), the size of the municipality and an inflation coefficient. Local authorities were given the power to adjust the rents in their housing stock in the light of local conditions through a special coefficient employed in the rent calculation (rent pooling); in reality, only a small portion of municipalities took advantage of this option. As a result, the limits of maximum rent per square metre of floor space in a first category flat[1] per month increased from the original CZK2.50 in 1991 to CZK37.07 in 2002 in Prague, CZK24.76 in cities with a population over 100,000, CZK18.31 in cities with a population of between 50,000 and 99,999, CZK16.42 in towns with a population between 10,000 and 49,999 people and CZK15.23 in towns and municipalities with a population below 10,000.

According to the Family Budget Survey (FBS) data, the average rent in an average rental flat increased nominally by 673% between 1990 and 2001. If we take into account changes in the general consumer price index, the real increase of the average rent would amount approximately to 300%, albeit from a very low starting point. Even in 2005 the huge gap between market and regulated rents in most Czech regions (the largest being in the capital Prague) is clear. Meanwhile, the prices of utilities were liberalised far more resolutely, which resulted in a sharp increase of the housing cost-to-income ratio. On average, rent accounts for only one third of the total housing expenditures of an average household; the remaining two thirds are utility payments. The government decree on rent regulation was abolished by the Constitutional Court in 2000 (and again in 2002). In 2002, rents were in effect frozen in nominal terms (and hence depreciated in real terms) as there was no further legislation passed in the parliament and rents could not be increased unilaterally by landlords.

Just like other housing policy instruments, the existence of rent regulation can be justified for two reasons: inefficient functioning of a market (low housing supply and housing shortage) and/or redistribution of income towards low-income households. The existing rent regulation in the Czech Republic is, however, completely unfounded. There is no reason for this form of state intervention for the purpose of increasing the efficiency of the housing market functioning. When we compare the commonly used housing indicators,[2] the Czech Republic does not suffer from a housing shortage compared to the old EU countries. The suspicion of an existence of a monopoly in private rental housing is also unjustified. The effectiveness of the current rent regulation system is also very poor. Figure 11.1 shows the percentage of households living in the rent-regulated housing sector in the total number of households in individual income deciles according to the total household income, or alternatively, household income per consumption unit (that is, income adjusted for the household size).

As is clear from Figure 11.1, rent regulation is almost equally applied to 'rich' and 'poor' households. As many as 10% of the wealthiest Czech households (according to income per consumption unit ranking in the tenth decile of the income distribution) live in a flat with regulated rent. This percentage is not significantly lower than among the poorest households (according to the household income per consumption unit in the first decile of the income distribution – 10.6%). Figure 11.2 shows how the total hidden subsidy following from rent regulation is

Figure 11.1: The percentage of households 'profiting' from regulated rent, Czech Republic

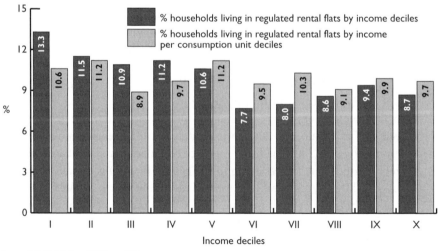

Source: FBS (2001) (n = 3,291, n = 857)

Figure 11.2: Distribution of the sum of the hidden subsidy from rent regulation according to household income, Czech Republic

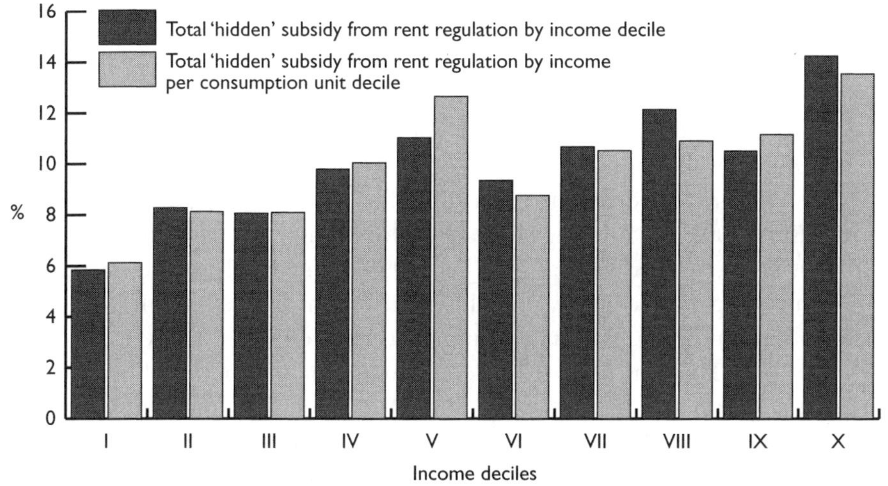

Source: FBS (2001), and author's calculations.

distributed, defined as a difference between the estimated equilibrium market rent (see Lux and Sunega, 2002) and the current regulated rent price, again according to the total household income or household income per consumption unit. It is clear from Figure 11.2 that it was especially the wealthiest and medium-income households that profited the most from rent regulation in 2001. In contrast, households with the lowest income relatively benefited the least from this hidden state subsidy.

The current unfair system of rent regulation has resulted in the creation of two segments in the rental housing market: rent-regulated rental housing and market rental housing. There is almost no effective tenure protection in market rental housing and 'market' rents are biased upwards due to the rent regulation itself (Lux and Sunega, 2002). Because of the gap in accessibility and affordability of housing between those two segments, the door is closed to any new incomers and so tenancy turnover is very low in the rent-regulated segment. This leaves newly established households without any effective help from the state. The accessibility and affordability of housing in transitional countries substantially decreased mainly, and often only, for households living in the unprivileged housing market segment. As these were mainly newly established, young households, this may be one of the reasons for the demographic changes connected with low fertility rates in most of the transitional countries. There was a challenge for housing allowances in those countries to meet this unfair policy outcome, but the response from the state administration, at least in the Czech Republic, completely missed the point, as we are going to see.

Housing allowances

The basic legislation concerning housing allowances in the Czech Republic is found in the current 1995 State Social Support Act, No 117; the whole Act came into effect in January 1996.[3] It defines the basic terms and conditions for recognising a claim to benefits of state social support, including housing allowance. Since its adoption, it has already been amended several times, as in April 1996 when the minimum level of housing allowance was set; another important amendment of 1 July 1998 increased the income ceiling for housing allowance applications. As of 1 April 2001, the housing allowance allocation period also changed.

It must be mentioned that, as of 1 July 1990, immediately at the start of the transformation period, a general social benefit was introduced in line with price liberalisation, known as the state compensatory allowance (Víšek et al, 1995; Dlouhý, 1997). This was designed to compensate for the increased living costs, particularly (but not only) food prices. In 1991 the circle of recipients began to be gradually restricted and the allowance was transformed from a general to a means-tested allowance. Apart from the state compensatory allowance, families at this time also received other social allowances, usually inherited from the previous regime. The characteristic features of the social support at that time were the lack of transparency, the large number of different social benefits (more than 60), ineffective targeting and a difficult uprating procedure. So a new general variable was sought which could be related to all current and new social benefits and this resulted in the introduction of the concept of the subsistence level.

The Czechoslovak Federal Republic's Federal Assembly passed the Subsistence Level Act in 1991. After 1993, when an independent Czech Republic was established, a more vigorous rent increase was expected, and therefore a new social allowance was created for tenants of rented and partly also of cooperative flats: a rent allowance. Its aim was to alleviate the social impact of the increase in gross rent (that is, rent including services and energy prices) in view of the initial 1993 level. The claim to this allowance was restricted by the family income from the previous half-year, which could not exceed 1.3 times the subsistence level. The level of the allowance, with certain restrictions, was defined as the difference between the level of rent as of the first day of the calendar half-year and the rent negotiated for December 1993. The force of the Act was fixed at two years. However, public interest for the entire period of this Act (from 1 January 1994 to 31 December 1996) was minimal. The next housing allowance scheme was introduced by the State Social Support Act, which came into force on 1 January 1996.

In the Czech Republic there are three basic components that form the social protection system (Víšek et al, 1995; Kepková, 1997): social insurance, social support and social assistance. Through social insurance citizens put aside part of their consumption against the event of any future uncertain social contingency, which could result in partial or full loss of income. The reasons for loss of income could be maternity, caring for a family member, illness, disability, old age, loss of provider or loss of employment. The aim of the insurance, in such a case, is to maintain a reasonable standard of living for the insured and their families. The social security insurance payable amounts to 12.5% of the gross income of employees. An additional 35% of the gross salary of employees paid by employers is transferred as social security contributions to the state budget.

Social support contributions help families to cover increased costs due to the presence of persons that are still not earning an income. They also help families that lack the power and resources to do so themselves to cope with specific life situations. Social support contributions may be divided into two subcategories according to the method by which financial resources are redistributed. If this concerns redistribution from families with and without children, then this is called horizontal redistribution. Contributions belonging to this category include: family, birth, funeral, charitable and guardian allowance. The payment of these allowances may be terminated depending on the achieved income level. If this concerns redistribution from high- to low-income families, this is called vertical redistribution. The level of allowances in this category is based on examining the real income situation of a family and this includes child allowance, additional social allowance and housing allowance. The level of allowance decreases as income rises, so the moment a family achieves a certain income level, its claim to benefit is terminated. Virtually the entire structure of social support allowances is based on the subsistence level concept that is used to determine the income ceiling ('*n*-multiple of the subsistence level').

Social assistance is designed for people (families) that are not able to secure their basic living requirements. In other words, social assistance is designed for families whose income is beneath the subsistence level. The basic level of this assistance in practice in most cases corresponds to the difference between the household's income and its subsistence level. When examining a household's claim, its property circumstances and possibilities of increasing its income are also considered.

The subsistence level, according to the Act, is defined as a socially recognised minimum income below which a state of material emergency occurs. It defines the level of necessary funds for a household to secure temporarily the basic living requirements of its members at a very modest level. The subsistence level in the Czech Republic consists of two components: the sum required to secure the needs of each person in the household and the sum required to secure the necessary expenses of the whole household. The first part of the subsistence level therefore applies to the basic personal requirements of each household member, which include food, clothing, footwear, industrial consumables, services and personal development. Five different levels are determined for the sums to secure personal requirements: four for children of various ages, the fifth for other citizens. The second part of the subsistence level serves to cover common household costs, that is, mainly housing costs and related services. The subsistence level is increased by a government decree, provided that the consumer price index (CPI) rises by at least 5%. If there is an extraordinarily high increase in consumer prices, the subsistence level sums may be increased outside the date of the regular uprating. However, since 2004 uprating the subsistence levels (and, via that, the social benefits) has been only an option for the government, not a duty.

In the Czech Republic, both homeowners and tenants (including housing cooperative members) are eligible to apply for a housing allowance, provided they are registered as permanently residing in the flat. They are entitled to receive an allowance if their after-tax household income is lower than the sum of their relevant household subsistence level multiplied by a coefficient of 1.60. Housing allowances are calculated according to the following equation:

$$HA = FC - \frac{FC \times Y}{SL \times 1.60}$$

where:

HA is the monthly level of housing allowance paid to the applicant;
FC is the tariff sum of family household costs (normative housing expenditures);
Y is the average monthly family income demonstrated in the calendar quarter; and
SL is the sum of the family subsistence level.

The allowance formula may be rewritten as follows:

$$HA = NE \ (1 - RY/MY)$$

where:

NE are the normative housing expenditures;
RY is the real monthly income;
MY is the maximum income (income ceiling).

If a household has a zero income, then the allowance has (for a particular size of household) maximal value; and if the household income has the maximum income (1.6 times the subsistence level), it receives no allowance. Housing expenditures are normative in the formula, that is, family household costs (*FC*). Family household costs are determined by the amount forming the second part of the household's subsistence level (the second component of the subsistence level securing necessary household costs). These normative costs include both rent (maintenance and management costs for homeowners or cooperative members) and utility payments. The allowance calculation formula takes into account, through the subsistence level, the size and structure of a household. All persons in the household who are registered as permanently residing there are included; no condition is required for these persons to be living together permanently and jointly paying the costs for their needs. At the same time, however, the district authority is entitled to exclude persons who have truly not been using the flat for at least a period of three months, although they are registered as its permanent residents.

The only criterion which is taken into account in its real value is the family income (*Y*). The decisive income is calculated as a net income, that is, after the deduction of expenses to achieve, secure and maintain it in the case of self-employed people or after the deduction of the social security premium, public health insurance premium and income tax in the case of employees. Assessable income includes income from employment and self-employment, capital assets, lease and other income under the Income Tax Act, income from state budget stipends, sickness benefits, pensions, unemployment benefit, income from abroad, family allowance, care allowance and child benefit. The decisive period during which the income is assessed is the calendar quarter preceding the calendar quarter in which the claim is processed. If the real income of a family does not attain the family's relevant subsistence level, the subsistence level amount is used for calculating the level of allowance.

Real housing expenses are not included in the calculation. What applies is that the lower the share of the household's decisive income (*Y*) in relation to the maximum income ($SL \times 1.60$), the bigger the part of housing costs tariff that is covered by the allowance. A normative housing expenditures burden rate in the Czech model is determined by the value of the $FC/(SL \times 1.60)$ share. So it only changes in relation to the size and structure of the household, which is variable and which affects the *FC* and *SL* values.

Housing allowances, as one of the social support benefits, fall under the jurisdiction of the Czech Ministry of Labour and Social Affairs. According to the law, allowances are paid to the claimants by the employment offices and the particular office is determined by the place where the applicant is registered as a permanent resident. The allowance is provided for a period of one year from 1 July to 30 June of the following calendar year. Proof of income must be provided each calendar quarter.

When originally introduced, the housing allowance was considered a benefit that would help low-income households to cope with increasing housing costs. The guiding variable, as for other social support benefits, became the official subsistence level. The advantage of such a link was automatic uprating in line with an increase in living costs, the greater transparency of the entire system, and lower administrative costs. The idea of using real housing costs in allowance equations was abandoned also due to the fact that some housing cost items (such as energy consumption) could be affected by the household. However, the division of the current allowance into rent allowance and allowance for other services related to housing (energy, utilities) was not discussed at that time. As a consequence, the normative costs do not, by far, reflect the regional differences in housing prices (particularly rents) or the much higher expenses of households living in the unprivileged market rental sector. Deducting the value of benefit from the subsistence level resulted instead in complete levelling out of the support for all types of households.

The statistics of the Ministry of Labour and Social Affairs concerning the housing allowance scheme and its recipients are considerably limited. Only the number of recipients and the average level of the allowance are systematically monitored (Průša, 2002). In 2000 the total amount spent on housing allowances was CZK2,518 million. This amount constituted 0.12% of GDP in current prices in 2000. In following years this ratio remained relatively stable – it was 0.10% in 2001, 0.11% in 2002 and 0.10% in 2003.

In December 2004, 268,345 households were receiving housing allowances (7% of all Czech households, according to the 2001 census), while the average level of the allowance was CZK712. In Table 11.2 it is evident that more than 47% of the total number of households receiving the allowance had an income lower than or equal to the official subsistence level. Of the total number of households receiving the allowance, the biggest were four- and three-member households (23.4% and 22.2% respectively).

Figure 11.3 shows the changes in the share of expenditure on housing allowances of the total social allowance expenditures between 1996 and 2004 (in December of each year).

Before 2003 there was no dataset available from which the housing allowance recipients could be identified. However, in 2003 the Family Budget Survey dataset (latest available) included information on the total (annual) amount of housing allowance received by each household, which makes it possible to identify the recipients of an allowance. If only actual recipients of housing allowances living in rental housing are considered, the average gross (before allowance) monthly rent-to-income ratio was 8.3% in 2003. After the deduction of an allowance from the rent paid by those households the average net rent-to-income ratio decreased for the recipients of an allowance to 5.2%.

The obligation of the applicant to furnish proof of duly paying rent or contributing to the repairs fund and of making payments for any consideration for using the flat or real estate tax payments was legally excluded in the course of time. The reason was the fact that residents of privately owned flats often had problems acquiring such confirmation. Instead, a new provision appeared in the

Table 11.2: Number of households receiving housing allowance, Czech Republic, December 2004, by income level and size of household

Number of people in household		Total with a family income up to:						
	Total	1.0 SL	1.1 SL	1.2 SL	1.3 SL	1.4 SL	1.5 SL	1.6 SL
1	54,037	26,174	2,019	2,648	5,586	5,767	6,704	5,139
2	50,653	28,406	3,958	4,452	3,901	4,359	3,376	2,201
3	59,505	30,579	5,022	5,203	5,063	6,021	4,491	3,126
4	62,678	22,869	4,969	7,288	6,855	7,517	7,683	5,497
5	27,224	10,709	2,621	2,940	3,292	3,139	2,766	1,757
6 or more	14,248	8,253	1,213	1,192	1,155	1,064	852	519
Total	**268,345**	**126,990**	**19,802**	**23,723**	**25,852**	**27,867**	**25,872**	**18,239**

Source: Ministry of Labour and Social Affairs of the Czech Republic.

Note: SL = 'subsistence level'.

―――

Figure 11.3: Housing allowance expenditures as share of total social allowances expenditure, Czech Republic, 1996–2004

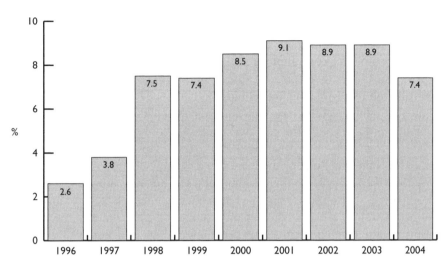

Source: Ministry of Labour and Social Affairs of the Czech Republic.

law, which allows housing allowances to be paid out to a person other than the claimant, that is, it is possible to pay out the allowance directly to the landlords. The law states that the employment office of the municipality may determine a 'substitute' recipient of the social benefit (for example, the landlord) in cases where the intended purpose of a benefit could not be achieved through the payment to the entitled beneficiary. Especially in the case of housing allowances, the law states that 'The substitute recipient is allowed to use the housing benefit without an approval of the entitled person for repayment of rent arrears'. The employment office can determine as a 'substitute' recipient both physical and legal persons.

According to Mareš (2001), low take-up is a major problem of the existing housing allowance, that is, the number of actual applicants is much lower than the number of the entitled households. "Generally, the 'non-take up of social security benefits' or non-withdrawal of social benefits by people to whom they are intended is mentioned as one of the forms of efficiency crisis of the welfare state – this crisis lies in the fact that the welfare state does not meet its objectives" (Mareš, 2001, p 3). According to the data stated in the study, less than 40% of entitled households applied for a housing allowance in 1996. Similarly, approximately 60% of respondents in a 1999 survey who were entitled to the housing allowance had not applied, were not applying, were not collecting or were not negotiating the housing allowance. Among the reasons for this situation, Mareš gives relatively general problems that pertain to all social benefits: values preventing people from becoming dependent on social benefits, rational calculation of the benefit in view of the costs related to the application, a lack of information, the effort to avoid stigmatisation, and a lack of skills (2001, p 12). However, there could be another very important and specific aspect in the case of housing allowances and that is the poor targeting of the allowance and thus its low effectiveness.

Based on simulations using the Family Budget Survey 2001 data, Figure 11.4 shows the allocation of the total housing allowance payment due in 2001 among households according to their total net income or, more precisely, according to the total income per consumption unit under the assumption of 100% take-up of the housing allowance. It is clear from Figure 11.4 that the housing allowance especially helps low-income households.

The major failure of the Czech housing allowance is the fact that real housing expenditures do not enter the equation but instead only the flat-rate component of the subsistence level (normative tariffs) is used. This failure is a very serious one, and it is probably one of the reasons why a large portion of entitled Czech households do not apply for this social benefit. The housing allowance is provided to homeowners who usually spend a relatively small portion of their income on housing, as well as tenants whose family budgets are far more burdened with housing costs (rents). The estimated distribution of the sum of potentially paid-out housing allowances among households with various degrees of housing cost-to-income ratios (first decile corresponds to the lowest housing cost-to-income ratio, tenth decile corresponds to the highest housing cost-to-income ratio) is shown in Figure 11.5 (under the assumption of 100% take-up).

The targeting of the housing allowance on households with a higher housing cost-to-income ratio is disputable, since, for example, 5% of the total sum of the housing allowance would potentially be distributed among households with the lowest housing cost-to-income ratio (first decile). Moreover, the current housing

Figure 11.4: Distribution of the total sum of housing allowance by household income, Czech Republic, 2001

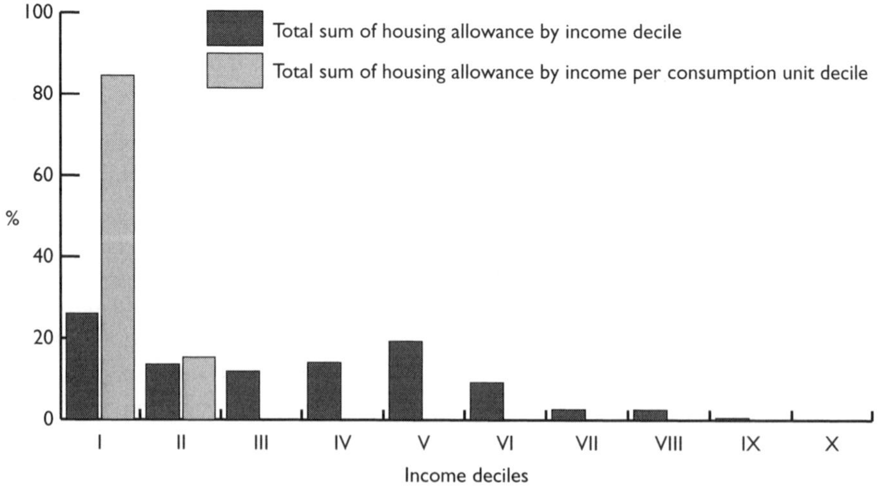

Source: FBS (2001) (n = 3,293)

Figure 11.5: Distribution of the total sum of housing allowance by total housing cost burden measure, Czech Republic, 2001

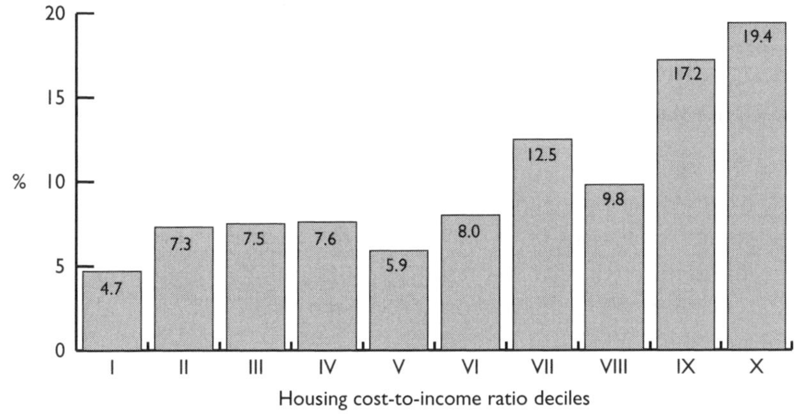

Housing cost-to-income ratio deciles

Source: FBS (2001) (n = 3,293)
Note: Only explicit costs were included in housing costs of homeowners, including the mortgage repayment due or expenditures on maintenance, repairs and modernisation of own houses and flats; imputed rent was neither calculated nor included in housing costs of homeowners.

allowance does not at all help households living in market rental housing because they usually reach an income over the 1.6 factor of the living minimum (otherwise they would not be able to live in the market rental sector at all) but their rent expenditures and thus the resulting housing cost-to-income ratio can be much higher than for many low-income households.

In the conditions of levelled-out (regulated) rent prices, the current form of housing allowance can fulfil its role relatively well, but not when the rent is considerably differentiated as a result of rent deregulation. Households with equally high income, who live in regions with different rent levels, are entitled, according to the current system, to the same level of allowance. The formula does not consider how great a part of their income households must really spend on housing. This has already led to the significant discrimination against households living in market rental housing. Hence, the housing allowance based on the subsistence level has several significant drawbacks. A comprehensive reform of the whole system of social protection is currently under discussion in the parliament but as there are several possible outcomes of this discussion we will not present them in this chapter. According to the proposal of the current government, the housing allowance should be paid both from the state and municipal budgets, which may create incentives for municipalities to hold the municipal housing stock for social purposes and not to sell it to current tenants. The income ceiling should be abolished and instead the concept of normative rate of burden (30% has been discussed) will be used in accordance with the standards of European continental housing allowances. However, the normative costs should be preserved in the allowance equation, which may lead to further discrimination of tenants living in the market rental sector who may pay higher average rents than those used as a ceiling in the allowance equation. A regional differentiation of normative costs will not be applied even though there are gaps in rent prices between different Czech regions.

Housing allowances in other Central Eastern European (CEE) countries

There is not much information about housing allowances in the CEE countries. We will briefly describe the models used in three other CEE countries and finally provide some conclusions from such international comparison. It is necessary to bear in mind, however, that information on housing allowances in other CEE countries relates to 2002, drawn from a comparative project on local government and housing (Lux, 2003).

Poland

Housing allowances were introduced in Poland as a kind of social assistance scheme for poor families (tenants and owners) in 1995 by the Law on Lease of Dwelling Premises and Housing Allowances, which was amended by the Law on Housing Allowances on 21 June 2001. The purpose of the amendment was to extend the number of potential beneficiaries by households living in the market rental sector (paying non-regulated market rent), households living in so-called 'social' housing dwellings and households conducting any kind of economic activity in their primary housing. In fact, no tenure is excluded from the right to apply for housing allowance, although important limits are applied in those cases when the household is not living in municipal rental housing.

To apply for the housing allowance, a household must not, in the last three months, have an income per head that is more than 125% of the lowest retirement pension for multiperson households; and not more than 175% of the lowest retirement pension for one-member households. The lowest retirement pension is announced by the president of the Social Assistance Office every month in the state official report 'Monitor Polski'. Income is defined as the net income of the household after deduction of taxes, social and health insurance payments (social transfers for orphans are not included into the income calculation).

The right to an allowance is restricted by the size of dwelling: the normative area of the dwelling is set at 35m² for one person, 40m² for two persons, 45m² for three, 55m² for four, 65m² for five, 70m² for six persons and for each additional person the normative area rises by 5m². In cases where the useful area of the dwelling is higher than the normative one, the average expenditures per one square metre are calculated and the result is multiplied by the normative area for the particular household. However, households are not entitled to a housing allowance if they are living in dwellings with an area higher than 30% (or 50% in cases when the area of habitable rooms and the kitchen does not exceed 60% of total area) of the normative area.

The allowance is equivalent to the difference between the real housing expenditures on the normative area of the dwelling (or real housing expenditures if the area of the dwelling is lower than the normative one) and the following percentage of household income: 15% of total income for one-member households, 12% of total income for two-, three- and four-member households and 10% of total income for five- and more member households. However, if income per head of household is higher than 150% of the lowest retirement pension in one-member households or 100% of the lowest retirement pension in multiperson households, the allowance is equivalent to the difference between the real expenses on the normative area of the dwelling and the following percentage of household income: 20% of total income for one-member households, 15% of total income for two-, three- and four-member households and 12% of total income for five- and more member households.

According to the specifications in the government decree approved on 28 August 2001 the housing expenditures include:

- in the case of tenants or subtenants in rental housing: rent, water charges, electricity and heating expenditures and expenditures on disposal of garbage;
- in the case of cooperative members and owners of dwellings in residential buildings: contribution to the fund on repairs and maintenance, water charges, electricity and heating expenditures, expenditures on disposal of garbage, real-estate tax and ground rent;
- in the case of family homeowners: electricity and heating expenditures, water charges and expenditures on disposal of garbage; and
- in the case of households without any legal title to the dwelling: the fee for occupation, electricity and water charges, heating expenditures, expenditures on disposal of garbage, real-estate tax and ground rent.

The Polish model of housing allowances therefore takes into account real housing costs. However, if the applicant lives in a home that is not a municipal rental dwelling (cooperative, own, free market rental housing) then the housing expenditures should be calculated in such a manner as if the applicant lives in municipal rental housing. This standardisation of expenditures has been done as a safeguard against unreasonably high housing expenditures. Such a standardisation is, however, confusing and is used mostly only for standardisation of market rents. Market rent expenditures are thus included into the calculation of housing allowances only within the limit of municipal rent expenditures for the same size of dwelling. In principle, the formula for housing allowances has the standard basic form of continental housing allowances in the EU countries:

$$HA = \min \ (HE, NHE) - NRB \times Y$$

where:

HA is the housing allowance;

HE   is real housing expenditure;

NHE   is normative housing expenditure (real housing expenditure on normative area of dwelling);

NRB   is the normative rate of burden (according to the size of household);

Y   is income.

Claimants have to declare their total net income by personal declaration every six months to obtain the housing allowance, and they are obliged to keep necessary confirmations of income (tax declaration, confirmation by employer) for a period of three years. The department can refuse to pay the allowance if there is a large discrepancy between declared income and the real wealth of the applicant household. The representative of the department can ask applicants to provide a schedule of assets of all household members, and if the applicant refuses to do so they will lose the right to apply for an allowance.

The allowance is paid directly to the person that has ownership title on the occupied dwelling, that is, directly to municipalities in the case of municipal rental housing, private landlords in the case of private rental housing, and housing cooperatives in the case of cooperative housing. If the household does not pay its housing liabilities – for rent, contribution to the homeowners' association, energy or water charges and so on – payment of the allowances will stop until the debt is paid. If the debt has not been paid within three months from the date at which payment of the housing allowance is interrupted, the applicant loses their right to the allowance and can apply again only after all debts are paid. The housing allowance recipient (that is, the housing cooperative, private landlord and so on) is obliged to inform the Department of Social Assistance in their municipality about defaults in payments by applicants within two months of the date at which the applicant stopped paying their housing obligations. If the recipient fails to meet this duty they will be obliged to repay all housing allowances paid during the time that claimant is default in payments.

Payment of allowances to persons living in all kinds of housing is the responsibility of municipalities (*gminas*), who get subsidies from the state budget covering on average half of the allowance paid. The *gmina* council can choose from two different relatively complex patterns of computation of state subsidy.

Slovakia

The housing allowance programme was introduced by the Housing Allowance Law passed by the Slovakian parliament in October 1999, which came into force on 1 January 2000. The housing allowance represents a means-tested benefit available to eligible households living in all different tenures (cooperative housing, rental housing, homeownership). The amount of the benefit is computed by a formula that takes into account the size of the household, net household income, the normative costs for the appropriate housing and the normative rate of burden (the share of income that each household should spend on housing expenditures).

The government decree passed in the first half of 2001 altered two parameters of the housing allowance system. First, it decreased the normative rate of the burden and, second, it increased the normative costs for the appropriate housing. In other words, the eligibility criteria became less restricted, enabled more households to apply for the housing allowance and increased the amount of the benefit for current recipients respectively.

Recognising that the housing allowance was the first demand-side housing subsidy in Slovakia, the Ministry of Labour and Social Affairs (MLSA) asked the United States Agency for International Development (USAID) to assist in the design and implementation of the housing allowance programme at the very beginning. The original feasibility study of a housing allowance programme was prepared for the Czech and Slovak Federal Republic in 1992. After the division of the country on 1 January 1993, the cooperation continued with the government of the Slovak Republic (Mikelson et al, 2000). The Slovak Republic 'inherited' the system of subsistence minimum and three-level social help (insurance, support and assistance) from the common Czechoslovak Republic, but the current housing allowance formula is different:

$$HA = MHC - (r \times Y)$$

where:

HA is the housing allowance paid monthly directly to the household;
MHC is the minimum housing costs (MHC), representing the normative monthly housing costs of appropriate housing, including utilities, for a household given size;
r is the normative rate of burden;
Y is the total net monthly income of the household during a previous half-year.

A household may receive a housing allowance payment only if the monthly amount of the housing allowance is SKK50 or more.

The *MHC* figures are based on the standard allotted living space (according to the size of household) multiplied by average regulated rent (per square metre) and average maintenance and energy fees. By the terminology established for housing allowance systems in the EU countries, *MHC* represents the maximum housing costs taken in calculating the benefit; any other costs must be covered solely by the household and do not enter into the calculation of benefit. The *MHC* are set by government decrees and were changed in proportion to the changes in the average housing costs (rent and energy prices deregulation). As can be seen from the formula, the real housing expenditures do not enter into the benefit calculation at all. If the real housing expenditures of particular households are above the *MHC* level the difference is fully paid by this household, and if the real housing expenditures are below the *MHC* level, the *MHC* level is used again. The value of the normative rate of burden *r* was at the start of the programme set at 0.30 (that is, households were expected to spend 30% of their own income on housing expenditures). Since 1 July 2001, r has had the value 0.29, based on a new government decree.

The total monthly income of the household, Y, consists of the monthly net income (after tax, social and health insurance payments are deducted) and monthly net incomes of people living permanently in the same dwelling. As well as the income from employment or entrepreneurship, this figure also includes contributions in case of illness, pensions, unemployment benefits, other regular social benefits (with the exception of supplement to child benefit) and income from abroad. However, social assistance benefits are excluded from the calculation.[4]

From the given formula it is apparent that as the income of the household rises, the amount of the allowance payment gradually decreases. When the household's income exceeds the level equal to the quotient $((MHC - 50)/r)$, a household is no longer eligible to receive an allowance. However, there are no explicit income ceilings as in the Czech or Polish models. The determination of the MHC and r levels gives to the government a powerful instrument affecting the number and type of household eligible to receive a housing allowance and the size of the benefits paid to households; this further influences the participation rate in the programme.

The application is made only for the period of the next half-year. Based on the information in the application, the district office determines whether the household qualifies for a housing allowance. As housing allowances form a part of the system of social support, households have to apply for housing allowances first before they can apply for social assistance (the benefit of last resort). If a household receives a housing allowance and social assistance benefit then the social assistance benefit is reduced by the amount of the housing allowance. In other words, those households who have income below the subsistence level and receive the social assistance benefit do not realise any new additional income from housing allowances and in the end receive the same amount of social transfers.

The normative calculation of housing expenditures (and not only of the dwelling area) remains the main barrier to the more effective application of the allowance. Regional differences in rent or other housing prices, and differences between the level of market rent and regulated rent prices, are not reflected in the current formula at all. Other deficiencies are connected with the flat normative rate of burden (coefficient r in the formula) with no relation to the real housing expenditures.

Estonia

The system of housing allowances in Estonia was introduced in 1992, and was considerably amended in 1994, 1997 and 2002. In the period from 1994 to 1996 there were two schemes to assist people in need: housing benefit (which was the more important of the two) and subsistence benefit. Housing benefit was paid to compensate for the part of the housing costs that, within the standard allotted living space, exceeded one third of the income of the household. The payment was organised by the Housing Board of the Ministry of Economic Affairs and the financial means came directly from the state budget. The two benefits (housing benefit and subsistence benefit) were integrated into a common subsistence benefit in 1997, with the exception of the capital, Tallin, where local government decided to continue with the old scheme of two different social transfers until 2000. The 2002 reform introduced fairly broad competencies for local government in setting the principles for paying the benefits and other aspects of their funding.

Since 1997 the subsistence benefit has been representing a universal social support for households in need. The benefit should help households to cover all costs of the primary needs, that is, not only the housing costs. Its calculation is based on minimal consumption costs on food, clothes, footwear and other goods and services to satisfy the primary needs (subsistence level). Both homeowners and tenants are eligible for benefit, the amount of which is the difference between the sum of household subsistence level and regular costs connected with permanent housing in the extent of the standard allotted living space and net (after-tax) monthly household income. The calculation of the subsistence benefit is based on the net income of all household members during the last month, the regular housing costs to the extent of standard allotted living space, and the approved subsistence level:

$$SB = (HC + SL) - Y$$

where:

SB is the subsistence benefit paid monthly to the household;
HC is the regular housing costs to the extent of standard allotted living space;
SL is the subsistence level calculated for a household (basic normative expenditures on other household consumption than housing);
Y is the household's monthly income.

The total net income of all family members (or all people sharing the same living space) is calculated; apart from the applicant, the incomes of the following persons are also taken into account: their spouse or partner, if any, their children, parents and other persons using one or more sources of income jointly with other members of the household (Purju, 2000). All social transfers are included in the income calculation with the following exceptions: one-off benefits (for example, birth benefit), certain social benefits paid to disabled persons, and child benefits.

An explicit income ceiling is not applied in Estonia. However, an implicit ceiling is apparent from the logic of the formula itself: the maximum household income is equal to the sum of the official subsistence level and regular housing costs to the extent of standard allotted living space (housing costs per square metre are also limited by municipalities, as described later) for the particular household.

The subsistence level is announced by the central government for each budgetary year; new levels cannot be lower than that of the previous year.

The standard allotted living space (normative area of dwelling according to the size of household) is as follows: 18m² per each household member and an additional 15m² per household itself. As in Poland, if the total area of an apartment is smaller than the standard allotted living space, the actual total area of the dwelling is taken for the calculation (Purju, 2000). However, if the number of rooms in an apartment is equal to the number of residents permanently living there and the total area of the apartment exceeds the standard allotted living space, the actual total area of an apartment is taken for the calculation. Moreover, single-pensioner households are allowed more advantageous conditions: the total area of two-room dwellings, and not more than 51m² in the case of dwellings with a higher number of rooms, is considered to be the standard allotted living space for these households.

The following expenses connected with permanent housing in the standard allotted living space are taken into account:

- rent or management costs (contribution to the homeowners' association);
- the heating costs and hot water charges;
- water supply and sewerage service costs;
- electricity costs;
- costs on fuels;
- land;
- the costs of housing insurance in accordance with the living space of the dwelling.

According to the legislation (since 2002), each municipality can decide on the limits applied on the above-mentioned costs. Until 2002 the local government had only responsibility for the allocation of benefit. They had to allocate benefits according to the principles stipulated in the law, but the finance needed for subsistence benefit came directly from the state budget. Since 2002 the benefits have been allocated from the local government's own budget, but necessary financial sources are transferred from the state budget according to the approximate sum of subsistence benefits in the previous period. In connection with this decentralisation strategy the municipalities were given the power to determine the principles for paying the allowances – that is, the maximum level of rent and housing costs to be compensated.

International comparison and conclusion

Table 11.3 summarises the comparison between housing allowances in the four CEE countries. The following figures (Figures 11.6–11.9) show the development in the amount of housing allowance related to the household income growth in the selected CEE countries.

Table 11.3: Comparison of housing allowances in four CEE countries, 2001

	Czech Republic	Estonia	Poland	Slovak Republic
Housing allowance is a separate benefit in social system designed particularly to cover housing costs	Yes	No (a common subsistence benefit was introduced for covering all primary needs)	Yes	Yes
All tenures are eligible for the housing allowance	Yes	Yes	Yes (but there are important limits in cases when household is not living in municipal rental housing)	Yes
Explicit or implicit income ceilings for housing allowance application	Yes, explicit (as a multiple of household's subsistence level)	Yes, implicit (as household's income after payment of limited housing expenditures must remain below the subsistence level)	Yes, explicit (as a percentage of the lowest retirement pension)	Yes, implicit (emerging from the formula used for housing allowance calculation)
What kind of income (net or gross) is used for the eligibility test or for the housing allowance calculation? Are other social benefits included?	Net income, including sick and retirement benefit, unemployment benefit, parents benefit, care benefit, child benefit. One-time benefits are not included	Net income, inclusive social benefits with a few exceptions: one-time benefits, certain benefits to disabled persons, child benefits	Net income, inclusive social benefits, with a few exceptions: one-time benefits and social transfers for orphans	Net income, inclusive other social benefits with a few exceptions: one-time benefits, social assistance
What housing expenditures are taken into account for housing allowance calculation?	Normative housing costs (part of a subsistence level) differentiated by household's size	Real housing costs to the extent of standard allotted living space and to the limits established by local authorities	Real housing costs to the extent of standard allotted living space (limits are applied mainly for households living in market rental sector)	Normative housing costs calculated on the basis of allotted living space for the household multiplied by average rent, maintenance and energy fees (per m²)
The share of households receiving housing allowance from total number of households	8.0% (December 2000)	12% (2001)	7.6% (2000)	4.2% (December 2001)

In the Czech Republic, if household income remains below the official subsistence level, the growth in income does not have any influence on the housing allowance; above the subsistence level the amount of housing allowance gradually decreases to zero. Households with incomes higher than 1.6 times the subsistence minimum lose their eligibility for the housing allowance.

Figure 11.6: Housing allowance amounts by household income, Czech Republic, 2001

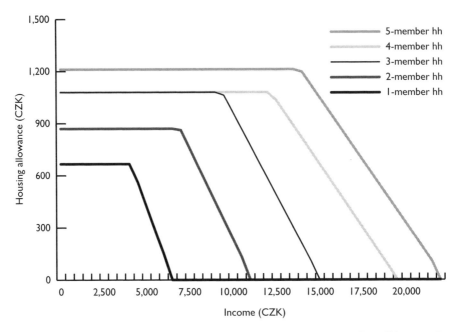

Notes: The following composition of households was assumed by calculation of values shown in Figure 11.1: one-member household: one adult; two-member household: two adults; three-member household: two adults and a child aged 6–10; four-member household: two adults, a child aged 10–15 and a child aged 15–26; five-member household: two adults, a child aged 6 and under, a child aged 6–10 and a child aged 15–26.

In Poland, the amount of housing allowance decreases with rising income. However, a noticeable decrease is apparent when household income per capita exceeds 150% of the lowest retirement pension in the case of one-member households and/or 100% of the lowest retirement pension in the case of multiperson households. When income per capita exceeds 175% of the lowest retirement pension in the case of one-member households or 125% of the lowest retirement pension in the case of multiperson households, the household is no longer entitled to the allowance (allowance is equal to zero).

Figure 11.7: Housing allowance amounts by household income, Poland

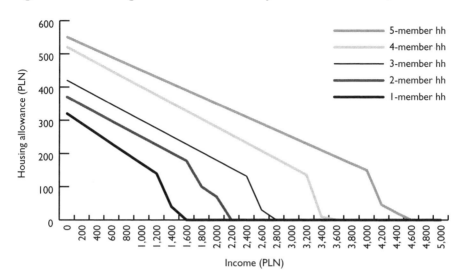

Notes: The following values of housing expenditures were taken into account by calculation of the benefit: PLN320 in case of one-member household, PLN370 in case of two-member household, PLN420 in case of three-member household, PLN520 in case of four-member household, and PLN550 in case of five-member household. The amount of the lowest retirement pension was set at PLN800.

From Figure 11.8 it is apparent that the amount of the housing allowance in the Slovak model gradually decreases with rising income. If the household's income reaches the level that implies an amount of the benefit lower than SKK50, the household loses its eligibility for the benefit.

Figure 11.8: Housing allowance amounts by household income, Slovakia

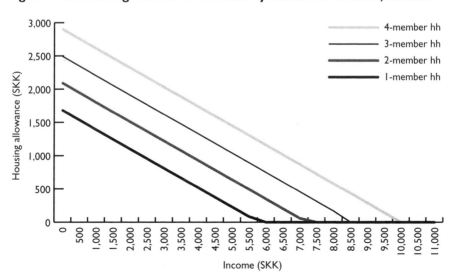

From Figure 11.9 it is apparent that the amount of the subsistence benefit in the Estonian model gradually decreases with rising income. If the household's income equals the sum of regular housing costs (to the extent of standard allotted living space) and the subsistence level for a given household, the subsistence benefit decreases to zero.

Figure 11.9: Housing allowance amounts by household income, Estonia

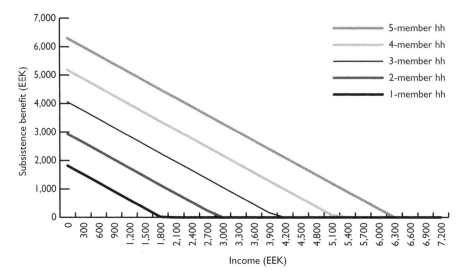

Notes: Standard size of the apartment (that is, 18m² per household member plus additional 15m² per household) and housing expenditures still covered by the municipality (Tartu case) were assumed. For example, a one-member household spends EEK1,320, two-member EEK2,040, three-member EEK2,760, four-member EEK3,480 and five-member EEK4,200.

A common feature of housing allowances in all selected CEE countries lies in their marginal significance; housing allowance serves rather as a support to the lowest-income families than effective demand–side housing policy instrument. This could be documented by the share of households receiving benefit from the total number of households in each country; this share does not exceed 8% in all countries except Estonia. The main goal of housing allowances is not the stimulation of the demand for housing, but the maintenance of the current housing standard by households in need. With caution it could be stated that there is no significant relationship between housing allowances and the supply side of the housing market in these transitional countries. The income support provided through the benefit is not sufficient to stimulate the demand for new housing with an adequate response in the supply.

Housing allowance programmes in the Czech Republic, Slovakia and Poland are targeted on low-income and disabled households. This could be demonstrated through the application of many restricted conditions, such as income ceilings and limits on housing expenditures. Two types of income ceilings could be distinguished: implicit and explicit. Implicit income ceilings arise from the formula used for calculation of the housing allowance, whereas explicit income ceilings are strictly set in legislation. The explicit income ceilings are used in the Czech and Polish systems – in both cases the rate of decrease in the allowance (the taper) is not constant with the rise in household income and there are significant breakpoints after which the value of the taper rises substantially (see previous figures). The explicit income ceiling thus could negatively affect the work incentives of the household members and lead to a poverty trap. Overall, however, the highest taper is in the Estonian allowance, which is part of the more general subsistence benefit.

Another common feature of the housing allowance systems is a disadvantageous position of households living in market rental housing. Generally, these households are not 'income poor' but may be labelled as 'housing poor' due to their high housing cost-to-income ratio. Restrictive income ceilings are complemented by the calculation of the allowance based on standard (normative) housing expenditures that are significantly lower than market rents. This is the case for the Czech Republic and Slovakia, but somewhat less so for Estonia (normative limits can be applied by local authorities) or Poland (reference rent in municipal housing can be used).

Another problem of the housing allowances in the selected CEE countries concerns the determination of the normative rate of burden. In all the selected countries the normative rate is established by one flat coefficient, albeit with two particular exceptions: the coefficient of the normative rate of burden differs by size and composition of a household in the Czech model and by income level in the Polish model. Although the Polish housing allowance model best meets the criteria of efficiency and equity (allowances are paid both from state and municipal budgets, real housing costs are included into the formula with only indirectly set limits, the normative rate of burden rises with household income) while holding an acceptable level of taper (taper for Estonian subsistence benefit is, for example, equal to one), it would not be fair to say that the Czech model of housing allowance is, in this comparative perspective, much worse than those in other transitional countries.

Notes

[1] The flats are categorised by law according to the quality of their equipment into four categories: the first category refers to the flats with the highest quality and the fourth category refers to the flats with the lowest quality.

[2] Most often the number of flats per 1,000 inhabitants.

[3] However part of the Act regulating the provision of benefits, regardless of the level of income, had already come into force on 1 October 1995.

[4] But a household must first apply for a housing allowance, then its eligibility for social assistance is tested.

References

Czech Statistical Office, *Census 1991, 2001*, www.czso.cz.

Czech Statistical Office, *Family budget surveys*, www.czso.cz.

Dlouhý, J. (ed.) (1997) *Životní minimum (The subsistence level)*, Prague: Socioklub.

Housing Allowance Act No 300/1999 Coll of the Slovak Republic

Kährik, A., Kõre, J., Hendrikson, M. and Allsaar, I. (2002) 'Local government and housing in estonia' study under the Local Government Policy Partnership programme, Tartu.

Kepková, M. (ed.) (1997) *Státní sociální podpora (State social support)*, Prague: Socioklub.

Kulesza, H. (2000) *Wydatki na mieszkanie w budzetach domowych*, Warsaw: Instytut gospodarki mieszkaniowej.

Lux, M. (ed.) (2003) *Housing policy: An end or a new beginning*, Budapest: LGI.

Lux, M. and Sunega, P. (2002) 'Modelování rovnovážné úrovně nájemného a důsledků aplikace vybraných nástrojů bytové politiky' ('Modelling of the equilibrium market rent and consequences of the application of selected housing policy instruments'), *Finance a úvěr*, vol 53, pp 31–59.

Mareš, P. (2001) *Problém nečerpání sociálních dávek (The problem of non-take-up of social benefits)*, Brno: VÚPSV.

Materials of the Ministry of Labour and Social Affairs of the Czech Republic, Internal unpublished documents.

Materials of the Ministry of Labour, Social Affairs and Family of the Slovak Republic (www.employment.gov.sk).

Mikelson, M., Tatian, P. and Zapletalova, J. (2000) *Slovakia housing allowance program – final report*, Washington, DC: Urban Institute.

Průša, L. (2002) 'Vývoj systému dávek státní sociální podpory ve druhé polovině devadesátých let' ('The development of the state social support in the second half of the 1990s'), *Veřejná správa*, vol 7, pp 24–7.

Purju, A. (ed.) (2000) *Living conditions*, Tallin: Statistical Office of Estonia.

State Social Support Act No 117/1995 Coll of the Czech Republic.

Subsistence Level Act No 463/1991 Coll of the Czech Republic.

Urbanska, W. (2000) *Ocena roli dodatków mieszkaniowych jako elementu polityki czynszowej*, Warsaw: Instytut gospodarki mieszkaniowej.

Víšek, P. (1995) *Náklady na děti: přístupy a aplikace v sociální politice (Child expenditures: approaches and applications in social policy)*, Prague: Foundation for Research on Social Transformation.

TWELVE

Housing allowances in the advanced welfare states

Peter A. Kemp

Introduction

This book has examined the context, role, design and impacts of income-related housing allowances in a variety of countries. Chapters Two to Ten looked at nine advanced welfare states, while Chapter Eleven explored the experience of the Czech Republic and made comparisons with several other transition economies. This final chapter draws upon the preceding chapters to reflect upon the role of housing allowances in the advanced welfare states. The first section describes the broad welfare regime and housing market context of the ten main countries covered in the book. The second section compares important features of income-related assistance with housing expenditures across these countries. The third section examines key reform pressures and debates about housing allowances and the fourth section focuses on 'housing vouchers' as a possible future for income-related assistance with housing expenditures. The final section presents some conclusions.

Contextualising housing allowances

Although housing allowances have become an important policy instrument in many of the advanced welfare states, they are embedded within different national contexts. Table 12.1 summarises some key features of the social protection systems in each country covered by this book. Nine of the 10 countries were included in Esping-Andersen's typology of welfare regimes (the exception being the Czech Republic). Australia, New Zealand, Canada, the US and Great Britain were described by him as liberal welfare regimes, characterised by a low level of benefits, reliance on means testing and a relative emphasis on private social provision.[1] France and Germany were classified as conservative welfare states, characterised by heavy reliance on status-maintaining social insurance schemes with relatively generous, earnings-related benefit levels and an emphasis on the 'male breadwinner family model'. Meanwhile, Sweden and (more controversially) the Netherlands were described as social democratic welfare states, with a commitment to generous and universal benefits, high quality services and an emphasis on the dual-earner family (Esping-Andersen, 1990). While this typology has been subject to criticism,

Table 12.1: Welfare regimes, benefit generosity and public social expenditure as a % of GDP

Country	Welfare regime classification[a]	Social insurance generosity index[b]	Public social expenditure as % of GDP[c]	Gini coefficient[d]
Australia	Liberal	0.99	20.4	0.31
New Zealand	Liberal	1.40	21.1	–
Canada	Liberal	2.14	20.4	0.31
US	Liberal	1.51	15.7	0.37
Great Britain	Liberal	1.45	25.4	0.35
France	Conservative	2.09	33.0	0.29
Germany	Conservative	2.09	30.6	0.25
Netherlands	Social democratic	2.33	24.3	0.25
Sweden	Social democratic	2.39	35.1	0.25
Czech Republic	–	–	22.2	0.26

Sources: Esping-Andersen (1990); Smeeding (2004); OECD (2005); Scruggs (2006).

Notes: [a] Esping-Andersen's classification, date circa 1980; [b] data for 2002, the higher the score, the greater the generosity, possible scores range from 0.0 to 3.0; [c] data for 2001; [d] various years, the higher the coefficient, the greater the inequality in disposable income; – Not available/applicable.

it nonetheless provides a useful summary description of institutional arrangements in respect of income protection in the advanced welfare states.

Broadly in line with this typology, with the exception of Canada, social insurance benefit generosity is lower in the liberal welfare states than in the conservative and especially the social democratic welfare states included in this book (Table 12.1). Further, with the exception of Britain, public social expenditure as a proportion of GDP is also lower in the liberal welfare states than in France, Germany, Sweden and to a lesser extent the Netherlands.[2] Finally, as measured by the Gini coefficient, there is a greater degree of inequality in disposable incomes in the five liberal welfare states than in the conservative or social democratic welfare states or the Czech Republic.

As well as social protection, the countries covered by this book also differ in respect of their housing systems (Table 12.2). The five liberal welfare states all have relatively high and similar levels of homeownership, ranging from 66% in Canada to 70% in Australia. With the exception of Great Britain, the liberal welfare states also have low levels of social housing and fairly high levels of private renting. In Great Britain, social renting exceeds private renting as a share of the housing market. Meanwhile, in the five other countries, homeownership does not dominate housing provision, the proportion of households owning their homes varying from 41% in Germany to 56% in France. Among these states, Germany has a very high level of private renting, the Netherlands has a high level of social housing, and both Sweden and the Czech Republic have a substantial amount of cooperative housing. Germany, the Netherlands and Sweden have what Kemeny (1995) describes as 'unitary' rental systems in which non-profit or social housing providers are encouraged to compete with for-profit private landlords and let

Table 12.2: Housing tenure in the early 2000s

Country	Owner-occupied	Private rented	Social rented	Other	Total
Australia	70	20	5	5	100
New Zealand	68	27	6	0	100
Canada	66	28	6	0	100
US	68	30	2	0	100
Great Britain	69	10	21	0	100
France	56	21	17	6	100
Germany	41	44	6	5	100
Netherlands	54	11	35	0	100
Sweden	46	21	18	15	100
Czech Republic	47	12	17	24	100

Source: OECD (2006, table 4.6); Statistics New Zealand (www.stats.govt.nz); CECODHAS (www.cedodhas.org)

Note: Totals may not sum to exactly 100 due to rounding.

their accommodation to a wide range of income groups. Meanwhile, Australia, New Zealand, Canada, the US and Great Britain have what Kemeny describes as 'dualist' rental systems in which social housing is separate from private rental housing and is targeted largely on the poor (cf Stephens et al, 2003).

Four of the liberal welfare regimes – Britain being the exception – charge income-related rents for some or all social (or other forms of subsidised) rented housing (Hulse, 2003). As I have pointed out, income-related rents are an implicit form of housing allowance (Kemp, 1997). Means testing rents in this way is not just a mechanism for ensuring that social housing is affordable to the very poor, it is also a way of ensuring that the amount of subsidy provided to social housing tenants is not more than they need. Income-related rents are therefore consistent with the liberal welfare regime outlined by Esping-Andersen (1990). However, they do not match the more socially inclusive approach to social housing pursued in countries such as Sweden and the Netherlands.

Notwithstanding these differences, some common patterns exist. In all nine of the advanced welfare states covered in this book, support for housing expenditures has shifted away from rent controls and bricks-and-mortar subsidies and towards housing allowances.[3] This shift has progressed to such an extent that housing allowances are the most important form of direct housing subsidy in these countries; and in the Netherlands and Sweden, almost the only housing subsidy.[4] The policy drivers behind this shift were outlined in Chapter One but, in summary, reflect both the influence of neo-liberal ideas (and in particular the importance given to markets) among many governments. Housing allowances are more in tune with neo-liberal thinking than either rent controls or bricks-and-mortar subsidies, not least because they appear to promote choice and help to underpin the market rather than subvert it. In an era of 'permanent fiscal austerity' (Pierson, 1994), housing allowances are seen to represent better value for money than bricks-and-mortar subsidies to governments influenced by neo-liberal ideas or concerned about national competitiveness in the global economy.

However, as noted in Chapter One, the shift towards housing allowances also reflects changing perceptions of the 'housing question', from a focus on the supply and quality of housing provision, to one that is more concerned with affordability (Kemp, 1990; Grigsby and Bourassa, 2003). Bricks-and-mortar subsidies were seen as important instruments for increasing the supply and improving the quality of rental housing in the first several decades after 1945 (Harloe, 1995). Even when housing shortages became a less pressing political issue, supply-side subsidies were still an important means of raising the quality of housing, including the refurbishment of older, private dwellings in central city locations. But once affordability becomes the more important problem, the rationale for bricks-and-mortar subsidies loses some of its force. Yet, ironically, one of the reasons why affordability has become a more pressing concern is precisely the shift towards market rents and decline of bricks-and-mortar subsidies. If the low-rent regimes established after the Second World War had remained in place, there would be less need for housing allowances today.

Nevertheless, housing affordability would probably still have become a more pressing issue for many governments, even if there had not been a move towards lower bricks-and-mortar subsidies and higher rents. That is because, as I pointed out in Chapter One, the shift towards housing allowances also reflects changes in 'needs' – or, to put it another way, in social risks – resulting from the social and economic trends that have accompanied the transition to post-industrial societies (on which see Esping-Andersen, 1999; Taylor-Gooby, 2005). Increased income inequality and the individualisation of social risks that has accompanied that transition make housing allowances a more suitable policy instrument than less targeted approaches such as bricks-and-mortar subsidies and rent controls.

Housing allowances and social risks

In this context, it is important to understand that the social risks tackled by housing allowances are subtly different from those addressed by social housing. The latter has generally involved subsidised, below market rent housing, often (though not exclusively) provided by not-for-profit organisations such as housing associations and public authorities (Ball et al, 1988; Harloe, 1995). The risks covered by social housing include both insufficient or substandard dwellings and high rent-to-income ratios. Depending upon the rules of access to such accommodation, the people benefiting from social housing have included both low- and moderate-income households in conservative and social democratic welfare regimes, and – with the exception of Britain prior to the 1980s – the poor in liberal welfare regimes. The provision of social rented housing on a substantial scale is more in tune with the social democratic and conservative welfare regimes than the liberal regime.

By contrast, housing allowances are more in tune with the liberal welfare regime and neo-liberalism more generally. They are means tested and very largely focused on poor and other low-income households, though the precise extent to which this is the case varies from one country to another. Thus housing allowances are almost by definition pro-poor (Gibbs and Kemp, 1993; Stephens, 2005). In contrast, social housing is not necessarily pro-poor and has often benefited the labour aristocracy (Harloe, 1995). The social risks covered by housing allowances are high housing expenditures and, at least indirectly, income risks such as unemployment, sickness and disability, old age and lone parenthood.[5] Housing allowances are focused more on the risk that housing is unaffordable to poor households than that it is substandard or in insufficient supply. Indeed, while housing allowances help to make housing more affordable, they do not necessarily guarantee that recipients live in minimally adequate housing. Nevertheless, unlike social housing, housing allowances are generally an entitlement to which people with a low income and relatively high housing expenses have a right.

The US is an important exception here in at least two respects. First, as Newman points out in Chapter Five, housing allowances in the US are not an entitlement: the Housing Choice Voucher programme is cash limited (see also Priemus et al, 2006). As a result, there are queues for housing vouchers among eligible applicants that cannot yet receive one because the money has run out. Second, housing vouchers are only payable to households living in minimally adequate housing. While this provision ensures that public money is not spent on paying for substandard accommodation, it does come at a significant price. As the US Experimental Housing Allowance Program (EHAP) found, the minimum standard rules disproportionately excluded the poorest households – including older people, ethnic minorities and large families – who could not gain access to housing above that standard (Bradbury and Downs, 1981). Hence, because they experienced some of the worst housing conditions they suffered the additional penalty of being ineligible for assistance with their housing expenditures under EHAP.

While housing allowances are more typically an entitlement programme, they are not necessarily universal schemes open to all low-income households. The risk groups covered by housing allowances vary according to the rules governing such schemes. For example, in some countries (such as Germany and Sweden) housing allowance schemes include both renters and homeowners, while in others (such as the Netherlands) they are confined to renters. And while in some countries (such as Australia) housing allowances are provided only to recipients of social assistance, in others (such as Britain) they are available to people with incomes above social assistance levels and even people in low-paid work. Likewise, some types of household may be excluded from eligibility, such as most students in Great Britain (Stephens, 1990) or single people and childless couples aged over 28 years in Sweden (see Chapter Ten). Thus, like other means-tested benefits, the groups of people that are eligible for housing allowances may be more or less circumscribed. As I argued in Chapter One, however, such inclusions and exclusions are not simply technical matters, but inherently political decisions with potentially important distributional implications.

Comparing housing allowances

The previous section showed that housing allowances exist within quite different institutional contexts, including a variety of housing market and income protection systems (Kemp, 1997; Hulse, 2003; Stephens et al, 2003). It is also apparent that the precise design of housing allowance schemes, including their rules on eligibility (who may apply) and entitlement (how much recipients are awarded), vary from one country to another. This section aims to draw some comparisons between housing allowances in the 10 countries covered in this book. Such comparisons are inevitably restricted by data limitations, quite apart from the difficulty of analysing the formal versus the nominal impact of such schemes. A comprehensive comparison would have required substantial research resources that were not available to the authors and hence this volume is a work of scholarship that is based on the existing literature and publicly available data. There is in fact a need for more research on housing allowances, particularly on their impact on recipient behaviour and their effects on the housing market more generally. Nevertheless, in the meantime some comparisons may usefully be made.

Table 12.3 presents a summary overview of the schemes providing income-related assistance with housing expenditure in each of the ten countries included in this book. It identifies three types of provision: (1) help with housing expenditures within social assistance benefits; (2) separate housing allowance schemes; and (3) income-related rents in social housing.

In six of the countries, the social assistance schemes include a top-up that covers *some* (the US and the Netherlands) or *all* 'reasonable' (Canada, Great Britain, Germany and Sweden) housing expenditure. In the British case, these housing top-ups apply only to homeowners. Nine of the countries have national housing allowance schemes, the exception being Canada, where such schemes exist only in some provinces and not at the national level. The Australian housing allowance applies only to eligible households (private renters) that are in receipt of social assistance. By contrast, in the remaining eight countries they are open to other – and hence generally better-off – households as well as those getting social assistance benefits. In five of the countries, New Zealand, France, Germany, Sweden and the Czech Republic, low-income homeowners are eligible to apply for housing allowances, but in Britain, Australia and the Netherlands they are available only to tenants. In practice, relatively few homeowners actually receive such payments in the countries where they are eligible to apply for them. This is at least partly because homeowners tend to have relatively high incomes compared with tenants. Finally, as noted previously, in four of the five liberal welfare regimes (the exception being Great Britain) social housing rents are generally income related, thereby obviating the need for housing allowances (Kemp, 1997).

Table 12.3: Summary of income-related assistance with housing costs

Country	Scheme	Tenure
Australia	Social assistance: rent allowances	Private tenants
	Income-related rents	Public housing
New Zealand	Separate housing allowance scheme	Private tenants and homeowners
	Income-related rents	Public housing
Canada	Social assistance: shelter addition	All tenures
	No separate housing allowance scheme[a]	
	Income-related rents	Social housing
US	Social assistance: covers some housing costs	All tenures
	Cash-limited housing vouchers	Private tenants
	Income-related rents	Public housing
Great Britain	Social assistance: housing additions	Homeowners
	Separate housing allowance scheme	Private and social tenants
France	Separate housing allowance schemes	All tenures
Germany	Social assistance: housing addition	All tenures
	Separate housing allowance scheme	All tenures
Netherlands	Social assistance: covers minimum housing costs	All tenures
	Separate housing allowance scheme	Private and social tenants
Sweden	Social assistance: housing addition	All tenures
	Separate housing allowance schemes	All tenures
Czech Republic	Separate housing allowance scheme	All tenures

Sources: Adapted from Wilcox (2001); country chapters.

Note: [a] Some provinces have housing allowance schemes (see Chapter Four).

Table 12.4 shows expenditure on housing allowance schemes as a percentage of gross domestic product (GDP) for the 10 countries included in the book.[6] It is clear from the table that spending on this policy instrument varies widely between these countries. Leaving aside Canada which does not have a national scheme, expenditure on housing allowance schemes ranges from 0.1% of GDP in both the US and the Czech Republic to 1.1% of GDP in Great Britain. The latter country and France (0.92%) devote considerably more of their GDP to housing allowance schemes than any of the other countries. This point is illustrated in the second column of Table 12.4, which shows expenditure in each country expressed as a percentage of the share of GDP that Great Britain devotes to housing allowances. From this it is clear that Sweden spends about half, the Netherlands a third, Germany a fifth, Australia a quarter and the US and Czech Republic only a tenth, of the amount that Britain spends on housing allowances as a share of GDP.

Table 12.4: Expenditure as a percentage of GDP and percentage of households receiving housing allowances[a]

	Housing allowance expenditure as a % of GDP	Expenditure on housing allowances as a % of the figure for Britain[b]	% of households in receipt of housing allowances
Australia	0.30	27	14
New Zealand	0.49	45	18
Canada	0.02	2	<1
US	0.10	9	2
Great Britain	1.10	100	16
France	0.92	84	23
Germany	0.23	21	9
Netherlands	0.35	32	14
Sweden	0.57	52	20
Czech Republic	0.10	9	7

Source: Country chapters, Uhry (2006); OECD Social Expenditure Database (www.oecd.org).

Notes: [a] Excludes housing additions incorporated in social assistance payments; [b] calculated from column 1.

Table 12.4 also shows the percentage of households receiving housing allowances in each country. The figures are very low in Canada because it has no national scheme and in the US because its voucher programme is cash limited and small in scale. Housing allowance receipt is highest in France (23%), followed by Sweden (20%), New Zealand (18%) and then Britain (16%). It is much lower in Germany (9%) and the Czech Republic (7%). Thus, although Great Britain devotes more of its GDP to housing allowances than the other countries, it does not have the highest proportion of households in receipt of housing allowances. Nonetheless, there is a fairly high correlation between expenditure as a share of GDP and the proportion of households in receipt of housing allowances. The correlation coefficient based on nine countries (that is, excluding Canada, for which an exact figure is not available) is 0.76; the corresponding figure based on rank order (for all 10 countries) is even higher at 0.90.[7] Hence, perhaps not surprisingly, countries that have a high proportion of households in receipt of housing allowances tend to spend a high share of GDP on such schemes.

Housing allowances form part of the 'income package' (Rein et al, 1986) that welfare states provide to low- and moderate-income households. Other elements of this package include social insurance, social assistance and family benefits such as child allowances. The precise configuration of this income package differs between different welfare states and also within them (varying, for example, by household type and employment record). Table 12.5 shows the importance of housing allowance schemes in relation to the income package received by newly unemployed one-earner families. The data are produced by the OECD for its benefits and wages series and are necessarily based on a number of assumptions (see OECD, 2002). In particular, the figures assume that the household is living in private rental housing and that it pays a rent equal to 20% of the earnings

Table 12.5: Composition of net benefit income of a one-earner couple with two children during the first month of unemployment[a]

Country	Unemployment insurance	Unemployment assistance	Family benefits	Housing benefits[c]	Income taxes	Total[d]	Net replacement rate[b]
Australia	–	60	32	8	0	100	62
New Zealand	–	82	19	11	–12	100	68
Canada	103	–	10	0	–13	100	91
US	103	–	0	–	–3	100	57
Great Britain	36	0	17	47	0	100	49
France	81	0	9	17	–7	100	72
Germany	72	0	17	11	0	100	70
Netherlands	97	0	8	16	–21	100	89
Sweden	119	0	14	5	–38	100	78
Czech Republic	77	–	10	0	–13	100	70

Source: OECD (2002, tables 3.4, 3.2).

Notes: [a] Data are for July 2002. The figures for unemployment insurance and unemployment assistance are before tax; [b] net benefit income as a % of average production worker (APW) earnings; [c] based on housing costs (rent) equal to 20% of the earnings of the APW; [d] assumes that the household has sufficient assets to be disqualified from social assistance.

of the 'average production worker' (APW). In this example, the figures are computed for a one-earner couple with two children where the 'breadwinner' is in the first month of unemployment and has a full contributory record for social insurance benefits where they exist. It further assumes that the household had an income prior to unemployment equal to 100% of the APW level; an important assumption, given that in some of these countries unemployment insurance is earnings related.[8] The example also assumes that the household has sufficient savings to disqualify them from social assistance. In the case of Great Britain, this assumption is arguably unrealistic because the great majority of people receiving unemployment insurance (*contributory* Jobseeker's Allowance) are also in receipt of social assistance (*income-based* Jobseeker's Allowance). In some of the countries, unemployment insurance and assistance are taxed, but in all of them housing allowances are not taxable.

It is clear from Table 12.5 that the contribution of housing allowances to the income package of newly unemployed single-earner couples with two children varies considerably between the 10 countries. It ranges from nil in the case of Canada and the US (for reasons previously discussed) to 47% in the case of Great Britain. However, if the assumption about disqualification from social assistance noted earlier is dropped, the figure for housing allowances in Britain falls to about 30%; a share that is still well above that for the other countries. One important reason why housing allowances represent such a large share of the incomes of unemployed households in Great Britain is that unemployment benefits in that country are flat rate rather than earnings related and relatively low (Kemp, 1997; Wilcox, 2001; Stephens et al, 2003). Table 12.5 shows that the net replacement rate is in fact much lower in Britain than in the nine other countries.[9]

The lower level of generosity of unemployment benefits in Britain in part reflects the fact that recipients who are renting their accommodation are not expected to use them to contribute to their housing expenses, but instead are meant to apply for help from the housing allowance scheme. In contrast, in the other countries, recipients are expected to make some contribution to their housing expenses from their unemployment benefit, a fact that is reflected in the 'housing gap' design of their housing allowance schemes (see Chapter One). In effect, therefore, some of the costs that are covered by housing allowances in Britain are covered by the unemployment schemes in the other countries (Kemp, 1997). Thus, to some extent the high level of housing allowances in the income support package in Britain reflects the different way that it provides income protection compared with the other nine countries. This implies that the income support package needs to be assessed as a whole rather than focusing only on one particular aspect of it in isolation. That makes it difficult to draw definitive conclusions about the role of individual benefits (including housing allowances) in the advanced welfare states.

Table 12.6 shows housing allowances as a percentage of the APW earnings and of rents for each country. This again shows that housing allowances in Britain are much larger than in all of the other countries, a result that (as noted previously)

Table 12.6: Housing benefit as a percentage of rent and APW earnings for a one-earner couple with two children during the first month of unemployment[a]

Country	Housing benefits as % of APW earnings[b]	Housing benefits as % of rent[c]
Australia	5.5	27.7
New Zealand	6.6	33.2
Canada	–	–
USA	–	–
Great Britain	20.0	100.0
France	5.3	26.5
Germany	4.6	23.1
Netherlands	3.0	15.1
Sweden	0.6	3.0
Czech Republic	6.1	30.3

Source: Calculated from OECD data on benefits and wages (www.oecd.org).

Notes: [a] Data are for July 2004 and are otherwise based on the same assumptions as in Table 12.5; [b] net benefit income as a % of average production worker (APW) earnings; [c] based on housing costs (rent) equal to 20% of the earnings of the APW.

reflects the design of the scheme and in particular the fact that benefits for social assistance recipients are not intended to cover the rental costs of tenants. Interestingly, although more households receive housing allowances in France and Sweden than in Britain, this benefit represents a much smaller percentage of the income package, APW earnings and rents in these two countries. Thus, while the coverage of housing allowances is somewhat greater in these two countries than in Britain, the amount received per household (at least in the case of newly unemployed, one-earner couples with two children) is much lower.

However, the net replacement rate, taking into account unemployment, family and housing benefits, is higher in France and Sweden (and the other seven countries) than in Great Britain (Table 12.5). Thus, relative to average earnings, unemployed, one-earner households are much worse off in Britain than their counterparts in the other nine countries, even when housing allowances are taken into account. The net replacement rate in Canada is much higher than in Britain and somewhat higher than in France and Sweden, even though in this example the household does not receive a housing allowance payment. This may explain why unemployed households in receipt of social insurance in Canada are able to manage without a separate housing allowance scheme. Meanwhile, social assistance recipients in Canada, as noted earlier, are entitled to a top-up to their benefit that covers their housing expenditures up to a rent ceiling.

Housing allowances under review

While income-related housing allowances are now a well-established and increasingly important policy instrument in many advanced welfare states, they have also faced a range of reform pressures in recent years. As the contributions to this book show, Britain, Germany, the Netherlands, New Zealand and Sweden have all implemented major reforms of housing allowances in recent years (see also Schwarz, 1991; Kuila, 1993; Priemus, 1998; Kemp, 2006). Germany has introduced changes that particularly affect recipients of social assistance. A radical reform was proposed in Australia in 1996 (Yates, 1997), but this was subsequently abandoned because of opposition from the states and concern about the potential cost involved. By contrast, in Canada and the US there has been relatively little change to housing allowances, though there is concern about the adequacy of their schemes in tackling affordability problems for low-income households. Additionally, in the US there is a debate in the housing arena about the lack of an entitlement to the housing voucher programme (Grigsby and Bourassa, 2004; Sard, 2004). Meanwhile, Satsangi reports in Chapter Seven that there is currently little political will in France for reform of their housing allowance programmes.

In general, policy makers have addressed five main concerns about housing allowances (see Priemus et al, 2006). The first is the cost of housing allowance programmes. Ironically, while the shift away from supply-side subsidies was partly motivated by a desire to use public money more efficiently, the reduction or phasing out of such subsidies has generally led to higher rents and, in turn, higher housing allowance expenditure. At the same time, for reasons that I discussed in Chapter One, housing allowance caseloads have tended to rise over time, thereby putting further pressures on scheme budgets.

Thus in Britain, the Netherlands and Sweden, the rising cost of housing allowances has been a major policy concern. In all three countries, this concern resulted in cutbacks being introduced during the 1990s in order to reduce costs. Scheme variables were adjusted in order to reduce entitlement levels and in Sweden to remove certain groups altogether from eligibility for assistance. This repeats a similar cycle – of reductions in bricks-and-mortar subsidies, higher unemployment, increased housing allowance caseloads and costs, followed by scheme cutbacks – which occurred in the 1980s in these three countries (Kemp, 2000c).

This cycle reflects a second major concern of policy makers, namely what the Dutch refer to as the 'uncontrollability' of housing allowance expenditure (Priemus, 1990). Because they are usually demand-led, when the number of claimants applying for housing allowances increases (say, because of rising unemployment), so too does the cost of the programme. Hence the demand-led nature of most housing allowance schemes means that costs increase during downturns in the economic cycle. This is, of course, true of social security benefits more generally. However, housing allowances are more prone to this problem because, unlike most other social security benefits, entitlement levels – that is, the amount of benefit paid to claimants – are not directly controllable. This is because entitlement is partly affected by the amount of rent paid by recipients. In other words, entitlement reflects not only political decisions about such key scheme variables as needs allowances, income tapers and the subsidy rate, but also the housing decisions that recipients take. These decisions determine the amount of rent that they pay, which in turn affects (in many countries) the amount of housing allowance that they receive (Kemp, 2000b). Moreover, if rents increase across the market, housing allowance expenditure will rise even if caseloads and scheme variables remain the same.

The extent to which housing allowance expenditure is 'uncontrollable' partly depends upon whether the variables that determine entitlement are indexed or not. In some of the countries covered in this book – Australia, the US, Great Britain and the Netherlands – the variables governing entitlement are uprated on a regular basis (generally yearly, but twice-yearly in Australia) to reflect the changing cost of living. This uprating serves to protect the degree of 'benefit adequacy' afforded by the scheme, but also helps to increase its cost in nominal terms. In contrast, some or all of the key housing allowance scheme variables are not regularly uprated in New Zealand, Canada, Germany or Sweden and hence inflation erodes their real value over time. This lack of benefit indexation has three important consequences: (1) it acts to reduce the number of households entitled to help; (2) it reduces the real value of the benefit provided to recipients; and (3) it reduces the real cost of the scheme over time.

Thus, as Weaver (1988) has pointed out, the non-indexation of welfare benefits means that retrenchment takes place automatically. Welfare states that do not automatically index housing allowances are implicitly prioritising cost containment over benefit adequacy. Moreover, where housing allowance scheme variables are not automatically indexed to inflation, increasing them – however infrequently – becomes a more obviously 'political' decision. It also gives the false appearance of being a scheme 'enhancement', thereby making such decisions more difficult to make than would otherwise be the case (Kemp, 2000c).

Third, policy makers appear to be increasingly concerned about the possibility that housing allowances may create work disincentives. The possibility that housing allowances may reduce labour market participation or work effort in part reflects the fact that they are means tested and, as noted in Chapter One, may consequently have poverty trap effects. Concern about possible unemployment trap effects may arise where income-related assistance with housing expenditure for people of working age is confined to households in receipt of social assistance (as in Australia or Canada) or the housing supplements in social assistance provide more generous support than the separate housing allowance scheme (as in Germany). Satsangi reports in Chapter Seven that in France there is concern about the impact of housing allowances on effective marginal tax rates and disincentives to take up low-paid work. In Britain, the high rate of withdrawal of benefit as income rises is the subject of frequent critical comment in the housing arena. Meanwhile, as Steele notes in Chapter Four, concern about work incentives is one reason why the Canadian provinces are reluctant to extend eligibility of their modest housing allowance programmes to people of working age.

Anxiety about the potential work disincentive effects of housing allowances has been given new impetus with the shift towards a welfare reform agenda in many advanced welfare states in recent years. This new agenda reflects a variety of pressures including a perceived need to increase the labour supply in the face of population ageing and global economic competition. Hulse defines 'welfare reform' as being the "reconceptualisation of income support for most people of workforce age as transitional and temporary cash assistance while recipients prepare for or actively seek work" (2003, p 38). Typically, welfare reform involves workfare programmes, work-focused interviews and help with job search, sometimes linked to increased benefit conditionality and sanctions for non-compliance (see Lodemel and Trickey, 2001). Within this reform agenda, governments have sought to reduce the barriers to work facing people on benefits, including recipients of housing allowances. Indeed, welfare reform has been the driving force behind housing allowance reforms in a number of countries including New Zealand in 1991 (Hulse, 2003; Thorns, Chapter Three) and Great Britain (Kemp, 2000a; Kemp, Chapter Six). In Australia, as Hulse notes in Chapter Two, recipients risk losing their rent allowance if they fail to comply with new requirements to participate in job search and training activities.

Fourth, in several countries policy makers and analysts have expressed concern about the possible impact of housing allowances on housing consumption incentives and, in particular, whether such schemes reduce recipients' incentive to shop around when looking for accommodation in the rental market. This concern about housing consumption incentives is most acute in Great Britain because the Housing Benefit scheme there currently covers 100% of the marginal cost of housing, albeit subject to a variety of regulations that seek to restrict assistance to 'reasonable' rents (Kemp, 2000b). The issue of housing consumption incentives is less extreme in 'housing gap' allowance schemes. This is because they (1) require recipients to make a minimum contribution to their rent; and (2) typically cover only a proportion of the difference between that minimum rent contribution and the eligible rent. This percentage (of the difference between the minimum rent and the eligible rent) defines the marginal rate of subsidy in the housing scheme, referred to here as the 'subsidy rate'.

There is a trade-off in housing gap schemes between the subsidy rate and housing consumption incentives. This is because the greater the subsidy rate, the lower the marginal cost of housing. In other words, with a high subsidy rate, most of the cost of an increase in rent falls on the taxpayer rather than the recipient. Meanwhile, there is also a trade-off between affordability and programme costs; the higher the subsidy rate, the smaller is the share of the rent paid for out of the recipient's own resources and hence the more affordable the rent is to the recipient, but the greater is the cost of the scheme. Both Australia and New Zealand have increased the subsidy rate in recent years in order to improve affordability for housing allowance recipients. Other things being equal, an increased subsidy rate will result in an increase in programme expenditure and, at least in theory, a reduced incentive for recipients to 'shop around' when looking for accommodation. Hence, as Turner and Elsinga (2005) have pointed out, the balance between affordability and the marginal cost of housing is a key policy dilemma for income-related housing allowances.

A related concern is that housing allowances will result in rent inflation within the housing market. The less incentive housing allowance recipients have to negotiate the rent or shop around for a good deal, the more likely it is that rents will rise. This may be particularly true if the allowance is spent on increasing housing consumption rather than reducing the rent burden (that is, the share of the household budget spent on housing). Expressed differently, the extent to which housing allowances result in higher market rents partly depends on the income elasticity of demand for housing. It is also likely to be affected by the proportion of households in receipt of allowances. One possible reason why the Experimental Housing Allowance Program did not result in a market-wide increase in rents is that only a small proportion of households were in receipt of an allowance. Also, recipients tended to spend the money on reducing their rental burden, thereby increasing their non-housing consumption (Bradbury and Downs, 1981). However, as Kofner points out in Chapter Eight, housing allowances are less likely to produce rent inflation in rent-regulated than in unregulated rental markets.

The concerns about housing consumption incentives and rent inflation link to the question of the 'controllability' of housing allowance budgets referred to above. The lack of controllability reflects the fact that housing allowance schemes are typically demand led and hence expenditure is (to some degree) counter-cyclical, their costs increasing during economic downturns and falling during upswings. However, it also reflects a more general concern about cost containment in an era of fiscal constraint (Pierson, 1994), albeit one that tends to become more urgent during recessions. In other words, the limited controllability of housing allowance programmes becomes especially important, quite apart from the economic cycle, in an era when governments feel under pressure to contain the cost of social protection. The concern about programme costs has also been fuelled by high levels of economic inactivity among people of working age and growing numbers of pensioners, both of which developments (as noted in Chapter One) have placed extra demands on housing allowance budgets.

Housing vouchers

In recent years, there has been growing interest in the idea of housing vouchers as an alternative to traditional housing allowance schemes. For instance, in the Netherlands, as Priemus and Elsinga report in Chapter Nine, there has been a lively debate about this subject. In a discussion paper on housing policy published by the Dutch housing ministry in 1999, vouchers were presented as a possible 21st-century replacement for housing allowances. Perhaps surprisingly, this debate was inspired by the US housing voucher scheme (Elsinga and Conijn, 2004). Although the idea seems to have been dropped for the time being, it may yet return to the policy agenda in the Netherlands. Meanwhile, at least two other European welfare states are known to be actively considering the possibility of replacing their housing allowance scheme with a housing voucher.[10] The Local Housing Allowance scheme for private tenants that is currently being tested in Great Britain prior to national implementation in 2008 (see Chapter Six) has also helped to raise interest in 'housing vouchers'.

Before progressing further it is helpful to clarify what, if anything, distinguishes a housing *allowance* from a housing *voucher*. In *Vouchers and the provision of public services*, Steuerle (2000, p 2) defines a voucher as "a subsidy that grants limited purchasing power to an individual to choose among a restricted set of goods and services" (see Priemus et al, 2006). Defined in this way, the essential characteristic of a voucher is that it is a payment to the individual, which may be used to purchase a particular type of good or service (such as education, health care or housing to rent). In Steuerle's view, a voucher can take the form of a direct subsidy or tax expenditure, and it may be made either to the individual or, on their behalf, to the provider of the good or service.[11] In other words, a voucher is simply a demand-side payment that may be made either directly or indirectly to an individual. It follows that, for Steuerle, housing allowances *are* vouchers.

In Chapter Five, Newman presents a different perspective on housing vouchers from Steuerle's. Whereas Steuerle sees housing allowances as a particular form of voucher, Newman sees housing vouchers as a particular form of housing allowance. Newman argues that, whereas housing allowances are typically cash transfers, housing vouchers in the US are not cash as such; instead, they are 'a promissory note from the government', albeit one with strings attached. In other words, a voucher is a *promise to pay* rather than the actual payment itself. Thus, in the US, housing voucher recipients do not cash the voucher at a bank, but instead hand it over to their landlord, who then redeems the payment from the public authority administering the scheme.[12] Thus, housing vouchers are akin to luncheon vouchers that some employers provide to their employees. This is a narrower definition of vouchers than that provided by Steuerle (2000) and, arguably, a much more helpful one.

However, the feature of US housing vouchers that has particularly interested policy makers in other countries is not the form that the payment takes; instead it is the fact that the amount to be paid is based on the 'fair market rent' for the local housing market rather than on the recipient's actual (or eligible) rent. By contrast, in most other housing allowance schemes, the amount paid is calculated on (some proportion of) the rent paid by the recipient. In other words, in this third perspective, what distinguishes a housing voucher from a housing allowance is not how it is *paid*, but how it is *calculated*.

Thus, the term 'housing vouchers' is being used in at least three different ways: (1) as a synonym for housing allowances; (2) as a particular form in which housing allowances are paid; and (3) as a certain way of calculating the payment.

All three definitions are valid uses of the term, but some definitions are arguably more useful than others. There seems little to gain analytically from using the terms housing allowances and housing vouchers interchangeably. Drawing on the example of luncheon vouchers, a cash payment is not a *voucher*; it is *cash* (or, increasingly, its electronic equivalent).[13] As such, and unlike a promissory note (voucher), the recipient could use the cash to pay for non-housing goods or services, so long as it is paid to them and not to their landlord. Indeed, for some policy makers, an advantage of vouchers is precisely that they can only legally be used to pay for the designated commodity. That is an important reason why, in the US, food stamps are paid instead of cash, to ensure that they are spent on food. Hence analytically there is considerable value in using the term 'vouchers' to describe demand-side subsidies that are paid in the form of promissory notes, in line with Newman's definition.

The third definition – that is, as a payment the amount of which is related to the average rent for the locality – seems to conflate this particular feature of the US housing allowance scheme with the name given to the programme (housing vouchers). Rather than necessarily being a feature that distinguishes housing vouchers from housing allowances, it reflects an important distinction between *ex ante* and *ex post* schemes (Gibb, 1995). In *ex post* schemes, the size of the housing allowance is related to the amount of rent that the recipient pays their landlord. By contrast, in *ex ante* schemes, the amount of the allowance is independent of the recipient's rent; it may instead be based on an arbitrary figure or a more 'objective' amount such as the average rent for the locality. From this perspective, housing vouchers are an *ex ante* form of housing allowance. In contrast, housing gap schemes – 'classic' housing allowances as Steele calls them in Chapter Four – are typically a form of *ex post* housing allowance. Likewise, the current British Housing Benefit scheme is also an *ex post* housing allowance. Thus, it is more accurate to describe payments that fall within the third definition as '*ex ante* housing allowances' rather than as 'housing vouchers'. Nevertheless, this third use of the term is likely to stick in the debate about the future of housing allowances, and for that pragmatic reason it is the one used in the remainder of this chapter.

For some policy makers, housing vouchers defined in the third sense – that is, as *ex ante* housing allowances – appear to offer the tantalising prospect of reconciling the trade-off between housing affordability for recipients and cost containment for taxpayers. This is because vouchers potentially reduce the perceived problem inherent in *ex post* housing allowances, that the amount of the payment is more or less closely related to the housing choices made by recipients. If recipients wish to spend more than the value of the voucher on the cost of their accommodation, that is their 'choice' and one that they and not the taxpayer pay for. By increasing the marginal cost of housing compared with a typical housing allowance, voucher recipients have a greater financial incentive to shop around for accommodation. Thus in theory, compared with housing allowances, vouchers reduce the scope for individual upmarketing or general rent inflation in the housing market.

Whether the trade-off between housing affordability and cost containment can be so easily resolved, remains to be seen. The Local Housing Allowance (LHA) that is due to replace the current Housing Benefit scheme for private tenants in Britain is an *ex ante* scheme (Kemp, 2006). The experience of the LHA so far has revealed little evidence of significantly greater shopping around for accommodation among recipients in the nine areas where it is being evaluated (Roberts et al, 2006; Walker, 2006). This muted impact of the LHA may reflect the fact that recipients have other factors in mind and not just the amount of the subsidy when looking for accommodation or deciding whether or not to move home. The transaction costs associated with moving house – search costs, letting agency fees, credit check charges, bonds/deposits, payment of rent in advance and removal costs, quite apart from the time involved – may inhibit recipients from moving house in order to get a better deal. Likewise, non-financial factors also tend to influence whether, and to where, people move (see Pawson and Sinclair, 2003). Hence, in the British context, the effects of housing allowances on moving decisions may be less important than many policy makers imagine (Kemp et al, 1994). Nevertheless, it seems likely that interest in housing vouchers (that is, *ex ante* housing allowances) as an alternative to *ex post* schemes will grow; and it is possible that other countries may follow the British example.

Conclusion

This book has drawn on existing research and data in a range of countries to examine the role and impact of housing allowances. As we have seen, housing allowance schemes exist within different welfare regime and housing market contexts. They are designed in different ways, but in general tend to be variants of the housing gap model, though the British scheme is an important exception (Kemp, 1997). Income-related assistance may be provided by separate housing allowance schemes and as a top-up to social assistance payments as well as implicitly via income-related rents in subsidised housing. This chapter has shown that the amounts spent on housing allowances vary considerably between different countries, as does the proportion of households in receipt of them. To some extent, these differences will reflect differences between countries in the way that housing supply is subsidised and priced.

However, it is clear from the evidence presented in this chapter that housing allowances are only one part of the wider income package provided by welfare states to meet social risks or other income protection goals. It is important, therefore, to examine housing allowances within that wider income package. Housing allowances are particularly important in the income package within Great Britain, both relative to other components of the package such as unemployment benefit, but also in relation to rents and average earnings. In all three respects, the British housing allowance is particularly 'generous' when compared with the other countries covered in this book. Nevertheless, the net replacement rate for newly unemployed insured workers is much lower in Britain relative to APW earnings than in the other nine countries. The highest net replacement rate is provided by Canada (closely followed by the Netherlands), which has no national housing allowance scheme. In other words, it seems that Britain has such an apparently generous housing allowance because the rest of its social security system is so mean. Meanwhile, it seems that newly unemployed Canadian families may be able to get by without a housing allowance because of the very high replacement rate in that country.

All of the countries have reduced their reliance on supply-side subsidies in recent decades and all with the partial exception of Canada have placed more emphasis on housing allowances. But while many governments see housing allowances as a more efficient and/or effective approach than supply-side subsidies to landlords, this has not exempted them from pressures to reform. They are often quite complex policy instruments precisely because they are targeted (that is, means tested) and may create disincentives in the labour market. The concern about the potential work disincentive effects of housing allowances has become more urgent with the need to reduce the number of economically inactive people and expand the labour supply in the face of fiscal austerity and an ageing population.

Being demand-led (outside the US) makes housing allowances prone to the so-called 'uncontrollability' problem, unlike bricks-and-mortar subsidies. This has arguably become a bigger issue as a result of the shift towards a post-industrial society, particularly in relation to the growth of precarious forms of employment, the fragmentation of families and increasing inequality of incomes, all of which create extra pressures on expenditure levels. In several countries, anxiety about housing allowance budgets appears to be heightened by concern about the impact of these schemes on housing consumption incentives. For policy makers concerned about budgetary pressures, housing vouchers (that is, *ex ante* housing allowances) appear to offer the prospect of a more stringent shopping incentive than is provided by *ex post* schemes, while at the same time ensuring that housing remains affordable to low-income households. Whether in practice such schemes prove to be quite so beneficial is likely to depend to some extent on the details of their design. Most crucially, it will also depend on how they influence the behaviour of recipients and other actors within the housing market, yet this is something about which we still do not know enough, especially from a comparative perspective.

Notes

[1] However, as O'Connor et al (1999) point out, there are in fact important differences between these countries in the extent to which they fit with the ideal-type characterisation of a liberal welfare regime.

[2] Public social expenditure includes health and education as well as income protection.

[3] There has also been a shift towards housing allowances in the Czech Republic, though starting from a very different housing system to those in the nine more advanced welfare states.

[4] However, it is important to note that in some countries, such as the Netherlands and the US, the biggest subsidy is mortgage interest tax relief and other forms of tax expenditure provided to homeowners.

[5] Hence 'housing gap' schemes restrict assistance to low-income households that have housing expenses that are in excess of a minimum threshold.

[6] It is important to remember that these figures will vary somewhat from year to year depending upon the economic cycle because (with the exception of the US) housing allowances in these and most other countries are demand-led schemes. The figures will also vary according to changes in the variables governing the scheme including measures that expand or contract benefit coverage or generosity.

[7] Both statistics are statistically significant. However, these correlation coefficients are calculated on a small number of cases and should be treated with caution.

[8] OECD also calculates net replacement rates for other percentages of APW earnings (OECD, 2002).

[9] However, if the assumption about disqualification to social assistance is dropped, the net replacement rate in Britain would be about 66%.

[10] Unfortunately, issues of confidentiality prevent me from identifying these two countries.

[11] Steuerle sees vouchers as an alternative to public provision of goods and services.

[12] The US Food Stamp programme operates in a similar way.

[13] If vouchers are to be regarded as a form of cash payment, then we need to have another term to describe payments that come in the form of a promissory note that is tied to a particular good or service. Although cheques may be regarded as promissory notes, unlike vouchers in the second sense of the term, they may be encashed at a bank.

References

Ball, M., Harloe, M. and Martens, M. (1988) *Housing and social change in Europe and the USA*, London: Routledge.

Bradbury, K.L. and Downs, A. (eds) (1981) *Do housing allowances work?*, Washington, DC: Brookings Institution.

Ditch, J., Lewis, A. and Wilcox, S. (2001) *Social housing, tenure and housing allowances: An international review*, Department for Work and Pensions, in-house report, London: Department for Work and Pensions.

Elsinga, M. and Conijn, J. (2004) 'Housing vouchers: An option for the Netherlands?', paper presented at the ENHR conference Housing Cultures – Convergence and Diversity, Vienna, July.

Esping-Andersen, G. (1990) *The three worlds of welfare capitalism*, Cambridge: Polity.

Fahey, T., Nolan, B. and Maitre, B. (2004) 'Housing expenditures and income poverty in EU countries', *Journal of Social Policy*, vol 33, no 3, pp 437–54.

Gibb, K. (1995) 'A housing allowance for the UK? Preconditions for an income-related housing subsidy', *Housing Studies*, vol 10, no 4, pp 517–32.

Gibbs, I. and Kemp, P.A. (1993) 'Housing benefit and income redistribution', *Urban Studies*, vol 30, no 1, pp 63–72.

Grigsby, W.G. and Bourassa, S.C. (2003) 'Trying to understand low-income housing subsidies: Lessons from the United States', *Urban Studies*, vol 40, no 5/6, pp 973–92.

Grigsby, W.G. and Bourassa, S.C. (2004) 'Section 8: The time for fundamental program change?', *Housing Policy Debate*, vol 15, no 4, pp 805–34.

Harloe, M. (1995) *The people's home? Social rented housing in Europe and America*, Oxford: Blackwell.

Hulse, K. (2003) 'Housing allowances and private renting in liberal welfare regimes', *Housing, Theory and Society*, vol 20, no 1, pp 28–42.

Hulse, K. and Randolph, B. (2005) 'Workforce disincentive effects of housing allowances and public housing for low income households in Australia', *European Journal of Housing Policy*, vol 5, no 2, pp 147–65.

Kemeny, J. (1995) *From public housing to the social market: Rental policy strategies in comparative perspective*, London: Routledge.

Kemp, P.A. (1990) 'Income related assistance with housing costs: A cross-national comparison', *Urban Studies*, vol 27, pp 795–808.

Kemp, P.A. (1997) *A comparative study of housing allowances*, London: Stationery Office.

Kemp, P.A (2000a) 'Housing benefit and welfare retrenchment in Britain', *Journal of Social Policy,* vol 28, no 2, pp 263–79.

Kemp, P.A (2000b) *'Shopping Incentives' and Housing Benefit Reform*, Coventry: Chartered Institute of Housing & Joseph Rowntree Foundation.

Kemp, P.A. (2000c) 'The role and design of income-related housing allowances', *International Social Security Review*, vol 53, no 3, pp 43–57.

Kemp, P.A. (2006) 'Housing benefit: Great Britain in comparative perspective', *Public Finance and Management*, vol 6, no 1, pp 65–87.

Kemp, P.A., Oldman, C., Rugg, J. and Williams, T. (1994) *The effects of benefit on housing decisions*, Department of Social Security research report no 26, London: HMSO.

Kuila, J. (1993) 'Integrating government assistance for accommodation', *Social Policy Journal of New Zealand*, vol 1, no 1, pp 44–50.

Lodemel, I. and Trickey, H. (2001) *'An offer you can't refuse': Workfare in international perspective*, Bristol: The Policy Press.

O'Connor, J.S., Orloff, A.S. and Shaver, S. (1999) *States, markets, families*, Cambridge: Cambridge University Press.

OECD (Organisation for Economic Cooperation and Development) (2002) *Benefits and wages: OECD indicators*, Paris: Organisation for Economic Cooperation and Development.

Pawson, H. and Sinclair, S. (2003) 'Shopping therapy? Incentive payments and tenant behaviour: Lessons from under-occupation schemes in the United Kingdom', *European Journal of Housing Policy*, vol 3, no 3, pp 289–311.

Pierson, P. (1994) *Dismantling the welfare state? Reagan, Thatcher and the politics of retrenchment*, Princeton: Princeton University Press.

Priemus, H. (1990) 'The uncontrollability of the housing allowance', *Netherlands Journal of Housing and Environmental Research*, vol 5, no 2, pp 169–80.

Priemus, H. (1998) 'Improving or endangering housing policies? Recent changes in the Dutch housing allowance scheme', *International Journal of Urban and Regional Research*, vol 22, no 2, pp 319–30.

Priemus, H., Kemp, P.A. and Varady, D. (2006) 'Housing vouchers in the United States, Great Britain, and the Netherlands: Current issues and future perspectives', *Housing Policy Debate*, vol 16, no 3/4, pp 575–609.

Rein, M., Rainwater, L. and Schwartz, J. (1986) *Income packaging in the welfare state: A comparative study of family income*, Oxford: Clarendon.

Roberts, S., Beckhelling, J., Phung, V.-H., et al (2006) *Living with the LHA: Claimants experiences after fifteen months of the LHA in the nine pathfinder areas*, Leeds: Corporate Document Services.

Sard, B. (2004) 'Comment on William G. Grigsby and Steven C. Bourassa's "Section 8: The Time for Fundamental Program Change"', *Housing Policy Debate*, vol 15, no 4, pp 835–49.

Schwarz, B. (1991) *The 1991 housing allowance reform in Sweden – Goals and effects*, Stockholm: Institute for Economic Research.

Scruggs, L. (2006) 'The generosity of social insurance, 1971–2002', *Oxford Review of Economic Policy*, vol 22, no 3, pp 349–64.

Smeeding, T.M. (2004) *Public policy and economic inequality: The United States in comparative perspective*, working paper no 367, Luxembourg: Luxembourg Income Study.

Stephens, M. (1990) 'Students and social security benefits', *Journal of Education Policy*, vol 5, no 1, pp 77–85.

Stephens, M. (2005) 'An assessment of the British housing benefit scheme', *European Journal of Housing Policy*, vol 5, no 2, pp 111–29.

Stephens, M., Burns, N. and MacKay, L. (2003) 'The limits of housing reform: British social rented housing in a European context', *Urban Studies*, vol 40, no 4, pp 767–89.

Steuvle, C.E. (2000) 'Common issues for voucher programs', in C.E. Steuvle, V.D. Ooms, G. Peterson and R.D. Reischauer (eds) *Vouchers and the provision of public services*, Washington DC: Brookings Institution.

Taylor-Gooby, P. (ed.) (2005) *New risks, new welfare*, Oxford: Oxford University Press.

Turner, B. and Elsinga, M. (2005) 'Housing allowances: Finding a balance between social justice and market incentives', *Journal of Housing Policy*, vol 5, no 2, pp 103–9.

Uhry, M. (2006) 'The right to housing and public responsibility in France', paper presented at the Helsinki Conference on Housing Rights, Helsinki, 18–19 September.

Walker, B. (2006) *Local housing allowance final evaluation: Implementation and delivery in the nine pathfinder areas*, Leeds: Corporate Document Services.

Weaver, R.K. (1988) *Automatic government: The politics of indexation*, Washington, DC: Brookings Institution.

Wilcox, S. (2001) 'Housing allowances in other countries', in S. Wilcox (ed.) *Housing finance review 2001/2002*, Coventry: Chartered Institute of Housing and Council of Mortgage Lenders.

Yates, J. (1997) 'Changing directions in Australian housing policies', *Housing Studies*, vol 12, no 2, pp 265–77.

Index